What makes an American?

Inspiring, heartfelt narratives of the immigrant experience—from the voices of America's adopted citizens.

Hector St. John de Crèvecoeur . . . Joseph Pickering . . .
Rebecca Burlend . . . Gro Svendsen . . . Margaret Anna
Cusack (The Nun of Kenmare) . . . Andrew Carnegie . . .
Jacob Riis . . . Henry Villard . . . Marie Zakrzewska . . .
Mary Antin . . . Edward Steiner . . . Anna Howard
Shaw . . . Edward Bok . . . Ludwig Lewisohn . . .
Michael Pupin . . . Constantine Panunzio . . . Dhan
Ghopal Mukerji . . . Abraham Rihbany . . . Etsu
Sugimoto . . . Claude McKay . . . No-Yong Park . . .
Carlos Bulosan . . . Ernesto Galarza . . . Mary Paik Lee

Immigrant Voices

Edited by Gordon Hutner

GORDON HUTNER is a professor of English at the
University of Wisconsin in Madison and the editor of
the journal *American Literary History*.

D0451438

IMMIGRANT VOICES

VOICES

Twenty-four Narratives on
Becoming an American

EDITED BY

Gordon Hutner

A SIGNET CLASSIC

SIGNET CLASSIC
Published by the Penguin Group
Penguin Putnam Inc., 375 Hudson Street,
New York, New York 10014, U.S.A.
Penguin Books Ltd, 27 Wrights Lane,
London W8 5TZ, England
Penguin Books Australia Ltd, Ringwood,
Victoria, Australia
Penguin Books Canada Ltd, 10 Alcorn Avenue,
Toronto, Ontario, Canada M4V 3B2
Penguin Books (N.Z.) Ltd, 182–190 Wairau Road,
Auckland 10, New Zealand

Penguin Books Ltd, Registered Offices:
Harmondsworth, Middlesex, England

Published by Signet Classic, an imprint of Dutton NAL,
a member of Penguin Putnam Inc.

First Signet Classic Printing, March, 1999
10 9 8 7 6 5 4 3 2 1

CONTENTS

INTRODUCTION

Americans like to think of themselves as a "nation of immigrants," an especially popular phrase during the second half of the twentieth century. The idea of seeing the country as constituted by such a heterogeneous people, with none more privileged than another, has proved crucial to our cultural imagination. Indeed, one of the liveliest and richest traditions in the literature of national definition lies in first-person accounts of the experience of becoming Americans. Even before there was a United States, there were narratives from newly arrived inhabitants about what life in America was like, what meanings were to be found, and what effects on the individual could be discerned.

Often, the record of these experiences took the form of diaries or letters—modes of life writing which encouraged introspection and meditation over storytelling. Or they were more straightforward travel reports (a form that persists, in this collection, in the hands of Joseph Pickering and Rebecca Burlend). These accounts of what happened to voyagers—met as these colonists were with expectations of thrilling adventures—generally found their origin as tales told for the benefit of readers at home rather than the colonists themselves. Written to inform as well as to delight potential settlers, these narratives also meant to entertain readers who stayed behind, even as they tried to warn prospective newcomers about the hardships and dangers awaiting them.

These travelers were emigrants: out of various intentions,

they had journeyed from one nation and pitched their fortune elsewhere. To be an immigrant, however, is perhaps to have a more certain destination, to the extent that immigrants might be more fully characterized by where it is they are going, while emigrants might best be understood by where they are coming from. British America did not offer much more of a national destination than merely being a colony, one very far away; as a matter of course, there were local ordinances and colony-wide conventions that predicted the experiment in democracy that, after the Revolution, would become famous all over the world. Still, in a manner of speaking, English, Welsh, Scottish, or Irish emigrants were no more immigrants to America than German, Dutch, or French sojourners. Most came out of a desire or a necessity to leave home, not out of a desire, specifically, to be in America. Few came in hopes of living under a new form of government, one created, in part, to accommodate an unprecedented mix of peoples. Perhaps only when America could offer the protections of being the United States does it make more useful cultural sense to delineate the beginning of a tradition of immigrant writing.

This tradition has been largely made up of first-person accounts that, by the second half of the nineteenth century, we recognize as clearly belonging to the genre of autobiography, or narratives that self-consciously set out to plot or relate the "story" of a career. Such plots, by their inclusion of some details and exclusion of others, mean to follow a pattern, one that creates a specific American identity out of a previously foreign one, and thereby converts the disorganized experiences of life into a coherent order. That order can be located in several places—in the understanding of social and psychological forces animating an author's life, in the models of previous autobiographers—immigrants or others—and in the visions of American identity prevailing at the time of the author's central experiences or even at the time of composition.

During the colonial era, there were enough eyewitness reports that they may be said to constitute a prehistory of the genre of immigrant autobiography. They were written out of a

variety of motives that would recur to later autobiographers—
to caution, to explain, to celebrate, to dramatize the circumstances of moving to America. By the time the New World
was portioned off into the political entities that include the
U.S., first-hand accounts of the challenges and rewards of
living there had already become a somewhat recognizable
form. The central and enduring convention in these descriptions, as we find in Pickering and Burlend, was that an
analysis of the topography also prompted characterological
assessment of the figures whom an author encountered.
Perhaps Hector St. John Crèvecoeur's *Letters from an
American Farmer* (1782) most fully represents this interest
in such social and geographical observation, even as it was
also very conscious that something in the complex social
experiment currently underway had the power to transform
individual identity.

Among the features of American life that most excited
Europeans was the presence of Indians, and these testimonies would be concerned not only to describe the natives
in detail (even when the authors had to invent them!), but
they also would refer to the effects on the European visitor that contact with Indians might yield. It has been argued
that the very first literary genre to which the New World
gave rise—the first mode of writing that seemed identifi-
ably, perhaps peculiarly American—was the captivity narrative, most notably Mary Rowlandson's account of her
physical and psychological "removes" from Puritan society.

Distantly related as captivity narratives are from immigrant autobiographies, they share some surprising affini-
ties. These accounts offered first-hand looks into life among
"hostiles" and conventionally sought to share insights into
the Indians' psychology and sociology. Such testimonies
might also enjoy a compelling occasion to examine one's
Puritan faith insofar as that faith would have sustained a
Christian in despair. Thus the interest of the Europeans' encounter with Indians lies less in the relishing of exotic sorts
of savagery than in proof of Old World ascendancy, a dominion that had to be construed as spiritual as it was political and military. Indian captivity narratives, like Hannah

Swarton's and John Williams's, could serve as witness to redemption and the victory over despondency, as if to suggest that America was an arena for a religious completion. That element of spiritual fulfillment would actuate the form: even later immigrants, some of whom never thought of coming to America as a result of religious persecution, like Etsu Sugimoto, would see their experience in the wilds of a new land in terms of salvation, redemption, and consolation. One thematic feature of captivity narratives that is widely, if unself-consciously, shared to this day among immigrant autobiographies is how America enables and perhaps encourages feelings, as it did for Abraham Rihbany and Edward Steiner, of being saved, not just as a metaphor for emotional, economic, or political freedom, but very much as a religious deliverance. In that, there is also a suggestion that the New World really does surpass the Old.

Thus from a very early moment in U.S. literary history, these stories about America's power of conferring new identities took shape as conversion narratives, stories about a change of identities that mark an exchange of old selves for new. The sentiment that "I was a sinner but now I am saved" loosely evolved to mean "I was a European, but now am American; I was an alien, but now I am a citizen." Then, such feelings might be reconceived in a way that draws an equation between civic and spiritual identities: I was lost (marginalized or dispersed) but now am found (assimilated). Other corollaries would also apply: I was poor, but now am rich, ignorant, but now am educated, anonymous, but now have status.

Out of the crucible of New World experience came a story of newly achieved selfhood, a tale of transformation that immigrant readers might use as a model for encountering their own fantasies, anxieties, even terrors. At the same time, the gratification for an audience of American citizens also lay in the authenticizing pleasure of observing the proof of others' assimilation. To this end, immigrant autobiography is closely tied to stories about the striving for legitimation, the up-by-the-bootstraps chronicle that brings together values of personal fulfillment with possibilities of cultural facilitation, stories that eventually signify the American dream. For the narrative impulse behind immigrant autobiographies, the complex motive such stories still share, derives from this dual need to testify simultaneously to the exceptionality of the author's experience and to the vision of its accessibility for others.

Immigrant autobiographies say that one's experience has been uniquely one's own (and proud the author is to recount it), even as they imply that something similar might happen to readers who were contemplating the journey to America or those already there but in need of direction or reassurance about the potential of their American experiment. Such readers, as the nineteenth century unfolds, will not discover the America of Indians and sublime landscapes, but instead will encounter strange inhabitants and their baffling ways—manners and codes which, to the foreigner, may first seem debilitating but which may yet become liberating and enhancing. Much is made, for example, of American amiability—the ready smile, and the friendly gesture—that the newly arrived mistrust or misinterpret. What the immigrants routinely find is that such conduct does not mean what it means at home—the promise of steadfastness—but merely represents how Americans are likely to treat each other at first, the social glue meant to solidify the sense of community. Indeed, immigrant autobiographers routinely include anecdotes of such misunderstanding, the ways that American life made them wary or confused, and, just as conventionally, remember parallel incidents about how such obstacles were later negotiated successfully.

By the mid-nineteenth century, the largest audience for immigrant autobiographies was not ultimately to be found in a writer's land of origin. Instead, these accounts of migration and assimilation were usually published here and were generally published by and for American readers. Memoirs written about coming to the U.S. were either intended for an audience whose place in America was secure—so that a tribute to a national ideal might be paid—or they were directed at new immigrants who might draw inspiration from the success stories that such autobiographies often readily endorsed. Of course, the autobiographies of newcomers who became eminent—Andrew Carnegie, Henry Villard, Michael Pupin, and especially Edward Bok—were popularly received, since their stories often appealed to both audiences. Yet even as the best-known of these works reached a broad readership, especially among the middle class, most immigrant autobiographies made little impact on the American reading public, if only because those who had the leisure to read were already "in."

Perhaps there is a tradition of autobiographical narratives of prospective American immigrants who returned frustrated or disgusted to their homelands. If so, such accounts might be less sentimental than the autobiographies that have been disseminated in English-speaking America, like Mary Antin's *Promised Land* (1912)—since they might be less concerned with the complex aspect of using the tales they relate to authenticate the authors' status as Americans and thus to testify to the effectuality of their conversion experience. Readers may seize, appreciatively or deprecatingly, on the celebratory tone of so many immigrant autobiographies, but they do so at the risk of missing what else these narratives teach. For so many of them follow a structure wherein the erstwhile immigrant meets several obstacles, of education and employment, for example, which are generally overcome or negated, often with the help of a cultural instructor (who might be an immigrant him- or herself). It even seems formulaic. Still, we might miss the nuance and variety in these experiences and thus lose something of what immigrants have surrendered; in addition, we might overlook the contributions that immigrants have made. These legacies might be well-known, like Pupin's contributions to telecommunications, but just as lasting are the ways that immigrants have shaped the life of ideas and social values, the very tone of American life. Obviously, these can be linguistic, culinary, or something in the nation's popular culture, but their social value lies in the way that America assimilates them. So assimilationist testimony in most autobiographies may only be the superficial story—the first and in some ways easiest reward to be found in these books. Such tales of "what America made of me" enjoy a patriotic appeal, but they leave out "what I made of America," how the country is changed not by what the most illustrious of immigrants have invented or given, but what the masses of "undistinguished" Americans have conferred upon the country's collective identity, which is, after all, what the famous ones typify.

Many of the authors collected here were not professional writers, though a significant number made their livelihood contributing to newspapers and magazines within their immigrant subcultures, especially in the earlier phases of their careers. Rather, the authors averred that they were not motivated by pecuniary interests but had been urged by wellmeaning friends and admirers, according to Anna Shaw and M. E. Zakrzewska, to tell their stories. In this endeavor, the autobiographers hope to inspire other immigrants and, in doing so, to participate in an ongoing battle —the controversy over the effects of immigration on American culture. Yet it was the contribution of immigrants to U.S. culture that many Americans of generations' standing feared most, especially at the turn of the century, when immigration reached peak levels and when so many of the new Americans came from southern and eastern Europe or from Asia. These autobiographies are, in a loose sense, reports from the front: on the one side, Americans of recent assimilation and of much-longer standing argued that the newer immigrants were moving up from the menial jobs that they were first admitted to the country to perform, and were thus competing with older inhabitants for entry into the middle class. In the process, they were surpassing and displacing workers, artisans, and merchants who had come before. In addition, anti-immigrationists held that these immigrants often brought with them such faulty political and economic ideas as unionism, socialism, and Marxism—radicalisms of every sort. (In fact, a few autobiographers, such as Antin and Constantine Panunzio, were at pains to dissociate themselves from such charges.) The new citizens were seen to impart alien folkways to American social life, a corruption of the dominant Anglo-American Protestant tradition and the capitalist entrepreneurial ideal. Not surprisingly, Asians, including No-Yong Park and Dhan Ghopal Mukerji, and Jews, such as Antin and Ludwig Lewisohn, were especially subject to such criticisms. And this political and cultural degradation, anti-immigrationists claimed, would be matched by a weakening of the gene pool through a mixing of bloods that would eventually destroy the "Caucasian race." (See E. A. Ross's *The Old World in the New* [1914] for a catalogue of such worries.)

On the other side were the newly arrived and their tale of achievement, love, and conversion. The political point that these autobiographies wished to carry, as we see in the writings of Rihbany, Sugimoto, and Steiner, was the aspiration to join the American community, an appreciation of the opportunity to uphold rather than disturb a way of life. Only when we get to Carlos Bulosan (1946) do we see an example of an autobiographer as an implacable critic, someone who writes to wake up Americans to the country's failure to accommodate the ambitions it inspires. Immigrant autobiographies were often written to argue that new Americans had something valuable and enhancing to give the culture. While it is certainly true that immigrant autobiographies, like Andrew Carnegie's, can claim a very legitimate connection to the vast literature of American success, from Benjamin Franklin through P. T. Barnum, we can also see in many of these accounts an ideological overlay that helps to explain the rhetoric of cultural triumph in the autobiographies.

The predominant mode is to see America as fundamentally good and of being equal to an immigrant's dreams of individual fulfillment and personal freedom. Such autobiographers, including Villard and Pupin, want to remind readers that immigrants should not inspire apprehensiveness but confidence. Sometimes, this urgency to achieve a fullness of American identity, to be completely assimilated, is so forceful that it will lead newcomers to give up their first religious training, along with their cultural backgrounds, for something they understand to be more wholly American. When autobiographers like Steiner and Sugimoto describe their taking up of Christianity as critical to their shaping as Americans, they tell of a conversion to a religious perspective to be sure, but their stories also bespeak an internalizing of the cultural vision of the host society. For it may have been less the general case that immigrants embraced one Protestant denomination or another out of a compelling experience of religious attainment than it was the cogent promise of Protestantism to certify social acceptability, to confirm the efficacy of assimilation, and to ensure Americanization.

Perhaps it is good for Americans to be sentimental about the folk story that so many carry close to their hearts, the animating narrative of how Grandma and Grandpa, escaping poverty or oppression or both, came to these shores, worked and saved, and got ahead. As a cultural legend—like the *Aeneid* or the *Odyssey*—it is a wonderful and powerful history of the founding of a civilization, an epic that dispenses heroic virtues more democratically than those of Rome or Greece. Yet as forcefully as these widely shared memories vivify and bolster the illusion of a coherent society enjoying a common history, this traditional American folk tale, as we see in Zakrzewska, Lewisohn, Mukerji, Park, and Paik Lee, often omits another story, a tale of exclusion, internalized prejudice, discrimination, and humiliation. The trauma of assimilation can be camouflaged or repressed in these autobiographies, for the cultural victory they enshrine often comes at a cost that later generations might consider distorting, even crippling. The price of assimilation may entail renunciation and alienation; and for some autobiographers, like Lewisohn and McKay, the ideal may not even be possible, much less desirable.

Whatever the larger cultural purpose of these immigrant autobiographies, their primary motive is pedagogic. They aim to impart lessons through the autobiographers' example of how to become successful Americans. The events they recall are seen as emblematic of the occasions whereby citizenship is earned. Details and themes are even slavishly chosen for this effect of abrogating an immigrant's alien status. So it is not surprising to learn that many of these writers found employment as lecturers; in this capacity, immigrants as different as No-Yong Park, Anna Shaw, Etsu Sugimoto, and Mary Antin became professional Americans, i.e., for a while they made their living by telling about their lives. A few became permanent "others," i.e., they succeeded insofar as they were understood to speak as representative Asians or Africans or Arabs. Some of these writers were identified solely by the voice or perspective that was associated with their race or previous nation. Thus they lectured as Syrians or Japanese or Jews, first and last, but always in the process of becoming Americans. So we might distinguish early and decisively between immigrant autobiographies and any other kind. Successful as the authors may have been in their worldly endeavors, their aims in telling the story of their Americanization encompass the art of their writing, virtually their whole power of representation. Some autobiographers will follow a model of transformation by endurance—like Zakrzewska's quest to become a doctor or Anna Shaw's to become a Methodist minister—or by assimilation, while others, like Bulosan or Mary Paik Lee, contribute to a countertradition of antisuccess literature, one that casts doubt on America's self-image of equal opportunity. Yet even these are true to type insofar as they cast America as the ideological entity that either enables or disables redemption or fulfillment.

For the greatest "character" in all these accounts is the very idea of America, which stands for the perceived totality of values and desires against which the immigrant marks his or her growth and development. That vision of America usually enjoys unspoken approval, and some autobiographers are unequivocal in their celebration of their new home. (As if to complete the passage into American citizenship, Panunzio recollects how, during World War I, he plants the American stars and stripes on Italian soil.) Often these autobiographers, like Villard and Carnegie, turn to philanthropy not only to relieve others' distress, but also to express their gratitude. Other autobiographers fix their attention on the state of U.S. society, especially its economic, social, and racial disparities. Social conditions, for these writers, are such that the true American is she or he who tries to aid the many indigent people in the land of plenty. Perhaps the nonpareil example among the writers collected here is Margaret Anna Cusack's survival manual for Irish-American female laborers and her campaign on behalf of these "working girls." Part of several autobiographers' story is their realization that their responsibility, as Jacob Riis so famously put it, is to expose "how the other half lives." For these cultural observers, like Ernesto Galarza, the true proportions of their American identities are achieved by dedicating themselves to relieving the privation of immigrants, whose entry into the country had been to provide cheap labor, not necessarily to foster religious or political freedom.

One occupation wide open to immigrants was a career in social work, if only because the help to be administered was so clearly present throughout the immigrant population. For some female autobiographers, this experience of helping and saving seems like a basic contribution to their community, as it does for Gro Svendsen, who taught English to other newcomers. Or it awakens another consciousness, a feminist one, such as we see not only in the story of Margaret Anna Cusack, but also in that of Anna Shaw, so that becoming an American is enmeshed with an account of the raising of one's consciousness as a woman. However, the bulk of immigrant autobiographies participate in a standard version of the gendered division of labor, with females entering service professions, like family medicine, social work, school, and church. Of course, some men may join in such endeavors, but for males the story of assimilation entails another sort of Americanization, whereby the transition from greenhorn to citizen yields the occasion to learn how to be a self-made American man.

Gender specifies the range of activities in and responses to America that the autobiographers can claim, but, male or female, these authors seldom discuss individual experiences of intimacy. A few won't mention anything at all about their spouses and children, a restraint that sometimes frustrates readers who wish to identify as closely as they can with these writers' self-characterizations. Why do authors so routinely rule out such personal experiences? Perhaps such experiences entail the privacy of loved ones and are well outside the categories that the immigrant author can recognize as a reader's legitimate interest. Yet it seems contrary to suppose that the difficulties of finding a mate, the trouble that one's children occasion, should have little resonance for a form that takes as its given the crucial interest of one person's experience. As Abraham Cahan, the editor of the *Jewish Daily Forward*, well understood in publishing an advice column to lovelorn or faint-hearted immigrants, the experience of love—who to marry over parental objections, who to spurn despite parental support—was, for many, many readers the most significant and tangible way they had of asserting an American identity. Few immigrants would rise to the status of a social arbiter, like Edward Bok, the editor of the *Ladies' Home Journal*, but all could entertain a fantasy of finding love in the land of opportunity, of creating a vital intimate life. Indeed, it may be one of the initial measures of assimilation, as it was for Park and Mukerji, to believe oneself deserving of a love match rather than the arranged marriages more typical of one's previous homeland.

While the ascendancy of European and East Asian immigration has declined, there are new immigrant experiences—Vietnamese, Haitian, Nigerian and Russian, among others—that are sure to be recollected and codified. Yet one wonders whether, collectively, Americans have lost a value for the instruction and inspiration that immigrant autobiographies give. One hundred years after the great wave of immigration, the nation might be less certain about what U.S. culture represents than previous generations of readers, so that the challenge of representing the experience of maneuvering through this society might meet with more apprehension than at the turn of the last century. Perhaps because so many Americans find this tale of learning a cultural identity so well rehearsed, its drama has dissipated; memories fade or distort Americans' sense of their own connection to immigration. Moreover, a century of wars in Europe and East

Asia, the Middle East, southeast Asia, and Latin America as well as the Cold War with the former Soviet Union has surely conditioned the national perception of foreigners so that, in the popular mind, they are perhaps more worrisome than their predecessors. At least since the first quarter of the twentieth century, the ideal of a melting pot has been challenged. Immigrants have been invited to understand their experience as "hyphenated" Americans, as if to say that the U.S. cannot be an *unum* drawn out of a *pluribus*, but a society that must be defined by its cultural pluralism, the conviction that the nation lives together out of separate, ultimately inassimilable cultural differences. Today, in an age that celebrates cultural diversity, the national ideal may well be one of hybridity, a multicultural American self, rather than the exalted one of assimilation.

As citizens, we can still enjoy the nuances and complexities in a story of a new American's experience of the U.S. And, as readers, we can still take pleasure in the spectacle of the earnest student of our society trying to make her or his way through its subtleties and paradoxes, its pitfalls, and deceptions. Reading immigrant autobiographers enables us to appreciate these features of their experience, even as it also enables us to see the shaping power of memory. Certainly, these autobiographers have their own stories to tell, though they may follow narrative conventions in doing so. Yet immigrant autobiography, as much as any work of fiction, contributes to the collective imagination of Americans. And as much as any work of history, they refine our understanding of what America is not as well as what it is.

I would like to thank my two research assistants, Erin Hanusa and Megan Waters, at the University of Wisconsin–Madison for their indispensable cooperation in preparing this volume. I would also like to dedicate this collection of autobiographies to the memory of my grandparents—Max and Esther Dollinger and Morris and Frances Hutner—who did not live to tell their stories to their great-grandsons, Daniel and Jacob.

—GORDON HUTNER

IMMIGRANT
VOICES

Letters from an American Farmer
Hector St. John de Crèvecoeur

Born in France, Hector St. John de Crèvecoeur (1735–1813) chose in 1759 to remain in the New World, where he had been sent as a military officer and mapmaker. He wandered from Quebec to the Ohio and Great Lakes regions, took out citizenship papers in New York in 1765, became a farmer in Orange county, and in 1769 married Mehitable Tippet, with whom he had three children. Unrest in Quebec had led Crèvecoeur to New England, but political instability would soon affect his new home also.

When the American Revolution broke out, Crèvecoeur found himself in the untenable position of having a wife from a Loyalist family and friends and neighbors among the opposite faction. Persecuted by both sides, he left the rebellious country only to languish for months in a British army prison before sailing for Europe in 1780. In London, he arranged for the publication of the twelve essays called *Letters from an American Farmer* (1782).

Within two years, this charmingly written, optimistic, and timely book saw eight editions in five countries and made its author famous. It gained him such influential patrons as Benjamin Franklin, a membership in France's Academy of Sciences, and an appointment as French Consul to three of the new American states.

On his return to America, Crèvecoeur found his wife dead, a daughter and son settled with strangers, and his farm burned as a result of anti-Loyalist sentiment.

Reunited with his family, he continued his interests in botany, agriculture, and medicine. A two-year furlough in Europe resulted in a larger, second version of the French edition of *Letters*. Once he was finally recalled from his consulship, Crèvecoeur wrote another book about his experiences in America, translated as *Travels in Upper Pennsylvania and New York* (1801). He lived quietly in France and Germany until his death in 1813.

In the 1920s, a bundle of unpublished essays was discovered in an attic in France and brought out as *Sketches of Eighteenth-Century America, or More Letters of an American Farmer*. Crèvecoeur's books outline the steps through which new immigrants passed, analyze the religious problems they faced, describe the life of Nantucket whalers as well as the anxieties of the colonial farmer. *Letters from an American Farmer* remains one of the crucial texts of the early Republic, and this excerpt from the third letter, "What Is an American?" has long been considered a defining statement of cultural identity in the United States.

LETTER III

WHAT IS AN AMERICAN?

I wish I could be acquainted with the feelings and thoughts which must agitate the heart and present themselves to the mind of an enlightened Englishman, when he first lands on this continent. He must greatly rejoice that he lived at a time to see this fair country discovered and settled. He must necessarily feel a share of national pride when he views the chain of settlements which embellish these extended shores. When he says to himself, this is the work of my countrymen, who, when convulsed by factions, afflicted by a variety of miseries and wants, restless and impatient, took refuge here. They brought along with them their national genius, to which they principally owe what liberty they enjoy and what substance they possess. Here he sees the industry of his native country displayed in a new manner, and traces, in their works, the embryos of all the arts, sciences, and ingenuity, which flourish in Europe. Here he beholds fair cities, substantial villages, extensive fields, an immense country filled with decent houses, good roads, orchards, meadows, and bridges, where, a hundred years ago, all was wild, woody, and uncultivated! What a train of pleasing ideas this fair spectacle must suggest! It is a prospect which must inspire a good citizen with the most heartfelt pleasure! The difficulty consists in the manner of viewing so extensive a scene. He is arrived on a new continent: a modern society offers itself to his contemplation, different from what he had hitherto seen. It is not composed, as in Europe, of great lords who possess every thing, and of a herd of people who have nothing. Here are no aristocratical families, no courts, no kings, no bishops, no ecclesiastical dominion, no invisible power giving to a few a very visible one, no great manufactures employing thousands, no great refinements of luxury. The rich and the poor are not so far removed from each other as they are in Europe. Some few towns excepted, we are all tillers of the earth, from Nova Scotia to West Florida. We are a people of cultivators, scattered over an immense territory, communicating with each other by means of good roads and navigable rivers, united by the silken bands of mild government, all respecting the laws, without dreading their power, because they are equitable. We are all animated with the spirit of an industry which is unfettered and unrestrained, because each person works for himself. If he travels through our rural districts, he views not the hostile castle and the haughty mansion contrasted with the clay-built hut and miserable cabin, where cattle and men help to keep each other warm, and dwell in meanness, smoke, and indigence. A pleasing uniformity of decent competence appears throughout our habitations. The meanest of our log-houses is a dry and comfortable habitation. Lawyer or merchant are the fairest titles our towns afford: that of a farmer is the only appellation of the rural inhabitants of our country. It must take some time ere he can reconcile himself to our dictionary, which is but short in words of dignity and names of honour. There, on a Sunday, he sees a congregation of respectable farmers and their wives, all clad in neat homespun, well mounted, or riding in their own humble waggons. There is not among them an esquire, saving the unlettered magistrate. There he sees a parson as simple as his flock, a farmer who does not riot on the labour of others. We have no princes, for whom we toil, starve, and bleed. We are the most perfect society now existing in the world. Here man is free as he ought to be; nor is this pleasing equality so transitory as many others are. Many ages will not see the shores of our great lakes replenished with inland nations, nor the unknown bounds of North America entirely peopled. Who can tell how far it extends? Who can tell the millions of men whom it will feed and contain? for no European foot has, as yet, travelled half the extent of this mighty continent.

The next wish of this traveller will be, to know whence came all these people? They are a mixture of English, Scotch, Irish, French, Dutch, Germans, and Swedes. From this promiscuous breed, that race, now called Americans, have arisen. The Eastern provinces must indeed be excepted, as being the unmixed descendents of Englishmen. I have heard many wish that they had been more intermixed also: for my part, I am no wisher, and think it much better as it has happened. They exhibit a most conspicuous figure in this great and variegated picture. They too enter for a great share in the pleasing perspective displayed in these thirteen provinces. I know it is fashionable to reflect on them, but I respect them for what they have done; for the accuracy and wisdom with which they have settled their territory; for the decency of their manners; for their early love of letters; their antient college, the first in this hemisphere; for their industry; which to me, who am but a farmer, is the criterion of every thing. There never was a people, situated as they are, who, with so ungrateful a soil, have done more in so short a time. Do you think that the monarchical ingredients, which are more prevalent in other governments, have purged them from all foul stains? Their histories assert the contrary.

In this great American asylum, the poor of Europe have by some means met together, and in consequence of various causes. To what purpose should they ask one another what countrymen they are? Alas, two thirds of them had no country. Can a wretch, who wanders about, who works and starves, whose life is a continual scene of sore affliction or pinching penury; can that man call England or any other kingdom his country? A country that had no bread for him; whose fields procured him no harvest; who met with nothing but the frowns of the rich, the severity of the laws, with jails and punishments; who owned not a single foot of the extensive surface of this planet. No! Urged by a variety of motives here they came. Every thing has tended to regenerate them. New laws, a new mode of living, a new social system. Here they are become men. In Europe they were as so many useless plants, wanting vegetative mould and refreshing showers. They withered; and were mowed down by want, hunger, and war; but now, by the power of transplantation, like all other plants, they have taken root and flourished! Formerly they were not numbered in any civil lists of their country, except in those of the poor: here they rank as citizens. By what invisible power hath this surprising metamorphosis been performed? By that of the laws and that of their industry. The laws, the indulgent laws, protect them as they arrive, stamping on them the symbol of adoption: they receive ample rewards for their labours: these accumulated rewards procure them lands: those lands confer on them the title of freemen, and to that title every benefit is affixed which men can possibly require. This is the great operation daily performed by our laws. Whence proceed these laws? From our government. Whence that government? It is derived from the original genius and strong desire of the people ratified and confirmed by the crown. This is the great chain which links us all; this is the picture which every province exhibits, Nova Scotia excepted. There the crown has done all. Either there were no people who had genius, or it was not much attended to. The consequence is, that the province is very thinly inhabited indeed. The power of the crown, in conjunction with the musketoes, has prevented men from settling there. Yet some parts of it flourished once, and it contained a mild harmless set of people. But, for the fault of a few leaders, the whole was banished. The greatest political error, the crown ever committed in America, was, to cut off men from a country which wanted nothing but men.

What attachment can a poor European emigrant have for a country where he had nothing? The knowledge of the language, the love of a few kindred as poor as himself, were the only cords that tied him. His country is now that which gives him his land, bread, protection, and consequence. *Ubi panis ibi patria* is the motto of all emigrants. What then is the American, this new man? He is neither an European, nor the descendent of an European: hence that strange mixture of blood, which you will find in no other country. I could point out to you a family, whose grandfather was an Englishman, whose wife was Dutch, whose son married a French woman, and whose present four sons have now four wives of different nations. He is an American, who, leaving behind him all his antient prejudices and manners, receives new ones from the new mode of life he has embraced, the new government he obeys, and the new rank he holds. He becomes an American by being received in the broad lap of our great *alma mater*. Here individuals of all nations are melted into a new race of men, whose labours and posterity will one day cause great changes in the world. Americans are the western pilgrims, who are carrying along with them that great mass of arts, sciences, vigour, and industry, which began long since in the east. They will finish the great circle. The Americans were once scattered all over Europe. Here they are incorporated into one of the finest systems of population which has ever appeared, and which will hereafter become distinct by the power of the different climates they inhabit. The American ought therefore to love this country much better than that wherein either he or his forefathers were born. Here the rewards of his industry follow, with equal steps, the progress of his labour. His labour is founded on the basis of nature, *self-interest*: can it want a stronger allurement? Wives and children, who before in vain demanded of him a morsel of bread, now, fat and frolicksome, gladly help their father to clear those fields whence exuberant crops are to arise, to feed and to clothe them all, without any part being claimed, either by a despotic prince, a rich abbot, or a mighty lord. Here religion demands but little of him; a small voluntary salary to the minister, and gratitude to God: can he refuse these? The American is a new man, who acts upon new principles; he must therefore entertain new ideas and form new opinions. From involuntary idleness, servile dependence, penury, and useless labour, he has passed to toils of a very different nature, rewarded by ample subsistence.—This is an American.

British America is divided into many provinces, forming a large association, scattered along a coast of 1500 miles extent and about 200 wide. This society I would fain examine, at least such as it appears in the middle provinces; if it does not afford that variety of tinges and gradations which may be observed in Europe, we have colours peculiar to ourselves. For instance, it is natural to conceive that those who live near the sea must be very different from those who live in the woods: the intermediate space will afford a separate and distinct class.

Men are like plants. The goodness and flavour of the fruit proceeds from the peculiar soil and exposition in which they grow. We are nothing but what we derive from the air we breathe, the climate we inhabit, the government we obey, the system of religion we profess, and the nature of our employment. Here you will find but few crimes; these have acquired as yet no root among us. I wish I were able to trace all my ideas. If my ignorance prevents me from describing them properly, I hope I shall be able to delineate a few of the outlines, which is all I propose.

Those, who live near the sea, feed more on fish than on flesh, and often encounter that boisterous element. This renders them more bold and enterprising: this leads them to neglect the confined occupations of the land. They see and converse with a variety of people. Their intercourse with mankind becomes extensive. The sea inspires them with a love of traffic, a desire of transporting produce from one place to another; and leads them to a variety of resources, which supply the place of labour. Those who inhabit the middle settlements, by far the most numerous, must be very different. The simple cultivation of the earth purifies them; but the indulgences of the government, the soft remonstrances of religion, the rank of independent freeholders, must necessarily inspire them with sentiments very little known in Europe among a people of the same class. What do I say? Europe has no such class of men. The early knowledge they acquire, the early bargains they make, give them a great degree of sagacity. As freemen they will be litigious. Pride and obstinacy are often the cause of law-suits; the nature of our laws and governments may be another. As citizens, it is easy to imagine that they will carefully read the newspapers, enter into every political disquisition, freely blame, or censure, governors and others. As farmers, they will be careful and anxious to get as much as they can, because what they get is their own. As northern men, they will love the cheerful cup. As Christians, religion curbs them not in their opinions: the general indulgence leaves every one to think for themselves in spiritual matters. The law inspects our actions; our thoughts are left to God. Industry, good living, selfishness, litigiousness, country politics, the pride of freemen, religious indifference, are their characteristics. If you recede still farther from the sea, you will come into more modern settlements: they exhibit the same strong lineaments in a ruder appearance. Religion seems to have still less influence, and their manners are less improved.

Now we arrive near the great woods, near the last inhabited districts. These men seem to be placed still farther beyond the reach of government, which, in some measure, leaves them to themselves. How can it pervade every corner, as they were driven there by misfortunes, necessity of beginnings, desire of acquiring large tracks of land, idleness, frequent want of œconomy, antient debts. The reunion of such people does not afford a very pleasing spectacle. When discord, want of unity and friendship,

when either drunkenness or idleness, prevail in such remote
districts, contention, inactivity, and wretchedness, must en-
sue. There are not the same remedies to these evils as in a
long-established community. The few magistrates they
have are, in general, little better than the rest. They are often
in a perfect state of war; that of man against man; sometimes decided by blows, sometimes by means of the law:
that of man against every wild inhabitant of these venerable
woods, of which they are come to dispossess them. There
men appear to be no better than carnivorous animals, of a
superior rank, living on the flesh of wild animals when they
can catch them, and, when they are not able, they subsist on
grain. He, who would wish to see America in its proper
light, and to have a true idea of its feeble beginnings and
barbarous rudiments, must visit our extended line of fron-
tiers, where the last settlers dwell, and where he may see the
first labours of settlement, the mode of clearing the earth, in
all their different appearances. Where men are wholly left
dependent on their native tempers and on the spur of uncertain industry, which often fails when not sanctified by the
efficacy of a few moral rules. There, remote from the power
of example and check of shame, many families exhibit the
most hideous parts of our society. They are a kind of forlorn hope, preceding, by ten or twelve years, the most respectable army of veterans which come after them. In that
space, prosperity will polish some, vice and the law will
drive off the rest, who, uniting again with others like themselves, will recede still farther, making room for more
industrious people, who will finish their improvements,
convert the log-house into a convenient habitation, and, rejoicing that the first heavy labours are finished, will change,
in a few years, that hitherto-barbarous country into a fine,
fertile, well-regulated, district. Such is our progress, such is
the march of the Europeans toward the interior parts of this
continent. In all societies there are off-casts. This impure
part serves as our precursors or pioneers. My father himself
was one of that class; but he came upon honest principles,
and was therefore one of the few who held fast. By good

conduct and temperance he transmitted to me his fair inheritance, when not above one in fourteen of his contemporaries had the same good fortune.

Forty years ago this smiling country was thus inhabited. It is now purged. A general decency of manners prevails throughout, and such has been the fate of our best countries.

Exclusive of those general characteristics, each province has its own, founded on the government, climate, mode of husbandry, customs, and peculiarity of circumstances. Europeans submit insensibly to these great powers, and become, in the course of a few generations, not only Americans in general, but either Pennsylvanians, Virginians, or provincials, under some other name. Whoever traverses the continent must easily observe those strong differences which will grow more evident in time. The inhabitants of Canada, Massachuset, the middle provinces, the southern ones, will be as different as their climates. Their only points of unity will be those of religion and language.

As I have endeavoured to shew you how Europeans became Americans, it may not be disagreeable to shew you likewise how the various Christian sects introduced wear out, and how religious indifference becomes prevalent. When any considerable number of a particular sect happen to dwell contiguous to each other, they immediately erect a temple, and there worship the Divinity agreeably to their own peculiar ideas. Nobody disturbs them. If any new sect springs up in Europe, it may happen that many of its professors will come and settle in America. As they bring their zeal with them, they are at liberty to make proselytes if they can, and to build a meeting, and to follow the dictates of their consciences; for neither the government nor any other power interferes. If they are peaceable subjects, and are industrious, what is it to their neighbours how and in what manner they think fit to address their prayers to the Supreme Being? But, if the sectaries are not settled close together, if they are mixed with other denominations, their zeal will cool for want of fuel, and will be extinguished in a little time. Then the Americans become, as to religion what they are as to country, allied to all. In them the name of

Englishman, Frenchman, and European, is lost, and, in like manner, the strict modes of Christianity, as practised in Europe, are lost also. This effect will extend itself still farther hereafter, and, though this may appear to you as a strange idea, yet it is a very true one. I shall be able perhaps hereafter to explain myself better; in the mean while, let the following example serve as my first justification.

Let us suppose you and I to be travelling. We observe that in this house, to the right, lives a Catholic, who prays to God as he has been taught, and believes in transubstantiation. He works and raises wheat, he has a large family of children, all hale and robust. His belief, his prayers, offend nobody. About one mile farther, on the same road, his next neighbour may be a good honest plodding German Lutheran, who addresses himself to the same God, the God of all, agreeably to the modes he has been educated in, and believes in consubstantiation; by so doing he scandalizes nobody. He also works in his fields, embellishes the earth, clears swamps, &c. What has the world to do with his Lutheran principles? He persecutes nobody, and nobody persecutes him; he visits his neighbours, and his neighbours visit him. Next to him lives a Seceder, the most enthusiastic of all sectaries; his zeal is hot and fiery; but, separated as he is from others of the same complexion, he has no congregation of his own to resort to, where he might cabal and mingle religious pride with worldly obstinacy. He likewise raises good crops, his house is handsomely painted, his orchard is one of the fairest in the neighbourhood. How does it concern the welfare of the country, or of the province at large, what this man's religious sentiments are, or really whether he has any at all? He is a good farmer, he is a sober, peaceable, good, citizen. William Penn himself would not wish for more. This is the visible character; the invisible one is only guessed at, and is nobody's business. Next again lives a Low Dutchman, who implicitly believes the rules laid down by the synod of Dort. He conceives no other idea of a clergyman than that of a hired man. If he does his work well he will pay him the stipulated sum; if not, he will dismiss him, and do without his sermons, and let his church be shut up for years. But, notwithstanding this coarse idea, you will find his house and farm to be the neatest in all the country; and you will judge, by his waggon and fat horses, that he thinks more of the affairs of this world than of those of the next. He is sober and laborious, therefore he is all he ought to be as to the affairs of this life; as for those of the next, he must trust to the great Creator. Each of these people instruct their children as well as they can, but these instructions are feeble compared to those which are given to the youth of the poorest class in Europe. Their children will therefore grow up less zealous and more indifferent in matters of religion than their parents. The foolish vanity, or rather the fury of making proselytes, is unknown here: they have no time: the seasons call for all their attention; and thus, in a few years, this mixed neighbourhood will exhibit a strange religious medley, that will be neither pure Catholicism nor pure Calvinism. A very perceptible indifference, even in the first generation, will become apparent; and it may happen that the daughter of the Catholic will marry the son of the Seceder, and settle by themselves at a distance from their parents. What religious education will they give their children? A very imperfect one. If there happens to be in the neighbourhood any place of worship, we will suppose a Quaker's meeting, rather than not shew their fine clothes, they will go to it, and some of them may perhaps attach themselves to that society. Others will remain in a perfect state of indifference. The children of these zealous parents will not be able to tell what their religious principles are, and their grandchildren still less. The neighbourhood of a place of worship generally leads them to it, and the action of going thither is the strongest evidence they can give of their attachment to any sect. The Quakers are the only people who retain a fondness for their own mode of worship; for, be they ever so far separated from each other, they hold a sort of communion with the society, and seldom depart from its rules, at least in this country. Thus all sects are mixed as well as all nations. Thus religious indifference is imperceptibly disseminated from one end of the continent to the other, which is at present one of the strongest characteristics of the Americans. Where this will reach no one can tell: perhaps it may leave a vacuum fit to receive other systems. Persecution, religious pride, the love of contradiction, are the food of what the world commonly calls religion. These motives have ceased here: zeal, in Europe, is confined; here, it evaporates in the great distance it has to travel; there, it is a grain of powder inclosed; here, it burns away in the open air, and consumes without effect.

But to return to our back settlers. I must tell you, that there is something in the proximity of the woods which is very singular. It is with men as it is with the plants and animals that grow and live in the forests. They are entirely different from those that live in the plains. I will candidly tell you all my thoughts, but you are not to expect that I shall advance any reasons. By living in or near the woods, their actions are regulated by the wildness of the neighbourhood. The deer often come to eat their grain, the wolves to destroy their sheep, the bears to kill their hogs, the foxes to catch their poultry. This surrounding hostility immediately puts the gun into their hands: they watch these animals; they kill some; and thus, by defending their property, they soon become professed hunters. This is the progress. Once hunters, farewel to the plough. The chase renders them ferocious, gloomy, and unsocial. A hunter wants no neighbour; he rather hates them, because he dreads the competition. In a little time their success in the woods makes them neglect their tillage. They trust to the natural fecundity of the earth, and therefore do little. Carelessness in fencing often exposes what little they sow to destruction: they are not at home to watch: in order therefore to make up the deficiency, they go oftener to the woods. That new mode of life brings along with it a new set of manners, which I cannot easily describe. These new manners, being grafted on the old stock, produce a strange sort of lawless profligacy, the impressions of which are indelible. The manners of the Indian natives are respectable compared with this European medley. Their wives and children live in sloth and inactivity, and, having no proper pursuits, you may judge what education the latter receive. Their tender minds have nothing else to contemplate but the example of their parents; like them they grow up a mongrel breed, half civilized, half savage, except nature stamps on them some constitutional propensities. That rich, that voluptuous, sentiment is gone, which struck them so forcibly. The possession of their freeholds no longer conveys to their minds the same pleasure and pride. To all these reasons you must add their lonely situation, and you cannot imagine what an effect on manners the great distances they live from each other has! Consider one of the last settlements in its first view: of what is it composed? Europeans, who have not that sufficient share of knowledge they ought to have, in order to prosper: people, who have suddenly passed from oppression, dread of government, and fear of laws, into the unlimited freedom of the woods. This sudden change must have a very great effect on most men, and on that class particularly. Eating of wild meat, whatever you may think, tends to alter their temper, though all the proof I can adduce is, that I have seen it; and, having no place of worship to resort to, what little society this might afford is denied them. The Sunday meetings, exclusive of religious benefits, were the only social bonds that might have inspired them with some degree of emulation in neatness. Is it then surprising to see men, thus situated, immersed in great and heavy labours, degenerate a little? It is rather a wonder the effect is not more diffusive. The Moravians and the Quakers are the only instances in exception to what I have advanced. The first never settle singly; it is a colony of the society which emigrates: they carry with them their forms, worship, rules, and decency. The others never begin so hard; they are always able to buy improvements in which there is a great advantage, for, by that time, the country is recovered from its first barbarity. Thus our bad people are those who are half cultivators and half hunters; and the worst of them are those who have degenerated altogether into the hunting state. As old ploughmen and new men of the woods, as Europeans and new-made Indians, they contract the vices of both. They adopt the moroseness and ferocity of a native, without his mildness, or even his industry at home. If manners are not refined, at least they are rendered simple and inoffensive by tilling the earth: all our wants are supplied by it: our time is divided between labour and rest, and leaves none for the commission of great misdeeds. As hunters, it is divided between the toil of the chase, the idleness of repose, or the indulgence of inebriation. Hunting is but a licentious idle life, and, if it does not alway pervert good dispositions, yet, when it is united with bad luck, it leads to want: want stimulates that propensity to rapacity and injustice, too natural to needy men, which is the fatal gradation. After this explanation of the effects which follow by living in the woods, shall we yet vainly flatter ourselves with the hope of converting the Indians? We should rather begin with converting our back-settlers; and now, if I dare mention the name of religion, its sweet accents would be lost in the immensity of these woods. Men, thus placed, are not fit either to receive or remember its mild instructions; they want temples and ministers; but, as soon as men cease to remain at home and begin to lead an erratic life, let them be either tawny or white, they cease to be its disciples.

Thus have I faintly and imperfectly endeavoured to trace our society from the sea to our woods; yet you must not imagine that every person, who moves back, acts upon the same principles, or falls into the same degeneracy. Many families carry with them all their decency of conduct, purity of morals, and respect of religion; but these are scarce, the power of example is sometimes irresistible. Even among these back-settlers, their depravity is greater or less, according to what nation or province they belong. Were I to adduce proofs of this, I might be accused of partiality. If there happens to be some rich intervals, some fertile bottoms, in those remote districts, the people will there prefer tilling the land to hunting, and will attach themselves to it; but, even on these fertile spots, you may plainly perceive the inhabitants to acquire a great degree of rusticity and selfishness.

It is in consequence of this straggling situation, and the astonishing power it has on manners, that the back-settlers of both the Carolinas, Virginia, and many other parts, have

been long a set of lawless people; it has been even dangerous to travel among them. Government can do nothing in so
extensive a country; better it should wink at these irregulari-
ties than that it should use means inconsistent with its usual
mildness. Time will efface those stains: in proportion as the
great body of population approaches them, they will reform, and become polished and subordinate. Whatever has
been said of the four New-England provinces, no such degeneracy of manners has ever tarnished their annals: their
back-settlers have been kept within the bounds of decency
and government, by means of wise laws, and by the influence of religion. What a detestable idea such people must
have given to the natives of the Europeans! They trade with
them; the worst of people are permitted to do that which
none but persons of the best characters should be employed
in. They get drunk with them, and often defraud the Indians.
Their avarice, removed from the eyes of their superiors,
knows no bounds; and, aided by a little superiority of
knowledge, these traders deceive them, and even sometimes shed blood. Hence those shocking violations, those
sudden devastations which have so often stained our fron-
tiers, when hundreds of innocent people have been sacrificed for the crimes of a few. It was in consequence of such
behaviour that the Indians took the hatchet against the Virginians in 1774. Thus are our first steps trodden, thus are
our first trees felled, in general, by the most vicious of our
people; and thus the path is opened for the arrival of a second and better class, the true American freeholders; the
most respectable set of people in this part of the world: respectable for their industry, their happy independence, the
great share of freedom they possess, the good regulation of
their families, and for extending the trace and the dominion
of our mother-country.

Europe contains hardly any other distinctions but lords
and tenants; this fair country alone is settled by freeholders,
the possessors of the soil they cultivate, members of the
government they obey, and the framers of their own laws,
by means of their representatives. This is a thought which
you have taught me to cherish; our distance from Europe,

far from diminishing, rather adds to, our usefulness and consequence as men and subjects. Had our forefathers remained there, they would only have crouded it, and perhaps prolonged those convulsions which had shaken it so long. Every industrious European, who transports himself here, may be compared to a sprout growing at the foot of a great tree; it enjoys and draws but a little portion of sap; wrench it from the parent roots, transplant it, and it will become a tree bearing fruit also. Colonists are therefore entitled to the consideration due to the most useful subjects; a hundred families, barely existing in some parts of Scotland, will here, in six years, cause an annual exportation of 10,000 bushels of wheat: 100 bushels being but a common quantity for an industrious family to fell, if they cultivate good land. It is here then that the idle may be employed, the useless become useful, and the poor become rich; but by riches I do not mean gold and silver, we have but little of those metals: I mean a better sort of wealth; cleared lands, cattle, good houses, good clothes, and an increase of people to enjoy them.

There is no wonder that this country has so many charms, and presents to Europeans so many temptations to remain in it. A traveller in Europe becomes a stranger as soon as he quits his own kingdom; but it is otherwise here. We know, properly speaking, no strangers; this is every person's country; the variety of our soils, situations, climates, governments, and produce, hath something which must please every body. No sooner does an European arrive, no matter of what condition, than his eyes are opened upon the fair prospect; he hears his language spoken, he retraces many of his own country manners, he perpetually hears the names of families and towns with which he is acquainted; he sees happiness and prosperity in all places disseminated; he meets with hospitality, kindness, and plenty, every where: he beholds hardly any poor, he seldom hears of punishments and executions; and he wonders at the elegance of our towns, those miracles of industry and freedom. He cannot admire enough our rural districts, our convenient roads, good taverns, and our many accommodations; he involuntarily loves a country where every thing is so lovely. When in England, he was a mere Englishman; here he stands on a larger portion of the globe, not less than its fourth part, and may see the productions of the north, in iron and naval stores; the provisions of Ireland, the grain of Egypt, the indigo, the rice, of China. He does not find, as in Europe, a crouded society, where every place is over-stocked; he does not feel that perpetual collision of parties, that difficulty of beginning, that contention which oversets so many. There is room for every body in America; has he any particular talent or industry? he exerts it in order to procure a livelihood, and it succeeds. Is he a merchant? the avenues of trade are infinite. Is he eminent in any respect? he will be employed and respected. Does he love a country life? pleasant farms present themselves; he may purchase what he wants, and thereby become an American farmer. Is he a labourer, sober and industrious? he need not go many miles, nor receive many informations before he will be hired, well fed at the table of his employer, and paid four or five times more than he can get in Europe. Does he want uncultivated lands? thousands of acres present themselves, which he may purchase cheap. Whatever be his talents or inclinations, if they are moderate, he may satisfy them. I do not mean that every one who comes will grow rich in a little time; no, but he may procure an easy decent maintenance by his industry. Instead of starving he will be fed, instead of being idle he will have employment; and these are riches enough for such men as come over here. The rich stay in Europe; it is only the middling and poor that emigrate. Would you wish to travel in independent idleness, from north to south, you will find easy access, and the most cheerful reception, at every house; society without ostentation, good cheer without pride, and every decent diversion which the country affords, with little expence. It is no wonder that the European, who has lived here a few years, is desirous to remain; Europe, with all its pomp, is not to be compared to this continent, for men of middle stations or labourers.

An European, when he first arrives, seems limited in his

intentions as well as in his views; but he very suddenly alters his scale; two hundred miles formerly appeared a very great distance, it is now but a trifle; he no sooner breathes our air than he forms schemes, and embarks in designs, he never would have thought of in his own country. There the plenitude of society confines many useful ideas, and often extinguishes the most laudable schemes which here ripen into maturity. Thus Europeans become Americans.

But how is this accomplished in that croud of low indigent people, who flock here every year from all parts of Europe? I will tell you; they no sooner arrive than they immediately feel the good effects of that plenty of provisions we possess: they fare on our best food, and are kindly entertained; their talents, character, and peculiar industry, are immediately inquired into; they find countrymen every where disseminated, let them come from whatever part of Europe. Let me select one as an epitome of the rest; he is hired, he goes to work, and works moderately; instead of being employed by a haughty person, he finds himself with his equal, placed at the substantial table of the farmer, or else at an inferior one as good; his wages are high, his bed is not like that bed of sorrow on which he used to lie: if he behaves with propriety, and is faithful, he is caressed, and becomes as it were a member of the family. He begins to feel the effects of a sort of resurrection; hitherto he had not lived, but simply vegetated; he now feels himself a man, because he is treated as such; the laws of his own country had overlooked him in his insignificancy; the laws of this cover him with their mantle. Judge what an alteration there must arise in the mind and the thoughts of this man; he begins to forget his former servitude and dependence, his heart involuntarily swells and glows; this first swell inspires him with those new thoughts which constitute an American. What love can he entertain for a country where his existence was a burthen to him? if he is a generous good man, the love of this new adoptive parent will sink deep into his heart. He looks around, and sees many a prosperous person, who, but a few years before, was as poor as himself. This encourages him much; he begins to form some little scheme, the first,

alas! he ever formed in his life. If he is wise, he thus spends
two or three years, in which time he acquires knowledge,
the use of tools, the modes of working the lands, felling
trees, &c. This prepares the foundation of a good name, the
most useful acquisition he can make. He is encouraged, he
has gained friends; he is advised and directed, he feels bold,
he purchases some land; he gives all the money he has
brought over, as well as what he has earned, and trusts to the
God of harvests to the discharge of the rest. His good name
procures him credit; he is now possessed of the deed, con-
veying to him and his posterity the fee simple and absolute
property of two hundred acres of land, situated on such a
river. What an epocha in this man's life! He is become a
freeholder, from perhaps a German boor; he is now an
American, a Pennsylvanian, an English subject. He is naturalized, his name is enrolled with those of the other citizens
of the province. Instead of being a vagrant, he has a place of
residence; he is called the inhabitant of such a country, or of
such a district, and, for the first time in his life, counts for
something; for hitherto he had been a cipher. I only repeat
what I have heard many say; and no wonder their hearts
should glow, and be agitated with a multitude of feelings,
not easy to describe. From nothing, to start into being; from
a servant, to the rank of a master; from being the slave of
some despotic prince, to become a free man, invested with
lands, to which every municipal blessing is annexed! What
a change indeed! It is in consequence of that change that he
becomes an American. This great metamorphosis has a double effect; it extinguishes all his European prejudices, he
forgets that mechanism of subordination, that servility of
disposition, which poverty had taught him; and sometimes
he is apt to forget it too much, often passing from one extreme to the other. If he is a good man, he forms schemes of
future prosperity, he proposes to educate his children better
than he has been educated himself; he thinks of future
modes of conduct, feels an ardour to labour he never felt before. Pride steps in, and leads him to every thing that the
laws do not forbid: he respects them; with a heart-felt gratitude he looks toward the east, toward that insular govern-

ment from whose wisdom all his new felicity is derived, and under whose wings and protection he now lives. These reflections constitute him the good man and the good subject. Ye poor Europeans, ye, who sweat, and work for the great; ye, who are obliged to give so many sheaves to the church, so many to your lords, so many to your government, and have hardly any left for yourselves, ye who are held in less estimation than favourite hunters or useless lap-dogs; ye, who only breathe the air of nature, because it cannot be withholden from you; it is here that ye can conceive the possibility of those feelings I have been describing; it is here the laws of naturalization invite every one to partake of our great labours and felicity, to till unrented, untaxed, lands! Many, corrupted beyond the power of amendment, have brought with them all their vices, and, disregarding the advantages held to them, have gone on in their former career of iniquity, until they have been overtaken and punished by our laws. It is not every emigrant who succeeds; no, it is only the sober, the honest, and industrious: happy those to whom this transition has served as a powerful spur to labour, to prosperity, and to the good establishment of children, born in the days of their poverty! and who had no other portion to expect but the rags of their parents, had it not been for their happy emigration. Others, again, have been led astray by this enchanting scene; their new pride, instead of leading them to the fields, has kept them in idleness; the idea of possessing lands is all that satisfies them; though surrounded with fertility, they have mouldered away their time in inactivity, misinformed husbandry, and ineffectual endeavours. . . .

After a foreigner from any part of Europe is arrived, and become a citizen, let him devoutly listen to the voice of our great parent, which says to him, "Welcome to my shores, distressed European; bless the hour in which thou didst see my verdant fields, my fair navigable rivers, and my green mountains!—If thou wilt work, I have bread for thee; if thou wilt be honest, sober, and industrious, I have greater rewards to confer on thee—ease and independence. I will give thee fields to feed and clothe thee; a comfortable fireside to sit by, and tell thy children by what means thou hast prospered; and a decent bed to repose on. I shall endow thee beside with the immunities of a freeman, if thou wilt carefully educate thy children, teach them gratitude to God, and reverence to that government, that philanthropic government, which has collected here so many men and made them happy. I will also provide for thy progeny; and to every good man this ought to be the most holy, the most powerful, the most earnest, wish we can possibly form, as well as the most consolatory prospect when he dies. Go thou, and work, and till; thou shalt prosper, provided thou be just, grateful, and industrious."

Inquiries of an Emigrant
Joseph Pickering

All that is known about Joseph Pickering's life is contained in his one known publication, *Inquiries of an Emigrant*, a guidebook for prospective travelers to the New World, first published in 1831. According to *Inquiries*, Pickering decided to emigrate to the United States in 1824 after losing his farm during an economic crisis in England following the War of 1812. Unable to find work in urban London, Pickering took the advice of the government fliers circulating at the time for landless Englishmen, and "sought some other business" in life in a more profitable nation. Believing Canada to be a frozen and untillable wasteland, Pickering settled on America as a place of agricultural opportunity.

Arriving in Baltimore, Pickering was disturbed by the spectacle of the slave trade and soon resolved to travel north, to New England and Philadelphia. He was not pleased with the customs of the locals in these areas, however, and soon crossed the border into more familiar British territory. In Ontario, Pickering saw that the land was not entirely covered with ice, and both comfort and land ownership were possible for a homesick Englishman. Although Pickering believed the United States to be a beautiful place full of fruitful farmland, he found American culture, particularly the institution of slavery, to be barbaric and alienating to British sensibilities of integrity and decorum.

Pickering is believed to have died in Canada, although

he did return to England in 1831 to publish his observations on American vegetation, farming, and culture. Chapters 1 and 2 of *Inquiries of an Emigrant* recount Joseph Pickering's motives for exile from a homeland which no longer had space for his endeavors.

CHAPTER 1

The Author's motives for Emigration—Preparations for the Voyage—Embarkation, and Passage out.

I shall premise the causes of leaving my native country, and reasons for preferring the United States; in doing which I am only describing the misfortunes and fate of thousands of my countrymen.

I took a farm previous to the close of the late war (about 1813), on a seven years' lease, and of course at a high rent. The year following, peace came, and with it ruin to nearly one-fourth of the agriculturists. My landlord compelled me to hold the farm for the term I had taken it, with but a small and insufficient abatement of rent. The consequence was, that with strict attention to economy and industry, at the close of my lease I had lost one-half of my little capital, the remains of which not being sufficient to stock the farm, I was obliged to give it up, although offered it at one-half the former rent. I then took his Majesty's ministers' advice, that, "if farming would not answer, farmers must engage in some other business." I engaged in another business, but through the shortness of my funds, and a combination of untoward circumstances, I lost the remainder of my property. I now determined to leave a country that no longer afforded me a respectable and comfortable subsistence, thinking no person with one spark of independent spirit, could hesitate a moment in a choice between honorable, though even laborious, exertion and dangers, with independence, to a dronish uselessness in society, or a mean ignoble dependence on friends.

Van Diemen's Land and the United States presented me with a choice of place for my exile. I weighed the inducements held out by each, deliberately, and their attractions counterpoised in the balance for some time, until the shortness and cheapness of the passage to the latter preponderated, and decided my choice: I then had not the least intention of going to Canada, a place I had been led to believe was frozen up two-thirds of the year, and scorched up the remainder; but on arriving in the United States, I procured better information, without seeking it.

In October, 1824, I engaged with an American captain of a brig, lying in the London Docks, bound to Baltimore, for a passage in the steerage, for six guineas, my finances not allowing me to go in the cabin; and being the only passenger on board (excepting two young American seamen who worked their passage) had the privilege of a small apartment to myself, dignified with the name of "state-room." Some days passed in providing provisions, &c. with great trouble in procuring the variety of articles wanted, to the best advantage, and on the 18th we sailed with the morning tide and a fair wind, down the river Thames; a frosty morning, but a fine pleasant day; numbers of vessels going out; and anchored off Gravesend for the night. I had paid 1£ to a person residing near the entrance of the Docks, for procuring me a "cocket" or clearance, which I am inclined to think was rather an imposition, but he said he would have procured the same for four or five passengers, had there been as many, for the same money; went on shore to the customhouse at Gravesend, to deliver the above cocket; was asked my name, and if an Englishman, and for a reference in London. I had nothing to pay, nor was any certificate of my occupation or identity, required, as I had been led to expect; some officers came on board, but did not examine my trunks, merely asked if they contained wearing apparel and personals only. The provisions I took for my passage were laid in for eight weeks' consumption, and I had no restriction in quantity or variety (there are restrictions in some ports respecting quantity, particularly if a considerable number of passengers are going in a ship); in the Appendix

I have stated particulars at length. We left Gravesend with a
fair wind, and pretty good spirits, my thoughts ranging
through the New World I had now fairly embarked for, and
then returning again to the land of my nativity, friends, and
former home, which, at times, would cause an involuntary
sigh; but the hopes and prospect ever-cheering fancy presented to my mind, dissipated all gloom, and I bade adieu to
Old England without much regret. The wind being a-head,
we tacked and came to anchor off Margate for the night; in
the morning beat up into the Downs, when the pilot left us;
a New York packet-ship, the Trident, passed in fine stile,
without tacking once, through her superior powers of sailing, and was in port three weeks before us; this may serve as
a hint to emigrants to engage a passage in a good sailing
vessel, which may be ascertained generally by inquiry, or
by the sharpness of their bows. I would also recommend
every one, before engaging his passage in a ship, to inquire
her age (from two to ten years is best), and to see if her sails,
rigging, anchors, and cables are good, and also if the captain is steady, respectable, and agreeable; a middle-aged
one I would generally prefer.

On leaving the Downs, we experienced a rough sea;
which produced sickness in the captain as well as myself;
the weather was quite warm, the thermometer being at
63; the wind increasing, we made considerable head-way,
and in two days lost sight of the Lizard Point, and a pigeon
passed us fifteen miles from the land; a packet spoke us
from the Straits, bound to Liverpool. There is no regard
paid to Sunday, as a sabbath, on board this vessel, indeed,
sometimes it would be impossible; on the 26th, a heavy gale
came on, and continued throughout the day; I could hardly
get from my berth or help tumbling out; no life nor power
to move—just enough to wish myself on some shore; the
wind dropped in the night, but the sea continued to roll its
mighty waves—

> Oh wonderful thou art, great element!
> And fearful in thy spleeny humours bent,
> Yet lovely in repose.

This was succeeded by a calm (three vessels in sight); ate a little gruel and a pancake only; a good deal of the latter used in the cabin. October 29th, another strong gale during the night, in which we again "lay too:" wind south-west, which drove us in sight of Cape Clear, in Ireland, by the morning, and in the heavy squall which followed, we had near been capsized through the negligence of the mate not taking in the sails soon enough; the captain, who was in bed when it came on, was instantly on deck, and gave the mate a deserved reprimand; one of the sails giving way, and the wind lowering, they were enabled to set all right again; the weather for several days various, and we felt a warmer climate, and longer days, north latitude 44 : 29—longitude, 12 : 30, west—thermometer 83. On the evening of Nov. 2d, a bank of clouds arose north-west, and a breeze sprung up in our favour; we had now been thirteen days at sea, and its effects were such, that provisions were in some measure useless, tea, gruel, pudding, or a roasted potatoe being all I could take, with soda-water, or a little warm porter for drink; but at this time the weather became pleasant and warm, with light wind, thermometer 65, and the sea being nearly smooth, partially restored my health, and I made ample amends in eating after my long abstinence; we now got so far from land that the gulls and other sea birds left us, and experienced a variety of winds, but generally warm weather, and the voyager would have some pleasure in agreeable and decorous company; whales sported about, and other large fish were occasionally near the vessel. The saline air caused my apparel to become damp and mouldy, and knives, &c. to rust; attention to these matters, assisted in passing time away, but occasional squalls would interrupt my business; in the twilight I often amused myself, when there was a gentle breeze fanning the surface of the water, by viewing the ripples it made with their white caps, it looked so much like an extensive fallow-field, with a slight scattering of snow on its unevennesses; and fancy, ever busy, conjured up in the distance some well-known familiar spot for the imagination to feast on, till the darkening shades of night, or the approach and noise of sailors, aroused me from my reverie:—ten days thus passed, when we had a heavy breeze all day, and took in the main top-gallant sails. Have seen of late a large brown bird of the gull species, which the sailors call a shear-water, and some small birds like martins they denominate Mother Cary's chickens. The ship's store of potatoes became half rotten through having been dug before they were ripe, and put on board in a wet state. Mine remained quite sound, but began to shoot, through the mild season. Rather disagreeable weather followed this gale, and several seas broke over the vessel: then a dead calm ensued, and the ship rolled much; but a smart breeze soon sprung up, north by east, which carried us eight knots per hour, and was the first wind the sailors called fair, that is, lying aft, or at the hind part of the vessel. The sea water is quite warm, and sparkles alongside the ship at night like fire; this appearance is caused, apparently, by the ship's side dashing the salt water into air-bubbles: some assert that this fiery appearance arises from a kind of animalculæ, but this opinion is evidently erroneous, for these animalculæ are never numerous enough in the water in any one place, and but occasionally to be met with at all, when these sparkles are everywhere to be seen in the night in salt water. The air from the waves which break at the ship's side, on leaning over, rises in the face like the steam from heated water. The vessel now made a good deal of water when the sea was rough.

The captain swears and storms like a madman; at one time cursing the men (by-the-by, some of them were a stupid set of fellows), then the ship, and the weather, and almost in the same breath saying, they could not have had a better day for the work they had to do, and that we had been highly favoured throughout: so inconsistent is human nature!

We were often compelled to lay to, in which there is little danger in any moderate gale, provided you have plenty of sea-room to drift, and the vessel has far less motion than if sailing in the same wind, or in a calm. In one of the late gales the tiller rope broke, when it threw down, and very much cut and bruised, the man steering. My butter was all spoiled through the warm weather, not having been potted close, and sufficient salt put in it.

Squalls, calms, head winds, &c. continue, and the captain says he never experienced so much bad weather and opposing winds before. A disagreeable life on board in such seasons: perhaps you are pitched head-foremost against one side of the vessel by a lee-lurch, or a roll, and before you have time to recover your legs, tumbled to the other side; or at dinner, the dishes and plates with their contents are suddenly dashed to the floor, when the potatoes, &c. are rolling about from one side of the vessel to the other, as if playfully amusing themselves; and, while attempting their recovery, you roll after them, or tumble head-foremost, to the no small amusement of the rest of the company.

We continued to experience westerly winds, which retarded our progress greatly, a proof of which was, that we spoke a brig from New York, bound to Buenos Ayres, out only eight days, and it took us three weeks to get into port; indeed, their prevalence is a strong reason why the voyage out should not be undertaken at this season, and that this period, or a little earlier, is often chosen to return to England. Appearances indicated an approach to the New World, and like similar circumstances to Columbus filled us with hope. Great quantities of sea or gulph-weed floated past us, and on the 4th of December we were in latitude 34 : 35, and southed a degree. Beautiful April-like weather, thermometer 71 in the shade, and 73 in the water; sometimes some light showers, with occasionally lightning in the evenings. The air exhibited a curious appearance, being of a yellowish red colour, and the clouds of a cinerous blue, which were in a thousand fantastic and singular forms, the sailors called them snow-clouds. Saw a number of flying fish pursued by a dolphin, and also numerous beautiful coloured nautilus or "men of war," with their sails expanded to the breeze, blown swiftly over the undulating waves. My bottled porter was excellent, and of great service now I had recovered from the sea-sickness; saw no more gulph-weed. We had now crossed the back stream, and were between the two; it runs down the eastern coast of America, across the banks of Newfoundland, round the Western Isles, and along the coast of Africa.

Dec. 6.—Squally again of late. Getting near the gulph-stream, which makes it warm, and great quantities of the gulph, or sea-weed is seen again; it nearly covers the surface of the water in some places, and in others it is extended for miles in parallel lines, north-east and south-west; I should suppose drifted from the side of the stream, which runs in that direction in this part.

Dec. 10.—Getting too far south, through the prevalence of north-west winds; latitude 33 : 30, thermometer 65 in the air, and 72 in the water. A shark ten or twelve feet in length came alongside the vessel, and a number of grampuses were seen at a distance. Fine weather, and would be delightful if on shore, and not altogether otherwise here.

Dec. 12.—Light wind, and smooth sea; clear, bright, warm day. Two dolphins came swimming about the vessel, one of which the captain struck with a fish-spear, and succeeded in getting it on board; they all said it was the largest they had ever seen, six feet seven and a half inches in length, and I should suppose weighed three quarters of a cwt. or more.

Dec. 13.—Hardly any wind of late, but a breeze sprung up this morning, and soon rose into a gale, and at noon blew violently from the southward. The foam flew like fine-drifted snow: the wind suddenly fell, and then chopped round to the north-west, and blew more moderate, when the grandest sight I had ever seen presented itself: the tremendous billows meeting in all directions formed a thousand fantastical shapes, sometimes running up into high peaks or spires, then suddenly sinking into vast abysses; or two large waves meeting, rose into an immense ridge; or meeting with violence, dashed their spray in all directions, as if in a rude, frolicsome play, while the vessel rose up their mountain sides most majestically, receiving now and then a salute from their gambols. Rain came on, and clouds were seen flying in various directions; the air remarkably warm. Thermometer in the morning 70, and in the water at noon 74; and before night 79; remaining at 70 in the air.—So we are in the Great Gulph stream at last!

Dec. 15.—Through the Gulph as it is called, and the air gets colder every hour. Shortened sail last night, and sounded without finding bottom. Found, by an observation taken at noon, we were in latitude 35 : 19. Just north of Cape Hattrass, a dangerous reef of sunken rocks, running forty miles into the sea, on the coast of Carolina. Sounded again in the evening, and found nineteen fathoms water. The thermometer had sunk in the air to 45, and in the water to 68. Water on soundings looks green, in the ocean a dark blue; this is universal, I am told.

Dec. 16.—Made land this morning opposite Roanoke Inlet, North Carolina, near the borders of Virginia, seventy miles too far south of the Chesapeak Bay; ranged within five miles of the shore all day, with a light breeze, and fine clear cold air. Cannot see anything of the country, but clay and sand banks, covered with pines and other trees; it is apparently a flat land along the sea-board; vessels sailing in different directions, and numbers of wild ducks seen along the shore.

Dec. 17.—As no pilot came on board last evening, a lantern was hung up in the night at the mast head, for a signal, and at two o'clock this morning one hove his boat alongside and was taken on board, who proceeded immediately with the vessel round Cape Henry, into the Chesapeak Bay; the wind having got south-east at the same time, with a stiff breeze, wafted us along faster than we had sailed all the time we had been out. Rain and hazy weather came on this evening, which compelled us reluctantly to come to an anchor for fear of the shoals. The Chesapeak is a very fine Bay, from ten or twelve to twenty miles across, and upwards of two hundred long; its low banks, fringed with trees, are all that is to be seen of the country, excepting here and there a house near the shore, and occasionally a small town or village. A great number of small craft, loaded with cord, wood for fuel, country produce, &c. for Baltimore market. Ten thousands of wild ducks, geese, swans, &c., almost covering the Bay, swimming and flying; an English sportsman would be in his Elysium here!

Dec. 18.—After a wet, blowing night, it cleared up soon after day-light this morning, when we weighed anchor, and proceeded up the Patapsco River. As beautiful a day as ever shone, with a serene mild air, and pleasant light breeze. Vessels of all sizes sailing in various directions, with well-dressed people on board; and Baltimore, with its white buildings rising to our view on the sides of the hills, as we approached it, had a most exhilarating effect on one whose vision had been confined to the monotonous rolling of the unstable waters for sixty-five days, which is deemed a very long passage.

CHAPTER 2

Arrival at Baltimore—Description of the Town, its Inhabitants, and Customs—Excursions in the neighbourhood, and continued residence—with a variety of miscellaneous Remarks.

My diary having been kept as a daily journal, I shall now offer it to the reader in that form, as exhibiting, better than any other mode, a narrative of my proceedings; and presenting to him the best means of understanding the occupations of my time, and the space I traversed.

On the 18th Dec., at two o'clock, the pilot laid the vessel alongside the wharf, when, in an instant its deck was covered with people of all sorts, looking about and asked question. After packing my luggage, I went into the town to procure something to eat, lodgings, &c., when I felt myself a stranger, on a foreign, although a kindred strand. After dining heartily on some excellent sausages, with some pleasant mild ale, I took a ramble through the city; but I hardly knew how to walk, the pavement seemed to have the motion of the vessel.

Baltimore is a large town, with some handsome public and private buildings; the streets are spacious, airy, and clean; the centres pitched with rock stone, and the side walks paved with red brick, of which also the houses are mostly built. Pratt-street, along tha water side, was all in a bustle, and apparently full of business, but the method of doing it evidently differs considerably from the manner in England.

Dec. 19. Sunday.—At one church, and two meeting-houses (no chapels here); some of them elegant buildings, with very respectable-looking congregations. Dined with the captain, whose treatment was hospitable. The manners of the Americans appear widely different to the English, particularly of the females, who are more easy and unembarrassed, yet reserved, in their address, than the retiring diffidence of the latter. Took lodgings at a respectable ship carpenter's, at three dollars, or 13*s*. 6*d*. sterling, per week, board, washing, and mending included.

Dec. 20.—A clear, bright, frosty air this morning. Thermometer in my sleeping room 43. Went to the custom-house, with the captain, to clear my luggage. Paid half a dollar to a notary (a very polite, agreeable person) for drawing up an inventory and certificate of my luggage, and 20 cents (one-fifth of a dollar, or about 11*d*. sterling) on presenting it; when the only question asked was, Will you swear this is a correct statement, and that the articles are for your own private use? I merely answered in the affirmative. Had a ramble through the town and its environs. Like the appearance of the Americans generally, and think the place prosperous, as the people appear to be all employed and busy, and have the air of ease and content in their countenances, with but little superciliousness. The markets are well supplied with meat as to quantity, but the quality not quite so good as in England, excepting the pork, which is fine; some little good beef, but veal and mutton very indifferent, nor is trouble taken to set it off to the best advantage. The vegetables brought to market now are chiefly potatoes, beets, and cabbages, great quantities of the latter, and mostly drumheads; some few carrots, turnips, onions, sweet potatoes, &c. at moderate prices. A great many negroes about the markets and wharfs, who appear far more lively and as independent as the whites, but are treated by the latter as inferior beings; will not eat at the same table, or walk in their company, and have separate places of worship.

There are five market houses in Baltimore, some of them large, and all conveniently built, very similar to the old Fleet Market in London. The centres, which are spacious, are occupied on each side by the butchers; on the outside of the butcher's stalls is also a passage on each side, with stalls on either hand, where vegetables, country produce, flour, meal, &c., ready-made clothes, shoes, tin-ware, &c. are exposed. The fish markets are at the ends of the others, and generally well supplied. To-day are their Christmas markets, at which there is great plenty of everything—some good beef, pork excellent, mutton thin and small, veal (calf) hardly fit to eat, killed too young. Beef, 2*d.* to 3½*d.* per pound; the best cuts, 4½*d.* (I have stated the prices in sterling money, being far more conveniently understood by the British reader); pork generally sold by the carcass, brought in by the farmers from the country, from 2*d.* to 3½*d.* per pound, and sometimes even lower; veal and mutton by the quarter, at 1*s.* 2*d.* to 2*s.* 3*d.* each; turkeys, 1*s.* 2*d.* to 2*s.* 3*d.* each; fowls, 6½*d.* to 9*d.* ditto; cabbages, (drumheads), 1*d.* to 2*d.* each; potatoes and turnips, 10*d.* to 1*s.* 2*d.* per bushel, &c. I was asked in the market 5*l.* for a cow and calf, worth in England 8*l.* or 10*l.* only five or six cows in the market; no fairs for cattle here, and but few sold in the markets; there are some farmers that deal in them, and supply those who want, and I am told do pretty well by it; wholesale butchers buy up the droves of cattle that are driven from Ohio and the west, slaughter, and sell them to the retail ones. The regulations respecting the markets in this warm climate are judicious; no slaughtering allowed in the town—no butchers' shops opened any where; the cattle are killed out of town, and the meat taken to the market houses early in the morning, where the inhabitants flock at break of day with their baskets, as every one carries home his purchases. The markets close in summer at eleven o'clock, in winter at one.

Great numbers of country waggons at the market every day through the fall, [autumn] winter, and spring, with country produce. Large quantities of water-fowl, from the Bay, brought to the markets during the winter; wild ducks, a great variety, from 3½d. to 5d. each; the canvas-back is large, and considered a delicacy, 1s. 1d. to 1s. 6d. each; partridges, 4d. to 7d. each; quails, 1d. to 2¼d. ditto; hares and rabbits, small, from 6d. to 1s. each.

The land round the city is hilly, commanding fine views down the Bay, and over the country. The soil in the vicinity is a mixture of dirty yellow clay, with sand and gravel, but the bottoms or small valleys which lie to the east and north-west are good, and here are the gardens that supply the markets. On the little hills and risings are situated some country seats, that the wealthy inhabitants retire to in summer; their whiteness, enlivened with the brightness of the sun, on opening to the view in different directions, from behind the slips of woods, reminds me of some spots in the neighbourhood of London, but on approaching them many are in a dilapidated state, and the gardens and fences in a slovenly, neglected condition.

Dec. 25.—Christmas-day: instead of ringing bells, &c. as in England (there are but few bells here to ring) it was ushered in by firing guns, squibs, and crackers all last night, and continues with intervals through the day. The moment I arose this morning, I was presented with a glass of "egg-mogg," as they termed it, a compound of rum, eggs, milk, and sugar, also with ginger-cake, and a cake with raisins in it, which is their "Christmas cake;" all for merry-making and "parties." I was pressed to one in the evening with the captain and his wife, a number of fine females and their beaus present; the time was spent with a variety of plays, singing songs, playing on the piano, eating cake, drinking toddy, peach brandy, &c., quite a sociable party, the female part easy and apparently unaffected; broke up early by the request of our host, the next day being Sunday. Americans use very little or no ceremony, except the introduction by shaking hands, &c.; each leaves table at meal-time as soon as done eating, and they are generally quick: no bidding good night, or other ceremony, on going to bed.

Dec. 26, Sunday.—The day as fine as the preceding, thermometer 47, with a clear bright air; the sun rises twenty-five minutes after seven o'clock on the shortest day, and sets thirty-five minutes past four. At the Roman Catholic cathedral this morning; it is just finished, and is a large elegant place, far superior to the one in Moorfields, London; there is another church here also of that persuasion, and a grand Unitarian one, but the latter has but a small congregation; there are besides, Episcopalians [church of England], Presbyterians, Congregationalists, Baptists, Quakers, and Methodists; the latter appear to be the most numerous, they having four or five large meetings, and all well attended. At one of them this evening; the male part of the audience on one side of the meeting, and the female on the other; the preacher respectable, but rather too noisy, yet he had to beg the attention of the congregation more than once; no pews, but long enclosed seats from one end to the other of the gallery, and below, from the aisles to the sides, and across between them; every one appeared to sit where he thought proper; the floors most disgustingly dirty from the effects of tobacco; more than half the males of the age of fourteen chew tobacco; and boys of ten or twelve years may often be seen smoking a cigar.

Dec. 27.—A thick fog this morning, wind east, and no frost; sun broke through the mist at noon, when it was quite warm. I took my gun into the woods, but found no game; on my return, by the race-ground, a number of persons had a bull tied to a stake for the purpose of baiting; I stopped to see a "set-to," as I had never seen one before; the bull was a fine, well-bred, gentle creature; seven or eight dogs were turned loose at him at once! They soon tore his ears off, and shockingly lacerated his head, which made the poor thing bellow hideously, and run about in every direction to the length of his chain, maddened with pain; in ten minutes he had killed one dog, and lamed others, when I turned away with disgust at the cruel sport; I was afterwards informed, the animal's head was literally torn to pieces! One might be led to suppose, by this spectacle, the Baltimoreans are a depraved set of beings, but I must say to their credit, I saw not more than ten or twelve of respectable looking people there, the others, about one hundred, consisted of the refuse of the place, and a number of them job butchers. Bull-baiting is not allowed in the liberties of the city, and means are about to be taken to put a stop to it altogether.

I have been looking out for some little business, or a situation as superintendent, or overseer of a farm, but have not yet succeeded; I find I am not prepared for the latter, because *I do not understand the management of Blacks*. I have been introduced to some Englishmen, but they, generally, have treated me with far more reserve and coolness than the Americans. One from the Isle of Wight, a Mr. S., says he was an extensive farmer and butcher there: he has been here about two years, and is doing pretty well as a butcher, having nothing much when he came, and has some ungracious feelings towards his native country. Another from Hampshire has been here fifty-six years, and is seventy-eight years of age. He shouldered his musket in the late war, he tells me, to defend his home.

Sunday, Jun. 2, 1825.—Some snow in the night, with rain, and afterwards frost, which makes the streets all ice; some few sleighs about to day, with bells, which I am told they are compelled to have by law, that they may not run foul of each other in the night. Heard a rather celebrated orator (a Methodist preacher from the back woods), hold forth in a meeting belonging to another denomination, in aid of a subscription for building an asylum for orphan females; a fluent speaker, but manner too theatrical, and language bombastic.

Jan. 10.—Frosty of late, when there were plenty of people to be seen skating. Been to ask the price of land to rent; one lot of fifty acres, only half cleared, four miles from town, 18*s.* per acre per annum: another of rich bottom land, or meadow, several miles off, near the river, I was asked 12 dollars, or 2*l.* 14*s.* per acre, rent. Great numbers of waggons from distant parts of the country every day, with barrels of flour for the merchants, and fat hogs, dead, for the market;

some come four hundred miles, the drivers sleeping in the waggons at night, and carry with them the horses' feed; the waggons are excellent, strong, and light; narrow wheels, narrow in the body, with tilts, seven or eight bows bent over, and remarkable at pleasure, these covered by a light-coloured fine canvass, drawn together at each end like a purse: the horses go double, with a pole, like a coach, generally four or six in each, sometimes five, the driver riding the near hind horse, with reins in one hand and whip in the other, and mostly go a trot. Smaller and very light waggons, drawn by one horse, called carry-alls, or carioles, are used to bring in milk, butter, eggs, fowls, &c. Vendues [auctions] of books, and almost every description of merchandise, are held every few days, and others at night. Sometimes things are sold very low,—I saw some British goods nearly as cheap as in London; American books much lower, but they are not quite so well printed, and paper generally inferior.

Sunday, Jan. 16.—Dull foggy day; frost out of the ground again. Witnessed a military funeral procession (General Harper, who died suddenly on Friday last); an early burial, we should think, yet here, I am told, it is the custom to inter a corpse the next, and often the same day of its decease. A grand parade of near 2000 soldiers, volunteers, there are no regulars in the city; there were three bands of music with muffled drums; each company having a peculiar dress made their appearance quite novel; two companies with different coloured plaid dresses; they all had frock jackets, I believe. The procession began with some officers, then some companies, and music playing various solemn airs; three or four more companies and music; then two brass field-pieces, and company of artillery-men; more music, and companies; then the hearse, (a small one, open on the side, as they all appear to be here); the General's horse, with sword, boots, &c.; mourning coaches; riflemen in companies; and closed with a great number of hackney coaches, and thousands of pedestrians. Some of the above companies are composed of respectable tradesmen, who have expensive dresses, with ostrich feathers on their caps, which gives them much the appearance of the ancient Spanish dress. General Harper was a Federalist, and like the whole of that party was looked upon with a kind of suspicion, as they are thought to have too great an attachment to the English constitution.

Jan. 23, *Sunday.*—At a Methodist meeting to-day; a woman cried out "mercy," and some others shouted "glory," and clapped hands, mostly women, and generally by the same persons; a common thing here I am told, which appears evident, as it excited little or no surprise, even amongst the most thoughtless; the preacher encouraged it, by preaching, or rather exclaiming louder as the women cried the more, till at last it amounted to almost raving; and because he could not make any apparent impression on the rest of the congregation, he accused them of hardness of heart, &c. I fear there is more weakness and enthusiasm than true devotion in such scenes as these; still custom makes it sufferable, and the Methodists have been rapidly increasing the last few years, and have evidently done much good; in most of the meetings here, of every denomination, they have another disgusting practice in the middle of the service, by holding a green bag at the end of a pole, in your face, along every seat, for money to purchase wood for the stove, candles, &c. Here I will say a word or two on the excessive fondness of Americans for stoves; each church and meeting has from two to four in each; hardly a poor family in Baltimore but has one or more, at which the cooking is all done in winter, which makes their rooms like ovens, and many people look as if half stewed. Lotteries are continually drawing here, and I believe have a bad tendency on the morals of the middle and lower classes. Almost every tavern keeps a bowling-alley, where the idle resort to play at ten pins (nine pins having been prohibited by law!) and various other games. Luxury and licentiousness appear to be usual in the lower part of the community, through the latitude and ability given by the republican institutions—as monarchial governments tend to the same effect in the upper classes of their subjects.

A True Picture of Emigration

Rebecca Burlend

The Illinois pioneer and author Rebecca Burton Burlend was born in 1793 to poor parents in Yorkshire, England. It is unknown when she married John Burlend, a teacher and farmer, but when Rebecca reached the age of thirty-eight, the couple emigrated to the United States due to financial concerns, with the younger five of their seven children. Letters of friends and relatives who had emigrated before them directed the Burlends to Pike City, Illinois. There, the English family labored on an eighty-acre plot. Wheat was planted, livestock bought, and animals were trapped for food.

With the subsequent success of the farm, Rebecca Burlend was able to travel back to England in 1846 and recount her pioneer story to her eldest son, Edward, a scholar and teacher with an interest in publishing, who had been left behind in 1831. Edward Burlend edited his mother's story, publishing it as "A True Picture of Emigration: Or fourteen Years in the Interior of North America; Being a Full and Impartial Account of the Various Difficulties and Ultimate Success of an English Family Who Emigrated from Barwick-in-Elmet near Leeds in the year 1831." Later, the text was republished as *The Wesleyan Emigrants* in 1856 or 1857. Like the letters of emigrants read by the Burlends in 1831, Rebecca's story helped convince others to emigrate from England including Mary Burlend Yelliot, the daughter she had left behind. At the age of seventy-seven Rebecca Burlend died among her large extended family on the Illinois plot she fought hard to maintain. In the third chapter of her memoir, a middle-aged Burlend recounts some of her first impressions of America while journeying from New Orleans to St. Louis aboard a steamboat. Though she eventually praised the American climate and its ability to produce a wealth of goods, Rebecca Burlend found a few difficulties in adjusting to the alien landscape around her.

CHAPTER 3

As I intimated in the preceding chapter, we reached New Orleans on Sunday morning; but when I came to survey the town more leisurely, I could scarcely believe it was the Lord's day. I remembered that frequently on our passage I had heard it remarked that the time varied with the time in England a few hours, and for a moment I supposed that the Sabbath varied also. The reader will perceive the cause of my surprise, when he is told that the shops were every where open, stalls set out in all directions, and the streets thronged with lookers-on more in the manner of a fair than a Christian Sabbath. This I was told was the general method of spending that day in New Orleans. With regard to the inhabitants, their appearance was exceedingly peculiar, their complexions varying almost as much as their features; from the deep black of the flat-nosed negro to the sickly pale hue of the American shopman. This city is a regular rendezvous for merchants and tradesmen of every kind, from all quarters of the globe. Slavery is here tolerated in its grossest forms. I observed several groups of slaves linked together in chains, and driven about the streets like oxen under the yoke. The river, which is of immense width, affords a sight not less unique than the city. No one, except eye-witnesses, can form an adequate idea of the number and variety of vessels there collected, and lining the river for miles in length. New Orleans being the provision market for the West Indies and some of the Southern States, its port is frequented not merely by foreign traders, but by thousands of small craft, often of the rudest construction, on which the settlers in the interior bring down the various produce of their climate and industry.[1] The town itself, from its low marshy situation, is very unhealthy; the yellow fever is an everlasting scourge to its inhabitants, annually carrying off great numbers. As a trading port, New Orleans is the most famous and the best situated of any in America; but whoever values a comfortable climate or a healthy situation, will not, I am sure, choose to reside there.

But to resume my narrative: having arrived at the port, it was our intention to proceed immediately up the river to St. Louis; but as no steam vessel left till the next day, we remained on board in front of the town. The custom-house officers had not yet been on board to examine the ship, but as we had nothing for which duty would be required, our captain gave my husband a document to present to the inspectors, by which we were allowed to pass early the next morning. Before entering the steam vessel, we got the remainder of our money, all in English sovereigns, exchanged into American dollars. We found that our expenses, since leaving home, amounted to about twenty-three pounds. On leaving the ship I felt a renewal of my home-sickness, to use a quaint expression; it seemed to be the only remaining link between me and England. I was now going to be an alien among strangers. Hitherto I had been accompanied by persons, who when my pain on leaving home manifested itself, could sympathize with me. I should have preferred the meanest passenger on the ship to any I saw on the packet. As, however, we were all in haste to be on our way, I had little time to spend on those tender associations. I certainly

[1] The flatboat commerce by which the surplus produce of the upper Mississippi Valley was brought to New Orleans flourished for a generation or more, until the era of railroad construction which immediately preceded the Civil War. An Illinois youth of recent adoption who made the long journey to New Orleans the year preceding Mrs. Burlend's arrival in America bore the name of Abraham Lincoln. The journey he made was typical of thousands of similar ones performed in the period here alluded to.

left the ship with an aching heart; the captain and cabin passengers had been very kind to us during the voyage, and on going away my children were severally presented with small tokens of approbation, of which they were not a little proud.

I must now leave the ship to pursue my route up the stream of the Mississippi to St. Louis, a distance of not less than thirteen hundred miles. The country on each side of the river is of a dead level, but to all appearance exceedingly productive, and cultivated with considerable pains. On account of the heat which prevails in these districts, the productions of tropical regions are here grown in great abundance. The extensive plantations, notwithstanding their flat appearance, are exceedingly beautiful; and if any thing could have made me forget that I was an unsettled exile, the scenery of the country bordering this river must have done it. There was, nevertheless, one drawback: these beautiful plantations are cultivated by slaves, many of whom we saw as we passed along. As we had regularly to stop by the way to obtain timber for our fires, that being the fuel invariably used by the steamers on this river, we had frequent opportunities of stepping ashore. On one occasion a passenger seeing a negro smoking his pipe by his little cabin, which was just at hand, took the liberty of going up to him for the purpose of begging a little fruit, which hung in plenty on the trees around. The negro, without hesitation, granted his request; and our hero immediately mounted a tree, which he partially stripped of its juicy burden. This little incident might have passed unnoticed, had not the intruder on descending from the tree made use of a kind of box, which was underneath, to break his fall; its structure was too slender for so unusual a load, and in consequence he burst in the top to the terror of the negro, who immediately darted across the orchard, leaving our companion to make the best of his misfortune. The latter was soon convinced that he had committed a blunder, as the box was a bee-hive, and its occupants, aware they had been insulted, would accept no apology, but drawing their sabres attacked their foe with tremendous fury. Poor Yankee was no Leonidas; but with all the speed his heels could muster betook himself to the packet, where he was greeted with roars of laughter by his less enterprising associates.

As we proceeded up the river the country assumed a more rude and uncultivated appearance: the date and plantain tree of the lower regions were exchanged for majestic forest trees and untrodden wilds. Further down it was delightfully pleasant; here magnificently grand eternal forests, in appearance as interminable as the universe, with here and there a patch of ground rudely cultivated by the hand of a lonely settler, constitute the scenery for thousands of miles contiguous to this matchless stream. As to the river itself, I shall not attempt a description of it; what has already been said proves its magnitude to be immensely great; even some of its branches, as the Ohio and the Missouri, are to be classed among the largest rivers in the world. The former[1] is noted for being very muddy, and hurrying in its ungovernable career vast quantities of floating timber, which, decayed by age or other causes, fall into it so as often to render it dangerous for the steamers to pass along. Of these the Mississippi contains acres, that coming from above, have in the lapse of years gradually settled together in places where the current is least active.

Proceeding with my narrative, I must confess I liked the packet much better than I expected. We had engaged to find our own provisions, but on account of their cheapness, or partly because I acted the part of matron to such as needed my assistance, we were frequently presented with young fowls, coffee, rice, &c. so that our food cost us very little on the river. During this transit we obtained considerable information respecting Illinois, which tended in some degree to lessen our disquietude. We were nevertheless very far from being at ease; our unsettled condition was ever the uppermost in our thoughts, and shed a settled gravity over our conduct. Whilst thus the subjects of painful uncertainty, we were one night much alarmed by the following attempt

[1]The river here alluded to is obviously the Missouri, rather than the Ohio.

to rob us: my husband and I were in our berths; I was fast asleep, but he was awake, musing upon our situation, when a black man, one of the crew, knowing we were going to settle in the country, and thinking no doubt we should have money with us, came to the side of our berths and began to search under my pillow, so softly indeed as not to awake me; he was going to examine under my husband's likewise, but as he was awake, he told him he could get him anything he wanted; such unexpected kindness was immediately understood, and the villain disappeared in a moment. Although this attempt proved a complete failure, we were induced to give up our money to the captain the following day, which he kept till we arrived at St. Louis. As my husband kept the money under his pillow, I have never looked back on this circumstance but with feelings of gratitude to Almighty God for his protecting providence, for had he succeeded, we should have been in a most miserable situation, not even able to reach the end of our journey;—destitute and penniless in a strange land, without friends and without home.

The time occupied in passing from New Orleans to St. Louis was about twelve days. We reached the latter place about noon, and found another steamer ready to convey us forward to the situation at which we purposed to remain. I had little opportunity of surveying the town, and therefore can say little respecting it; but was somewhat surprised to find that this noted city should be built principally of wood; its situation is not the most eligible as it regards health, being near the confluence of the Missouri and the Illinois. It is however on that very account likely to become a large and wealthy city, and is indeed by some described as such already.[1] On entering the second steamer I found I had made a poor exchange; the weather was beginning to feel

---

[1]Although St. Louis dates from 1764, the increase in population was extremely slow for several decades. Upon incorporation as a city in 1823, there were only a few hundred inhabitants. By 1830, the year prior to Mrs. Burlend's visit, the number had increased to almost 5,000. One hundred years later (1930) the U. S. census revealed a population of 821,960, amply fulfilling the forecast of the humble English immigrant of 1831.

uncommonly chill, and our accommodation was here very inferior, so that we felt exceedingly anxious to be at our journey's end.

The place at which we intended to leave the river was not more than one hundred and twenty miles from St. Louis; we therefore comforted ourselves with the idea that we should soon be there. We were finally to disembark at Phillip's Ferry, according to the directions sent by the aforementioned Mr. B. to his brother. We should then be within two miles of his residence. Mr. B., therefore, and Phillip's Ferry, occupied our thoughts almost to the exclusion of every other subject. We had already travelled nearly seven thousand miles. Our food had been principally dried provisions. For many long weeks we had been oppressed with anxious suspense; there is therefore no cause for wonder, that, jaded and worn out as we were, we felt anxious to be at our destined situation. Our enquiries of the sailors 'how much further we had to go,' almost exhausted their patience. Already we had been on the vessel twenty-four hours, when just at nightfall the packet stopped: a little boat was lowered into the water, and we were invited to collect our luggage and descend into it, as we were at Phillip's Ferry;[1] we were ut-

---

[1]Philips Ferry is still conducted, on or near the original site, at Valley City, where the present Editor utilized it late in the month of August, 1936. The ferry was established by Garret Van Dusen in 1822, who two years later transferred it to Nimrod Philips.

The latter had come from Kentucky to Pike County about 1821; he died here a decade later. By his will, made in 1826, he bequeathed the ferry to his son, Andrew. This document, still on file in the Court House at Pittsfield, we copy in full for the entertainment of the reader:

"Illinois pike County in the name of God Amen I Nimrod Philips of the State and County aforesaid inten to travel and Not knowing but I may die before I return do make this my last will and testament   first I give to Zerrelda Jean my youngest child five head of Cattle a cow cald Cherry and her Caves a horse Cald Jack three beds and furniture and all the kitchen furniture and utensils   this I give to my youngest child by Nancy Philips onst Nancy Norris Zerrelda Jean Philips is her name   I give to Nancy Philips my wife one loom and its furniture 3 breeding Sows and their pigs six barrows for her meat   She is to have her choise of

terly confounded: there was no appearance of a landing place, no luggage yard, nor even a building of any kind within sight; we, however, attended to our directions, and in a few minutes saw ourselves standing by the brink of the river, bordered by a dark wood, with no one near to notice us or tell us where we might procure accommodation or find harbour. This happened, as before intimated, as the evening shades were rapidly settling on the earth, and the stars through the clear blue atmosphere were beginning to twinkle. It was in the middle of November, and already very frosty. My husband and I looked at each other till we burst into tears, and our children observing our disquietude began to cry bitterly. Is this America, thought I, is this the reception I meet with after my long, painfully anxious and bereaving voyage? In vain did we look around us, hoping to see a light in some distant cabin. It was not, however, the time to weep: my husband determined to leave us with our luggage in search of a habitation, and wished us to remain where we then stood till he returned. Such a step I saw to be necessary, but how trying! Should he lose himself in the wood, thought I, what will become of me and my helpless offspring? He departed: I was left with five young children, the youngest at my breast. When I survey this portion of my history, it looks more like fiction than reality; yet it is the precise situation in which I was then placed.

After my husband was gone I caused my four eldest children to sit together on one of our beds, covered them from the cold as well as I could, and endeavoured to pacify them. I then knelt down on the bare ground, and committed myself and little ones to the Father of mercies, beseeching him

---

the above named Hoggs   She is to live where I now live at the ferry My part of the crop of corn that has been on the place this year to be hers She is to live on the place until Zerrelda is of age and have the benefit of the improved land   Zerrelda is to have six dolers for 3 years Scholling 18 dollars

I give to Elizabeth Elledge my oldest daughter one doller the rest of my estate and property is to be equaly divided between my 3 children Andrew Philips, Selah Philips, Asa Philips except Andrew is to have the ferry   this is my last will and testament 'to be a lantern to my feet, a light unto my path, and to establish my goings.' I rose from my knees considerably comforted, and endeavoured to wait with patience the return of my husband. Above me was the chill blue canopy of heaven, a wide river before me, and a dark wood behind. The first sound we heard was that of two dogs that came barking towards us, so as greatly to increase our alarm; the dogs came up to us, but did us no harm, and very soon after I beheld my dear husband, accompanied by a stranger, who conducted us to his habitation, whither our luggage was shortly afterwards removed in a waggon.

My husband had followed a sort of cattle track, which led him to the house, which had been concealed by trees and underwood growing around it. And now, for the first time in my life, did I fairly see the interior of a log-house, which, however rude I might think it, I felt, as the reader will readily believe, most happy to enter. It was much more comfortable to sleep on a bed laid on the floor before a fire of glowing embers, than it would have been on the cold ground, which a short time before I feared would be my lodging. The following morning, after a comfortable night's repose, we felt our health and spirits improved. My husband began to examine the soils and produce of the country, and I to collect what information I could respecting American housewifery, manners, religion, &c. Our hostess was a little woman, exceedingly fond of smoking, as the Americans generally are, particularly the females. Before leaving England I had heard a great deal said in behalf of American hospitality, but these encomiums certainly require to be qualified: they are exceedingly hospitable to gentlemen who may be making a tour, likewise amongst themselves as neighbours; but when they know a person really must trouble them, they appear to be aware they are conferring a favour, and expect an equivalent. The little lady I have been describing knew little of generosity; we understood very soon that we should be expected to pay for our harbour, although we used our own provisions. I am forgetting that on one occasion she generously told me I might give my children the broth in which she had boiled some cabbage, if I thought they would drink it; I told her they had not been accustomed to such fare. We remained here three days, during which I became tolerably conversant in the theory of American housekeeping, and as Mrs. Phillips[1] (that was the name of our hostess) was very loquacious, she initiated me into the peculiarities of Illinois politeness. No person, however slender his pretensions to knighthood, or how long soever the time since his small-clothes were new, is addressed without the courteous epithet of 'Sir;' and this practice is observed by the members of the same family in their intercourse with each other; of course the females are in like manner honoured with 'Madam,' *Ubi tu Caius, ego Caia.* It is not etiquette in Illinois to sit at the table after you have done eating; to remain after you have finished your meal implies that you have not had sufficient. This custom I subsequently found a very convenient one.

But I am forgetting the house. It was a fair specimen of a log-house, and therefore a description of it will give the reader a pretty correct idea of the American peasantry. There were two rooms, both on the ground floor, separated from each other with boards so badly joined, that crevices were in many places observable. The rooms were nearly square, and might contain from thirty to forty square yards each; beneath one of the rooms was a cellar, the floor and sides of which were mud and clay, as left when first dug out; the walls of the house consisted of layers of strong blocks of timber, roughly squared and notched into each other at the corners; the joints filled up with clay. The house had two doors, one of which is always closed in winter, and open in summer to cause a draught. The fire was on the floor at the end of the building, where a very grotesque chimney had been constructed of stones gathered out of the land, and

[1]The will of Nimrod Philips seems to indicate that the Mrs. Philips whom Mrs. Burlend knew was a second wife of Nimrod, whose maiden name was Nancy Norris. Of her we have learned nothing apart from the vivacious picture limned by our author. An earlier wife of Philips who was a member of the Elledge family intermarried with the Boones, and on coming to Illinois settled in Scott County on the east side of the Illinois River from Pike.

walled together with clay and mud instead of cement. It was necessarily a great width, to prevent the fire from communicating with the building. The house was covered with oak shingles; that is to say, thin riven boards nailed upon each other, so as just to over-reach. The floors of the house were covered with the same material, except a large piece near the fire, which was paved with small stones, also gathered from the land. There was no window to the house I am describing, although many log-houses may now be found having glass windows. This inconvenience I pointed out to my hostess, who replied, 'upon the whole it was as well without, for in winter the house was warmer and in summer they had always the door open, which was better than any window.' It is in reality true, that the want of light is felt very little in a log-house; in winter they are obliged to keep fine blazing fires, which, in addition to the light obtained from their low wide chimneys, enable the inmates to perform any business that is requisite.

It is however by no means to be understood that an American log-house equals in comfort and convenience a snug English cottage. It is quite common to see, at least, one bed in the same room as that in which the fire is kept; a practice which invariably gives both the bed and house a filthy appearance. There was no chamber, only a sort of loft, constructed rather with a view to make the house warmer, than to afford additional room. Adjoining one side were a few boards nailed together in the form of a table, and supported principally by the timber in the wall. This was dignified with the name 'sideboard.' In the centre of the room, stood another small table, covered with a piece of coarse brown calico; this was the dining table. The chairs, four in number, were the most respectable furniture in the house, having bark of ichory platted for bottoms. Besides these there were two stools and a bench for common use,—a candlestick made from an ear of Indian corn, two or three trenchers and a few tin drinking vessels. One corner of the house was occupied with agricultural implements, consisting of large hoes, axes, &c., for stubbing, called in America grubbing, flails and wooden forks, all exhibiting specimens of workmanship rather homely. Various herbs were suspended from the roof with a view of being medicinally serviceable, also two guns, one of them a rifle. There were also several hams and sides of bacon, smoked almost till they were black; two or three pieces of beef, &c. Under one of the beds were three or four large pots filled with honey, of which Mrs. P. was not a little lavish, as she used it to every meal along with coffee. The furniture in the other room consisted of two beds and a hand-loom, with which the family wove the greater part of their own clothes. In the cellar I observed two or three large hewn tubs, full of lard, and a lump of tobacco, the produce of their own land, in appearance sufficient to serve an ordinary smoker his life.

During our sojourn at Mr. Phillips', my husband found Mr. B., and on the third day after our arrival, brought that gentleman's team, two stiff oxen yoked to a clumsy sledge; on which we placed our beds, boxes, &c. and bid good by to Mrs. P., who, as we paid her for our harbour, contrived to shed a tear or two at the thoughts of parting. After arriving at Mr. B.'s house, I certainly felt I had been a little cajoled. My husband had seen him the day before, but had made no mention of his condition. He was in the fields when we arrived; but as the door was unlocked, or rather lockless, we took the liberty of introducing ourselves and luggage. Mr. B. was at once a bachelor and solitaire. He had left England precipitately, and what is more unusual, a great part of his money, which at this time he was daily expecting by a remittance. The property he had taken with him was all expended in land and cattle, so that a little money was a desideratum. Shortly after our arrival, Mr. B. made his appearance, which, as I before intimated, was rather mysterious. In his letters sent to England, he had spoken of his situation as 'a land flowing with milk and honey'; but I assure you patient reader, his appearance would have led any one to suppose that he gathered his honey rather from thorns than flowers. He was verily as ragged as a sheep: too much so for decency to describe. And his house was more like the cell of a hermit who aims at super-excellence by enduring privations than the cottage of an industrious peasant.

The bed on which he slept was only like a bolster which he had used on shipboard, and laid upon a kind of shelf of his own constructing. Then again the walls of his house were of hewn timber as others, but the joinings or interstices were left quite open. The first night I passed in this miserable abode I was almost perished. My husband was obliged to heat a flat iron, and after wrapping it in flannel, apply it to my feet, so little were we protected from the inclemency of the weather. Finding our comforts here so few, we determined to have a home of our own as soon as possible. Mr. B. was too busy in his farm to render my husband much assistance in selecting a piece of ground. Besides the condition of his *haut-de-chausse*[1] rendered it almost imperative upon him to keep near home, especially as he was a bachelor.

Before I proceed any further with my narrative, perhaps it will be of advantage to the reader to explain the method of purchasing land in the United States. The land in the various states has all been surveyed by direction of the government, and divided into portions of eighty acres each. For the sale of the land thus surveyed and laid down on large plans, a land-office is established in various central situations, where all the allotments of a certain district are sold, and the purchasers' names registered. Any person, therefore, who wishes to purchase one or more of these subsections, can see the plan, and select any that are unsold. They will even sell as small a quantity as forty acres; but as they do this merely to accommodate new settlers, no person already possessing eighty acres, can purchase a smaller quantity than that at a time. In some of the older states the government lands are all sold off. It must there be bought of private owners; but in Illinois and other new states there is plenty unsold. The government price everywhere is one hundred dollars for eighty acres. As there are myriads of acres yet in its native luxuriant wildness, any person may with impunity cultivate as much as he chooses without paying anything; and, as a further inducement, when a person begins thus to cultivate, no other person can legally purchase

---

[1]Meaning, his trousers.

this land, till four years have expired from the time of his beginning to cultivate. By obtaining what is termed a preemption the improvement arising from his own industry is as secure to him for four years as if he was the actual owner. Should, however, he fail to pay for the land before the term expires, an indifferent person may then purchase it; but this seldom happens. Every person purchasing land at the office, must declare upon oath, if required, that no other party has an improvement on it. And, if it be proved to be otherwise, such purchase is in every case invalid; and the fraudulent party liable to a heavy fine.

An improved eighty acres was the first land we purchased: we obtained it in the following manner:—A person named Mr. Oakes[1] having heard that a family about to settle was sojourning at Mr. B.'s came to invite my husband to buy some venison, which he had killed with his rifle just before. My husband went with him, and in conversation found he was disposed to sell his improvement right; for the four years were not expired, and he had not entered it at the landoffice. For this right he wanted sixty dollars. My husband told him he would call upon him the next day, and returned to Mr. B.'s after buying a quantity of nice venison at a halfpenny per pound. The following day, my husband and I visited at Mr. Oakes's, who took us round the estate, shewed us the boundaries, which were marked out by large stones set at each corner, termed the corner stones.

On the land there were about four hundred sugar maples

[1]There were, commonly, three waves of migration in the settlement of any given portion of the frontier. First of all came the traders, hunters, and trappers, with no particular intention of improving the country. Second came the "squatters," who occupied (without troubling to buy legal title) a tract of land and made some slight improvements on it, frequently building a cabin and reducing one or more acres to cultivation, but relying largely upon hunting and on the natural products of the forest for their support. In the wake of the squatter came the permanent settler, who acquired legal title to the soil and developed a home with the intention of passing it on to his children. Oakes, the individual here noted, was evidently a squatter, who has left no record of his sojourn in the community. Of him and his kind, Mr. Jess M. Thompson, local historian, observes, "All seem to have vanished from the community at an early day."

which Mr. Oakes had tapped the preceding year. These trees grow plentifully in the United States, and promise with proper culture to supersede the use of West Indian sugar in America. They like a low situation and a deep soil, and grow to a larger size than any trees in this country. They are said to thrive the better the oftener they are pierced. The method of obtaining sugar from them is very simple. A small cabin, or, as it is there termed, camp, is built in the midst of the trees; two or three large coppers, holding from five to ten gallons each, are set within it, to boil the liquor, which being drained from the trees into hewn wooden troughs, is carried into the camp. The incisions are made with an auger in the beginning of March, when the sap is beginning to rise. Into each of these holes a tube is inserted, about an inch in diameter, so as just to fill the hole, through this the liquor flows as through a spout. The tree from which these tubes are made, is admirably adapted for the purpose, growing somewhat like the elder, only its branches are straighter and contain more pith. It is usually called in Illinois the shoemaker's tree,[1] its botanical name I do not know. The most suitable weather for the discharge of this liquor is when the days are fine and the nights frosty. After the liquor is thus collected, it is boiled down to the consistency of thin treacle. It is then strained through a coarse woollen cloth, and afterwards boiled again at a slower fire till it becomes hard and firm like raw sugar. It is at present much used in the United States, and always sells at a higher rate than that from the West Indies. On the land now under consideration, Mr. Oakes had broken up about twelve acres, three of which were sown with wheat, and the remaining nine ready to be sown with Indian corn, oats, &c. the following spring. As we liked the situation and land very much and were wishful to be settled, the agreement was completed that evening, and the money paid and possession obtained the following day. The reader is aware that the sixty dollars given to Mr. Oakes, were only for his house, im-

---

[1] Apparently the co-author of Mrs. Burlend's narrative nodded here. The tree in question is the sumac.

provement right, sugar-making utensils, &c. One hundred more we paid at the land office, at Quincy, and we obtained the usual certificate or title deeds; and thus by the first of December, having spent about thirty pounds in travelling, thirty-five more in land, &c. we were the rightful owners of a farm of eighty acres, with a log-house in the centre of it.[1] What more could we require? The reader will perceive in the next chapter.

[1] The farm which the immigrants thus obtained for their home is legally known as the northeast ¼ of Section 6, Twp. 5 S, R. 2 W. of the Fourth P. M. It lies about two miles east of Bethel Cemetery, and about three miles north of the village of Detroit, in northwestern Detroit Township. Three miles to the northeast lies Valley City, formerly Philips Ferry. The approach of the Burlends to the farm site was, of course, by way of Philips Ferry. The original cabin site was on the face of a sloping hillside, a few rods from a spring which still gives forth a stream of clear, cool water.

Autobiography of Andrew Carnegie
Andrew Carnegie

It was poverty that encouraged the parents of millionaire industrialist Andrew Carnegie to emigrate to America in 1848. Born in Dunfermline, Scotland, in 1835, Carnegie recollected very little about his homeland. Better remembered is the Pennsylvania of his youth where Carnegie began his legendary career in Allegheny, first as a bobbin boy in a cotton factory, then as a messenger in a telegraph office, and later as a head of the Pennsylvania Railroad's western division in 1859. During this rise, however, Carnegie's father encouraged him to read, write, and attend night school. Without these skills, Carnegie's success was meaningless, according to his father, who had been an educated and politically active man in Scotland. Later, this encouragement would inspire Carnegie's far-reaching philanthropic interests in university funds, research and teaching grants, and libraries.

In 1873 Carnegie founded the J. Edgar Thomson Steel Works with money gleaned from different investments in oil fields, locomotive works, and iron mills. By using every new advance in the steel industry and overseeing each step in the steel-making process from manufacturing to transportation, Carnegie created an incredibly lucrative "vertical" monopoly, renamed Carnegie Steel in 1889. Although many Americans admired Carnegie's ingenuity, others found fault with his methods. As an increased awareness toward the rights of workers emerged at the turn of the century, accusations arose concerning labor practices at Carnegie Steel. Carnegie avoided this controversy to some extent in 1900 when he sold Carnegie Steel to J. P. Morgan for $250,000,000 and began a retirement devoted to philanthropy.

Among Carnegie's writings, the most notable is a collection of essays entitled *The Gospel of Wealth*, published in 1900, which stemmed from an earlier text, "Wealth," published in 1889. *The Gospel of Wealth* maintains that a man acquires riches through his natural talents and education, and it is his duty to use his wealth to the benefit of society. According to Carnegie, to die rich is a disgrace, although this element of the doctrine is often overlooked in American culture. Andrew Carnegie died on August 12, 1919, perhaps richer than he would have liked to be, but still indebted to the poverty of his childhood. In the chapters "Arrival in New York" and "Pittsburgh and Work" from the *Autobiography of Andrew Carnegie*, published posthumously in 1920, the author recalls his eagerness to rid his immigrant family of debt by immersing himself in work as a boy of thirteen.

ARRIVAL IN NEW YORK

I had left school forever, with the exception of one winter's night-schooling in America, and later a French night-teacher for a time, and, strange to say, an elocutionist from whom I learned how to declaim. I could read, write, and cipher, and had begun the study of algebra and of Latin. A letter written to my Uncle Lauder during the voyage, and since returned, shows that I was then a better penman than now. I had wrestled with English grammar, and knew as little of what it was designed to teach as children usually do. I had read little except about Wallace, Bruce, and Burns; but knew many familiar pieces of poetry by heart. I should add to this the fairy tales of childhood, and especially the

"Arabian Nights," by which I was carried into a new world. I was in dreamland as I devoured those stories.

On the morning of the day we started from beloved Dunfermline, in the omnibus that ran upon the coal railroad to Charleston, I remember that I stood with tearful eyes looking out of the window until Dunfermline vanished from view, the last structure to fade being the grand and sacred old Abbey. During my first fourteen years of absence my thought was almost daily, as it was that morning, "When shall I see you again?" Few days passed in which I did not see in my mind's eye the talismanic letters on the Abbey tower—"King Robert The Bruce." All my recollections of childhood, all I knew of fairyland, clustered around the old Abbey and its curfew bell, which tolled at eight o'clock every evening and was the signal for me to run to bed before it stopped. I have referred to that bell in my "American Four-in-Hand in Britain"[1] when passing the Abbey and I may as well quote from it now:

As we drove down the Pends I was standing on the front seat of the coach with Provost Walls, when I heard the first toll of the Abbey bell, tolled in honor of my mother and myself. My knees sank from under me, the tears came rushing before I knew it, and I turned round to tell the Provost that I must give in. For a moment I felt as if I were about to faint. Fortunately I saw that there was no crowd before us for a little distance. I had time to regain control, and biting my lips till they actually bled, I murmured to myself, "No matter, keep cool, you must go on"; but never can there come to my ears on earth, nor enter so deep into my soul, a sound that shall haunt and subdue me with its sweet, gracious, melting power as that did.

By that curfew bell I had been laid in my little couch to sleep the sleep of childish innocence. Father and mother, sometimes the one, sometimes the other, had told me as they bent lovingly over me night after night, what that bell said as it tolled. Many good words has that bell spoken to me through their translations. No wrong thing did I do through the day which that

---

[1] *An American Four-in-Hand in Britain.* New York, 1886.

voice from all I knew of heaven and the great Father there did not tell me kindly about ere I sank to sleep, speaking the words so plainly that I knew that the power that moved it had seen all and was not angry, never angry, never, but so very, *very* sorry. Nor is that bell dumb to me to-day when I hear its voice. It still has its message, and now it sounded to welcome back the exiled mother and son under its precious care again.

The world has not within its power to devise, much less to bestow upon us, such reward as that which the Abbey bell gave when it tolled in our honor. But my brother Tom should have been there also; this was the thought that came. He, too, was beginning to know the wonders of that bell ere we were away to the newer land.

Rousseau wished to die to the strains of sweet music. Could I choose my accompaniment I could wish to pass into the dim beyond with the tolling of the Abbey bell sounding in my ears, telling me of the race that had been run, and calling me, as it had called the little white-haired child, for the last time—*to sleep.*

I have had many letters from readers speaking of this passage in my book, some of the writers going so far as to say that tears fell as they read. It came from the heart and perhaps that is why it reached the hearts of others.

We were rowed over in a small boat to the Edinburgh steamer in the Firth of Forth. As I was about to be taken from the small boat to the steamer, I rushed to Uncle Lauder and clung round his neck, crying out: "I cannot leave you! I cannot leave you!" I was torn from him by a kind sailor who lifted me up on the deck of the steamer. Upon my return visit to Dunfermline this dear old fellow, when he came to see me, told me it was the saddest parting he had ever witnessed.

We sailed from the Broomielaw of Glasgow in the 800-ton sailing ship Wiscasset. During the seven weeks of the voyage, I came to know the sailors quite well, learned the names of the ropes, and was able to direct the passengers to answer the call of the boatswain, for the ship being under-manned, the aid of the passengers was urgently required. In consequence I was invited by the sailors to participate on Sundays, in the one delicacy of the sailors' mess, plum duff. I left the ship with sincere regret.

The arrival at New York was bewildering. I had been taken to see the Queen at Edinburgh, but that was the extent of my travels before emigrating. Glasgow we had not time to see before we sailed. New York was the first great hive of human industry among the inhabitants of which I had mingled, and the bustle and excitement of it overwhelmed me. The incident of our stay in New York which impressed me most occurred while I was walking through Bowling Green at Castle Garden. I was caught up in the arms of one of the Wiscasset sailors, Robert Barryman, who was decked out in regular Jack-ashore fashion, with blue jacket and white trousers. I thought him the most beautiful man I had ever seen.

He took me to a refreshment stand and ordered a glass of sarsaparilla for me, which I drank with as much relish as if it were the nectar of the gods. To this day nothing that I have ever seen of the kind rivals the image which remains in my mind of the gorgeousness of the highly ornamented brass vessel out of which that nectar came foaming. Often as I have passed the identical spot I see standing there the old woman's sarsaparilla stand, and I marvel what became of the dear old sailor. I have tried to trace him, but in vain, hoping that if found he might be enjoying a ripe old age, and that it might be in my power to add to the pleasure of his declining years. He was my ideal Tom Bowling, and when that fine old song is sung I always see as the "form of manly beauty" my dear old friend Barryman. Alas! ere this he's gone aloft. Well; by his kindness on the voyage he made one boy his devoted friend and admirer.

We knew only Mr. and Mrs. Sloane in New York—parents of the well-known John, Willie, and Henry Sloane. Mrs. Sloane (Euphemia Douglas) was my mother's companion in childhood in Dunfermline. Mr. Sloane and my father had been fellow weavers. We called upon them and were warmly welcomed. It was a genuine pleasure when Willie, his son, bought ground from me in 1900 opposite our New

York residence for his two married daughters so that our children of the third generation became playmates as our mothers were in Scotland.

My father was induced by emigration agents in New York to take the Erie Canal by way of Buffalo and Lake Erie to Cleveland, and thence down the canal to Beaver—a journey which then lasted three weeks, and is made to-day by rail in ten hours. There was no railway communication then with Pittsburgh, nor indeed with any western town. The Erie Railway was under construction and we saw gangs of men at work upon it as we traveled. Nothing comes amiss to youth, and I look back upon my three weeks as a passenger upon the canal-boat with unalloyed pleasure. All that was disagreeable in my experience has long since faded from recollection, excepting the night we were compelled to remain upon the wharf-boat at Beaver waiting for the steamboat to take us up the Ohio to Pittsburgh. This was our first introduction to the mosquito in all its ferocity. My mother suffered so severely that in the morning she could hardly see. We were all frightful sights, but I do not remember that even the stinging misery of that night kept me from sleeping soundly. I could always sleep, never knowing "horrid night, the child of hell."

Our friends in Pittsburgh had been anxiously waiting to hear from us, and in their warm and affectionate greeting all our troubles were forgotten. We took up our residence with them in Allegheny City. A brother of my Uncle Hogan had built a small weaver's shop at the back end of a lot in Rebecca Street. This had a second story in which there were two rooms, and it was in these (free of rent, for my Aunt Aitken owned them) that my parents began housekeeping. My uncle soon gave up weaving and my father took his place and began making tablecloths, which he had not only to weave, but afterwards, acting as his own merchant, to travel and sell, as no dealers could be found to take them in quantity. He was compelled to market them himself, selling from door to door. The returns were meager in the extreme.

As usual, my mother came to the rescue. There was no keeping her down. In her youth she had learned to bind shoes in her father's business for pin-money, and the skill then acquired was now turned to account for the benefit of the family. Mr. Phipps, father of my friend and partner Mr. Henry Phipps, was, like my grandfather, a master shoe-maker. He was our neighbor in Allegheny City. Work was obtained from him, and in addition to attending to her household duties—for, of course, we had no servant—this wonderful woman, my mother, earned four dollars a week by binding shoes. Midnight would often find her at work. In the intervals during the day and evening, when household cares would permit, and my young brother sat at her knee threading needles and waxing the thread for her, she recited to him, as she had to me, the gems of Scottish minstrelsy which she seemed to have by heart, or told him tales which failed not to contain a moral.

This is where the children of honest poverty have the most precious of all advantages over those of wealth. The mother, nurse, cook, governess, teacher, saint, all in one; the father, exemplar, guide, counselor, and friend! Thus were my brother and I brought up. What has the child of millionaire or nobleman that counts compared to such a heritage?

My mother was a busy woman, but all her work did not prevent her neighbors from soon recognizing her as a wise and kindly woman whom they could call upon for counsel or help in times of trouble. Many have told me what my mother did for them. So it was in after years wherever we resided; rich and poor came to her with their trials and found good counsel. She towered among her neighbors wherever she went.

PITTSBURGH AND WORK

The great question now was, what could be found for me to do. I had just completed my thirteenth year, and I fairly panted to get to work that I might help the family to a start in the new land. The prospect of want had become to me a frightful nightmare. My thoughts at this period centered in the determination that we should make and save enough of money to produce three hundred dollars a year—twenty-five dollars monthly, which I figured was the sum required to keep us without being dependent upon others. Every necessary thing was very cheap in those days.

The brother of my Uncle Hogan would often ask what my parents meant to do with me, and one day there occurred the most tragic of all scenes I have ever witnessed. Never can I forget it. He said, with the kindest intentions in the world, to my mother, that I was a likely boy and apt to learn; and he believed that if a basket were fitted out for me with knick-knacks to sell, I could peddle them around the wharves and make quite a considerable sum. I never knew what an enraged woman meant till then. My mother was sitting sewing at the moment, but she sprang to her feet with outstretched hands and shook them in his face.

"What! my son a peddler and go among rough men upon the wharves! I would rather throw him into the Allegheny River. Leave me!" she cried, pointing to the door, and Mr. Hogan went.

She stood a tragic queen. The next moment she had broken down, but only for a few moments did tears fall and sobs come. Then she took her two boys in her arms and told us not to mind her foolishness. There were many things in the world for us to do and we could be useful men, honored and respected, if we always did what was right. It was a repetition of Helen Macgregor, in her reply to Osbaldistone in which she threatened to have her prisoners "chopped into as many pieces as there are checks in the tartan." But the reason for the outburst was different. It was not because the occupation suggested was peaceful labor, for we were taught that idleness was disgraceful; but because the suggested occupation was somewhat vagrant in character and not entirely respectable in her eyes. Better death. Yes, mother would have taken her two boys, one under each arm, and perished with them rather than they should mingle with low company in their extreme youth.

As I look back upon the early struggles this can be said:

there was not a prouder family in the land. A keen sense of honor, independence, self-respect, pervaded the household. Walter Scott said of Burns that he had the most extraordinary eye he ever saw in a human being. I can say as much for my mother. As Burns has it:

> Her eye even turned on empty space,
> Beamed keen with honor.

Anything low, mean, deceitful, shifty, coarse, underhand, or gossipy was foreign to that heroic soul. Tom and I could not help growing up respectable characters, having such a mother and such a father, for the father, too, was one of nature's noblemen, beloved by all, a saint.

Soon after this incident my father found it necessary to give up hand-loom weaving and to enter the cotton factory of Mr. Blackstock, an old Scotsman in Allegheny City, where we lived. In this factory he also obtained for me a position as bobbin boy, and my first work was done there at one dollar and twenty cents per week. It was a hard life. In the winter father and I had to rise and breakfast in the darkness, reach the factory before it was daylight, and, with a short interval for lunch, work till after dark. The hours hung heavily upon me and in the work itself I took no pleasure; but the cloud had a silver lining, as it gave me the feeling that I was doing something for my world—our family. I have made millions since, but none of those millions gave me such happiness as my first week's earnings. I was now a helper of the family, a breadwinner, and no longer a total charge upon my parents. Often had I heard my father's beautiful singing of "The Boatie Rows" and often I longed to fulfill the last lines of the verse:

> "When Aaleck, Jock, and Jeanettie,
> *Are up and got their lair*,[1]
> They'll serve to gar the boatie row,
> And lichten a' our care."

[1] Education.

I was going to make our tiny craft skim. It should be noted here that Aaleck, Jock, and Jeanettie were first to get their education. Scotland was the first country that required all parents, high or low, to educate their children, and established the parish public schools.

Soon after this Mr. John Hay, a fellow-Scotch manufacturer of bobbins in Allegheny City, needed a boy, and asked whether I would not go into his service. I went, and received two dollars per week; but at first the work was even more irksome than the factory. I had to run a small steam-engine and to fire the boiler in the cellar of the bobbin factory. It was too much for me. I found myself night after night, sitting up in bed trying the steam gauges, fearing at one time that the steam was too low and that the workers above would complain that they had not power enough, and at another time that the steam was too high and that the boiler might burst.

But all this it was a matter of honor to conceal from my parents. They had their own troubles and bore them. I must play the man and bear mine. My hopes were high, and I looked every day for some change to take place. What it was to be I knew not, but that it would come I felt certain if I kept on. Besides, at this date I was not beyond asking myself what Wallace would have done and what a Scotsman ought to do. Of one thing I was sure, he ought never to give up.

One day the chance came. Mr. Hay had to make out some bills. He had no clerk, and was himself a poor penman. He asked me what kind of hand I could write, and gave me some writing to do. The result pleased him, and he found it convenient thereafter to let me make out his bills. I was also good at figures; and he soon found it to be to his interest— and besides, dear old man, I believe he was moved by good feeling toward the white-haired boy, for he had a kind heart and was Scotch and wished to relieve me from the engine— to put me at other things, less objectionable except in one feature.

It now became my duty to bathe the newly made spools in vats of oil. Fortunately there was a room reserved for this purpose and I was alone, but not all the resolution I could muster, nor all the indignation I felt at my own weakness, prevented my stomach from behaving in a most perverse way. I never succeeded in overcoming the nausea produced by the smell of the oil. Even Wallace and Bruce proved impotent here. But if I had to lose breakfast, or dinner, I had all the better appetite for supper, and the allotted work was done. A real disciple of Wallace or Bruce could not give up; he would die first.

My service with Mr. Hay was a distinct advance upon the cotton factory, and I also made the acquaintance of an employer who was very kind to me. Mr. Hay kept his books in single entry, and I was able to handle them for him; but hearing that all great firms kept their books in double entry, and after talking over the matter with my companions, John Phipps, Thomas N. Miller, and William Cowley, we all determined to attend night school during the winter and learn the larger system. So the four of us went to a Mr. Williams in Pittsburgh and learned double-entry bookkeeping.

One evening, early in 1850, when I returned home from work, I was told that Mr. David Brooks, manager of the telegraph office, had asked my Uncle Hogan if he knew where a good boy could be found to act as messenger. Mr. Brooks and my uncle were enthusiastic draught-players, and it was over a game of draughts that this important inquiry was made. Upon such trifles do the most momentous consequences hang. A word, a look, an accent, may affect the destiny not only of individuals, but of nations. He is a bold man who calls anything a trifle. Who was it who, being advised to disregard trifles, said he always would if any one could tell him what a trifle was? The young should remember that upon trifles the best gifts of the gods often hang.

My uncle mentioned my name, and said he would see whether I would take the position. I remember so well the family council that was held. Of course I was wild with delight. No bird that ever was confined in a cage longed for freedom more than I. Mother favored, but father was disposed to deny my wish. It would prove too much for me, he said; I was too young and too small. For the two dollars and a half per week offered it was evident that a much larger boy was expected. Late at night I might be required to run out into the country with a telegram, and there would be dangers to encounter. Upon the whole my father said that it was best that I should remain where I was. He subsequently withdrew his objection, so far as to give me leave to try, and I believe he went to Mr. Hay and consulted with him. Mr. Hay thought it would be for my advantage, and although, as he said, it would be an inconvenience to him, still he advised that I should try, and if I failed he was kind enough to say that my old place would be open for me.

This being decided, I was asked to go over the river to Pittsburgh and call on Mr. Brooks. My father wished to go with me, and it was settled that he should accompany me as far as the telegraph office, on the corner of Fourth and Wood Streets. It was a bright, sunshiny morning and this augured well. Father and I walked over from Allegheny to Pittsburgh, a distance of nearly two miles from our house. Arrived at the door I asked father to wait outside. I insisted upon going alone upstairs to the second or operating floor to see the great man and learn my fate. I was led to this, perhaps, because I had by that time begun to consider myself something of an American. At first boys used to call me "Scotchie! Scotchie!" and I answered, "Yes, I'm Scotch and I am proud of the name." But in speech and in address the broad Scotch had been worn off to a slight extent, and I imagined that I could make a smarter showing if alone with Mr. Brooks than if my good old Scotch father were present, perhaps to smile at my airs.

I was dressed in my one white linen shirt, which was usually kept sacred for the Sabbath day, my blue roundabout, and my whole Sunday suit. I had at that time, and for a few weeks after I entered the telegraph service, but one linen suit of summer clothing; and every Saturday night, no matter if that was my night on duty and I did not return till near midnight, my mother washed those clothes and ironed them, and I put them on fresh on Sabbath morning. There was nothing that heroine did not do in the struggle we were making for elbow room in the western world. Father's long factory hours tried his strength, but he, too, fought the good fight like a hero and never failed to encourage me.

The interview was successful. I took care to explain that I did not know Pittsburgh, that perhaps I would not do, would not be strong enough; but all I wanted was a trial. He asked me how soon I could come, and I said that I could stay now if wanted. And, looking back over the circumstance, I think that answer might well be pondered by young men. It is a great mistake not to seize the opportunity. The position was offered to me; something might occur, some other boy might be sent for. Having got myself in I proposed to stay there if I could. Mr. Brooks very kindly called the other boy—for it was an additional messenger that was wanted—and asked him to show me about, and let me go with him and learn the business. I soon found opportunity to run down to the corner of the street and tell my father that it was all right, and to go home and tell mother that I had got the situation.

And that is how in 1850 I got my first real start in life. From the dark cellar running a steam-engine at two dollars a week, begrimed with coal dirt, without a trace of the elevating influences of life, I was lifted into paradise, yes, heaven, as it seemed to me, with newspapers, pens, pencils, and sunshine about me. There was scarcely a minute in which I could not learn something or find out how much there was to learn and how little I knew. I felt that my foot was upon the ladder and that I was bound to climb.

Frontier Mother
Gro Svendsen

Born into an upper-class, rural family in Hallingdal, Norway, Gro Gudmundsrud (1841–1878) grew up in a happy home of green valleys, many relatives, and books. Although the Gudmundsruds were well educated, employed servants, and lived comfortably, the family often aided their less fortunate neighbors through political action and social work. Gro's father, Nils Knudsen Gudmundsrud, was known as both a community leader and a teacher who campaigned for literacy among rural Norwegians. Gro's mother also taught school and often lent volumes from her extensive library to interested students. Closely knit and content, the Gudmundsruds were frightened by their daughter's decision to marry Ole Svendsen and to leave for the United States in 1861. Unlike Nils Gudmundsrud, Ole was landless, and his only hope for a higher social standing existed in America. The Gudmundsruds understood this dilemma and eventually reconciled themselves to the idea of their daughter's emigration. Gro comforted her parents with promises of exciting stories and many letters to come. These letters home would eventually be collected by historians at the University of Minnesota and published by the Norwegian-American Historical Association as Gro Svendsen's autobiography, *Frontier Mother* (1950).

In America, Ole and Gro settled in St. Ansgar, Iowa, but later moved to the nearby town of Estherville. Both

communities were almost entirely composed of Scandi-
navians, and the Svendsens struggled to learn English in
an area where Norwegian was commonly taught in grade
schools. Soon after the couple arrived in America, Ole
was sent to serve in the Civil War, leaving Gro alone
with children and a farm to take care of. In her letters
home, Gro showed surprise at the hard work necessary
to earn a living in rural America, worried for her husband's safety, and learned for the first time how to be
alone. To help her cope, Gro's mother sent her books as
often as possible. Upon Ole's return, Gro occupied herself teaching school. She taught herself English by using
a primer brought home by her son, Sven. Svendsen died
in 1878 soon after giving birth to her tenth child.

In the letters following "One Must Learn Everything
All Over Again" taken from her autobiography *Frontier
Mother*, the newly arrived Gro Svendsen expresses the
many powerful ties she still felt to Norway through a
correspondence full of news, books, and her own prefer-
ences and habits.

ONE MUST LEARN EVERYTHING
ALL OVER AGAIN

Sando, November 20, 1862

Dearest Mother and Brother:

With tears of joy I read your letter. You can never imagine
how happy I was to hear from you who are always in
my thoughts. When I learned that you are all well, I wept
from sheer joy. Now and then I reproach myself for leaving
you alone at a time when you needed my help, but what's
done is done. On the other hand, you mustn't think for a moment that I regret my choice. I felt then and even more so
now that we were destined for each other, and you must
never think that I regret not taking any of my other suitors. I

knew then that he [Ole] loved me deeply and sincerely, and every day, in countless ways, I have constant proof of his love. He would fulfill my smallest wish, so you may tell my sister that I don't think she is any happier with her Henrik than I am with my husband. We may be less prosperous, but we have all the necessities. Indeed, I assure you that I do not in the least envy the rich folks at home.

You may say "that I haven't sailed very far down the fjord yet." To this I would answer, well begun is half done. My husband fully understands what sacrifices I made when I left everything most precious to me to go with him into the unknown. Therefore, when I am lonely, he tries to comfort me. With him alone can I share my joys and sorrows, so even when the darkest moods of loneliness come upon me, I feel infinitely better when I have talked with him. So, my dear mother, you must not worry about me and my happiness. As long as my husband is kind to me, I shall never complain.

I also want to tell you that we bought a cow for which we paid fifteen dollars, and she now has a little calf. Then, too, we bought a pair of oxen for thirty dollars. They are old enough to use for driving. My Ole is doing his best to learn to drive them. For a newcomer he is doing very well. Many people never learn, but he can already manage them alone. The harness used for the oxen is very strange. I think you, little Brother, would like to see a sketch of it. The yoke is placed round the neck of the poor creatures. Then the wagon-tongue is put into the center ring of the bar or yoke, and in this way they draw the load.

Life here is very different from life in our mountain valley. One must readjust oneself and learn everything all over again, even to the preparation of food. We are told that the women of America have much leisure time, but I haven't yet met any woman who thought so! Here the mistress of the house must do all the work that the cook, the maid, and the housekeeper would do in an upper-class family at home. Moreover, she must do her work as well as these three together do it in Norway.

Clothes are washed in a very unusual way. First one must

prepare the lye. This is poured into boiling water, and immediately the lye forms a white scum something like thick sour milk. The frothy scum must be skimmed off before one puts the clothes into the water. The lye is very strong and must be removed, so you see there is a lot of extra work in washing clothes. Without this treatment the water is much too hard.

In like manner, many other things, too, are very different from things at home. I believe that I can truthfully say that the only things that seem to be the same are the fleas, for their bite is as sharp and penetrating here as elsewhere.

I want to tell you so much about the customs of this land, but there is too much to tell. Another time—if God will give me the strength so that I may write you and hear from you again. Tell Engebret of Gudmundsrud that he must be good.

BY ALL MEANS BRING SOME BOOKS

[Undated and incomplete—probably November 1862]

Although you gave me many books to bring along with me, I nevertheless miss many of those we had at home. To be sure there are books enough, such as they are, to be had here, but the print is poor, by no means as good as the print in the Norwegian books. So it is with everything: shoddy and careless workmanship everywhere. Therefore I have praised and defended Norway and things Norwegian so much that I have had heated arguments with some people who believe this land is paradise. Since I can't accept this point of view, and since I shall never be able to place this country above my own fatherland, I shall never be overwhelmed by superficial comparisons. My love for my native land is far too deep and too sacred. I could never prefer any other country to my own.

Speaking of Norwegian books, there are none to be had for miles and miles. Besides, they are high-priced and not at all worth while. Therefore, if anyone should be coming next summer, he should by all means bring some books along. And those who have children must not forget school-books. They are better by far than those we have here.

Norwegian clothes, too, are better and much warmer. We can get nothing but cotton goods, and unfortunately, on account of the war, they are getting more expensive every day. Tobacco, too, is expensive. Cotton and tobacco are both imported from the South; hence the high price.

One advantage, at least, they do have here. They get new clothes more often than we did in Norway, simply because the clothes here don't last. Working people wear out their clothes in just a few weeks.

I remember that Tollef Hagene asked me to tell him something about the climate here in America. The climate in Norway is indeed more temperate. Here we always have extremes. If it's warm, it's warmer by far than our Norwegian summer. The wind is more violent; the rain comes down in torrents; electric storms with terrifying thunder and lightning are more frequent. On summer nights the dew is so heavy that if one walks through the grass, one's feet get soaked. People often get sick from this exposure. The winters, I am told, are colder, with more snow. Up to this time we have had only one snowfall. On the second of November, we had a little snow—just a light fall that disappeared after a couple of hours.

The leaves on the oak trees have not fallen yet, but they have turned a golden brown.

I can't say whether the climate is healthful or not. I have not suffered any ill effects, but then I have not taken chances by doing things that I have been warned not to do.

Just as an example: A man named Knud K. Guldbrands-gaard came over here last year. On his way to Assor Grøth's he spent the last night sleeping on the ground, and since that day he has been a sick man. He is not able to do any work and can barely plod along. He firmly maintains that his illness is due to this climate.

At any rate people are not so strong and healthy as in Norway, whatever the reasons may be. You will have to draw your own conclusions. Even at that, this part of the country is supposed to be far more healthful than the land farther to the south. Whatever the climate may or may not be, I can safely say that it is not so invigorating as that of Norway.

I could tell you all sorts of things, but the letters would cost too much by the time they reach you. Incidentally, it would be interesting to know what you actually do have to pay for postage.

I must close this letter. When you write me, tell me if anyone is planning to come over next summer. If anyone should be coming, I recommend their signing up with Captain Deckman from Aasgaardstrand. He is a good man, kind to and considerate of his passengers. He told me that he expected to go to Aal and sign up his passengers himself. He promised to look up my parents.

Good-by, all of you. Greetings to my friends, E. Noss and Plym, and everyone in the parsonage. Tell all who ask about us that we are fine. A special greeting to you, my dearest ones. God bless you all.

Your daughter in a faraway land.

CHRISTMAS IS DRAWING NEAR

[December 1862]

My dear Ones:

Many days have passed since I wrote these first letters, but I haven't been able to get them to the post office before now, so I shall add a few words.

I have almost completed my first month of school, and the results are quite good. The first week I taught in the home of a man by the name of Erik Espedalen. His place is about as far from our home as Gudmundsrud is from Hagene. The second week we were at the home of Hans Olsen Rust, the distance there being about as far as to Pladsen. The last two weeks we have held school in our own little home here at Sando.

On the whole, the children are poor readers, and they are

very slow to comprehend. The reason, no doubt, is that the Norwegian school term is so short and so irregular. The English school must come first, and no religion is taught there. I suppose I shall carry on for the rest of the term. The farmers seem to be satisfied with me. I told you what they pay me, but when I teach here at home, I board myself, and they do not compensate me for this.

The clergyman here is a Dane named Clausen. He is a good preacher. At present he is in the South, serving as a chaplain in the war. He was here last August and conducted two services. I thought he was very able. Two other clergymen have been here, but they were not so good as Clausen.

The local government is different from that at home. The sheriff and the judge and all the rest are elected just as the foremen are elected at home.

I could tell you a great deal more, but I must cut this short. Christmas is drawing near. With all my heart I want to wish you a joyous Christmas and a happy New Year. It will be most strange to be so far away from all of you on that most hallowed night. I shall be happy enough here, but I should be far happier if so many of my dear ones had not been left behind. Never to be with you again on Christmas Eve, that festive, exalted, and holy night, when we were all so happy! I can't think of it without weeping. God make us strong! Give us patience and a firm faith!

Enough of this. Farewell. Do write soon. Our one great joy is to hear from you. Don't forget to tell me all the news—particularly the outcome of the *clergyman's case*. Tell me in detail everything about yourselves.

Ole sends greetings to Knud H. Sorteberg and his wife, also to John S. Sundie, and to all who ask about us. And don't forget Tante.

I might tell you that the Indian revolt has been somewhat subdued, so we feel much safer than we did awhile ago. It isn't enough merely to subdue them. I think that not a single one who took part in the revolt should be permitted to live. Unfortunately, I cannot make the decision in the matter. I fear that they will be let off too easily.

Good-by, once again, and do not worry about us. Have no

fears about me. If we put our trust in Almighty God, He will protect us, and we shall survive, in spite of all dangers—if that is our destiny. God bless you all! He will reward you for all your kindness. May we all pray that He will continue to bless us so that we may meet each day with confidence. With all my heart this is my wish for you.

May God be with you.

Your daughter,

Gro Nielsdatter

Our address is Mr. Ole Svendsen Skrattegaarden, St. Ansgar P.O., Mitchell County, Iowa, Nordamerika.

CHURCH, CATTLE, AND BOOKS

March 25, 1863

Precious Parents, Brothers, and Sisters:

On the fifth of March we received your letter of January 16th, and we were very happy to know that you all were well. I can't tell you how glad I am to hear from you. Only he who has been separated from his loved ones could ever know how I feel. To have the assurance that you all were well! So far, we, too, have been in good health and are fortunate indeed. The black measles are raging in the neighborhood. The innkeeper, or tavernkeeper as he is called here, in the village of St. Ansgar, only two and a half miles away, became sick and died. Ole Sando's oldest son, Erik, has not yet recovered, although he is now up and around.

We have had no snow this winter. When the snow does fall, it's gone within two or three days. Going to church on Christmas Day, we didn't see even a particle of snow, something I have never experienced before. I had another strange experience on that same trip. Coming into town where the church services were to be held, we saw the Americans working just as on any other day. I saw carpenters, woodsmen, and the like working out of doors as the weather was very mild. It was disturbing, accustomed as we are to the quiet and peace of the Sabbath.

I said "going to church," but we really have no church. We do expect to have one, however. So far $1,550 has been collected, but a great deal more is needed in order to build. In America money was said to be so plentiful, and it may be. But it's hard to get any of it when it's to be used for the common good, for such as teachers' salaries, ministers' salaries, and other expenses connected with the church. The men assigned to collect this money are called trustees. They go about with a list, soliciting from the farmers and getting contributions in the same way as we collected the personal property tax and the church tax at home.

Speaking of the minister, he has no fixed salary. The farmers pledge what they will give each year, and with that amount he must be satisfied. Our pastor, who has been serving as a chaplain in the army, came home for Christmas. He is a good and conscientious man and works to the best of his ability for things temporal and spiritual. So far as I can tell, he is a sound Lutheran. He resembles you, my oldest brother, and always reminds me of you.

As a *klokker* we have the son of a man from Gol by the name of Mikkel Ruust or Golberg. The son's name is Tollef. He sings well. He is also the sheriff and one of the directors of the public school.

The sheriff and the judge are elected in the same way as the mayors were at home.

You ask me why we use oxen. There are many reasons. In the first place, it is better to have cattle than cash. Currency fluctuates constantly—I have never heard nor seen the like— a very deplorable situation. Paper money is printed in every town. Then after a short time it disappears from circulation or loses its value. We actually have nothing but paper money. There is no sign of gold or silver money. So you see it's far better to have cattle than the practically worthless paper money. If one had gold or silver, one would get only 30 or 40 percent on the dollar. The price of cattle, on the other hand, does not fluctuate so much, and the young oxen will rise in value each year. If we were to sell them in the fall, we would surely get 45 or 50 dollars a yoke, good returns for the winter fodder. They continue to rise in value till they are eight years old, when they will bring anywhere from 80 to 100 dollars. When they are fully grown, they can do all the work. Therefore, anyone who intends to buy land should buy and raise young oxen. They are easy to care for, hay is plentiful, and in a very short time they are old enough to work. Then, too, one can hire them out by the day. Even if one doesn't plan to buy land, it is wise to raise oxen and sell them, because of the profit. We do not intend to sell ours, however. They are now three years old, and they seem to be strong and healthy. The larger one is reddish brown. He has long horns and his name is "Braid." The other one, slightly younger and not so large, is a lighter color and has white spots. His name is "Bok." The two of them are "Bok" and "Braid" [*Buck and Bright?*].

From what I have said you can readily see that it's wise to raise oxen. Our cow, Braanda, is dark-brindled. She is four years old and is a good milker. We managed to buy a little calf, too, for five dollars. He will be one year old this July. He is a lighter brown, so we call him "Risenjer." We are told that he is of good breed, and he seems to be strong and alert.

Since I've been talking about cattle, I might tell you what [Americans] say when they call animals. Whenever one calls a horse one says, "Kop, Kop, Kop." To call a cow one says, "Come Boss, come Boss"; to call a sheep one says, "Sheep, Sheep, Sheep"; a pig, "Pig, Pig, Pig"; and a dog, "Heah, Heah." If one wants to rouse a dog one calls, "Sekken, Sekken" [*Sic him*]. To a cat one says, "Ketty, Ketty, Kete." When one wants to stop a horse one cries a long "Haav." Horses, too, have special names, and there are always two to a wagon. Some horses' names are "Kjale" and "Beel" [*Charley and Bill*], "Dola" and "Fana" [*Dolly and Fanny*], and so forth. They are not paired according to color. One rarely sees a cart with one horse; in fact, it's as rare as seeing two horses driven at home. Enough of this!

You may think that all this is pure nonsense, but I thought it very interesting when I first heard it and wanted to share it with you. Don't read this part of the letter to anyone who would chide me for being so childish.

The newspapers you mention are not to be had here. Some people farther to the south take them, but they pay a great deal for the subscription. We get *Emigranten,* and there is always one article about Norway. I wish you would send in an article from Hallingdal, as we have had several articles about Norway's mountain districts.

It would be wonderful to get the books. Whenever you have the opportunity, send them—but I don't want to inconvenience you too much. I got a small grammar by S. Kroble from my little brother, and I have read it through several times. I should have mastered this book when I was at home, but it is good to have it here now.

It would be fun to have a good monochord (*salmodikon*) and a good book of chorals. We do have monochords here, but they are not good and they are expensive. I also long for a good alpenhorn. We have no evergreen trees here. Only foliage trees, and the wood from these is not suited for making a good instrument. There are many other kinds of trees, but I can't dwell on all that now. I must put an end to this letter. Good-by.

The address is Ole Svendsen Skrattegaarden, St. Ansgar P.O., Mitchell County, Iowa.

DIFFERENT WAYS OF
DOING EVERYTHING

1863

Dear Parents, Sisters, and Brothers (always in my thoughts):

I have often thought that I ought to tell you about life here in the New World. Everything is so totally different from what it was in our beloved Norway. You never will really know what it's like, although you no doubt try to imagine what it might be. Your pictures would be all wrong, just as mine were.

I only wish that I could be with you to tell you all about it. Even if I were to write you countless pages, I still could not tell you everything.

I remember I used to wonder when I heard that it would be impossible to keep the milk here as we did at home. Now I have learned that it is indeed impossible because of the heat here in the summertime. One can't make cheese out of the milk because of flies, bugs, and other insects. I don't know the names of all these insects, but this I do know: If one were to make cheese here in the summertime, the cheese itself would be alive with bugs. Toward late autumn it should be possible to keep the milk. The people who have more milk than they need simply feed it to the hogs.

It's difficult, too, to preserve the butter. One must pour brine over it or salt it; otherwise it gets full of maggots. Therefore it is best, if one is not too far from town, to sell the butter at once. This summer we have been getting from eight to ten cents a pound. Not a great profit. For this reason people around here do not have many cows—just enough to supply the milk needed for the household. It's not wise to have more than enough milk, because the flies are everywhere. Even the bacon must be preserved in brine, and so there are different ways of doing everything.

I have so much to tell you. We have no twilight here in the summertime. Even in June, on the longest day of the year, the sun doesn't rise before 4:23 and sets at 7:40. The nights are as dark as they are at home in autumn. We never have rain without thunder and lightning. The thunderstorms are so violent that one might think it was the end of the world. The whole sky is aflame with lightning, and the thunder rolls and crashes as though it were right above our heads. Quite often the lightning strikes down both cattle and people, damages property, and splinters sturdy oak trees into many pieces. Even though one did not fear the thunder in Norway, one can easily become frightened here.

Then there is the prairie fire or, as they call it here, "Faieren." This is terrifying, and the fire rages in both the spring and the fall. Whatever it leaves behind in the fall, it consumes in the spring, so there is nothing left of the long grass on the prairies, sloughs, and marshes. It is a strange and terrible sight to see all the fields a sea of fire. Quite often the scorching flames sweep everything along in their path—people, cattle, hay, fences. In dry weather with a strong wind the fire will race faster than the speediest horse. No one dares to travel without carrying matches, so that if there is a fire he can fight it by building another and in this way save his life and prevent burns, which sometimes prove fatal.

Snakes are found here in the summertime and are also a worry to us. I am horribly afraid of them, particularly the rattlesnake. The rattlesnake is the same as the *klapperslange*. I have seen many of them and thousands of ordinary snakes.

I could tell you even more, but possibly many who read this letter may think I am exaggerating. I assure you that all that I have told you I have experienced myself. If they do not believe me, they should come over and find out for themselves. Then they would tell you the same things I tell you.

By the way, no one leaving Norway should sell all his possessions as most people do. Everything that is useful in Norway is also useful here. The women can make use of all their clothes, with the exception of their headdress, bodice, jackets, and kerchiefs. All these they could sell, but all the other clothes they could make over and wear here. Everything Norwegian is of better quality than what can be bought here. So I am very grateful to you, my parents, every time I touch anything I have received from you. Bedding, too, should be brought along, as it's colder here in the winter than in Norway. Even those who criticize Norway and praise America must admit this. I could tell you much more but haven't time.

This winter I shall teach a few weeks of Norwegian school, but more about that another time.

IT'S A FINE PIECE OF LAND

Skrattegaarden
July 25, 1863

Dear Parents (always in my thoughts):

I am not at all sure whether or not I should be writing you
at this time, but I am going to anyway and at least tell you
how we are faring.

First, I want to say that I received your letter mailed from
Drammen on the sixth of June on the twenty-fifth of July. I
was very happy to learn that you all were well and especially happy to learn that you have a new daughter-in-law
and we, a new sister-in-law. We sincerely wish the young
couple a happy future. The news of this marriage had already reached us through a letter sent to Juli.

Although I am expecting a letter from you any day, I
shall write now. However, as soon as I receive your letter,
I shall write you again.

On May 26th we left Sando's and moved up to Ole's parents. I think I told you in my last letter that Ole was eager to
go out to get some land. He left in April and came back in
May, after having secured a quarter section of land in Em-
mett County, Iowa. Ole's quarter section borders on Lars
Poulsen Trøos or Sumbreen's land [*claim*]. Many others
have also settled there. My husband found land that he liked
and staked his claim. I shall describe the land to you when I
have seen it. One thing certain—it's a fine piece of land. Ole
Sando and sons are eager to go and settle there, too. More
about that another time.

So little Svend and I are here with my parents-in-law for
the time being. On the first of June Ole went west again to
work for an American farmer. At the same time he is guarding his claim because quite often others come around, pull
up the stakes, and claim the land. So he has to be near by in
order to watch and protect it. His daily wage is very good,
and he likes his work. He expects to come back in Septem-

ber, and we shall move there sometime this fall. That's our plan for the present, if everything [*Ms. illegible*].

I have had two letters from him since he left [*Ms. illegible*]. In the meantime I am here, feeling fine, and getting along. However, the statement that one often finds in letters from America—that one wouldn't care to be back in Norway for all the world, or words to that effect to assure those at home that they like it here—such a statement I could never make as I should not be telling the truth. I recall, too, that very pious religious utterances are found in so many of the letters that people at home have thought that people here in America are more devout. But that is certainly not the truth. I know only one person, an old woman from Flo, who, I think, is sincerely religious. I don't think people are any worse, but they are certainly not any better. Life just isn't the same, even in this respect. But enough of this.

I have told you that I am happy here, and I really am. If I haven't anything else to do, I take my little boy in my arms and go over to the public school. It's not very far away (as far as to Bakken). What a remarkable change! A few months ago I was the teacher. Now I am the student and a very poor one at that. I can't boast of having learned very much. I can read just a little, but I do understand a few of the stories in the English books.

My little boy is growing fast. He is a restless little fellow. He is everybody's favorite, his grandfather's as well as his uncles', and they all help to take care of him. I haven't seen his aunt since the Pentecost holidays. At that time she was moving to the home of a Yankee in St. Ansgar. She expects to work there four months at one dollar a week. Little Ole is working for a man from Gol and will get sixty dollars for the four months. All are well and getting along fine. Engebret and the boys are here helping the old folks.

When you write me again, I wish you would send me the price of everything that you have bought and sold this past year, particularly the price of coffee, sugar, tobacco, cotton goods, yarn, and the like. Everything here is very expensive. Those who do not have Norwegian clothes or cloth, and are forced to buy everything they need, certainly come to know and feel that times are hard. One yard of cotton costs forty cents or a half dollar, according to the quality of the cloth. What we pay thirty or forty cents for is about like what they paid eight skillings for at home. Colored cotton goods, which we call calico, here costs from twenty, twenty-five, to thirty, yes, even forty cents a yard. Spool cotton, which we paid two or three skillings for there, costs ten cents a spool here, and everything else is in the same ratio. We get only two or two and a half pounds of coffee for one dollar. Tobacco costs one dollar a pound. Everything is so expensive—unreasonably so. Prices have risen unbelievably high in such a short time.

I said at the beginning of my letter that I didn't know what I should write you, but now I see that I have covered the page with these few items. I shall write you more next time. I have more to tell you but must close. Good-by and God bless you. This is my deepest wish.

Your daughter and sister
Gro Nielsdatter

To Nils Knudsen Gudmundsrud

The Nun of Kenmare

Margaret Anna Cusack

Margaret Anna Cusack, born in 1829 in Coolock, Ireland, was a woman known by many names: Margaret Anna, Sister and Mother Mary Francis Clare, and most popularly, the Nun of Kenmare. The spiritual journey that endowed Margaret Anna with so many names began early in her life. Though her family had once lived comfortably as landholding aristocrats, financial debts and health problems caused Cusack's parents to separate in 1843. Mrs. Cusack took Margaret Anna and a son, Samuel, to Exeter, England, where Margaret Anna turned to religion as a way of dealing with the pain of losing her father. Cusack found her mother's belief in Episcopalian Christianity gloomy and isolating, however, and found solace in the social activism of a nearby Anglican church. Soon after, Margaret Anna became an Anglican sister and devoted her life to working for the good of society rather than for the self.

Convent life was not what she expected it to be. Cusack became disillusioned with a church that spent money on expensive train trips for clergy rather than helping to feed the hungry. Impressed by the compassion for the poor of the Order of the Poor Clares in Newry, Ireland, Cusack became confirmed by the Catholic Church in 1858. A year later she entered a cloistered life of intense study, writing, and contemplation as Sister Mary Francis of the Poor Clares. One of Cusack's more famous historical works, *History of the Kingdom of Kerry*

(1868), was written during this period. It was also during this period that the Nun of Kenmare earned her name by founding a new Order of the Poor Clares in Kenmare, Kerry, a particularly impoverished region of Ireland.

The lack of decent wages, an equal distribution of food, and educational institutions in Kerry concerned Cusack and prompted her to begin a campaign against Irish landlords that was unprecedented by a Catholic nun. To draw attention to the plight of the poor among the Irish at large, Cusack stormed into government offices, was outspoken at upper-class dinners and benefits, and sent delegates among Catholic officials to spread the news of Irish impoverishment to America. In fact, Cusack addressed her first published work of social reform, *Advice to Irish Girls in America* (1872), to Irish-Americans with the hope that the stories of underprivileged Irish people on both sides of the Atlantic would be heard. Although this work was banned in Ireland, McGee of New York acted as publisher, and it circulated widely within Irish-American communities. Believing that such immigrants would support an Order of the Poor Clares in America, the Nun of Kenmare traveled to New York in 1884 in search of funding for a new convent.

In New York, the Nun happily found champions for the "working girl" among suffragettes and industry owners, but many important Irish-American ecclesiastics and politicians prevented her from getting even a night's shelter. The Nun attributed such slights to the patriarchal nature of both her religion and her homeland. Unable to fend off the countless taunts of cardinals and archbishops, the aging Margaret Anna Cusack went to England in 1888 to write her autobiography. Before her death the following year, Cusack, having been shunned by so many from the religious community, now wavered between Anglicanism, Presbyterianism, Methodism, and Baptism.

In "Arrival in New York," Chapter 22 of her autobiography, *The Nun of Kenmare* (1888), Cusack relates the period of her never-ending struggles among Ameri-

can church officials. Intending to open a convent to train
girls for domestic life, the Nun is continually denied financial or spiritual assistance.

CHAPTER 22

ARRIVAL IN NEW YORK

*Refused an Interview by Cardinal McClosky and Bishop
Corrigan—Inexcusable Discourtesy—Comment of Mgr.
Capel—Word of Avoidance Passed Around—Opposed
by Mgr. Quinn—Letter to Cardinal McClosky—Circular
in Aid of Immigrants—Miss Charlotte O'Brien—The
Bishop of Cloyne—His Interest—Forbidden to Work
at Castle Garden—Father Riordan's Mission there.*

Canon Monaghan had brought with him all the necessary
credentials from our English ecclesiastical superior,
and he waited on Cardinal McCloskey to present them in
person. The canon and myself were peremptorily refused an
interview, not only by the cardinal but by Archbishop Corrigan, then coadjutor bishop. For this marked discourtesy,
there was no excuse, and it had the effect which was no
doubt intended. The reader may imagine my grief and dismay; I had been received with marked kindness and I might
say respect in Rome, but as Canon Monaghan said, "I was
good enough for the Vatican, but I was not good enough for
the Episcopal Palace in New York."

But there was at this time, a visitor in New York who received very different treatment. Mgr. Capel had preceded
me, and was duly honored by Archbishop Corrigan and his
friends, who gave him leave to preach and lecture where
he pleased. He soon heard of the very different reception
which was given to me and called on me at the hotel where
I was staying, with an offer of his services and many expressions of indignation for the way in which I was treated.

"Indeed," he said, with some contempt, "if they were

gentlemen, at least, they would treat a lady differently." I declined his offers of services, very much to the disappointment of Canon Monaghan. If I had accepted them and arranged for a series of lectures, as he proposed, no doubt I should have realized a very large sum of money for the support of our institution. But I did not think that money obtained in this way would have any special grace, though I have no doubt, it would have obtained some favor from those who appreciate success, and honor wealth at the expense of poverty.

There were many circumstances over which I had no control connected with my coming to America which were very much to my disadvantage; at the same time, I must say that if there had been an intelligent, perhaps I should rather say a Christian interest in my work, they should not have had the least weight. They were such circumstances as would not have been considered for a moment, unless there was an object in finding fault. But they were just the circumstances which could be used to my disadvantage by those who wanted to prevent the success of this work. It is sad to say this, but it is true. When I arrived in America, I had not the least idea where I was to stay; I never thought of asking to go to a convent, and even if I had thought of it, I would probably not have asked, with my former experience. Besides, I had been long enough a sister to know how often jealousy interferes with good works. But the arrangements that were made for me were singularly unfortunate. I was so ill going from Liverpool to Queenstown that I was obliged to remain in Queenstown a week before I was able to continue my journey to New York. Canon Monaghan who travelled with us, insisted on going on to New York without me. I requested him not to do anything until I arrived, but he thought it too long to wait, and his mistaken zeal led to consequences which were not to our mutual advantage.

A place should have been taken for me in a quiet, private house, and not in a public and expensive hotel. Of all these arrangements I was totally ignorant, until I arrived, and it was too late to alter them; and, as I have said, if I had been received in a friendly spirit, all would have been well. But those who were looking for causes against me found them ready to their hand.

In addition to this, reports were given out, either to injure me, or from ignorance, that I was come to collect an immense sum of money for a cathedral in Nottingham, which report had the effect which was intended. The Irish people were more or less deliberately deceived about the circumstances under which I had left Knock, and it was not difficult to excite feeling against me.

Further, I learned later that some one in Ireland had been busy writing to the American bishops against me. Why they had preferred believing these false reports to the testimony of the Pope and Propaganda, I cannot tell.

I heard from a gentleman who had good opportunities of knowledge, that the Jesuit fathers had been specially warned against me, which was curious, considering that it was a Jesuit father who had been my great helper and encourager in all my troubles, as his letters show. However, I came to know later that there is not quite as much harmony even in the religious orders of the Roman Catholic church as those outside suppose.

I now met with a very serious accident, which compelled me to remain longer at the hotel than I wished. Again I was at the mercy of circumstances, over which I had no control, and at the mercy of people who did not concern themselves to inquire whether their denunciations of my character were justified by facts.

How far his Eminence Cardinal McCloskey was or was not able to attend to affairs at this time personally, I do not know, but his name was used by Mgr. Preston in a letter to Canon Monahan, now before me. It is no wonder that all the rumors which were carefully circulated about me were believed, when those who circulated them could say, that the archbishop had refused even to see the Nun of Kenmare; and this refusal to see me told on the public, as no doubt it was intended to do. Every one knew how cordially other sisters had been received, how priests came to New York and were often allowed to collect, whose missions certainly were not so specially and openly approved by the Holy Father and Propaganda as mine was.

I could not understand how it was every one avoided me. Later on, I learned that the word had been passed around through the priests, that I was not to be received by any one. The working men and women of New York, I have heard, were longing to see me. They knew my work for the old land, but they did not know what to do. They were expecting day after day that there would be a lecture or a meeting, or some public notice of my arrival. Reports were widely circulated against me, notwithstanding the authorization I had brought with me from the Holy See. It was said that I had been disobedient to my bishop in Ireland, though no one seemed to know who the bishop was. It was, indeed, a time of darkness and sorrow to me, and I had not then realized the utter hopelessness of trying to carry on work to which the bishops were determinedly opposed, no matter what papal sanction I might have.

One of my principal opponents was the late Mgr. Quinn; he even went so far as to tell a Protestant lady, who was very much interested in my plans for working girls, that I was disobedient to my bishop in Ireland, and to try to prevent her from interesting herself in my work.

Canon Monahan was by no means easily discouraged; he made repeated offers to see Mgr. Preston and to explain matters to him, but he was always put off with an evasive and not very courteous answer.

Finding that matters were becoming more and more hopeless, I thought that I had better address a letter to Cardinal McCloskey myself, knowing that if it did not reach him, it must reach his assistant, Archbishop Corrigan. I have kept a copy of the letter, which I append here.

December 31, 1884.

MY DEAR LORD CARDINAL,—As I find that false and very cruel reports are circulating about me amongst your eminence's clergy, I write to beg most earnestly that you will allow me an interview with you, when I can show you letters from Archbishop Croke and other Irish ecclesiastical dignitaries, any one of which will prove that I have been very cruelly and unjustly slandered.

My Lord Cardinal, we are neither of us young, and we must both stand before the judgment seat of God shortly; if your eminence will do me an act of justice, God will repay you in that awful hour. My lord let me not plead with you in vain.

The matter is one of great moment to me, and it is of still more moment to our holy Faith. It is very natural that the refusal of the ecclesiastical authorities in New York even to see me has occasioned a belief in these false and scandalous reports.

The principal scandals which were circulated about me were: that I left Kenmare without leave, and that I took money from Knock which belonged to it; both of these charges were as false as they were malicious. I am no saint, but your eminence has read the lives of the saints, and you know how often and how cruelly the founders of religious orders were belied and misrepresented even by good people. Surely, the Holy Father's approval of my work should be sufficient to bring the encouragement of every bishop in the land. I remain, my Lord Cardinal,

Your obedient servant,
SISTER MARY FRANCIS CLARE,
Mother-General of the Sisters of Peace.

To this letter I received no reply, and this was the first of many appeals which I have made unsuccessfully to the Roman Catholic bishops of America to give me a few moments of their time to see for themselves what was true and what was false. Nor could it be said that the work which I asked to do was not wanted in America. Never was such a work more needed, and this has been made evident by the large number of homes and institutions for girls which have been established within the last two years by Protestant ladies. These homes are open to Roman Catholics, and Roman Catholic girls make large use of them, finding no such help in their own community.

My first consideration in America was the work for immigrant girls. As we had large schools in Kenmare, I knew the difficulties of these girls in obtaining employment. And with strange ignorance of their own best advantage, Irish landlords are unwearied in getting rid of their tenants, and girls are sent in droves to America.

In the summer of 1881 I issued a circular, which will be found below, and to which I desire to call special attention, in view of circumstances to be related presently.

Miss Charlotte O'Brien, a near relative of Mrs. Monsell, of the Clewer sisterhood, and who was also a relative of mine, came to me to Kenmare, on the subject of protecting emigrant girls, before she went to America for the same purpose.

I was always ready to help a good work, especially where girls were concerned; but there were many difficulties in my way. I sent this circular to all the bishops in Ireland, and had some warm letters of recommendation and encouragement—:

EMIGRANTS' AID AND PROTECTION SOCIETY.

It is proposed to form an Emigrant's Aid and Protection Society, with the sanction of ecclesiastical authority, under the protection of Our Lady Star of the Sea and St. Raphael. The special sanction of his lordship the Bishop of Cloyne has been obtained.

The necessity for such a society need scarcely be insisted on. Every day thousands of our people are leaving Ireland and England for America, and too often they go as little prepared spiritually as temporarily; hence so many are lost to the faith. Whatever opinion many of us may have as to the cause of emigration, of the fact there is no question. The society of Our Lady Star of the Sea will not interfere in any way for or against emigration. Its object is purely to give spiritual aid to those who will and do emigrate. But even in a temporal point of view such aid cannot fail to be beneficial.

We cannot but hope that in saving thousands of immortal souls from danger, we shall also help them to be better citizens of their new country, and thus to benefit even the country of their birth. Miss Charlotte O'Brien, with a most commendable zeal, has called public attention to the fearful dangers through which our emigrants, and especially our female emigrants, pass. She has urged the writer of this, in words of no ordinary fervor, to undertake the promotion of a society for their protection. She says, 'Of gold and silver or merchandise, careful invoices are kept, but of the human soul no word is known.' The object of this society will be human souls, the most glorious object which we can possibly have, since it was the one object of the life of our divine Lord on earth.

The Work of This Society.

It is proposed that this society should be placed under the protection of the most reverend, the archbishops and the bishops of the whole English-speaking world.

1. That the society should be under the direction of a priest, whose exclusive work it shall be. God will provide one.

2. That as soon as possible, a congregation of priests should be located at Queenstown, Cork, and in New York, devoted to this special work. God will inspire some of our religious orders to take up this work. We have already hopes that a congregation of missionary priests will take it up as part of their work. One of these priests, if possible, and if a sufficient staff can be had, would go out in each vessel with emigrants.

3. Corresponding secretaries would be appointed at Queenstown and in New York, to look after the embarkation and the debarkation of emigrants, to take charge of those who are friendless until they are placed in the hands of friends, or in respectable situations, and to advise the pastors of American cities and other places of new additions to their flocks. It is hoped that this would save thousands, if not millions, from falling away from the church, and that it would probably be the means of reclaiming multitudes who have so fallen.

4. In order to make the working of this society as

perfect as possible, it is proposed that an organization should be formed in every parish in Ireland and America, and, as far as possible, in the large English towns where there is a large Irish population, and that all Catholics should be asked to join the society as honorary or active members; the parish priest in all cases to be the president; the active members to form a small committee, with a secretary and treasurer.

The duty of the secretary will be to ascertain the names and the addresses of the persons about to emigrate, which could be easily obtained from the emigration agents, as well as from other sources; to ascertain the destination of the emigrants, and to forward the name and particulars to the secretary in Queenstown or New York, as may be arranged. The treasurer will collect and receive donations for the general fund, which need not be large, as we know what has been done for the propagation of the faith by the pence of the poor.

All the members, whether honorary or active, to contribute one penny per month to the general fund, and to say daily one Hail Mary for all emigrants, and the invocation "Our Lady, Star of the Sea, protect us until we reach the safe haven of eternity; St. Raphael, friend of wanderers, be our guide through life!"

5. The active members will undertake to do their best to induce all emigrants to approach the sacraments before leaving Ireland, and, where it may be necessary, to bring them to a priest or nun for instruction; or, should this help not be available, to give them the necessary instruction. Even those who are most occupied during the week could find time on Sundays for this good work, and thus obtain for themselves and families a great reward from God.

As this society is intended for all—both young and old, rich and poor—it is hoped that it may be the means of helping the spiritual life of all.

Since we are all travellers to another country, we need, each and all, the succor of Our Lady Star of the Sea to protect us in our passage over the stormy ocean of life to the haven of rest. We need the help of dear St. Raphael for ourselves, our families, our friends, for all our little or our great adventures in life. Hence, this is a society for all—a help for all. If, indeed, hard times are coming for the church of God, we need to cling closer to each other to help and support each other with the love and fervor of the early Christians. And how many there are who are heartbroken, because some friend or brother has been swamped or shipwrecked in the treacherous sea of temptation. Do we not need the prayers of such a society to reclaim them? And then in helping others we are helping ourselves, and obtaining new strength and grace for our own journey and for its happy termination.

6. The national schoolmasters of Ireland, who have been so faithful to their great trust, will, no doubt, help this well. If the confraternity was established in every convent school, it could be made a centre of salvation, not only for the children of the school—so many of whom will emigrate—but for all others in the parish, who could be most effectively reached in this way.

It is hoped that, after a time, the Holy See will approve of this association, and allow it to be erected into a confraternity.

SISTER MARY FRANCIS CLARE.

KENMARE CO., KERRY.
Feast of Corpus Christi, 1879.

Indeed I had been so long interested in the whole question of preparation for emigration, that some time before I had written a paper on the subject for the Social Science Congress in Dublin. This paper, which gave rise to a great deal of useful discussion, was read for me by Dr. Mapother, the President of the College of Surgeons, Dublin. Thus it will be seen that I was long at work on this important subject, and could not be accused of having taken it up as any new idea of interfering with Father Riordan's plans. Indeed I have heard from several persons that it was my persistent agitation of the subject which made him take it up. Be this as it may, there was a great field for us both.

Soon after, the Bishop of Cloyne, the Right Rev. Dr. Mc-
Carthy, sent a priest to me to Kenmare, to see what could be
done about establishing a place in Queenstown, where a
special house for emigrant girls is quite as much needed as
in New York, and towards this project Miss O'Brien promised liberal help. But, as I have said, there were difficulties
put in my way by the sisters.

When I was on my way to America, I saw the Bishop of
Cloyne at Queenstown, and had every expectation of get-
ting a house established there, to correspond with one in
America, for emigrant girls.

I believe the opposition to this plan, which I met from ecclesiastical authority in New York, was caused partly by a
very absurd idea that my arrangements might interfere with
those of Father Riordan, who had opened a sort of mission
for girls at Castle Garden, and who was anxious to build
a church there, on the somewhat romantic idea that the
girls who landed from Ireland should see a church immediately on their arrival. Certainly, if they had not learned their
religion in Ireland, seeing a church when they landed in
America would not teach them much. But building churches
is always acceptable to certain ecclesiastics, and will always be encouraged, no matter how unnecessary they may
be, or how heavy the debt incurred in consequence.

It was at once decided that I should not be allowed to establish any kind of home in Castle Garden, or have any connection with it. Yet, to say the least, what harm could I have
done there? And what could a man do in such a position? It
was woman's work essentially. Poor Father Riordan is gone
now,—what harm would it have done him if he had allowed
me to join in his work, and to do what he could not do? In
fact he really spent a very small portion of his time in Castle
Garden, for I called there many times to see him, and he was
almost always absent. Still, no doubt, the protection of a
priest was desirable and useful.

A Woman's Quest

Marie Zakrzewska

Marie Elizabeth Zakrzewska, one of America's most successful early female physicians, was born on September 6, 1829, in Berlin, a descendant of a powerful Polish family. Like her mother before her, Zakrzewska was schooled in midwifery, and had earned a position of authority at the Hospital Charitie of Berlin. When further occupational success led to a professorship at a prominent medical school, however, Zakrzewska lost the support of her peers and was demoted. Although women were accepted in Prussian society as midwives or as aides to doctors during births, it was inconceivable that they might act as superiors within the field. Although Zakrzewska emigrated to the United States in 1853 with hopes of practicing medicine freely, she would unfortunately experience worse prejudice among Americans.

Zakrzewska came to the United States with a younger sister and immediately discovered that women physicians were considered disreputable, even dangerous to most of the population. Unwilling to give up, Zakrzewska worked as a seamstress until she met an important contact in 1854: America's first female doctor, Dr. Elizabeth Blackwell (1821–1910). An immigrant from England, Dr. Blackwell suffered adversity similar to Zakrzewska's, only to secure a degree from Cleveland Medical College in 1849. With Blackwell's help, Zakrzewska entered the college in 1854, and graduated two years later. Neither woman could find work in any established American hospitals, however, and they were forced to create their own institution, the New York Infirmary for Women and Children, in 1857. To counteract further exclusion of females from the medical profession, Blackwell and Zakrzewska employed an all-female staff at their infirmary.

Though practicing medicine was Marie Zakrzewska's triumph, it was not the only social service to which she committed herself. Known for her empathy and support of the disadvantaged, Zakrzewska opened a lunchroom for poor working girls, spoke out for the emancipation of slaves, and was an active member of the suffrage movement. Through these endeavors, Zakrzewska made herself known in the Boston area, where she accepted a position as Chair of Obstetrics at the New England Female Medical College in 1859, and opened the highly regarded New England Hospital for Women and Children in 1862. Zakrzewska spent the rest of her life as a hospital administrator and professor as well as a social advocate. A unique success story among nineteenth-century women and immigrants alike, Zakrzewska died in 1902.

Dr. Marie Zakrzewska's autobiography, *A Woman's Quest*, mainly contains passages taken from a lifetime of letters to relatives and friends. It was published posthumously in 1924. The following section, Chapter 11, details a low period in a long career as the newly arrived Zakrzewska wonders how she can possibly support both her professional dreams and her family in the face of an uncertain future.

CHAPTER 11

*Social relations largely limited to learning the lives of
her employees and helping them by work, by sympathy
and by friendliness, and sometimes by taking them into
her house to tide over an emergency. (Twenty-four
years of age: 1853.)*

I must tell you here something of the social life that we led.
We had brought a number of friendly letters with us from
our acquaintances in Berlin to their friends and relatives in
America; all of which upon our arrival we sent by post, with
the exception of two—the one sent by a neighbor to his son,
Albert C., the other to a young artist, both of whom called
for their letters.

About four weeks after we were settled in New York, we
received a call from some young men whose sisters had
been schoolmates of my sisters in Berlin, who came to inquire of us where to find Mr. C. We could give them no information, as we had not seen him since he called for his
letter; neither did we now see anything of the G.'s. But the
acquaintance thus formed with these young men was continued, and our solitude was now and then enlivened by an
hour's call from them. Soon after I had commenced my new
business, they came one day in company with Mr. C., whom
they had met accidentally in the street, and, on his expressing a wish to see us, had taken the liberty to bring him to our
house.

My business continued to prosper, and by constantly offering none but the best quality of goods for sale, in a very
short time I had so much to do that my whole time in the day
was occupied with out-door business, and I was forced to sit
up at night with my sister to prepare work for the knitters.

At one time, we had thirty girls constantly in our employ,
and in this way I became acquainted with many of those un-
fortunates who had been misled and ruined on their arrival

by persons pretending friendship. Two of these in particular interested me greatly.

One, the granddaughter of a famous German and bearing his name, was the daughter of a physician. She had come to this country hoping to find a place as governess. Poor girl! She was a mere wreck when I found her, and all my efforts to raise her up were in vain. She was sick and in a terrible mental condition. We took her into our house, nursed her and cared for her. When she recovered, we supplied her with work for which we paid her so well that she always had three dollars a week, which paid for her board and washing. It was twice as much as she could earn, yet not enough to make her feel reconciled with life.

At one time, she did not come to us for a whole week. I went to see her, and her landlady told me that she was melancholy. I persuaded her to come and stay with us for a few days, but in spite of all my friendly encouragement, I could not succeed in restoring her to cheerfulness. She owned that she could not work merely to live; she did not feel the pangs of hunger, but she felt the want of comforts to which she had been accustomed and which in our days are regarded as necessities.

She attempted to find a situation as governess, but her proficiency in music, French and drawing counted as nothing. She had no city references, and though having been two years in New York, dared not name the place to which she had been conducted on her arrival. She left us at last in despair after having been a week with us. She never called again and I could not learn from her landlady where she had gone.

Three months afterwards, I heard from one of the girls in our employ that she had married a poor shoemaker in order to have a home, but I never learned whether this was true. About a year later, I met her in the Bowery, poorly but cleanly dressed. She hastily turned away her face on seeing me, and I only caught a glimpse of the crimson flush that overspread her countenance.

The other girl that I referred to was a Miss Mary ————, who came with her mother to this country, expecting to live with a brother. They found the brother married and unwilling to support his sister, while his wife was by no means friendly in her reception of his mother. The good girl determined to earn support for her mother, and a pretended friend offered to take care of their things until she could find work and rent lodgings. After four weeks' search, she found a little room and bedroom in a rear building in Elizabeth Street at five dollars a month, and was preparing to move when her "friend" presented a bill of forty dollars for his services. She could only satisfy his rapacity by selling everything that she could possibly spare, after which she commenced to work, and as she embroidered a great deal besides working for me (for which I paid her six dollars a week), for a time she lived tolerably well.

After some time, her mother fell ill, and she had to nurse her and attend to the household as well as to labor for their support. It was a trying time for the poor girl. She sought her brother, but he had moved to the West. I did all that I could for her, but this was not half enough. And after I had quitted the manufacturing business and left the city, my sister heard that she had drowned herself in the Hudson, because her mother's corpse was lying in the house while she had not a cent to give it burial or to buy a piece of bread unless she sold herself to vice.

Are not these two terrible romances of New York life? And many besides did I learn among these poor women, so many indeed that I forget the details of them all. Stories of this kind are said to be without foundation, but I say that there are more of them in our midst than it is possible to imagine.

Women of good education but without money are forced to earn their living. They determine to leave their home, either because false pride prevents their seeking work where they have been brought up as ladies, or because this work is so scarce that they cannot earn by it even a life of semi-starvation, while they are encouraged to believe that in this country they will readily find proper employment.

They are too well educated to become domestics, better

educated indeed than half the teachers here, but modesty, and the habit of thinking that they must pass through the same legal ordeal as in Europe, prevent them from seeking places in this capacity. They all know how to embroider in the most beautiful manner, and knowing that this is well paid for in Europe, they seek to find employment of this kind in the stores.

Not being able to speak English, they believe the stories of the clerks and proprietors, are made to work at low wages, and are often swindled out of their money. They feel homesick, forlorn and forsaken in the world. Their health at length fails them, and they cannot earn bread enough to keep themselves from starvation. They are too proud to beg, and the consequence is that they walk the streets or throw themselves into the river.

I met scores of these friendless women. Some I took into my house; for others I found work and made myself a sort of guardian; while to others I gave friendship to keep them morally alive. It is a curious fact that these women are chiefly Germans. The Irish resort at once to beggary or are inveigled into brothels as soon as they arrive, while the French are always intriguing enough either to put on a white cap and find a place as *bonne*, or to secure a *private* lover.

I am often in despair about the helplessness of women, and the readiness of men to let them earn money in abundance by shame while they are ground down to the merest pittance for honorable work.

Shame on society, that women are forced to surrender themselves to an abandoned life and to death when so many are enjoying wealth and luxury in extravagance! I do not wish the rich to divide their estates with the poor—I am no friend to communism in any form. I only wish institutions that shall give to women an education from childhood that will enable them, like young men, to earn their livelihood. These weak women are the last to come forth to aid in their emancipation from inefficient education. We cannot calculate upon these; we must educate the children for better positions, and leave the adults to their destiny.

How many women marry only for a shelter or a home!

How often have I been the confidante of girls who the day before, arrayed in satin, had given their hands to rich men before the altar, while their hearts were breaking with suppressed agony! And this, too, in America, this great free nation, which, notwithstanding, lets its women starve.

It is but lately that a young woman said to me, "I thank Heaven, my dear doctor, that you are a woman, for now I can tell you the truth about my health. It is not my body that is sick, but my heart. These flounces and velvets cover a body that is sold—sold legally to a man who could pay my father's debts."

Oh! I scorn men, sometimes, from the bottom of my heart. Still, this is wrong, for it is the fault of the woman—of the mother—in educating her daughter to be merely a beautiful machine fit to ornament a fine establishment; not gaining this, there is nothing left but wretchedness of mind and body.

Women, there is a connection between the Fifth Avenue and the Five Points! Both the rich and the wretched are types of womanhood, both are linked together forming one great body, and both have the same part in good and evil. I can hardly leave this subject, though it may seem to have little to do with my American experience, but a word spoken from a full heart not only gives relief but may carry a message to at least one listening ear with far-reaching results.

Story of a Pioneer

Anna Howard Shaw

Anna Howard Shaw, born in Newcastle-upon-Tyne, England, February 14, 1847, was a politically active minister, medical doctor, and leader of the American women's suffrage movement. As a small child, Shaw emigrated to the United States with her poor farming family in 1851, first settling in Massachusetts and then in the wilderness of Michigan. Once grown, Shaw left her pioneer family to return to the east coast where she was able to pursue degrees in theology and medicine.

As the only female member of her class at Boston University in the late 1870s, Shaw became increasingly concerned with the place of women in American institutions. To create a livable income and to voice her political views, she began a series of religious lecture tours before receiving a degree in Theology from Boston College in 1879. With a desire to be fully accepted as a minister, Shaw petitioned the Methodist Episcopal Church that same year, but was denied ordination. This act only inspired her religious pursuits further, and, in 1880, she became the first female pastor accepted by a Protestant denomination in America: the Methodist Church. To further supplement her Christian role as spiritual "healer," Shaw received an M.D. from Boston Medical School in 1885.

Now a fully ordained preacher and certified doctor, Shaw formally left the Church a year later to lead a variety of women's rights organizations, including the

National American Woman Suffrage Association (1904–1915). This career acquainted Shaw with many American luminaries such as John Greenleaf Whittier, Ralph Waldo Emerson, and Louisa May Alcott, but her closest association would be with the inspirational Susan B. Anthony, a life-long mentor and friend beginning in 1888. Both women received national attention for their work (Shaw received the Distinguished Service Medal during World War I as chair of the Women's Committee of the Council of National Defense), but neither lived to see the Federal Suffrage Amendment added to the Constitution of the United States in 1920. Shaw died while supporting the League of Nations on July 2, 1919.

In the chapter entitled "The Great Cause," from her memoirs, *Story of a Pioneer* (1915), Anna Howard Shaw describes the natural transition from her first love, ministry, to her life's greatest work: the suffrage movement.

7

THE GREAT CAUSE

There is a theory that every seven years each human being undergoes a complete physical reconstruction, with corresponding changes in his mental and spiritual make-up. Possibly it was due to this reconstruction that, at the end of seven years on Cape Cod, my soul sent forth a sudden call to arms. I was, it reminded me, taking life too easily; I was in danger of settling into an agreeable routine. The work of my two churches made little drain on my superabundant vitality, and not even the winning of a medical degree and the increasing demands of my activities on the lecture platform wholly eased my conscience. I was happy, for I loved my people and they seemed to love me. It would have been pleasant to go on almost indefinitely, living the life of a country minister and telling myself that what I could give to my flock made such a life worth while.

But all the time, deep in my heart, I realized the needs of the outside world, and heard its prayer for workers. My theological and medical courses in Boston, with the experiences that accompanied them, had greatly widened my horizon. Moreover, at my invitation, many of the noble women of the day were coming to East Dennis to lecture, bringing with them the stirring atmosphere of the conflicts they were waging. One of the first of these was my friend Mary A. Livermore; and after her came Julia Ward Howe, Anna Garlin Spencer, Lucy Stone, Mary F. Eastman, and many others, each charged with inspiration for my people and with a special message for me, which she sent forth unknowingly and which I alone heard. They were fighting great battles, these women—for suffrage, for temperance, for social purity— and in every word they uttered I heard a rallying-cry. So it was that, in 1885, I suddenly pulled myself up to a radical decision and sent my resignation to the trustees of the two churches whose pastor I had been since 1878.

The action caused a demonstration of regret which made it hard to keep to my resolution and leave these men and women whose friendship was among the dearest of my possessions. But when we had all talked things over, many of them saw the situation as I did. No doubt there were those, too, who felt that a change of ministry would be good for the churches. During the weeks that followed my resignation I received many odd tributes, and of these one of the most amusing came from a young girl in the parish, who broke into loud protests when she heard that I was going away. To comfort her I predicted that she would now have a man minister—doubtless a very nice man. But the young person continued to sniffle disconsolately.

"I don't want a man," she wailed. "I don't like to see men in pulpits. They look so awkward." Her grief culminated in a final outburst. "They're all arms and legs!" she sobbed.

When my resignation was finally accepted, and the time of my departure drew near, the men of the community spent much of their leisure in discussing it and me. The social center of East Dennis was a certain grocery, to which almost every man in town regularly wended his way, and from which all the gossip of the town emanated. Here the men sat for hours, tilted back in their chairs, whittling the rungs until they nearly cut the chairs from under them, and telling one another all they knew or had heard about their fellow-townsmen. Then, after each session, they would return home and repeat the gossip to their wives. I used to say that I would give a dollar to any woman in East Dennis who could quote a bit of gossip which did not come from the men at that grocery. Even my old friend Captain Doane, fine and high-minded citizen though he was, was not above enjoying the mild diversion of these social gatherings, and on one occasion at least he furnished the best part of the entertainment. The departing minister was, it seemed, the topic of the day's discussion, and, to tease Captain Doane one young man who knew the strength of his friendship for me suddenly began to speak, then pursed up his lips and looked eloquently mysterious. As he had expected, Captain Doane immediately pounced on him.

"What's the matter with you?" demanded the old man. "Hev you got anything agin Miss Shaw?"

The young man sighed and murmured that if he wished he could repeat a charge never before made against a Cape Cod minister, but—and he shut his lips more obviously. The other men, who were in the plot, grinned, and this added the last touch to Captain Doane's indignation. He sprang to his feet. One of his peculiarities was a constant misuse of words, and now, in his excitement, he outdid himself.

"You've made an incineration against Miss Shaw," he shouted. "Do you hear—*an incineration!* Take it back or take a lickin'!"

The young man decided that the joke had gone far enough, so he answered, mildly: "Well, it is said that all the women in town are in love with Miss Shaw. Has that been charged against any other minister here?"

The men roared with laughter, and Captain Doane sat down, looking sheepish.

"All I got to say is this," he muttered: "That gal has been in this community for seven years, and she 'ain't done a thing during the hull seven years that any one kin lay a finger on!"

The men shouted again at this back-handed tribute, and the old fellow left the grocery in a huff. Later I was told of the "incineration" and his eloquent defense of me, and I thanked him for it. But I added:

"I hear you said I haven't done a thing in seven years that any one can lay a finger on?"

"I said it," declared the Captain, "and I'll stand by it."

"Haven't I done any good?" I asked.

"Sartin you have," he assured me, heartily. "Lots of good."

"Well," I said, "can't you put your finger on that?"

The Captain looked startled. "Why—why—Sister Shaw," he stammered, "you know I didn't mean *that*! What I meant," he repeated, slowly and solemnly, "was that the hull time you been here you ain't done nothin' anybody could put a finger on!"

Captain Doane apparently shared my girl parishioner's prejudice against men in the pulpit, for long afterward, on one of my visits to Cape Cod, he admitted that he now went to church very rarely.

"When I heard you preach," he explained, "I gen'ally followed you through and I knowed where you was a-comin' out. But these young fellers that come from the theological school—why, Sister Shaw, the Lord Himself don't know where they're comin' out!"

For a moment he pondered. Then he uttered a valedictory which I have always been glad to recall as his last message, for I never saw him again.

"When you fust come to us," he said, "you had a lot of crooked places, an' we had a lot of crooked places; and we kind of run into each other, all of us. But before you left, Sister Shaw, why, all the crooked places was wore off and everything was as smooth as silk."

"Yes," I agreed, "and that was the time to leave—when everything was running smoothly."

All is changed on Cape Cod since those days, thirty years ago. The old families have died or moved away, and those

who replaced them were of a different type. I am happy in
having known and loved the Cape as it was, and in having
gathered there a store of delightful memories. In later
strenuous years it has rested me merely to think of the place,
and long afterward I showed my continued love of it by
building a home there, which I still possess. But I had little
time to rest in this or in my Moylan home, of which I shall
write later, for now I was back in Boston, living my new
life, and each crowded hour brought me more to do.

We were entering upon a deeply significant period. For
the first time women were going into industrial competition
with men, and already men were intensely resenting their
presence. Around me I saw women overworked and under-
paid, doing men's work at half men's wages, not because
their work was inferior, but because they were women.
Again, too, I studied the obtrusive problems of the poor and
of the women of the streets; and, looking at the whole social
situation from every angle, I could find but one solution
for women—the removal of the stigma of disfranchisement.
As man's equal before the law, woman could demand her
rights, asking favors from no one. With all my heart I joined
in the crusade of the men and women who were fighting for
her. My real work had begun.

Naturally, at this period, I frequently met the members of
Boston's most inspiring group—the Emersons and John
Greenleaf Whittier, James Freeman Clark, Reverend Minot
Savage, Bronson Alcott and his daughter Louisa, Wendell
Phillips, William Lloyd Garrison, Stephen Foster, Theodore
Weld, and the rest. Of them all, my favorite was Whittier.
He had been present at my graduation from the theological
school, and now he often attended our suffrage meetings.
He was already an old man, nearing the end of his life; and I
recall him as singularly tall and thin, almost gaunt, bending
forward as he talked, and wearing an expression of great serenity and benignity. I once told Susan B. Anthony that if I
needed help in a crowd of strangers that included her, I
would immediately turn to her, knowing from her face that,
whatever I had done, she would understand and assist me. I
could have offered the same tribute to Whittier. At our

meetings he was like a vesper-bell chiming above a battle-field. Garrison always became excited during our discussions, and the others frequently did; but Whittier, in whose big heart the love of his fellow-man burned as unquenchably as in any heart there, always preserved his exquisite tranquillity.

Once, I remember, Stephen Foster insisted on having the word "tyranny" put into a resolution, stating that women were deprived of suffrage by the *tyranny* of men. Mr. Garrison objected, and the debate that followed was the most exciting I have ever heard. The combatants actually had to adjourn before they could calm down sufficiently to go on with their meeting. Knowing the stimulating atmosphere to which he had grown accustomed, I was not surprised to have Theodore Weld explain to me, long afterward, why he no longer attended suffrage meetings.

"Oh," he said, "why should I go? There hasn't been any one mobbed in twenty years!"

The Ralph Waldo Emersons occasionally attended our meetings, and Mr. Emerson, at first opposed to woman suffrage, became a convert to it during the last years of his life—a fact his son and daughter omitted to mention in his biography. After his death I gave two suffrage lectures in Concord, and each time Mrs. Emerson paid for the hall. At these lectures Louisa M. Alcott graced the assembly with her splendid, wholesome presence, and on both occasions she was surrounded by a group of boys. She frankly cared much more for boys than for girls, and boys inevitably gravitated to her whenever she entered a place where they were. When women were given school suffrage in Massachusetts, Miss Alcott was the first woman to vote in Concord, and she went to the polls accompanied by a group of her boys, all ardently "for the Cause." My general impression of her was that of a fresh breeze blowing over wide moors. She was as different as possible from exquisite little Mrs. Emerson, who, in her daintiness and quiet charm, suggested an old New England garden.

Of Abby May and Ednah Cheney I retain a general impression of "bagginess"—of loose jackets over loose waistbands, of escaping locks of hair, of bodies seemingly one size from the neck down. Both women were utterly indifferent to the details of their appearance, but they were splendid workers and leading spirits in the New England Woman's Club. It was said to be the trouble between Abby May and Kate Gannett Wells, both of whom stood for the presidency of the club, that led to the beginning of the anti-suffrage movement in Boston. Abby May was elected president, and all the suffragists voted for her. Subsequently Kate Gannett Wells began her anti-suffrage campaign. Mrs. Wells was the first anti-suffragist I ever knew in this country. Before her there had been Mrs. Dahlgren, wife of Admiral Dahlgren, and Mrs. William Tecumseh Sherman. On one occasion Elizabeth Cady Stanton challenged Mrs. Dahlgren to a debate on woman suffrage, and in the light of later events Mrs. Dahlgren's reply is amusing. She declined the challenge, explaining that for anti-suffragists to appear upon a public platform would be a direct violation of the principle for which they stood—which was the protection of female modesty! Recalling this, and the present hectic activity of the anti-suffragists, one must feel that they have either abandoned their principle or widened their views.

For Julia Ward Howe I had an immense admiration; but, though from first to last I saw much of her, I never felt that I really knew her. She was a woman of the widest culture, interested in every progressive movement. With all her big heart she tried to be a democrat, but she was an aristocrat to the very core of her, and, despite her wonderful work for others, she lived in a splendid isolation. Once when I called on her I found her resting her mind by reading Greek, and she laughingly admitted that she was using a Latin pony, adding that she was growing "rusty." She seemed a little embarrassed by being caught with the pony, but she must have been reassured by my cheerful confession that if *I* tried to read either Latin or Greek I should need an English pony.

Of Frances E. Willard, who frequently came to Boston, I saw a great deal, and we soon became closely associated in our work. Early in our friendship, and at Miss Willard's suggestion, we made a compact that once a week each of us would point out to the other her most serious faults, and thereby help her to remedy them; but we were both too sane to do anything of the kind, and the project soon died a natural death. The nearest I ever came to carrying it out was in warning Miss Willard that she was constantly defying all the laws of personal hygiene. She never rested, rarely seemed to sleep, and had to be reminded at the table that she was there for the purpose of eating food. She was always absorbed in some great interest, and oblivious to anything else. I never knew a woman who could grip an audience and carry it with her as she could. She was intensely emotional, and swayed others by their emotions rather than by logic; yet she was the least conscious of her physical existence of any one I ever knew, with the exception of Susan B. Anthony. Like "Aunt Susan," Miss Willard paid no heed to cold or heat or hunger, to privation or fatigue. In their relations to such trifles both women were disembodied spirits.

Another woman doing wonderful work at this time was Mrs. Quincy Shaw, who had recently started her day nurseries for the care of tenement children whose mothers labored by the day. These nurseries were new in Boston, as was the kindergarten system she also established. I saw the effect of her work in the lives of the people, and it strengthened my growing conviction that little could be done for the poor in a spiritual or educational way until they were given a certain amount of physical comfort, and until more time was devoted to the problem of prevention. Indeed, the more I studied economic issues, the more strongly I felt that the position of most philanthropists is that of men who stand at the bottom of a precipice gathering up and trying to heal those who fall into it, instead of guarding the top and preventing them from going over.

Of course I had to earn my living; but, though I had taken my medical degree only a few months before leaving Cape Cod, I had no intention of practising medicine. I had merely wished to add a certain amount of medical knowledge to my mental equipment. The Massachusetts Woman Suffrage Association, of which Lucy Stone was president, had frequently employed me as a lecturer during the last two years of my pastorate. Now it offered me a salary of one hundred dollars a month as a lecturer and organizer. Though I may not have seemed so in these reminiscences, in which I have written as freely of my small victories as of my struggles and failures, I was a modest young person. The amount seemed too large, and I told Mrs. Stone as much, after which I humbly fixed my salary at fifty dollars a month. At the end of a year of work I felt that I had "made good"; then I asked for and received the one hundred dollars a month originally offered me.

During my second year Miss Cora Scott Pond and I organized and carried through in Boston a great suffrage bazaar, clearing six thousand dollars for the association—a large amount in those days. Elated by my share in this success, I asked that my salary should be increased to one hundred and twenty-five dollars a month—but this was not done. Instead, I received a valuable lesson. It was freely admitted that my work was worth one hundred and twenty-five dollars, but I was told that one hundred was the limit which could be paid, and I was reminded that this was a good salary for a woman.

The time seemed to have come to make a practical stand in defense of my principles, and I did so by resigning and arranging an independent lecture tour. The first month after my resignation I earned three hundred dollars. Later I frequently earned more than that, and very rarely less. Eventually I lectured under the direction of the Slaton Lecture Bureau of Chicago, and later still for the Redpath Bureau of Boston. My experience with the Redpath people was especially gratifying. Mrs. Livermore, who was their only woman lecturer, was growing old and anxious to resign her work. She saw in me a possible successor, and asked them to take me on their list. They promptly refused, explaining that I must "make a reputation" before they could even consider me. A year later they wrote me, making a very good offer, which I accepted. It may be worth while to mention here that through my lecture-work at this period I earned all the money I have ever saved. I lectured night after night, week after week, month after month, in "Chautauquas" in the summer, all over the country in the winter, earning a large income and putting aside at that time the small surplus I still hold in preparation for the "rainy day" every working-woman inwardly fears.

I gave the public at least a fair equivalent for what it gave me, for I put into my lectures all my vitality, and I rarely missed an engagement, though again and again I risked my life to keep one. My special subjects, of course, were the two I had most at heart—suffrage and temperance. For Frances Willard, then President of the Woman's Christian Temperance Union, had persuaded me to head the Franchise Department of that organization, succeeding Ziralda Wallace, the mother of Gen. Lew Wallace; and Miss Susan B. Anthony, who was beginning to study me closely, soon swung me into active work with her, of which, later, I shall have much to say. But before taking up a subject as absorbing to me as my friendship for and association with the most wonderful woman I have ever known, it may be interesting to record a few of my pioneer experiences in the lecture-field.

In those days—thirty years ago—the lecture bureaus were wholly regardless of the comfort of their lecturers. They arranged a schedule of engagements with exactly one idea in mind—to get the lecturer from one lecture-point to the next, utterly regardless of whether she had time between for rest or food or sleep. So it happened that all-night journeys in freight-cars, engines, and cabooses were casual commonplaces, while thirty and forty mile drives across the country in blizzards and bitter cold were equally inevitable. Usually these things did not trouble me. They were high adventures which I enjoyed at the time and afterward loved to recall. But there was an occasional hiatus in my optimism.

One night, for example, after lecturing in a town in Ohio, it was necessary to drive eight miles across country to a tiny railroad station at which a train, passing about two o'clock in the morning, was to be flagged for me. When we reached the station it was closed, but my driver deposited me on the platform and drove away, leaving me alone. The night was cold and very dark. All day I had been feeling ill, and in the evening had suffered so much pain that I had finished my lecture with great difficulty. Now toward midnight, in this desolate spot, miles from any house, I grew alarmingly worse. I am not easily frightened, but that time I was sure I was going to die. Off in the darkness, very far away, as it seemed, I saw a faint light, and with infinite effort I dragged myself toward it. To walk, even to stand, was impossible; I crawled along the railroad track, collapsing, resting, going on again, whipping my will power to the task of keeping my brain clear, until after a nightmare that seemed to last through centuries I lay across the door of the switch-tower in which the light was burning. The switchman stationed there heard the cry I was able to utter, and came to my assistance. He carried me up to his signal-room and laid me on the floor by the stove; he had nothing to give me except warmth and shelter; but these were now all I asked. I sank into a comatose condition shot through with pain. Toward two o'clock in the morning he waked me and told me my train was coming, asking if I felt able to take it. I decided to make the effort. He dared not leave his post to help me, but he signaled to the train, and I began my progress back to the station. I never clearly remembered how I got there; but I arrived and was helped into a car by a brakeman. About four o'clock in the morning I had to change again, but this time I was left at the station of a town, and was there met by a man whose wife had offered me hospitality. He drove me to their home, and I was cared for. What I had, it developed, was a severe case of ptomaine poisoning, and I soon recovered; but even after all these years I do not like to recall that night.

To be "snowed in" was a frequent experience. Once, in Minnesota, I was one of a dozen travelers who were driven in an omnibus from a country hotel to the nearest railroad station, about two miles away. It was snowing hard, and the driver left us on the station platform and departed. Time passed, but the train we were waiting for did not come. A true Western blizzard, growing wilder every moment, had set in, and we finally realized that the train was not coming, and that, moreover, it was now impossible to get back to the hotel. The only thing we could do was to spend the night in the railroad station. I was the only woman in the group, and my fellow-passengers were cattlemen who whiled away the hours by smoking, telling stories, and exchanging pocket flasks. The station had a telegraph operator who occupied a tiny box by himself, and he finally invited me to share the privacy of his microscopic quarters. I entered them very gratefully, and he laid a board on the floor, covered it with an overcoat made of buffalo-skins, and cheerfully invited me to go to bed. I went, and slept peacefully until morning. Then we all returned to the hotel, the men going ahead and shoveling a path.

Again, one Sunday, I was snowbound in a train near Faribault, and this time also I was the only woman among a number of cattlemen. They were an odoriferous lot, who smoked diligently and played cards without ceasing, but in deference to my presence they swore only mildly and under their breath. At last they wearied of their game, and one of them rose and came to me.

"I heard you lecture the other night," he said, awkwardly, "and I've bin tellin' the fellers about it. We'd like to have a lecture now."

Their card-playing had seemed to me a sinful thing (I was stricter in my views then than I am to-day), and I was glad to create a diversion. I agreed to give them a lecture, and they went through the train, which consisted of two day coaches, and brought in the remaining passengers. A few of them could sing, and we began with a Moody and Sankey hymn or two and the appealing ditty, "Where is my wandering boy to-night?" in which they all joined with special zest. Then I delivered the lecture, and they listened attentively. When I had finished they seemed to think that some slight return was in order, so they proceeded to make a bed for me. They took the bottoms out of two seats, arranged them crosswise, and one man folded his overcoat into a pillow. Inspired by this, two others immediately donated their fur overcoats for upper and lower coverings. When the bed was ready they waved me toward it with a most hospitable air, and I crept in between the overcoats and slumbered sweetly until I was aroused the next morning by the welcome music of a snow-plow which had been sent from St. Paul to our rescue.

To drive fifty or sixty miles in a day to meet a lecture engagement was a frequent experience. I have been driven across the prairies in June when they were like a mammoth flower-bed, and in January when they seemed one huge snow-covered grave—my grave, I thought, at times. Once during a thirty-mile drive, when the thermometer was twenty degrees below zero, I suddenly realized that my face was freezing. I opened my satchel, took out the tissue-paper that protected my best gown, and put the paper over my face as a veil, tucking it inside of my bonnet. When I reached my destination the tissue was a perfect mask, frozen stiff, and I had to be lifted from the sleigh. I was due on the lecture platform in half an hour, so I drank a huge bowl of boiling ginger tea and appeared on time. That night I went to bed expecting an attack of pneumonia as a result of the exposure, but I awoke next morning in superb condition. I possess what is called "an iron constitution," and in those days I needed it.

That same winter, in Kansas, I was chased by wolves, and though I had been more or less intimately associated with wolves in my pioneer life in the Michigan woods, I found the occasion extremely unpleasant. During the long winters of my girlhood wolves had frequently slunk around our log cabin, and at times in the lumber-camps we had even heard them prowling on the roofs. But those were very different creatures from the two huge, starving, tireless animals that hour after hour loped behind the cutter in which I sat with another woman, who, throughout the whole experience, never lost her head nor her control of our frantic horses. They were mad with terror, for, try as they would, they could not outrun the grim things that trailed us, seemingly not trying to gain on us, but keeping always at the same distance, with a patience that was horrible. From time to time I turned to look at them, and the picture they made as they came on and on is one I shall never forget. They were so near that I could see their eyes and slavering jaws, and they were as noiseless as things in a dream. At last, little by little, they began to gain on us, and they were almost within striking distance of the whip, which was our only weapon, when we reached the welcome outskirts of a town and they fell back.

Some of the memories of those days have to do with personal encounters, brief but poignant. Once when I was giving a series of Chautauqua lectures, I spoke at the Chautauqua in Pontiac, Illinois. The State Reformatory for Boys was situated in that town, and, after the lecture the superintendent of the Reformatory invited me to visit it and say a few words to the inmates. I went and spoke for half an hour, carrying away a memory of the place and of the boys which haunted me for months. A year later, while I was waiting for a train in the station at Shelbyville, a lad about sixteen years old passed me and hesitated, looking as if he knew me. I saw that he wanted to speak and dared not, so I nodded to him.

"You think you know me, don't you?" I asked, when he came to my side.

"Yes'm, I do know you," he told me, eagerly. "You are Miss Shaw, and you talked to us boys at Pontiac last year. I'm out on parole now, but I 'ain't forgot. Us boys enjoyed you the best of any show we ever had!"

I was touched by this artless compliment, and anxious to know how I had won it, so I asked, "What did I say that the boys liked?"

The lad hesitated. Then he said, slowly, "Well, you didn't talk as if you thought we were all bad."

"My boy," I told him, "I don't think you are all bad. I know better!"

As if I had touched a spring in him, the lad dropped into the seat by my side; then, leaning toward me, he said, impulsively, but almost in a whisper:

"Say, Miss Shaw, *some of us boys says our prayers!*"

Rarely have I had a tribute that moved me more than that shy confidence; and often since then, in hours of discouragement or failure, I have reminded myself that at least there must have been something in me once to make a lad of that age so open up his heart. We had a long and intimate talk, from which grew the abiding interest I feel in boys today.

Naturally I was sometimes inconvenienced by slight misunderstandings between local committees and myself as to the subjects of my lectures, and the most extreme instance of this occurred in a town where I arrived to find myself widely advertised as "Mrs. Anna Shaw, who whistled before Queen Victoria"! Transfixed, I gaped before the billboards, and by reading their additional lettering discovered the gratifying fact that at least I was not expected to whistle now. Instead, it appeared, I was to lecture on "The Missing Link."

As usual, I had arrived in town only an hour or two before the time fixed for my lecture; there was the briefest interval in which to clear up these painful misunderstandings. I repeatedly tried to reach the chairman who was to preside at the entertainment, but failed. At last I went to the hall at the hour appointed, and found the local committee there, graciously waiting to receive me. Without wasting precious minutes in preliminaries, I asked why they had advertised me as the woman who had "whistled before Queen Victoria."

"Why, didn't you whistle before her?" they exclaimed in grieved surprise.

"I certainly did not," I explained. "Moreover, I was never called 'The American Nightingale,' and I have never lectured on 'The Missing Link.' Where *did* you get that subject? It was not on the list I sent you."

The members of the committee seemed dazed. They withdrew to a corner and consulted in whispers. Then, with clearing brow, the spokesman returned.

"Why," he said, cheerfully, "it's simple enough! We mixed you up with a Shaw lady that whistles; and we've been discussing the missing link in our debating society, so our citizens want to hear your views."

"But I don't know anything about the missing link," I protested, "and I can't speak on it."

"Now, come," they begged. "Why, you'll have to! We've sold all our tickets for that lecture. The whole town has turned out to hear it."

Then, as I maintained a depressed silence, one of them had a bright idea.

"I'll tell you how to fix it!" he cried. "Speak on any subject you please, but bring in something about the missing link every few minutes. That will satisfy 'em."

"Very well," I agreed, reluctantly. "Open the meeting with a song. Get the audience to sing 'America' or 'The Star-Spangled Banner.' That will give me a few minutes to think, and I will see what can be done."

Led by a very nervous chairman, the big audience began to sing, and under the inspiration of the music the solution of our problem flashed into my mind.

"It is easy," I told myself. "Woman is the missing link in our government. I'll give them a suffrage speech along that line."

When the song ended I began my part of the entertainment with a portion of my lecture on "The Fate of Republics," tracing their growth and decay, and pointing out that what our republic needed to give it a stable government was the missing link of woman suffrage. I got along admirably, for every five minutes I mentioned "the missing link," and the audience sat content and apparently interested, while the members of the committee burst into bloom on the platform.

Memoirs of Henry Villard
Henry Villard

Henry Villard, born Heinrich Gustav Hilgard, in Speyer, Bavaria, April 11, 1835, became a major journalist and railroad financier in the United States. A rebellious child, Villard shocked his father by supporting democratic revolutionaries in early nineteenth-century Bavarian government rather than the king (Louis I). Sent to a French boarding school as a young adult for disciplinary purposes, Villard further outraged his father by taking the surname of a fellow student in 1853. The newly named Villard left for America that same year, but he retained his ties with Germany through frequent family visits and politically important German business connections.

These connections in particular led Villard to his greatest financial success in the United States: ownership of the Northern Pacific Railroad in 1881. Acting as a representative for German bondholders of an American railroad in 1874, Villard gained the respect of both investors and company owners on both sides of the Atlantic. This diplomatic edge allowed Villard to mastermind the "blind pool" of 1881, a controversial buyout of the extremely lucrative Northern Pacific Railroad by a concealed group of German funds. Villard's position as president of this company would be short-lived, however, as he was forced to resign in 1884 due to grievous financial miscalculations and management errors. Though his millionaire status was brief, Villard gave thousands of his earnings to orphan asylums, hospitals, and immigrant scholarship funds. Such contributions were often overlooked by the press, who pictured Villard as an inexperienced and greedy "robber baron" at the end of his life.

Before this dramatic rise and fall, however, Villard pursued a lengthy career in journalism at the forefront of American politics. As a writer and editor for both German-speaking and American dailies before and during the Civil War, Villard covered the Lincoln-Douglas debates for a German-American newspaper, the *Staats-Zeitung* (1860) and the Battle of Bull Run for *The New York Tribune* (1862). Villard's journalistic career also brought him into the home of William Lloyd Garrison in Boston, where he met his future wife, Fanny Garrison, in 1863. The chapter "Through Politics to Journalism— 1856–7" of Henry Villard's autobiography, *Memoirs of Henry Villard*, published posthumously in 1904, records the beginnings of his first career. "Through Politics to Journalism" describes an inexperienced immigrant in the middle of a metamorphosis. While attempting to secure a charter for a German settlement and learning about American politics and business practices, Villard discovers a career as a newspaper publisher.

CHAPTER 4

THROUGH POLITICS TO JOURNALISM.—1856–7

On applying at the store of the booksellers, at that time the leading firm in the trade in the Northwest, I was taken to the partner in charge of the subscription department. He was a gentleman in speech and manner. He took my measure at once as a youthful enthusiast with a lively imagination and but little judgment. He did not at all urge me on, but spoke very disinterestedly of the uncertainties of the canvassing business; but he failed to sober me. I told him rather proudly that I had been in the business before and knew what special capacities it required, and that I possessed them. He said, finally, that as I insisted upon it, he would be glad to let me make a trial. There would not be much risk in it for me, as I need buy only one copy of the work at a discount. He would assign me to an entirely unexplored and very promising field, the city of Milwaukee. I was to be allowed a commission of thirty-three per cent. on all subscriptions obtained. Being provided with a full equipment of subscription-books and circulars, I lost no time in starting for the scene of my future operations.

Milwaukee has always been an almost German city. In 1856, the preponderance of the German element was even greater than at present; in fact, its Americanization, which has in the meantime progressed very rapidly, had then hardly begun. It was known among German-Americans as "Deutsch-Athen," and, comparatively speaking, deserved the name. There was a large number of educated and accomplished men among my countrymen, and in them the love of music and histrionic art was very marked. Under the leadership of Hans Balatka, who still wields the baton in Chicago, good orchestral and vocal music was more liberally provided for than in any other city in the West. There was also a very good German theatre. Another attraction was the Hotel Weltstein, the best German inn in the United States. It was named after the proprietor, who had belonged to a learned profession in the fatherland, and was a most intelligent, well-informed, and entertaining host, though too fond of a glass of good wine. He was killed twenty-five years afterwards by a fall from a window. He kept his house very neat and clean, furnished an excellent table, and his charges were reasonable.

I obtained quarters there and quickly became acquainted with a number of the leading Germans, who were either regular guests or who had the habit of enjoying a social glass there. I felt at first encouraged by the fact that my work would be mostly among my own countrymen. But I soon found out that it was, on the contrary, a disadvantage, for most of those I approached knew nothing of American literature and did not care much for it. They had not been in the country long enough for that, and, moreover, their purely German surroundings naturally kept their interest in American affairs at a low point. I was made to feel, before long, that they had not become sufficiently emancipated from their feelings of caste not to look down upon me, more or less, as a book-peddler. I strove very hard to obtain subscribers, and regularly set out every morning and devoted all the day to going about from store to store and office to office. I have a lively recollection of a very heavy snowstorm that raged for several days, and was followed by a bitter cold spell which made canvassing very irksome physically. By degrees, the meagre fruits of my efforts caused my sanguine hopes to vanish, and made me uneasy as to the final outcome. At the end of three weeks, I had sold only thirty-five copies in all, twenty-seven to Americans and eight to Germans. I believe that I am correct in saying that only one out of every twelve attempts to sell was successful. I need not mention that that meant all sorts of experiences for me, mostly of a disagreeable character. I had, as a rule, to drink continually of the cup of humiliation. I had the satisfaction of having tried my best, and enjoyed, upon the whole, a good time, socially. Of course, this did not suffice, as I had failed in my real object, which was to make money. The net pecuniary result was that I spent, all in all, five more dollars than I received during the three weeks, though I really had exhausted the field from which I expected so much.

I returned to Chicago much disheartened, and at a loss what to do. I ought to have said ere this that my confidence in the success of the venture had been so great that, before starting for Milwaukee, I had written to Messrs. Manning & Merriman that I had decided to give up the law temporarily, in order to engage in a most promising business that had unexpectedly come in my way.

I was fortunate enough to find what promised to be a suitable place in the office of a firm of real-estate agents, within a few days, by answering a "want" advertisement. The firm name was Staples & Sims, and they had a fine office at the corner of Dearborn and Clark Streets, fronting on Court-House Square. Staples was a retired merchant and capitalist, Sims a Scotch doctor who had not been able to find a satisfactory practice. It was a queer combination and did not last very long, as it turned out. The firm tried to do a commission business—that is, sell other people's real estate on commission. My special function was to attract German customers, and, accordingly, my name appeared under that of the firm, as salesman, in the advertisements in the German papers. My salary was fifty dollars a month and a small interest in the commission business secured by me. There was also a French clerk, as a bait to French buyers and sellers, who besides acted as draughtsman. I was very much set up when I secured the place, and in this hopeful frame of mind I completed my twenty-first year on April 10, 1856.

It was at this time that I received my first lesson in practical politics, so to speak, in this country. I had long before become a regular reader of newspapers, and fully understood the political questions of the day. The deliberate attempts of the Democrats in the South, aided by the bulk of their Northern sympathizers, to secure an extension of the territory open to slavery, in connection with the organization of Kansas as a Territory, was the all-absorbing and all-exciting topic. The formation of a new party out of the elements opposed to the admission of slavery into Kansas and Nebraska had already begun. Free soil was fast becoming a leading issue, not only in national and State, but even in local elections. It was also made the dividing line in the Chicago municipal election that spring. Of course, I had no right to vote, but that did not prevent me from enlisting as a violent partisan on the anti-Democratic side. The contest was fought directly over slavery. The Democratic nominee for Mayor was Thomas Dyer, and the leader of the opposition Frank C. Sherman. The canvass was made by both sides in the usual way, through public meetings, processions, and a most violent newspaper war. I engaged in it with heart and soul. Every evening I attended a meeting, used my voice as loudly as anybody in cheering and shouting, and joined in a torch-light procession. On election day,

I acted as ticket-distributor, and had then my first sight of violent scenes and rioting at the polls. The "right" and "wrong" seemed to be so clearly defined that I could not understand how any intelligent mind could be at all in doubt. That the ignorant, priest-ridden Irish should support the Democratic candidates was comprehensible, but it aroused my disgust and indignation that there were Germans on the Democratic ticket, a German newspaper and prominent Germans who actually supported it. I looked upon them as contemptible apostates. I was confident, too, that the unholy combination would be overwhelmingly defeated. My unutterable humiliation and grief may be imagined, therefore, when the Democrats obtained a decisive victory. Influenced by the predictions of the dire, irremediable evils that would befall the country if the Democrats carried the day, I felt wofully depressed in spirit. It seemed to me almost as if the world would come to an end. It took me weeks to forget this grievous disappointment. A certain compensation for it lay in the extensive acquaintance which I secured through my political début.

My connection with Messrs. Staples & Sims continued only till the end of May. They were new to the business, having embarked in it only a few months before they engaged me, and they failed to secure the expected custom. They had also entertained extravagant expectations, which remained unfulfilled, of obtaining German customers through me. At the time mentioned, they proposed to change the terms of my engagement so that I should not be paid a salary, but only be allowed commissions on business secured by me. As I had so far not derived more than twenty-five dollars in this way, I could not possibly accept, and therefore left them.

The loss of my place did not at all trouble me, for I had conceived and was full of a scheme from the realization of which I expected much honor and great profit. It will be remembered that, at that time, both the proslavery and antislavery parties respectively were engaged in promoting with all their might emigration into the disputed Territory of Kansas. In the North as well as in the South, from the

New England States to the Mississippi, a lively agitation was going on for the formation of "Kansas emigration societies." Quite a number of such had already been formed and were sending settlers into Kansas. The newspapers announced almost daily the arrival of more or less numerous parties on their way West. My project was nothing less than the forming of a society among the young Germans throughout the Northwest to secure a large tract of land in Kansas and settle the members upon it. The colony was to be, like the other Northern settlements, a vanguard of liberty, and to fight for free soil, if necessary.[1] Of course, I aspired to be the head of the organization. I wrote out a regular plan for it, and, as soon as I was free from office duties, I proceeded to push it. I had no difficulty in interesting in it quite a number of young men, "Turners" and members of political clubs. There was enough enthusiasm among us, but no capital. No one of us could do more than pay a moderate weekly contribution into the treasury. At my suggestion, it was resolved to try and interest local capitalists in our undertaking, and the task devolved upon me. I called upon a number of well-known and wealthy antislavery men, and obtained a dozen subscriptions ranging from fifty to a hundred dollars. Of course, this was not sufficient capital. It then occurred to me that we could far more readily obtain this in the large Eastern cities, which accordingly I persuaded my associates to authorize me to visit for the purpose of soliciting further subscriptions. I made them also instruct me to go to Washington, with a view to getting a donation of land for our purposes from Congress or the Government. I need not say that this feature of the venturesome enterprise was attributable to the fact that I had not the remotest idea of the insuperable difficulties of obtaining any sort of bounty from the Federal authorities.

I went direct from Chicago via Baltimore to the national capital. I had obtained letters of introduction from local

---

[1] He "came very near joining one of the companies of Sharp's riflemen that were being formed all over the North in order to save that Territory to freedom."   .

political leaders to United States Senators and several members of the House from Illinois. The letters did not endorse my scheme, but said that I would explain what I wanted, simply vouching for my reliability. I devoted one day to sight-seeing before presenting them. Aside from the stately public buildings, Washington presented, thirty years ago, the appearance of a shabby, lifeless Southern town. The former dwarfed the masses of mean buildings around them, making them look shabbier and more insignificant. Intense July heat had set in, and hardly anybody was to be seen on the immense streets. The large colored population, exhibiting characteristics indicative of slavery, was a negatively interesting feature to me. But my general impression of the place was very unsatisfactory.

I had little difficulty in getting at the Illinois Senators, Lyman Trumbull and Stephen A. Douglas, and saw them both. Trumbull was a new member and had not made much of a reputation, while Douglas was at that time the most prominent political character before the American public, owing to his growing opposition to the extreme proslavery demands of his party, so that I considered the chance to see and talk with him quite a feather in my cap. Mr. Trumbull had heard of me as a former student in his brother's office; he knew my relatives, and so gave me a kindly reception. I found him very much like his brother, though of more commanding presence. I submitted our printed colonization plan to him. After reading it through, he asked what he was expected to do about it. Thereupon I dwelt as eloquently as I could upon our wishes for either executive or legislative aid from the Government. I saw a smile steal over his face, which produced a feeling of embarrassment in me; but I went through with my argument. "Young friend," the Senator answered, "I regret that you have incurred the trouble and expense of coming to Washington, for your mission is absolutely hopeless. What you seek is contrary to law and usage, and especially ill-advised in the face of the pending party struggle, in and out of Congress, over Kansas." He could but counsel me to abandon at once all contemplated attempts and to return home. This was a cold-water douche indeed, and I left him very crestfallen.

Nevertheless, during the day, I resolved to try my luck with Senator Douglas. Going to his hotel the next morning, I found more than a dozen callers ahead of me, and it was fully two hours before I stood before the "Little Giant," as he was already dubbed by his party. The phrase was well suited to him. He was very small, not over four and a half feet high, and there was a noticeable disproportion between the long trunk of his body and his short legs. His chest was broad and indicated great strength of lungs. It took but a glance at his face and head to convince one that they belonged to no ordinary man. No beard hid any part of his remarkable, swarthy features. His mouth, nose, and chin were all large and clearly expressive of much boldness and power of will. The broad, high forehead proclaimed itself the shield of a great brain. The head, covered with an abundance of flowing black hair just beginning to show a tinge of gray, impressed one with its massiveness and leonine expression. His brows were shaggy, his eyes a brilliant black. He glanced at the letters I handed to him, and asked, with his deep, sonorous voice, that never failed to tell upon popular audiences, what he could do for me. I handed him our prospectus, when he remarked: "Can you tell me its substance? My time is so limited that I cannot read it." I tried to explain, but I had hardly alluded to our object when he cut me short, saying: "Never mind, I understand it all, but I can do nothing for you. Similar requests are addressed to me almost daily by societies formed in the interest of the South, and, even if legal difficulties were not in the way, it would never do for me to favor either side in the national controversy, for political reasons." With this brief and emphatic reply I had to be satisfied, and took my leave. It seemed useless to continue my efforts among the members of the House to whom I had recommendations, and hence I took the first train for Philadelphia.

I spent a whole week in the "City of Brotherly Love" in pursuit of my purpose. I had only one letter of introduction, to William D. Kelley, who was even then playing a leading part in the formation of the opposition to the proslavery Democracy into a new party, and who afterwards achieved national distinction as a member of Congress representing the same Philadelphia district for over a generation. He received me very kindly, but did not hold out much encouragement as to local success in my mission. He went so far as to go around with me personally to wealthy political sympathizers. They were nearly all business men; among them was Mr. Drexel, the senior member of the great banking-firm of Drexel & Co. Several of them, and especially Mr. Drexel, examined me closely as to the details of my project, and particularly regarding the precise uses which we proposed to make of the capital I was trying to raise. I was much embarrassed by being unable to answer some of their questions. My plan did not cover the point whether the subscribers would get something like shares in the company in return for their money, or whether they were expected simply to make gifts. The truth was, that my business knowledge had not been sufficient to make me qualified to elaborate the scheme on a joint-stock basis, and that what I really wanted was outright donations. I remember very distinctly how confounded I was by Mr. Drexel's remarks: "Supposing that your enterprise were really laudable enough to deserve pecuniary help from me and others, why should you and your associates alone have all the benefits reaped from such assistance?" I got out of the quandary as best I could by stating that the subscribers who desired it could, of course, have their contributions treated by the company as loans. But, as I was utterly unprepared to give any guarantees or to show that the proper legal forms had been provided for in that respect, I not only failed to obtain subscriptions, but evidently became an object of suspicion.

Depressed and humiliated, I proceeded to New York. I put up at the Prescott House, a well-known and well-kept German hotel, mainly patronized by the Germans of the better classes from all parts of the United States and from the old country. One of the first persons I saw among the guests was "Colonel" Blenker, who had acquired considerable notoriety, during the rising in the Palatinate in 1849, as the commander of a so-called "free corps," an independent battalion of young ultra-radicals, who proved, however, more determined in the display of red emblems than on the battle-field. I became acquainted with him at the table d'hôte. He was tall, well-built, with fine manners, but his features, so far as they were not covered by his full beard, had the coloring of a confirmed toper. He was a very loud talker, and, when he did not brag of his martial achievements, could not say enough in denunciation of the United States, where his merits hitherto had not been recognized. I soon found out that the cause of his disgust with the country was the fact that he was obliged to eke out a precarious living as a small market-farmer in Rockland County, New York. He supplied the hotel with vegetables and fruit, and, strange to say, took his pay mostly in dinners and wine. He subsequently played quite a part on the Northern side during the War of the Rebellion.

I had a letter to Dr. Hexamer, a German physician of very high professional and social standing, and also a leader of the local German wing of the newly-formed Republican party. Had he lived, he would doubtless have had a brilliant career, but he was consumptive and had then but a short time to live, as he told me himself. He was one of the kindest and most delightful men in every way that I ever met, ready at once to help my scheme, with which he was much impressed. He introduced me personally to Friedrich Kapp, which proved the beginning of a lifelong intimacy. Kapp was engaged in the practice of law, so he seemed to be just the man I needed to put my project into legal shape. He was very willing, too, to give me the benefit of his advice. He agreed with my Philadelphia critics that I and my associates could not expect the public to place a large sum of money unconditionally in our hands, to be used as we saw fit. He advised me strongly to abandon all efforts to raise money under my original plan, and proposed to me to organize a joint-stock company. However, even a brief discussion of the details of the methods to be followed in acting on his proposition was sufficient, little as I then knew of business

affairs, to satisfy me that, in the first place, having no acquaintance, no influence, and no means with which to meet
the preliminary expenses, it would be utterly impossible for
me to effect such an organization. Secondly, even if I succeeded in forming a company, I could not expect to realize
my ambitious dream of controlling it, as I had nothing to
contribute towards its capital.

Thus I was compelled to come to the conclusion that my
scheme would have to be dropped. I was not inclined, however, to accept it at once, and my mind only gradually
worked up to the recognition of that disagreeable necessity.
But my reluctance was due as much to lack of conviction as
to the recognition of the awkward position in which the
miscarriage of my plans would inevitably place me—for
had I not collected considerable money in Chicago, which
was then spent for travelling expenses?

Meantime, I enjoyed an interesting political experience.
Deep excitement over the memorable Presidential election
of that year was felt throughout the country. The nomina-
tion of John C. Frémont as the candidate for the White
House and the opponent of the further extension of slavery
had, more than all others, produced intense enthusiasm, in
which I shared. Hexamer and Kapp were very active in organizing German Republican clubs in New York and the adjoining cities. I accompanied them regularly to the meetings
held for the purpose. Their propaganda was not as widely
successful as they thought it would be, for the mass of our
countrymen showed a stubborn adhesion (born of ignorance and their traditional voting for the Democratic ticket)
to the Democratic party. I was also a regular frequenter of
the Republican headquarters, which were established at
Clinton Hall on Broadway, nearly opposite Clinton Place.
The chairman of the Republican Central Committee was
Simeon Draper, a well-known real-estate dealer. I remember well the admiration I felt every time I saw his commanding figure and heard his stentorian voice. I was also
present when a serenade was given to "John and Jessie"
(Colonel Frémont's wife, *née* Benton), who occupied a

house on Clinton Place, and I had the good fortune to shake hands with them both on that occasion.

I thus loitered in New York for several weeks before returning to Chicago to explain to my associates the reasons for my failure. Most of them were slow to accept my statement that I had tried my best but failed, owing to the nature of our scheme, and criticised my staying in the East longer than was necessary. In settling my account, there was strong opposition to allowing me all that I claimed for travelling expenses, in consideration of which I reduced my claim considerably, though I had charged for only part of my stay in New York. The result of it all was that I resigned and that the "land association" thereupon collapsed.

This sorry ending reduced me again to pecuniary embarrassment. I had not felt justified in drawing the monthly allowance from my father, after leaving Peoria. Thus I found myself with less than thirty dollars in my possession. I had intended to return to New York, feeling sure that, with the aid of my new acquaintances, I could find an acceptable position, but this was now out of the question. At this juncture, I learned accidentally of an opening that seemed to me especially attractive. The Republicans of Racine, Wisconsin, on the direct railroad line between Chicago and Milwaukee, were anxious to win over to their party the large German vote in their city, and for that purpose planned to buy the Democratic German paper and convert it into a Republican organ. They had asked the editors of the Illinois *Staats-Zeitung* to recommend a suitable person to take charge of the concern, and I had heard of the matter through one of them. I was convinced that I was sufficiently familiar with current politics, and that, as for the rest of the needed qualifications, the natural ability which I claimed for myself, together with the energy and enthusiasm that I should bring to the new occupation, would enable me to acquire them speedily. I saw a direct road to literary and political distinction before me. Accordingly, I lost no time in pursuing that great chance. I persuaded my informant to give me a letter of introduction to the Republican Executive Committee of

Racine, and took the next train for that place. This was about the end of August, 1856.

Racine was then, and, I am told, still is, a beautiful town. It is situated right on the shore of Lake Michigan, of which it commands a grand view. There was one long, broad street, lined on both sides with business buildings. The residence part consisted of fine shaded avenues intersecting each other at right angles, with numerous attractive homes. The city was the seat of the county authorities, and of a well-frequented college which always enjoyed a good reputation among Western educational institutions. It contained about twelve thousand inhabitants, one-third of whom were Germans. The county population was also largely German. My first impressions of the place were so favorable as to make me doubly anxious to secure the acceptance of my services. The chairman of the Republican Committee, a bright young lawyer, received me with evident pleasure. I felt much relieved on learning from him that I had no competitor. He at once called a meeting of the committee and presented me to them. They asked no questions at all and engaged me on the spot, with expressions of great satisfaction. The committee had a secret option from the publisher of the German paper to buy it at a certain price, and they resolved to proceed at once to raise the necessary money and exercise it. I was to have eighteen dollars a week salary—princely pay, as it seemed to me—and the sole editorial and business management on behalf of the new owners. The chairman at once set out with me to find a suitable boarding-place, and I obtained a very satisfactory one in a genteel private family, for the low price of five dollars a week for a nice room and all my meals. Thus, literally, in less than twenty-four hours after leaving Chicago, I was at anchor in what appeared to be a permanent haven of rest and promise. A feeling of security and hopefulness came over me which I had not experienced to the same degree since I landed on American soil. As it took the committee several days to close the purchase, I had sufficient leisure to see the town and vicinity thoroughly and to make acquaintances. I was charmed with all I saw and heard.

This happiness was somewhat dimmed when the committee had concluded their bargain and I took possession of the weekly *Volksblatt* printing-office for them and ascertained the exact condition of the paper. The man who had sold it was a printer by trade, and had, with one assistant, edited and printed the paper. The supply of type was limited and nearly worn out. There was only an old-style handpress, on which six hundred copies could be printed in a working-day of twelve hours. The appearance of the paper was indeed wretched, and its contents no better. It had been edited mainly with the aid of scissors, but the selections plainly indicated absence of both taste and judgment. There was very little editorial matter, and what there was consisted of commonplace stuff expressed in ungrammatical language. Indeed, the author of it, who was not at all an educated man, confessed that he never had attempted to write out anything, but that it was his regular practice to put such thoughts as he had directly into type. Under the circumstances, it was not to be wondered at that the subscription-list always remained small. There were nominally about three hundred and eighty names on the books, but a close examination proved that many of the rural subscribers had either not paid at all for years, or paid in farming produce—butter, eggs, chickens, potatoes, corn, and the like. Further inquiries also showed that the subscribers were almost entirely made up of shopkeepers, saloon-keepers, mechanics, and farmers, and that two German doctors were the only representatives of the higher education among them. That with such readers there was not much chance for "literary distinction" was plain enough. As the paper was to raise boldly, between two issues, the Republican instead of the Democratic flag in its columns, the effect of this somersault upon the subscribers remained to be seen. It was clear that, as a preventive of numerous desertions among them, the contents of the paper ought to be very much improved; but the poor material equipment rendered this out of the question.

Still, I resolved to try my best. New as I was to the calling, the first weeks were full of hard work and nervous anxiety. I believe that I wrote and re-wrote the editorials in the first number issued under my control half a dozen times, until I could persuade myself that they would pass muster. I worked literally night and day, succeeding, I can say without self-flattery, in producing very respectable papers. There were at the time only three other German Republican papers published in Wisconsin, as against a score of Democratic, but they all complimented my work. The Democratic organs, as was to be expected, raised a great outcry against the political conversion of the *Volksblatt,* and at once began to abuse me as its originator, with much wrath and unanimity of feeling. The change in the politics of the paper provoked also a declaration, by about a score of old subscribers, published in a Milwaukee German paper, that the "treason" of the paper was due to the mercenariness and bad faith of the publisher, who had no right to sell it, as leading Democrats had originally supplied the capital. This added fuel to the flame, and made the war I waged in my columns against political opponents hotter from week to week. More than half of the subscribers stopped their paper; but I did not mind this, as the local managers of the campaign ordered as large an edition as we could print with our facilities, till after the election.

I was not expected to do anything except, through the newspaper, to persuade the local German voters to go with the Republican party. But I was too earnest, and too full of the intense excitement that took possession of the whole Union during the memorable Presidential contest of that year, to confine my activity to writing. I volunteered to organize a German wing of the local Republican club, and, although this was no easy task, owing to the stolid allegiance of my countrymen to the other party, I succeeded in working up a membership of nearly fifty from the smallest beginnings. We held frequent meetings, which gave me the long-desired opportunity to practise public speaking. I readily got over the first embarrassment, common to all beginners in that art, and acquired considerable fluency. I even addressed some gatherings of German voters especially brought together to listen to me. I was so much encouraged that I even ventured on two occasions on the bold experiment of speaking in English before general meetings of the Republican club. I was well prepared, and, as a double precaution against failure, spoke but briefly. It helped me very much to have the opportunity to listen to a number of prominent politicians and fine speakers from other States who came to Racine to address mass-meetings. There were also some very good speakers among the local leaders, whom I heard regularly in the club. The most prominent among them was Judge Doolittle, afterwards United States Senator.

Notwithstanding these political preoccupations, I found time to form a regular connection, as Western political correspondent, with the *Neue Zeit*, a weekly of the highest aspirations, founded by an enterprising German publisher in New York. It numbered among its contributors all the leading German-American writers, as well as eminent literati and journalists in the old country. It was edited with great care, and every number was replete with fine articles on politics, literature, science, music, and other subjects. I had become acquainted with its editors in New York, and had an ambitious longing to be permitted to write for it. Shortly after reaching Racine, I prepared a long letter on the general political situation in the Northwest. I spent much time and labor on it and sent it to the editors at a venture. To my intense joy, there came an answer from them within a week, saying that it was gladly accepted, and that further contributions were desired from me. My compensation was to be five dollars a letter, which was not a liberal allowance, considering the hard work involved in it for me; still, it was adding just so much to my income, and, moreover, I thought it such an honor to write for the *Neue Zeit* that I would gladly have corresponded with it without pay.

I vividly recollect to this hour the feverish anxiety into which I had worked myself by the time of the near approach of the election. I became so restless that even my editorial duties seemed very irksome. I did outside political work from morning till midnight. The night following the elections, I stayed up with the local Republican leaders till the small hours of the morning. The election returns were not encouraging when we finally sought our quarters, but there was no ground for giving up hope. I need hardly say that I felt indescribably woful when it became a cruel certainty on the following day that, instead of achieving a sweeping victory, the Republicans had suffered an overwhelming, humiliating defeat. My inexpressible disgust made me shun the sight of everybody, and it took me nearly a week to recover my balance.

There was enough in the condition of the *Volksblatt* to sober me entirely. As already mentioned, its sudden political conversion had resulted in a considerable melting away of the subscription-list. The election being over, all the campaign subscriptions stopped, of course, and the fact stared me in the face that there remained only about two hundred and fifty names that could be positively relied on for the future. The advertising patronage, too, was slim. The total gross income of the paper from both sources was not more than eighteen hundred dollars. A close calculation showed that it would take nearly twice as much to pay my salary, the wages of two printers, the cost of paper, ink, etc. Moreover, the renewal of type was imperative. During the campaign, the paper had been allowed a subsidy of fifty dollars a week out of the party funds, and, in view of the condition described, it was of vital importance to me to know whether this stipend would be continued. Hence, I naturally communicated without delay with the Republican Committee on the subject, only to discover, however, that all their enthusiasm had evaporated with the lost election. I received, too, my first lesson in that common experience in this and every other free country, that there is the greatest difference between the promises of politicians before an election and their fulfillment after it. I was informed at once that not only had the campaign fund been entirely exhausted, but the committee was still in debt for electioneering expenses, and that hence they could not contribute another dollar towards the *Volksblatt*. Nor was this all. I now learned for the first time that the greater part of the purchase price of the paper was still unpaid—that, indeed, only one-fourth of it had been paid down in cash, and that the balance would become due in six months from the date of purchase and was secured by a mortgage on the whole concern. This revelation was accompanied by the suggestion, which, under the circumstances, sounded a good deal like mockery, that, in view of my zealous services during the campaign, the committee would be willing to waive all claim for the cash payment, and turn the paper over to me, to be dealt with as best I could, upon the sole condition that I should continue to advocate the Republican cause.

The double task was thus to be put upon me of increasing the income of the paper to a living point and making provision within less than four months for the payment of the remaining three-quarters of the purchase price—a decidedly appalling outlook. But my enthusiasm and confidence in myself were greater than my business experience, so, after considering the question for a couple of days, I decided to accept the committee's proposal. I had persuaded myself that, with strong personal efforts, I might succeed in securing considerable additions to the subscription-list. Then I had reason to think that, by adding a job-printing outfit to the establishment, a new source of income might be found. As regarded the unpaid purchase money, I got over the difficulty by assuring myself that, if I was successful in my efforts in other directions and could make a small additional payment, the creditor would probably be willing to grant an extension of time. There remained the necessity of procuring a new lot of type for the paper. I had heard that it was not difficult to obtain credit from type-makers, and that was sufficient to do away with my hesitation on that score.

I can affirm that I left no stone unturned in my subsequent endeavors to establish the *Volksblatt* on a paying basis. I devoted all the time I could spare from my office labors as editor and publisher to a persistent canvass for new subscribers and advertisers. I solicited not only in Racine, but in three other smaller towns in the county. I even visited Milwaukee repeatedly, but at the end of the year I had secured only a hundred and thirty subscribers more and about seven hundred dollars' worth of advertising—about one-third of the amount needed to keep up the paper. A good part of the new receipts, too, I had to use for travelling expenses.

This meagre result brought me to the end of my wits. I had exhausted the whole field in which anything was to be gathered. I might have bought job and ordinary type on credit, if I had made myself personally liable for it, but I was afraid to do so, and did not buy. The inevitable end of my newspaper ownership came early in January, 1857. Unable to pay the wages of the compositors any longer, I advised the chairman of the Republican Committee of my state of stress. He authorized me to turn the concern over to the former owner, who reluctantly accepted it and forthwith changed it back into a Democratic organ. He claimed at the time that the committee, and I myself as its successor in the control of the paper, were liable to him for the balance due, but he had no legal remedy and did not attempt to enforce his claim. Twenty-four years later, when at the height of my prosperity, I received a letter from this same person, saying that he had been ruined by relieving me of the paper and asking for some recognition on my part. I sent him a check for one thousand dollars.

The Making of an American
Jacob Riis

Danish-born Jacob August Riis is best known in America as a ground-breaking photographer, journalist, and social reformer who changed the face of New York's tenement district forever. As the author of *How the Other Half Lives* (1890), Riis gained international fame for revealing the truth of the horrific living conditions in the Lower East Side through words and photographs. Riis's success prompted him to speak out publicly against a myriad of social ills in New York such as unventilated sweatshops, deficient school systems, and ill-kept public water supplies. For his frankness, future president Theodore Roosevelt deemed Riis "the ideal American," and offered that he "would come to help." Most important to Riis, however, was the attention his work attracted at the New York Board of Health where changes for the worst tenement sections were immediately implemented.

Before his fame, the author worked as a carpenter in Denmark, where he had been born to middle-class parents in 1849. Riis emigrated to America in 1870 after a thwarted love affair, and spent seventeen years reporting on police activity in the tenements for the *New York Tribune*. This experience gave Riis first-hand knowledge of the people he would eventually describe in *How the Other Half Lives*, and inspired a sense of duty to help their plight. Unfortunately, as recounted in his autobiography, *The Making of an American*, published in 1901,

Riis could not force any change in the situation around him through speeches, letters, or articles. It was only with his use of the newly invented "flashbulb" in 1890 that Riis captivated the public with dramatic photographs of the dark tenement interiors pictured in *How the Other Half Lives*. This dismayed Riis, and to compensate for the sensational attention his heavily shadowed flashbulb photos caused, the activist made national lecture tours dealing with social issues until his death in 1914.

While *How the Other Half Lives* created an awareness of poverty previously unheard of in America, *The Making of an American* was criticized by the press as poorly written and self-praising. No critic has ever found fault with Jacob Riis's contributions to society, however, and the chapter "I Become an Author and Resume My Interrupted Career As a Lecturer" offers a unique look into the publication of the book that changed its author's life as much as it changed the lives of others.

CHAPTER 12

I BECOME AN AUTHOR AND RESUME MY INTERRUPTED CAREER AS A LECTURER

For more than a year I had knocked at the doors of the various magazine editors with my pictures, proposing to tell them how the other half lived, but no one wanted to know. One of the Harpers, indeed, took to the idea, but the editor to whom he sent me treated me very cavalierly. Hearing that I had taken the pictures myself, he proposed to buy them at regular photographer's rates and "find a man who could write" to tell the story. We did not part with mutual expressions of esteem. I gave up writing for a time then, and tried the church doors. That which was bottled up within me was, perhaps, getting a trifle too hot for pen and ink. In the church one might, at all events, tell the truth unhindered. So I thought; but there were cautious souls there, too, who held the doors against Mulberry Street and the police reporter. It was fair, of course, that they should know who I was, but I thought it sufficient introduction that I was a deacon in my own church out on Long Island. They did not, it seemed. My stock of patience, never very large, was showing signs of giving out, and I retorted hotly that then, if they wanted to know, I was a reporter, and perhaps Mulberry Street had as much sanctity in it as a church that would not listen to its wrongs. They only shut the doors a little tighter at that. It did not mend matters that about that time I tried a little truth-telling in my own fold and came to grief. It did not prove to be any more popular on Long Island than in New York. I resigned the diaconate and was thinking of hiring a hall—a theatre could be had on Sunday—wherein to preach my lay sermon, when I came across Dr. Schauffler, the manager of the City Mission Society, and Dr. Josiah Strong, the author of "Our Country." They happened to be together, and saw at once the bearing of my pictures. Remembering my early experience with the magic lantern, I had had slides made from my negatives, and on February 28, 1888, I told their story in the Broadway Tabernacle. Thereafter things mended somewhat. Plymouth Church and Dr. Parkhurst's opened their doors to me and the others fell slowly into line.

I had my say and felt better. I found a note from Dr. Schauffler among my papers the other day that was written on the morning after that first speech. He was pleased with it and with the collection of $143.50 for the mission cause. I remember it made me smile a little grimly. The fifty cents would have come handy for lunch that day. It just happened that I did not have any. It happened quite often. I was, as I said, ever a bad manager. I mention it here because of two letters that came while I have been writing this, and which I may as well answer now. One asks me to lift the mortgage from the writer's home. I get a good many of that kind. The writers seem to think I have much money and might want to help them. I should like nothing better. To go around, if one were rich, and pay off mortgages on little homes, so that the

owners when they had got the interest together by pinching
and scraping should find it all gone and paid up without
knowing how, seems to me must be the very finest fun in all
the world. But I shall never be able to do it, for I haven't any
other money than what I earn with my pen and by lecturing,
and never had. So their appeals only make me poorer by a
two-cent stamp for an answer to tell them that, and make
them no richer. The other letter asks why I and other young
men who have had to battle with the world did not go to the
Young Men's Christian Association, or to the missionaries,
for help. I do not know about the others, but I did not want
anybody to help me. There were plenty that were worse off
and needed help more. The only time I tried was when Pater
Breton, the good French priest in Buffalo, tried to get me
across to France to fight for his country, and happily did not
succeed. As to battling with the world, that is good for a
young man, much better than to hang on to somebody for
support. A little starvation once in a while even is not out of
the way. We eat too much anyhow, and when you have
fought your way through a tight place, you are the better for
it. I am afraid that is not always the case when you have
been shoved through.

And then again, as I have just told, when I did go to the
ministers with a fair proposition, they did not exactly jump
at it. No, it was better the way it was.

The thing I had sought vainly so long came in the end by
another road than I planned. One of the editors of *Scribner's
Magazine* saw my pictures and heard their story in his
church, and came to talk the matter over with me. As a result
of that talk I wrote an article that appeared in the Christmas *Scribner's*, 1889, under the title "How the Other Half
Lives," and made an instant impression. That was the beginning of better days.

Before I let the old depart I must set down an incident of
my reporter's experience that crowds in with a good hearty
laugh, though it was not the slum that sent me to the Church
of the Holy Communion over on Sixth Avenue. And though
the door was shut in my face, it was not by the rector, or
with malice prepense. A despatch from the Tenderloin po-

lice station had it that the wife of the Rev. Dr. Henry Mottet
was locked up there, out of her mind. We had no means of
knowing that Dr. Mottet was at that time a confirmed bachelor. So I went over to condole with him, and incidentally to
ask what was the matter with his wife, any way. The servant
who came to the door did not know whether the doctor was
in; she would go and see. But even as she said it the wind
blew the door shut behind her. It had a snap-lock.

"Oh!" she said, "I am shut out. If the doctor isn't in the
house, I can't get in."

We rang, but no one came. There was only one way: to try
the windows. The poor girl could not be left in the street. So
we went around the rectory and found one unlatched. She
gave me a leg up, and I raised the sash and crawled in.

Halfway in the room, with one leg over the sill, I became
dimly conscious of a shape there. Tall and expectant, it
stood between the door-curtains.

"Well, sir! and who are you?" it spoke sternly.

I climbed over the sill and put the question myself: "And
who are you, sir?"

"I am Dr. Mottet, and live in this house." He had been in
after all and had come down to hear what the ringing was
about. "And now may I ask, sir—?"

"Certainly, you may. I am a reporter from Police Headquarters, come up to tell you that your wife is locked up in
the Thirtieth Street police station."

The doctor looked fixedly at me for a full minute. Then
he slowly telescoped his tall frame into an armchair, and
sank down, a look of comic despair settling upon his face.

"O Lord!" he sighed heavily. "A strange man climbs
through my parlor window to tell me, a bachelor, that my
wife is locked up in the police station. What will happen
next?"

And then we laughed together and made friends. The
woman was just an ordinary lunatic.

I was late home from the office one evening the week my
Christmas article was printed. My wife was waiting for me
at the door, looking down the street. I saw that she had

something on her mind, but the children were all right, she said; nothing was amiss. Supper over, she drew a chair to the fire and brought out a letter.

"I read it," she nodded. It was our way. The commonest business letter is to me a human document when she has read it. Besides, she knows so much more than I. Her heart can find a way where my head bucks blindly against stone walls.

The letter was from Jeanette Gilder, of the *Critic,* asking if I had thought of making my article into a book. If so, she knew a publisher. My chance had come. I was at last to have my say.

I should have thought I would have shouted and carried on. I didn't. We sat looking into the fire together, she and I. Neither of us spoke. Then we went up to the children. They slept sweetly in their cribs. I saw a tear in her eye as she bent over the baby's cradle, and caught her to me, questioning.

"Shall we lose you now?" she whispered, and hid her head on my shoulder. I do not know what jealous thought of authors being wedded to their work had come into her mind; or, rather, I do. I felt it, and in my heart, while I held her close, I registered a vow which I have kept. It was the last tear she shed for me. Our daughter pouts at her father now and then; says I am "fierce." But She comes with her sewing to sit where I write, and when she comes the sun shines.

Necessarily, for a while, my new work held me very close. "How the Other Half Lives" was written at night while the house slept, for I had my office work to attend to in the day. Then it was my habit to light the lamps in all the rooms of the lower story and roam through them with my pipe, for I do most of my writing on my feet. I began the book with the new year. In November it was published, and on the day it came out I joined the staff of the *Evening Sun.* I merely moved up one flight of stairs. Mulberry Street was not done with me yet, nor I with it.

I had had a falling out with the manager of the Associated Press Bureau,—the *Tribune* had retired from the copartnership some years before,—and during one brief summer ran an opposition shop of my own. I sold police news to all the papers, and they fell away from the Bureau with such hearty unanimity that the manager came around and offered to farm out the department to me entirely if I would join forces. But independence was ever sweet to me, and in this instance it proved profitable even. I made at least three times as much money as before, but I did it at such cost of energy and effort that I soon found it could not last, even with the phenomenal streak of good luck I had struck. It seemed as if I had only to reach out to turn up news. I hear people saying once in a while that there is no such thing as luck. They are wrong. There is; I know it. It runs in streaks, like accidents and fires. The thing is to get in the way of it and keep there till it comes along, then hitch on, and away you go. It is the old story of the early bird. I got up at five o'clock, three hours before any of my competitors, and sometimes they came down to the office to find my news hawked about the street in extras of their own papers.

One way or another, a fight there was always on hand. That seemed foreordained. If it was not "the opposition" it was the police. When Mulberry Street took a rest the publisher's "reader" began it, and the proof-reader. This last is an enemy of human kind anyhow. Not only that he makes you say things you never dreamed of, but his being so cocksure that he knows better every time, is a direct challenge to a fight. The "reader" is tarred with the same stick. He is the one who passes on the manuscript, and he has an ingrown hatred of opinion. If a man has that, he is his enemy before he ever sets eye on him. He passed on my manuscript with a blue pencil that laid waste whole pages, once a whole chapter, with a stroke. It was like sacking a conquered city. But he did not die in his sins. I joined battle at the first sight of that blue pencil. The publishers said their reader was a very capable man. So he was, and a fine fellow to boot; had forgotten more than I ever knew, except as to the other half, of which he did not know anything. I suggested to the firm that if they did not think so, they had better let him write a book to suit, or else print mine as I wrote it. It was fair, and they took my view of it. So did he. The blue pencil went out of commission.

How deadly tired I was in those days I do not think I myself knew until I went to Boston one evening to help discuss sweating at the Institute of Technology. I had an hour to spare, and went around into Beacon Street to call upon a friend. I walked mechanically up the stoop and rang the bell. My friend was not in, said the servant who came to the door. Who should she say called? I stood and looked at her like a fool: I had forgotten my name. I was not asleep; I was rummaging in an agony of dread and excitement through every corner and crevice of my brain for my own name, but I did not find it. As slowly as I could, to gain time, I reached for my card-case and fumbled for a card, hoping to remember. But no ray came. Until I actually read my name on my card it was as utterly gone as if I had never heard it. If the people of Boston got anything out of my speech that day they did better than I. All the time I spoke something kept saying over within me: "You are a nice fellow to make a speech at the Institute of Technology; you don't even know your own name."

After that I was haunted by a feeling that I would lose myself altogether, and got into the habit of leaving private directions in the office where I would probably be found, should question arise. It arose at last in a Brooklyn church where I was making a speech with my magic-lantern pictures. While I spoke a feeling kept growing upon me that I ought to be down in the audience looking at the pictures. It all seemed a long way off and in no way related to me. Before I knew it, or any one had time to notice, I had gone down and taken a front seat. I sat there for as much as five minutes perhaps, while the man with the lantern fidgeted and the audience wondered, I suppose, what was coming next. Then it was the pictures that did not change which fretted me; with a cold chill I knew I had been lost, and went back and finished the speech. No one was any the wiser, apparently. But I was glad when, the following week, I wrote the last page in my book. That night, my wife insists, I deliberately turned a somerset on the parlor carpet while the big children cheered and the baby looked on, wide-eyed, from her high chair. . . .

For myself I have never been able to satisfactorily explain the great run "How the Other Half Lives" had. It is a curiously popular book even to-day. Perhaps it was that I had had it in me so long that it burst out at last with a rush that caught on. The title had a deal to do with it. Mr. Howells asked me once where I got it. I did not get it. It came of itself. Like Topsy, it growed. It had run in my mind ever since I thought of the things I tried to describe. Then there was the piece of real good luck that Booth's "In Darkest England" was published just then. People naturally asked, "how about New York?" That winter Ward McAllister wrote his book about society as he had found it, and the circuit was made. Ministers preached about the contrast. "How the Other Half Lives" ran from edition to edition. There was speedily a demand for more "copy," and I wrote "The Children of the Poor," following the same track. Critics said there were more "bones" in it, but it was never popular like the "Other Half."

By "bones" I suppose they meant facts to tie to. They were scarce enough at that stage of the inquiry. I have in my desk a table giving the ages at which children get their teeth that bears witness to that. I had been struggling with the problem of child-labor in some East Side factories, and was not making any headway. The children had certificates, one and all, declaring them to be "fourteen," and therefore fit to be employed. It was perfectly evident that they were not ten in scores of cases, but the employer shrugged his shoulders and pointed to the certificate. The father, usually a tailor, would not listen at all, but went right on ironing. There was no birth registry to fall back on; that end of it was neglected. There seemed to be no way of proving the fact, yet the fact was there and must be proven. My own children were teething at the time, and it gave me an idea. I got Dr. Tracy to write out that table for me, showing at what age the dog-teeth should appear, when the molars, etc. Armed with that I went into the factories and pried open the little workers' mouths. The girls objected: their teeth were quite generally bad; but I saw enough to enable me to speak positively. Even allowing for the backwardness of the slum, it was clear that a child that had not yet grown its dog-teeth was not "fourteen," for they should have been cut at twelve at the latest. Three years later the Reinhardt Committee reported to the Legislature that the net result of the Factory Law was a mass of perjury and child-labor, and day began to dawn for the little ones, too.

Rough ways and rough work? Yes, but you must use the tools that come to hand, and be glad for them, if you want to get things done. Bludgeons were needed just then, and, after all, you can get a good deal of fun out of one when it is needed. I know I did. By that time the whole battle with the slum had evolved itself out of the effort to clean one pig-sty, and, as for my own share in it, to settle for one dead dog. It was raging all along the line with demands for tenement-house reform and the destruction of the old rookeries; for parks for the people who were penned up in the slum; for playgrounds for their children; for decent teaching and decent schools. There were too many dark spots in New York where we had neither. So dense was the ignorance of the ruling powers of the needs and real condition of the public schools, which, on parade days, they spoke of sententiously as the "corner-stone of our liberties," while the people cheered the sentiment, that it was related how a Tammany Mayor had appointed to the office of school trustee in the Third Ward a man who had been dead a whole year, and how, when the world marvelled, it had been laughed off at the City Hall with the comment that what did it matter: there were no schools in the ward; it was the wholesale grocery district. I do not know how true it was, but there was no reason why it might not be. It was exactly on a par with the rest of it. I do not mean to say that there were no good schools in New York. There were some as good as anywhere; for there were high-souled teachers who redeemed even the slough we were in from utter despair. But they were there in spite of it and they were far from being the rule. Let us hope for the day when that shall have been reversed as a statement of fact. No one will hail it more gladly than I. There is an easy way of putting it to the test; we did it once before. Broach a measure of school reform and see what the question is that will be asked by the teachers. If it is, "How is it going to benefit the children?" hoist the flag; the day of deliverance is at hand! In the battle I refer to that question was not asked once. The teachers stood shoulder to shoulder for *their* rights, let the children fare as they might.

However, that is an old grievance. We had it out over it once, and I have no mind to rip it up again unless it is needed. My own father was a teacher; perhaps that is one reason why I revere the calling so that I would keep its skirts clear of politics at any hazard. Another is that I most heartily subscribe to the statement that the public school is the corner-stone of our liberties, and to the sentiment that would keep the flag flying over it always. Only I want as much respect for the flag: a clean school under an unsoiled flag! So we shall pull through; not otherwise. The thing requires no argument.

My own effort in that fight was mainly for decent schoolhouses, for playgrounds, and for a truant school to keep the boys out of jail. If I was not competent to argue over the curriculum with a professor of pedagogy, I could tell, at least, if a schoolroom was so jammed that to let me pass into the next room the children in the front seat had to rise and stand; or if there was light enough for them to see their slates or the blackboard. Nor did it take the wisdom of a Solomon to decide that a dark basement room, thirty by fifty feet, full of rats, was not a proper place for a thousand children to call their only "playground." Play, in the kindergarten scheme, is the "normal occupation of the child through which he first begins to perceive moral relations." Nice kind of morals burrowed there for him! There was, in the whole of Manhattan, but a single outdoor playground attached to a public school, and that was an old burial-ground in First Street that had been wrested from the dead with immense toil. When I had fed fat my grudge upon these things, I could still go where the public school children came, and learn, by a little judicious pumping, how my friend, the professor, had stored their minds. That is, if they did not come to me. Many hundreds of them did, when under Roosevelt we needed two thousand new policemen, and it was from some of them we learned that among the thirteen States which formed the Union were "England, Ireland, Wales, Belfast, and Cork"; that Abraham Lincoln was "murdered by Ballington Booth," and that the Fire Department was in charge of the city government when the Mayor was away. Don't I wish it were, and that they would turn the hose on a while! What a lot of trouble it would save us in November.

As for a truant school, the lack of one was the worst outrage of all, for it compelled the sending of boys, who had done no worse harm than to play hooky on a sunny spring day, to a jail with iron bars in the windows. For the boy who did this wicked thing—let me be plain about it and say that if he had not; if he had patiently preferred some of the schools I knew to a day of freedom out in the sunshine, I should have thought him a miserable little lunkhead quite beyond hope! As for those who locked him up, almost nothing I can think of would be bad enough for them. The whole effort of society should be, and is getting to be more and more, thank goodness and common sense, to keep the boy out of jail. To run to it with him the moment the sap begins to boil up in him and he does any one of the thousand things we have all done or wanted to do if we dared, why, it is sinful folly. I am not saying that there are not boys who ought to be in jail, though to my mind it is the poorest use you can put them to; but to put truants there, to learn all the tricks the jail has to teach, with them in the frame of mind in which it receives them,—for boys are not fools, whatever those who are set over them may be, and they know when they are ill-used,—I know of nothing so wickedly wasteful. That was our way; is still in fact, to a large extent, though the principle has been disavowed as both foul and foolish. But in those days the defenders of the system—Heaven save the mark!—fought for it yet, and it was give and take right along, every day and all day.

Before this, in time to bear a strong hand in it all, there had come into the field a new force that was destined to give both energy and direction to our scattered efforts for reform. Up till then we had been a band of guerillas, the incentive proceeding usually from Dr. Felix Adler, Mrs.

Josephine Shaw Lowell, or some one of their stamp; and the rest of us joining in to push *that* cart up the hill, then taking time to breathe until another came along that needed a lift. The social settlements, starting as neighborhood guilds to reassert the lost brotherhood, became almost from the first the fulcrum, as it were, whence the lever for reform was applied, because the whole idea of that reform was to better the lot of those whom the prosperous up-town knew vaguely only as "the poor." If parks were wanted, if schools needed bettering, there were at the College Settlement, the University Settlement, the Nurses' Settlement, and at a score of other such places, young enthusiasts to collect the facts and to urge them, with the prestige of their non-political organization to back them. The Hull House in Chicago set the pace, and it was kept up bravely at this end of the line. For one, I attached myself as a kind of volunteer "auxiliary" to the College Settlement—that was what the girls there called me—and to any one that would have me, and so in a few years' time slid easily into the day when my ruder methods were quite out of date and ready to be shelved.

How it came about that, almost before I knew it, my tongue was enlisted in the fight as well as my pen I do not know myself. It could not be because I had a "silver-tongue," for I read in the local newspaper one day when I had been lecturing in the western part of the state that "a voluble German with a voice like a squeaky cellar-door" had been in town. It seems that I had fallen into another newspaper row, all unsuspecting, and was in the opposition editor's camp. But, truly, I lay no claim to eloquence. So it must have been the facts, again. There is nothing like them. Whatever it was, it made me smile sometimes in the middle of a speech to think of the prophecies when I was a schoolboy that "my tongue would be my undoing," for here it was helping right wrongs instead. In fact, that was what it had tried to do in the old days when the teachers were tyrannical. It entered the lists here when Will Craig, a clerk in the Health Department, with whom I had struck up a friendship, helped me turn my photographs into magic-lantern slides by paying the bills, and grew from that, until now my winters are spent on the lecture platform altogether. I always liked the work. It tires less than the office routine, and you feel the touch with your fellows more than when you sit and write your message. Also, if you wish to learn about a thing, the best way is always to go and try to teach some one else that thing. I never make a speech on a subject I am familiar with but that I come away knowing more about it than I did at the start, though no one else may have said a word.

Then there is the chairman. You never can tell what sort of surprise is in store for you. In a Massachusetts town last winter I was hailed on the stage by one of his tribe, a gaunt, funereal sort of man, who wanted to know what he should say about me.

"Oh," said I, in a spirit of levity, "say anything you like. Say I am the most distinguished citizen in the country. They generally do."

Whereupon my funereal friend marched upon the stage and calmly announced to the audience that he did not know this man Riis, whom he was charged with introducing, never heard of him.

"He tells me," he went on with never a wink, "that he is the most distinguished citizen in the country. You can judge for yourselves when you have heard him."

I thought at first it was some bad kind of joke; but no! He was not that kind of man. I do not suppose he had smiled since he was born. Maybe he was an undertaker. Assuredly, he ought to be. But he had bowels after all. Instead of going off the stage and leaving me blue with rage, he stayed to exhort the audience in a fifteen minutes' speech to vote right, or something of that sort. The single remark, when at last he turned his back, that it was a relief to have him "extinguished," made us men and brothers, that audience and me. I think of him with almost as much pleasure as I do of that city editor chap out in Illinois who came blowing upon the platform at the last minute and handed me a typewritten speech with the question if that would do. I read it over. It began with the statement that it was the general impression that all newspapermen were liars, and went on by easy stages to point out that there were exceptions, myself for in-

stance. The rest was a lot of praise to which I had no claim.
I said so, and that I wished he would leave it out.

"Oh, well," he said, with a happy smile, "don't you see it
gives you your cue. Then you can turn around and say that
anyway I am a liar."

With tongue or pen, the argument shaped itself finally
into the fundamental one for the rescue of the home imper-
illed by the slum. There all roads met. Good citizenship
hung upon that issue. Say what you will, a man cannot live
like a pig and vote like a man. The dullest of us saw it. The
tenement had given to New York the name of "the homeless
city." But with that gone which made life worth living, what
were liberty worth? With no home to cherish, how long before love of country would be an empty sound? Life, liberty,
pursuit of happiness? Wind! says the slum, and the slum is
right if we let it be. We cannot get rid of the tenements that
shelter two million souls in New York to-day, but we set
about making them at least as nearly fit to harbor human
souls as might be. That will take a long time yet. But a beginning was made. With reform looming upon the heels of
the Lexow disclosures came the Gilder Tenement-House
Commission in the autumn of 1894.

Greater work was never done for New York than by that
faithful body of men. The measure of it is not to be found in
what was actually accomplished, though the volume of that
was great, but in what it made possible. Upon the foundations they laid down we may build for all time and be the
better for it. Light and air acquired a legal claim, and where
the sun shines into the slum, the slum is doomed. The worst
tenements were destroyed; parks were opened, schools
built, playgrounds made. The children's rights were won
back for them. The slum denied them even the chance to
live, for it was shown that the worst rear tenements murdered the babies at the rate of one in five. The Commission
made it clear that the legislation that was needed was "the
kind that would root out every old ramshackle disease-
breeding tenement in the city." That was the way to begin it.
As to the rest of them, it laid the foundation deeper yet, for
it made us see that life in them "conduces to the corruption

of the young." That told it all. It meant that a mortgage was put on the civic life of the morrow, which was not to be borne. We were forewarned.

The corruption of the young! We move with rapid strides in our time. That which was a threat, scoffed at by many, has become a present and dreadful peril in half a dozen brief years. We took a short cut to make it that when we tried to drain the pool of police blackmail of which the Lexow disclosures had shown us the hideous depths. We drained it into the tenements, and for the police infamy got a real-estate blackmail that is worse. The chairman of the Committee of Fifteen tells us that of more than a hundred tenements, full of growing children, which his committee has canvassed, not one had escaped the contamination that piles up the landlord's profits. Twelve dollars for an honest flat, thirty for the other kind and no questions asked! I find in my scrap-book this warning, sounded by me in the Christmas holidays, 1893, when the country was ringing with Dr. Parkhurst's name:—

"I would not, whatever else might happen, by any hasty or ill-advised system of wholesale raids crowd these women into the tenements and flats of our city. That is what will surely happen, is happening now. It is a danger infinitely greater than any flowing from their presence where they are, and as they are. Each centre of moral contagion by this scattering process becomes ten or twenty, planted where they will do the most possible harm. Think of the children brought in daily, hourly contact with this vice! Think of the thousands of young women looking vainly for work this hard winter! Be there ever so little money for woman's honest work, there is always enough to buy her virtue. Have tenement houses moral resources that can be trusted to keep her safe from this temptation?

"This is a wicked villany that must not be permitted, come whatever else may. We hear of danger to 'our young men,' from present conditions. What sort of young men must they be who would risk the sacrifice of their poorer sisters for their own 'safety'? And it is being risked wherever houses of this kind are being shut up and the women turned into the streets, there to shift for themselves. The jail does not keep them. Christian families will not receive them. They cannot be killed. No door opens to them: yet they have to go somewhere. And they go where they think they can hide from the police and still ply the trade that gives them the only living society is willing they shall have, though it says it is not."

And they did go there. Dr. Parkhurst was not to blame. He was fighting Tammany that dealt the cards and took all the tricks, and for that fight New York owes him a debt it hardly yet knows of. Besides, though those raids hastened the process, it was already well underway. The police extortion of itself would have finished it in time. A blackmailer in the long run always kills the goose that lays his golden egg. His greed gets the better of his sense. The interview I quoted was not a plea for legalizing wrong. That will get us no farther. It was rather a summons to our people to cease skulking behind lying phrases and look the matter squarely in the face. With a tenement-house law, passed this winter, which sends the woman to jail and fines the landlord and his house $1000, we shall be in the way shortly of doing so. Until we do that justice first, I do not see how we can. Poverty's back is burdened enough without our loading upon it the sins we are afraid to face. Meanwhile we shall be getting up courage to talk plainly about it, which is half the battle. Think of the shock it would have given our grandmothers to hear of a meeting of women in a public hall "to protest against protected vice." On a Sunday, too. Come to think of it, I do not know but that wholesome, plain speech on this subject is nearer the whole than half the battle. I rather guess it is.

The Promised Land
Mary Antin

Mary Antin, born Maryashe Antin in 1881, made it her mission in life to reconcile turn-of-the-century American immigration policies with the democratic ideals outlined in the Constitution of the United States. Born in Polotzk, Russia, Antin lived in a world of extreme inequality called "the Pale of Settlement," an impoverished community allotted to Jews by the Czar. Antin's father, Israel Antin, had once been a rabbi, but then rejected orthodox Judaism, and encouraged his daughter to read and write (a privilege not granted to women in conservative Polotzk). He was united with his community, however, against the abuses all Jews suffered at the hands of Gentiles in late nineteenth-century Russia. The elder Antin sought to free his family from this daily ridicule and menace of death by bringing his wife and children to the United States. The Antins arrived in Boston in 1894, when Mary was thirteen.

Conflicts in American society posed less harsh, but similar problems for this immigrant family. In Boston, Mary attended the Girls Latin School, a private Catholic institution, where she learned that even a poor Jewish girl born into the persecution of the Pale like herself was a "fellow citizen" of George Washington, according to the Constitution of the United States. An overwhelming admiration and faith in the American legal system followed these childhood lessons and would remain with Antin until her death at the age of sixty-eight. Social activists such as Josephine and Emma Lazarus further inspired Antin to defend freedom and equality among all American citizens, and with her father's lessons in literacy as power in mind, Antin wrote an autobiographical text laced with political commentary entitled *The Promised Land* in 1912.

Like her other notable work on immigration, *They Who Knock at Our Gates*, published in 1914, *The Promised Land* was criticized as idealistic and riddled with pro-assimilation doctrine. Antin's explicit message in both texts, however, that "Ellis Island is just another name for Plymouth Rock," was praised by some as a much-needed personal link between the first immigrants of the United States and those that followed them. As a result of this effort, Antin crossed America as a lecturer from 1913 to 1918 along with other famous social activists like Jacob Riis, and received many literary and civic honors. She died in Suffern, New York, in 1949.

Although icons like George Washington helped make American ideals of freedom and equality easily comprehensible to Mary Antin as a child, she struggled throughout her life to equate her reverence for democracy with the reverence for God others felt. In a moving description of the prejudices sometimes caused by religious differences entitled "Miracles" (taken from *The Promised Land*), Mary Antin describes a difficult emancipation process from the "yoke" of religious belief to the "freedom" of democratic thinking. Whether or not the young Antin truly escapes the laws of American Christian society, however, is unclear by the chapter's end.

CHAPTER 12

MIRACLES

It was not always in admiration that the finger was pointed at me. One day I found myself the centre of an excited group in the middle of the schoolyard, with a dozen girls interrupting each other to express their disapproval of me. For I had coolly told them, in answer to a question, that I did not believe in God.

How had I arrived at such a conviction? How had I come, from praying and fasting and Psalm-singing, to extreme impiety? Alas! my backsliding had cost me no travail of spirit. Always weak in my faith, playing at sanctity as I played at soldiers, just as I was in the mood or not, I had neglected my books of devotion and given myself up to profane literature at the first opportunity, in Vitebsk; and I never took up my prayer book again. On my return to Polotzk, America loomed so near that my imagination was fully occupied, and I did not revive the secret experiments with which I used to test the nature and intention of Deity. It was more to me that I was going to America than that I might not be going to Heaven. And when we joined my father, and I saw that he did not wear the sacred fringes, and did not put on the phylacteries and pray, I was neither surprised nor shocked, remembering the Sabbath night when he had with his own hand turned out the lamp. When I saw him go out to work on Sabbath exactly as on a week day, I understood why God had not annihilated me with his lightnings that time when I purposely carried something in my pocket on Sabbath: there was no God, and there was no sin. And I ran out to play, pleased to find that I was free, like other little girls in the street, instead of being hemmed about with prohibitions and obligations at every step. And yet if the golden truth of Judaism had not been handed me in the motley rags of formalism, I might not have been so ready to put away my religion.

It was Rachel Goldstein who provoked my avowal of atheism. She asked if I wasn't going to stay out of school during Passover, and I said no. Wasn't I a Jew? she wanted to know. No, I wasn't; I was a Freethinker. What was that? I didn't believe in God. Rachel was horrified. Why, Kitty Maloney believed in God, and Kitty was only a Catholic! She appealed to Kitty.

"Kitty Maloney! Come over here. Don't you believe in

God?—There, now, Mary Antin!—Mary Antin says she does n't believe in God!"

Rachel Goldstein's horror is duplicated. Kitty Maloney, who used to mock Rachel's Jewish accent, instantly becomes her voluble ally, and proceeds to annihilate me by plying me with crucial questions.

"You don't believe in God? Then who made you, Mary Antin?"

"Nature made me."

"*Nature* made you! What's that?"

"It's—everything. It's the trees—no, it's what makes the trees grow. *That's* what it is."

"But *God* made the trees, Mary Antin," from Rachel and Kitty in chorus. "Maggie O'Reilly! Listen to Mary Antin. She says there is n't any God. She says the trees made her!"

Rachel and Kitty and Maggie, Sadie and Annie and Beckie, made a circle around me, and pressed me with questions, and mocked me, and threatened me with hell flames and utter extinction. I held my ground against them all obstinately enough, though my argument was exceedingly lame. I glibly repeated phrases I had heard my father use, but I had no real understanding of his atheistic doctrines. I had been surprised into this dispute. I had no spontaneous interest in the subject; my mind was occupied with other things. But as the number of my opponents grew, and I saw how unanimously they condemned me, my indifference turned into a heat of indignation. The actual point at issue was as little as ever to me, but I perceived that a crowd of Free Americans were disputing the right of a Fellow Citizen to have any kind of God she chose. I knew, from my father's teaching, that this persecution was contrary to the Constitution of the United States, and I held my ground as befitted the defender of a cause. George Washington would not have treated me as Rachel Goldstein and Kitty Maloney were doing! "This is a free country," I reminded them in the middle of the argument.

The excitement in the yard amounted to a toy riot. When the school bell rang and the children began to file in, I stood out there as long as any of my enemies remained, although it was my habit to go to my room very promptly. And as the foes of American Liberty crowded and pushed in the line, whispering to those who had not heard that a heretic had been discovered in their midst, the teacher who kept the line in the corridor was obliged to scold and pull the noisy ones into order; and Sadie Cohen told her, in tones of awe, what the commotion was about.

Miss Bland waited till the children had filed in before she asked me, in a tone encouraging confidence, to give my version of the story. This I did, huskily but fearlessly; and the teacher, who was a woman of tact, did not smile or commit herself in any way. She was sorry that the children had been rude to me, but she thought they would not trouble me any more if I let the subject drop. She made me understand, somewhat as Miss Dillingham had done on the occasion of my whispering during prayer, that it was proper American conduct to avoid religious arguments on school territory. I felt honored by this private initiation into the doctrine of the separation of Church and State, and I went to my seat with a good deal of dignity, my alarm about the safety of the Constitution allayed by the teacher's calmness.

This is not so strictly the story of the second generation that I may not properly give a brief account of how it fared with my mother when my father undertook to purge his house of superstition. The process of her emancipation, it is true, was not obvious to me at the time, but what I observed of her outward conduct has been interpreted by my subsequent experience; so that to-day I understand how it happens that all the year round my mother keeps the same day of rest as her Gentile neighbors; but when the ram's horn blows on the Day of Atonement, calling upon Israel to cleanse its heart from sin and draw nearer to the God of its fathers, her soul is stirred as of old, and she needs must join in the ancient service. It means, I have come to know, that she has dropped the husk and retained the kernel of Judaism; but years were required for this process of instinctive selection.

My father, in his ambition to make Americans of us, was rather headlong and strenuous in his methods. To my mother, on the eve of departure for the New World, he wrote boldly that progressive Jews in America did not spend their days in praying; and he urged her to leave her wig in Polotzk, as a first step of progress. My mother, like the majority of women in the Pale, had all her life taken her religion on authority; so she was only fulfilling her duty to her husband when she took his hint, and set out upon her journey in her own hair. Not that it was done without reluctance; the Jewish faith in her was deeply rooted, as in the best of Jews it always is. The law of the Fathers was binding to her, and the outward symbols of obedience inseparable from the spirit. But the breath of revolt against orthodox externals was at this time beginning to reach us in Polotzk from the greater world, notably from America. Sons whose parents had impoverished themselves by paying the fine for nonappearance for military duty, in order to save their darlings from the inevitable sins of violated Judaism while in the service, sent home portraits of themselves with their faces shaved; and the grieved old fathers and mothers, after offering up special prayers for the renegades, and giving charity in their name, exhibited the significant portraits on their parlor tables. My mother's own nephew went no farther than Vilna, ten hours' journey from Polotzk, to learn to cut his beard; and even within our town limits young women of education were beginning to reject the wig after marriage. A notorious example was the beautiful daughter of Lozhe the Rav, who was not restrained by her father's conspicuous relation to Judaism from exhibiting her lovely black curls like a maiden; and it was a further sign of the times that the rav did not disown his daughter. What wonder, then, that my poor mother, shaken by these foreshadowings of revolution in our midst, and by the express authority of her husband, gave up the emblem of matrimonial chastity with but a passing struggle? Considering how the heavy burdens which she had borne from childhood had never allowed her time to think for herself at all, but had obliged her always to tread blindly in the beaten paths, I think it greatly to her credit that in her puzzling situation she did not lose her poise entirely. Bred to submission, submit she must; and when she perceived a conflict of authorities, she prepared to accept the new order of things under which her children's future was to be formed; wherein she showed her native adaptability, the readiness to fall into line, which is one of the most charming traits of her gentle, self-effacing nature.

My father gave my mother very little time to adjust herself. He was only three years from the Old World with its settled prejudices. Considering his education, he had thought out a good deal for himself, but his line of thinking had not as yet brought him to include woman to the intellectual emancipation for which he himself had been so eager even in Russia. This was still in the day when he was astonished to learn that women had written books—had used their minds, their imaginations, unaided. He still rated the mental capacity of the average woman as only a little above that of the cattle she tended. He held it to be a wife's duty to follow her husband in all things. He could do all the thinking for the family, he believed; and being convinced that to hold to the outward forms of orthodox Judaism was to be hampered in the race for Americanization, he did not hesitate to order our family life on unorthodox lines. There was no conscious despotism in this; it was only making manly haste to realize an ideal the nobility of which there was no one to dispute.

My mother, as we know, had not the initial impulse to depart from ancient usage that my father had in his habitual scepticism. He had always been a nonconformist in his heart; she bore lovingly the yoke of prescribed conduct. Individual freedom, to him, was the only tolerable condition of life; to her it was confusion. My mother, therefore, gradually divested herself, at my father's bidding, of the mantle of orthodox observance; but the process cost her many a pang, because the fabric of that venerable garment was interwoven with the fabric of her soul.

My father did not attempt to touch the fundamentals of her faith. He certainly did not forbid her to honor God by loving her neighbor, which is perhaps not far from being the whole of Judaism. If his loud denials of the existence of God influenced her to reconsider her creed, it was merely an incidental result of the freedom of expression he was so eager to practise, after his life of enforced hypocrisy. As the opinions of a mere woman on matters so abstract as religion did not interest him in the least, he counted it no particular triumph if he observed that my mother weakened in her faith as the years went by. He allowed her to keep a Jewish kitchen as long as she pleased, but he did not want us children to refuse invitations to the table of our Gentile neighbors. He would have no bar to our social intercourse with the world around us, for only by freely sharing the life of our neighbors could we come into our full inheritance of American freedom and opportunity. On the holy days he bought my mother a ticket for the synagogue, but the children he sent to school. On Sabbath eve my mother might light the consecrated candles, but he kept the store open until Sunday morning. My mother might believe and worship as she pleased, up to the point where her orthodoxy began to interfere with the American progress of the family.

The price that all of us paid for this disorganization of our family life has been levied on every immigrant Jewish household where the first generation clings to the traditions of the Old World, while the second generation leads the life of the New. Nothing more pitiful could be written in the annals of the Jews; nothing more inevitable; nothing more hopeful. Hopeful, yes; alike for the Jew and for the country that has given him shelter. For Israel is not the only party that has put up a forfeit in this contest. The nations may well sit by and watch the struggle, for humanity has a stake in it. I say this, whose life has borne witness, whose heart is heavy with revelations it has not made. And I speak for thousands; oh, for thousands!

My gray hairs are too few for me to let these pages trespass the limit I have set myself. That part of my life which contains the climax of my personal drama I must leave to my grandchildren to record. My father might speak and tell how, in time, he discovered that in his first violent rejection of everything old and established he cast from him much that he afterwards missed. He might tell to what extent he later retraced his steps, seeking to recover what he had learned to value anew; how it fared with his avowed irreligion when put to the extreme test; to what, in short, his emancipation amounted. And he, like myself, would speak for thousands. My grandchildren, for all I know, may have a graver task than I have set them. Perhaps they may have to testify that the faith of Israel is a heritage that no heir in the direct line has the power to alienate from his successors. Even I, with my limited perspective, think it doubtful if the conversion of the Jew to any alien belief or disbelief is ever thoroughly accomplished. What positive affirmation of the persistence of Judaism in the blood my descendants may have to make, I may not be present to hear.

It would be superfluous to state that none of these hints and prophecies troubled me at the time when I horrified the schoolyard by denying the existence of God, on the authority of my father; and defended my right to my atheism, on the authority of the Constitution. I considered myself absolutely, eternally, delightfully emancipated from the yoke of indefensible superstitions. I was wild with indignation and pity when I remembered how my poor brother had been cruelly tormented because he did not want to sit in heder and learn what was after all false or useless. I knew now why poor Reb' Lebe had been unable to answer my questions; it was because the truth was not whispered outside America. I was very much in love with my enlightenment, and eager for opportunities to give proof of it.

It was Miss Dillingham, she who helped me in so many ways, who unconsciously put me to an early test, the result of which gave me a shock that I did not get over for many a day. She invited me to tea one day, and I came in much trepidation. It was my first entrance into a genuine American household; my first meal at a Gentile—yes, a Christian—board. Would I know how to behave properly? I do not know whether I betrayed my anxiety; I am certain only that I was all eyes and ears, that nothing should escape me which might serve to guide me. This, after all, was a normal state for me to be in, so I suppose I looked natural, no matter how much I stared. I had been accustomed to consider my table manners irreproachable, but America was not Polotzk, as my father was ever saying; so I proceeded very cautiously with my spoons and forks. I was cunning enough to try to conceal my uncertainty; by being just a little bit slow, I did not get to any given spoon until the others at table had shown me which it was.

All went well, until a platter was passed with a kind of meat that was strange to me. Some mischievous instinct told me that it was ham—forbidden food; and I, the liberal, the free, was afraid to touch it! I had a terrible moment of surprise, mortification, self-contempt; but I helped myself to a slice of ham, nevertheless, and hung my head over my plate to hide my confusion. I was furious with myself for my weakness. I to be afraid of a pink piece of pig's flesh, who had defied at least two religions in defence of free thought! And I began to reduce my ham to indivisible atoms, determined to eat more of it than anybody at the table.

Alas! I learned that to eat in defence of principles was not so easy as to talk. I ate, but only a newly abnegated Jew can understand with what squirming, what protesting of the inner man, what exquisite abhorrence of myself. That Spartan boy who allowed the stolen fox hidden in his bosom to consume his vitals rather than be detected in the theft, showed no such miracle of self-control as did I, sitting there at my friend's tea-table, eating unjewish meat.

And to think that so ridiculous a thing as a scrap of meat should be the symbol and test of things so august! To think that in the mental life of a half-grown child should be reflected the struggles and triumphs of ages! Over and over and over again I discover that I am a wonderful thing, being human; that I am the image of the universe, being myself; that I am the repository of all the wisdom in the world, being alive and sane at the beginning of this twentieth century. The heir of the ages am I, and all that has been is in me, and shall continue to be in my immortal self.

From Alien to Citizen
Edward Steiner

Edward Alfred Steiner was born to German-Jewish parents on November 1, 1866, in Slovakia, then ruled by Hungary. In Europe, Steiner excelled academically while attending public school in Vienna, *gymnasium* in Bohemia, and college at the universities of Heidelberg, Gottingen, and Berlin. In his memoirs, *From Alien to Citizen*, Steiner would muse that his only interest in America as a child was purely financial (Steiner once stated that he would go to America and marry a rich woman). Politically radical viewpoints and an interest in the work of Tolstoy, however, brought the scholar to the attention of German authorities fearful of communism. To avoid questioning, Steiner left Germany in the late 1880s for New York.

From New York, Steiner migrated deep into America's heartland as a student, Protestant minister, and professor. This journey began in Pittsburgh where the immigrant dreamed of attending Princeton University while he worked at Carnegie Steel. The Presbyterian Theological Seminary at Oberlin College in Ohio, however, became Steiner's school of choice after he gained a working knowledge of English and converted to Christianity. Steiner left the Presbyterian faith soon after his graduation in 1891, and served as a Congregational minister for the next ten years in Ohio, Illinois, and Minnesota. Among the Congregationalists, a parent denomination of the Unitarian Church, Steiner preached for the inclusion of immigrant populations among Protestants in America. This sentiment was welcomed at least in theory among Steiner's rural congregations in the Midwest. Far from the urban tenement districts of New York, San Francisco, and Chicago, Midwesterners listened to Steiner's own success story of conversion and assimilation through faith, and the message that a Christian America could melt all people into one strong society.

Later in life, Steiner made this message more public as an author and professor of Applied Christianity at Grinnell College in Iowa, were he was appointed in 1903. At Grinnell, he wrote fifteen books concerned with immigration, including *On the Trail of the Immigrant* (1906) and *The Making of a Great Race* (1929). Steiner died at the age of ninety in 1956. In the following passage from *From Alien to Citizen* (1914), Edward Steiner reflects on the religious awakening that made these intellectual pursuits possible for a Slovakian Jew.

16

THE GATE INTO CHICAGO

An entanglement of railroad tracks, miles of hot sand dunes, a stretch of inland sea; the sky line assaulted by gigantic elevators and smokestacks, a block or two crowded by houses dropped into an empty prairie—that is the beginning of Chicago. Certainly it began too soon for a certain footsore traveller, who thought he had arrived—then found that the guide-post promised fifteen miles more of labyrinthine tracks, of sand dunes fashioned into scrubby streets, of multiplied elevators and smokestacks and more miles of sporadically settled prairie. Chicago held out no illusions; she promised nothing but toil, grime, sore feet and a ceaseless struggle for just shelter and a mouthful of food. To me, accustomed to the beauties of large cities in the Old World, she seemed forbiddingly, hopelessly ugly and pitiless. Even now, after having discovered the soul and the heart of her— I have a distinct feeling of fear when I arrive there, although I step from a Pullman car and feel safe, at least from want.

The process of selection takes place in hobo land as it does everywhere else, and out of the army of tramps which I met, a rather decent Bohemian attached himself to me. He had been in Chicago before, and failing to gain a foothold at that time was returning to try again. He had some very attractive schemes for beginning to make a fortune for both of us, and the one which seemed to him most alluring was to go into the saloon business under the patronage of some beer-brewer. Neither capital nor character being needed, and having had the necessary experience with liquor on both sides of the bar, his future seemed rosy indeed, and generous fellow that he was, he was ready to share its glow with me.

Being blessed by a temperate ancestry, liquor was repugnant to me, whether to buy or sell; so I did not embark in the saloon business, although for a man situated as I was, entrance into Chicago almost invariably lay through that avenue.

I often wish back the opportunity of receiving the first impression of places and cities I have seen, but never of Chicago.

What the Loop, that congested, noise-girdled shopping district, is to those privileged to spend money, Canal Street and West Madison Street are to those compelled to earn it in the hardest way. How can one describe them?

Solid phalanxes of saloons, reeking from stale beer odours, mechanical music, blatant and harsh; long lines of men leaning over brass trimmed bars, poor, wasted remnants of womanhood, brazen creatures, pitilessly repellent, offering up all that is left them on the altar of man's lust; whirling wheels of chance and poor, duped humanity crowding about, eager to stake the last cent remaining from a hard-earned wage. Anxious groups surrounding bulletin boards which announced hard work for little pay, criers for boarding houses pulling and cajoling their victims, and the watchful Jewish trader eager for bargaining—that was the Chicago to which my hobo comrade introduced me.

He knew where to get the largest schooner of beer and the best free lunch. He opened to me the door into Chicago through that degrading, demoralizing institution, the saloon; and the more I saw of it, the more I became convinced that the selling of liquor was the most harmless of all its functions. Beneath it, above it and in the rear, it dealt out damnation indescribable and unmentionable.

Leaving my comrade absorbed in a free lunch and beer, the drink paid for out of my meagre purse, I started down Canal Street, studying the posters of various labour agencies which at that time were invariably connected with saloons.

A man who evidently had watched me, stopped with me in front of one of those places and cordially invited me to enter and consider an attractive situation. I was eager for work and went in with him. I was asked to step in front of the bar—then I felt something give way I was hurled into darkness. I knew nothing until late at night I felt myself being dragged out into an alley and abandoned.

No one came in answer to my feeble cries, so I summoned enough strength to crawl back to the street. As I came staggering out of the darkness a policeman caught me by the back of the neck, dragged me to a street lamp and in a few minutes I could hear the tramping of horses. At the time I did not know that it was a patrol wagon into which I was roughly pushed, and after a short ride, during which no explanation was vouchsafed me, I was deposited at the Harrison Street Police Station.

There is a tradition that one ought not to speak ill of the dead; I suppose not even of dead police stations. Fortunately, this horrible man trap is no more—but without slandering the "dear departed," I can say that it was worse than the saloon in which I was knocked down and robbed of the little I had—and that is saying a great deal.

That night I spent in a huge basement cell, a sort of general depository of the day's unsorted human refuse. Men were fighting for room to stretch out and rest their miserable bodies, and they fought like savages. Some were drunk and delirious, some sick and sore, others were hungry and dirty; all were crying, laughing or singing until an insane asylum would have seemed like a child's nursery in comparison with that bedlam. There was just one time when the room was comparatively quiet, when men were sleeping. Then it was more gruesome than the noise, for they talked in their sleep.

I heard snatches of tender words, angry curses, the ravings of men under the spell of hideous dreams; then some one chuckled as if enjoying a brief breath of happiness, and one man woke and began to curse his dreaming neighbour, who too awoke. Blow followed blow and men lived in hell again until daybreak.

I have said that I should not care to have my first impressions of Chicago repeated, yet I have shared with thousands of men and women their experience, more or less like my own.

Until very lately the immigrant in Chicago, unless he had waiting friends, found no gateway open to him except the saloon, the brothel, the cheap lodging house and finally the "lock up."

The agencies which began the assimilative process were all anti-social, greedy for their prey and, worst of all, the police was in league with them and protected them. There was nothing left to do but walk up and down in impotent rage and inveigh against a city which permitted its newest and most potential human material to be polluted, if not corrupted, at the very entrance into its life.

I have repeatedly snatched men from the doors of gambling-rooms, from fake labour agencies and from greedy hotel runners, only to find myself unpleasantly involved with the police; while I usually got a cursing, if not worse, for my pains.

An Immigrant Protective League and the Y.M.C.A. are now doing fine work in directing and sheltering the newcomers. Nevertheless, it is a reflection upon the spirit which governs the city that *private individuals* had to organize a sort of vigilance committee to do this most elementary work of justice for helpless strangers.

There are now two forces which do the fundamental work for the assimilation of our immigrant. One of them is the anti-social group of agencies which I have mentioned, and until very lately it did its work unchallenged. The other is the privately organized associations which under the recent growth of the social conscience have multiplied and, in a measure at least, checked the enemy.

The American people as a whole clamour with a kind of savage hunger for the assimilation of the immigrant; but the question into what he is to be assimilated has not agitated them to any marked degree. Whether or not we threw the immigrant to the dogs did not matter, so long as he was eaten up and his bones gnawed free of anything foreign which adhered to his nature.

However, when that which is eaten by the dogs becomes dog, sometimes very savage dog, we develop a national hydrophobia which manifests itself in great aversion to the immigrant in general. We load him with all the curses of our civilization and blame him for all its ills, from race suicide to the I.W.W.

When I finally escaped this primary influence which had so rudely touched me, I had as yet no special grievance against society, but I had a clear understanding of the suffering of the new-comer to an American city. I also had a profound sympathy with those who were at war against a government which seemed not only stupid, but venal, and which on the face of it was no better than the most brutal autocracy, although it called itself a "government of the people, and for the people."

This sympathy I was eager to express, but the immediate physical necessities silenced for a while my burning idealism.

In my aimless wandering I drifted beyond the territory marked by the red line of crime and misery. I walked endless stretches of maddening streets as hopeless as they were straight, hot and ugly. North as far as the picturesque water tower on Lake Michigan, south as far as the city had gone on its conquering way. The few remaining landmarks, whenever I see them, remind me of hunger, weariness and despair.

Chicago is full of friends now. I need never go to an hotel for shelter. I need not even travel on a street car; I have spoken in its fashionable churches and been banqueted in the gilded caverns of its sumptuous hostelries; but best of all, I have been drawn into the blessed circle of those who are giving wealth and time and life for the bettering of the very conditions from which I once suffered.

Yet I have never been able to love Chicago. Perhaps I ought to love it, if only because it reminds me of "how deep the hole out of which I was drawn, and how horrible the pit out of which I was digged."

17

AMONG THE BOHEMIANS

After a fruitless search for work which would give me a chance to rehabilitate myself, I returned to the West Side; but fortunately wandered beyond the limits of that awful portal and found myself, to my great delight, in Chicago's "Bohemia."

I shall never forget the joy I felt in reading Czechish names and signs, and hearing again the language which was as familiar to me as my mother tongue.

I always felt a close kinship with the Bohemian people, whose unhappy history I knew and whose genius I understood and valued. I suppose while "blood is thicker than water," language is thicker than blood, and the larger relationship rests more upon ability to understand another people's ideals and share them, than upon general hereditary factors.

Perhaps more than any other people, the Bohemians have been able to transplant their national ideals and characteristics to the new soil, developing them to a marked degree. This may be due to the great difficulties under which they have lived in the Old World, so that when, in this country, they can speak and print their beloved language, they do it with a fierce passion as if to make up for lost time.

The contradictory characteristics of these, the most talented of the Slavic peoples, give them uncommon interest. Their light-heartedness and sadness, hospitality and hostility, industry and idleness, their passionate loves and hates, their devotion to art, their piety, infidelity and materialism— all seemed to be running at full tide when I happened upon "Bohemia in Chicago," in my quest for work. Had there been the least opposition to their expression, these people might have built a mediæval castle wall around themselves and annexed their territory to the Kingdom of Bohemia.

I was walking through one of those West Side streets which differ from others in nothing but the name, when I saw men digging for the foundation of a house. Upon asking in Bohemian for a job, I got my opportunity, not only to work, but also to enter into the life of the most radical section of the Bohemian community.

The man who employed me was a tailor who, with the thrift of his race, had saved enough money to build a house. It was most fortunate for me that when the evening of the first day's labour came, he had discovered that I was homeless and offered me lodging under his roof, which, of course, I most gratefully accepted.

Not only was the place scrupulously clean, but there were music and good literature. The latter was decidedly radical, ranging from Spencer to Ingersoll. The home also brought me in contact with people of some education.

At that time the social life of the men still centred almost entirely around the saloon, an institution which unfortunately and invariably takes on Anglo-Saxon qualities, no matter with what national elements it is started, or by what name it is called. It might be a matter of some interest to discover why this is so; but whatever the reason, it is certain that the saloon plays an important part in the Americanization of the immigrant. It frequently aims to preserve his social tendencies and usually harbours the national societies which spring up in every immigrant group.

The saloon patronized by my host and employer was located on Halstead Street and bore all the outer marks of its American prototype, although within were the Bohemian elements which gave it something of a home or club atmosphere.

What attracted me was the newspapers which were kept on file and the meetings of a Freethinkers' Club, which had its headquarters there.

I was in the mood to yield myself completely to its influence and rejoiced in its intellectual atmosphere, which meant more to me than bread and meat after my recent stultifying experiences.

This radical movement which seemed so natural to the Bohemian communities at that time was an inevitable reaction from their intolerant past in which Church and State, bishop and king had each been bad, and together did their worst.

Out of an environment of superstition and oppression these people had come into the buoyant atmosphere of religious freedom, and they were breathing like men escaped from a tomb. Much of their speech was like the raving of madmen, but, after all, it was a fine idealism to which they tried to give expression, and this movement, harmful as it must have been in some directions, saved them from a gross materialism to which they were naturally inclined.

This group, which I joined, was then reading the essays of Thomas Paine, and no matter what one may think of his philosophy or his attitude toward traditional religion—it seemed to me wonderful, to see ditch diggers, tailors and cobblers, at the end of the day's work discussing such serious literature so earnestly. This movement among the Bohemians has been severely attacked as atheistic. It never deserved that opprobrium, for at its heart it was religious, only it was seeking a high, free level. It never was dangerous, because, in spite of the attempt to inoculate the younger generation, the virus never took.

For some reason, anti-religious movements cannot be propagated in this country. No matter how virile the movement in its beginning, it dwindles and dies, and the second generation of even the most radical propagandists, becomes either respectably religious, or blends with that great mass of people who are neither hot nor cold in their attitude toward the things of the spirit.

During this period I came in touch with a number of anarchists and heard their vehement onslaught against organized government. While I never was carried away by their extreme individualism, and never was in danger of becoming an assassin, I felt keenly the injustice they deplored, and sympathized deeply with them in their protest against the brutal hanging of some of their number, which not long before had startled the United States.

In the exercise of justice, governments are apt to be both cruel and unjust, and I am not sure but that the verdict against the Chicago anarchists will one day be revised by a generation of men far enough removed from the hate and prejudice gendered at that time to judge the matter impartially.

I heard Mrs. Parsons, the wife of one of the condemned anarchists, and suffered greatly as I listened to her. While I never plotted violent deeds, I appreciated her desire to avenge what she called judicial murder. After all, it is easy for us who are safely removed from the suffering and need of the toilers, to condemn the radicals or label men and movements with a name which smacks of the plague or the pestilence. It was a crowd like that which said of Jesus, "He hath a devil," and joined in the ready cry: "Crucify Him!"

The one thing we are all apt to forget is, that anarchy and kindred movements grow out of a soil made stony and hard by injustice. They are symptoms of a disease in the body social, and the ill cannot be cured by jailing or hanging or crucifying the men who feel the hurt most and cry out in their agony.

It was in this Chicago Bohemian saloon that I began to speak in public, and I delivered a series of talks on Bakunin and Tolstoy.

The latter's religious idealism gave no little offence to my auditors, but to me it was the saving element in the situation and kept my soul alive during that most critical period. These talks were exceedingly informal, broken into by questions, jests and ridicule. Although I always began with a definite theme, all the affairs of the universe which needed righting were usually touched upon before I finished.

The startling thing to me was then, and now is, the latent idealism in these immigrant groups which can make of even a saloon something resembling a people's university. Unfortunately, this idealism does not survive long, for in that very saloon where at that time men sat and leisurely drank their beer, while they discussed the philosophy of Bakunin and Tolstoy, they now stand before the bar and make a business of drinking. They may discuss a prize fight or the latest news from the baseball field, but nothing more elevating.

The social settlement which might have given me a grappling place for the higher things, if it existed at all, was in its swaddling clothes, and the so-called respectable people never wandered into my social sphere.

When the house of my Bohemian host was finished I found a job in a machine shop and gradually lifted myself to a position of leadership among my shopmates. During the noon hour they would ask me questions and once I attempted to deliver an address, but the foreman interfered, a quarrel ensued and I was summarily discharged.

I had little money saved, but I had some good clothing and an accumulation of paper-bound books.

Then began a weary journey from shop to mill in a vain search for work; until my last penny was eaten up, all my surplus clothing had become security for my lodging and the books were sold for a pittance.

It was a year of great industrial depression; on one side, over-production, and on the other, under-consumption. Strikes and riots combined to make the situation abnormal, and after even the casual jobs failed I again turned westward, this time to the great harvest fields of Minnesota.

24

FROM ALIEN TO CITIZEN

Some time ago, it devolved upon me to guide through a portion of this country a Royal Commission from Germany that came to study some of our social problems, and the institutions which have been created to meet them or to solve them. What most astonished the members of the Commission was the idealistic current of our national life. One of them frankly confessed that he had always believed us to be the most materialistic and practical people in the world.

"When we landed in New York," he said, "we spent a sleepless night in one of your gigantic hotels, in rooms which faced three busy corners. Above them, high in air, were three huge and ingenious electric signs, compelling our attention. At one corner we saw the face of a woman emerging out of the night, winking her right eye as she disappeared and reappeared.

"Over the second corner a large whiskey bottle emptied its flaming contents into a glass, renewing the process every few minutes.

"The most wonderful sign was that which seemed to completely cover the heavens. It represented a chariot race. Fierce, fiery, tramping steeds were urged on by a reckless driver standing in his chariot; but while its wheels moved faster and faster, it never reached the goal.

"Those three signs appeared to us to represent the American spirit. The woman who seems to rule everything, the whiskey which symbolizes your love of pleasure, and the horses, the rush of trampling trade.

"Since that first impression, however, we have discovered that the unseen and unadvertised forces are stronger here than we believed. We have ceased to be startled by your materialistic symbols; but each day brings its new surprises in the sphere of ideals."

Such a judgment passed by keen students of abnormal

social phenomena, was exceedingly gratifying to me; for long ago I realized that fact, which was first impressed upon me in the little college town, where I discovered the real and the less known America.

Founded upon an ideal, the town was put down into a flat, uninviting, uninspiring landscape, which offered no commercial advantages whatever. It did give brave men a chance to build a community in which to realize their ideals, a college through which to propagate them and a church wherein to keep them vitalized by contact with God. The three—community, college and church—were so blended that one scarcely knew where one began and the other ended. Work, education and religion were steeped in an atmosphere of prayer; while fanaticism, narrow-mindedness and hypocrisy, if they existed, and no doubt they were there, never dominated.

While life may have been sombre, the real joys were not crowded out; for the college became a noted centre of musical education, an art gallery containing a good collection of paintings was developed, and last but not least, the championship in many forms of athletics has been in the keeping of the institution for many seasons.

Great men lived there, unconscious of their greatness, achieving far-reaching results in a modest way; many had suffered derision and even imprisonment for their convictions, and, dying, asked no other reward than the approval of their conscience and their God.

That which, more than anything else, lifted the place in my estimation and inspired my love for it and for the country in which such a community was possible, was the fact that here there was no difference of race or of sex; that all were God's children with a full chance to prove their worth.

This was my home for three years; as far as their value to my life was concerned, they might have been as many decades. While many other forces and other people in other places were at work to make and shape my mind and character, here I put off much of the "old man" and put on the new. It was a daily conversion, a process which I know is never finished, and in this process, community, college and church each had its share.

It was a busy as well as a self-renewing life; for not only did I study theology, I taught in the modern language department of the college, preached every Sunday and did some manual labour. Such a mixture of occupations not only kept me from becoming one-sided or growing into a pious prig, but helped pay my expenses.

My passion for all sorts and conditions of people was kept alive by the fact that I had to live in close proximity to several Negroes who attended the college and seminary. One of the brightest students in the academy was a black boy who learned German from me so alarmingly fast that I could scarcely keep up with him.

The man who knew Hebrew most thoroughly and had the Hebrew spirit at its best, was a young mulatto with whom I frequently talked about the tragedy of race. I have never been weaned from this sense of kinship with all men, and for this gift I thank God more than for any other that he has given me.

It would be futile to try to tell of the many jubilant notes which my seminary experiences brought into the hitherto minor chords of my life in America. One epoch-making event, however, I must record. During that period I became an American citizen. On a certain never-to-be-forgotten day I walked to the county seat, about seven miles away, to get my papers. What seemed to me should be a sacred rite proved to be an uninspiring performance. I entered a dingy office where a commonplace man, chewing tobacco, mumbled an oath which I repeated. Then he handed me a document for which I paid two dollars. When I held the long-coveted paper in my hand, the inspiring moment came, but it transpired in my own soul.

"Fellow-citizen with the saints! Fellow-citizen with the saints!" I repeated it many times all to myself.

I scarcely noticed the straight, monotonous seven miles back. I was travelling a much longer road; I was reviewing my whole life. Far away across the ocean I saw the little village in the Carpathian Mountains, with its conglomerate of warring races among which I lived, a despised "Jew boy." Loving them all, I was hated by all.

I heard the flogging of the poor Slovak peasants, the agonized cries of Jewish men and women incarcerated in their homes, while these same peasants, inflamed by alcohol but still more by prejudice, were breaking windows and burning down houses.

I saw myself growing into boyhood more and more separated from my playmates, until I lived, a youth without friends, growing into a "man without a country!"

Again I felt the desolation of the voyage on the sea, relived the sweat shop experience in New York, the hard labour in mill and mine, tramped across the plains and suffered anew all the agonies of the homeless, hungry days in Chicago. Then came the time when faith began to grow and the Christ became real: the reaction from a rigid theology and a distasteful, dogmatic atmosphere. After that, once more a stranger in a strange but holy place, and then a "Fellow-citizen with the saints!" "Fellow-citizen with the saints!"

It is no wonder that strangers like myself love this country, and love it, perhaps, as the native never can. Frequently I have wished for the careless American citizen, who holds his franchise cheap, an experience like my own, that he might know the value of a freeman's birthright. It would be a glorious experience, I am sure, to feel that transition from subject to citizen, from scarcely being permitted to say, "I," to those great collective words: "We, Fellow-citizens."

If I have preached this doctrine of fellowship in a hundred variations from one end of the country to the other—and I have done it almost with a fanatic's zeal—those who have read the story of my life will understand the reason. I have preached this doctrine with a passion, not only because America gave me the chance to achieve certain things, or because it has granted me certain rights and privileges, but because this country ought to be able to keep itself young and virile and vital enough, to bestow these blessings upon all who crowd our shores, filling our cities and entering daily into our inner life.

A hard and an almost impossible task it is, unless we can bring our idealistic forces to bear upon these unformed and rude elements which come to "spy out the land."

More and more I realize that the right of citizenship has been too easily given, because it is too lightly held; that the time must come when homeborn and stranger shall learn to realize that it is not only a gift but a privilege which must be earned, and whose right to hold must be proved by him who holds it. The community, the church, the schools and the other new, articulated ideals which are being born in these better days, must become so aggressive and so vital, that even these unlettered folk shall know that the three electric signs on Broadway are not the symbols which dominate our life. They must learn that outside this illumined triangle in which the great tragedies of life take place, there is a vast, unlimited field over which broods the spirit of a noble idealism, the spirit of America.

It is a cause for sincere gratitude that we are becoming more and more conscious of the power of ideals in our national life, and that these ideals bid fair to conquer.

Another great day came to me when I graduated from the seminary. I remember everything connected with that momentous exercise. The baccalaurcate sermon was preached by the professor of Hebrew, who had in the meanwhile become president of the college. The text was, "For unto me, who am less than the least of all saints, was this grace given to preach the Gospel." It was a call to a humble spirit, a courageous and sincere pride in the vocation upon which we were entering. It fitted into my mood, for I did feel the sense of humility and gratitude. I did appreciate the high privilege which awaited me.

The theme of my address on Commencement Day was: The Old Prophets and the New Problems. I have always been rather prodigal of what I have written, and that paper long ago disappeared; but its spirit has remained with me. I have never outgrown the theme, even as perhaps I have never attained the ideal I held out.

At last the exercises were concluded and I received my diploma. The tender words spoken as it was given me I also have not forgotten. The mere bowing of the head, that conventional form by which we expressed our thanks, seemed to me most inadequate. Had we been in a different environment, or at least in one where emotions were not held in check, I would have kissed the hand which bestowed it upon me.

Life was all joy that morning. It was a magnificent May day, the eleventh of that superb month. The town was at its best, buried in blossom-crowned trees and carpeted in flowers. It was a glad day and yet a sad one. Three sheltered, glorious years were at an end; years in which everything was given me freely, as God gives freely. I had come a stranger into a strange place, in a strange country. Now I had friends, dear and loyal friends. The unsettled, unformed and undirected life was shaped for service.

The class in which I graduated was typical of the product of the institution. It was made up of a mixture of races and nationalities. A number of them went into the foreign field as missionaries, and one died a martyr's death in China during the Boxer uprising of 1900; a close, personal friend, whose zeal and courage I always envied, has been one of the moulding forces of the unfortunate Balkan states.

Most of the class have done a valuable, if sometimes humble, service in country and town, carrying wherever they went the idealism they had absorbed.

Some of them have achieved conspicuous success. None of them left Oberlin, the School of the Prophets, with profounder gratitude than I. While I left there with a sense of regret, I went out with joy, for I was leaving it: "No more Stranger, but Fellow-citizen with the Saints."

A Far Journey
Abraham Rihbany

From an early age, Abraham Mitrie Rihbany's heart was divided between his native home of Syria and a land across the sea: America. Born to illiterate, strict Greek Orthodox parents in 1870, Rihbany first began to learn his father's trade of stonemasonry at the age of nine. The lure of an education in philosophy and letters, however, at an American Protestant mission school near Beirut, drew Rihbany away from the skilled trade of his forefathers or the possibility of a career in the Greek Orthodox priesthood. By the age of twenty-two, Rihbany had converted to Protestantism and left Syria for America. Only in America, Rihbany believed, could he avoid the clan feuds and suppression of individual rights that had arisen in the political climate of his homeland. The young man wished to labor with Protestant philosophy in a democratic state, while his kin remained laborers of a dry and much disputed land.

In America, Rihbany improved his English and exercised his mind as a bookkeeper, a member of the Syrian Scientific and Ethical Society, and as literary editor of the short-lived paper *The Kowkub America* (Star of America) (1892). In his writings, Rihbany tried to counteract the commonly held image in America of the Syrian immigrant as a "dingy peddler" by encouraging his fellow Syrians to embrace American customs and to pursue an education. With plans to avoid this stereotype himself, Rihbany gave religious lectures across the Midwest, and entered Ohio Wesleyan University in 1895. Once ordained as a Unitarian minister in 1900, Rihbany spent the rest of his life preaching and writing about the religion that inspired both his intellect and his immigration. Rihbany died at the age of seventy-four in Connecticut. His publications include *Syrian Christ*, *Seven Days with God*, *Militant America*, and an autobiography, *A Far Journey*, which was serialized in *The Atlantic Monthly* in 1914.

In these chapters from *A Far Journey*, Abraham Rihbany examines the difficult joy he felt when leaving a closely knit extended family to pursue a new education.

CHAPTER 10

OUT FROM MY KINDRED

It should be borne in mind, however, that my decision to depart from New York altogether was only in a small part the result of my dissatisfaction with my lot as editor. The real cause lay much deeper. The Syrian colony in New York seemed to me to be simply Syria on a smaller scale. During my stay of nearly eighteen months in it I did not have occasion to speak ten sentences in English. We ate the same dishes, spoke the same language, told the same stories, indulged in the same pleasures, and were torn by the same feuds, as those that had filled our lives on the Eastern shores of the Mediterranean. I seemed to be almost as far from the real life of America as if I had been living in Beyrout or Tripoli. The only glimpses I had of the higher life of this country came to me through the very few enlightened Syrians who mingled extensively with the better class of Americans, and who only occasionally visited our colony.

The sum total of my year-and-a-half's experience in New York convinced me that it was most difficult, if not impossible, for a foreigner to become really Americanized while living in a colony of his own kinsmen. Just as the birth of a new species can never take place without a radical break with the parent stock, so the thorough transformation of a foreigner into an American can never be accomplished without the complete departure, inwardly and outwardly, of that individual from his kindred.

The Syrian colony in New York rendered me all the service it could by providing me with a home for about eighteen months among those whose language was my language and whose habits were my habits. Its Oriental atmosphere with its slight Occidental tinge protected me from the dangers of an abrupt transition. Had I been thrust into American society upon my arrival in this country, penniless and without serviceable knowledge of the English language, the change in environment might have proved too violent for me to endure with any comfort. To me the colony was a habitat so much like the one I had left behind me in Syria that its home atmosphere enabled me to maintain a firm hold on life in the face of the many difficulties which confronted me in those days, and just different enough to awaken my curiosity to know more about the surrounding American influences.

The "gregarious habits" of foreigners in this country are deplored by those who have the welfare of both the foreigner and America at heart. It is evident to such well-wishers that the congregating of aliens together, especially in the large cities, tends to encourage in them the naturally strong desire to cling to their inherited modes of thought and life, and to make the task of Americanizing them doubly difficult. This inference is substantially correct. Nevertheless the fact remains that, but for these "gregarious habits," a multitude of the less aggressive foreigners, by being scattered prematurely among an alien population, would very likely lose their bearings, suffer disheartening loneliness and dejection, and become public charges. The law of the "survival of the fittest" rules in those "foreign colonies" in American cities, just as it does everywhere else. The multitude of "commoners" furnish the conditions necessary to produce the small minority of eager, aggressive idealists, whose restless spirits soon break through the barriers of inherited customs and respond with avidity to the challenges of a higher civilization. To such the word America soon takes the form of Opportunity, and is understood in terms of incentive and room for soul expansion. The loose composition of a population of many and mutually exclusive nationalities, the grotesque manners, and the multitude of saloons and other haunts of vice and crime in the "lower regions" of American cities, where the foreign colonies are generally located, soon tend to awaken in the mind of that foreigner, who finds himself yearning for a better order of things, the significant question, Where is America?

I often asked myself, in those days, where and how do the real Americans live? Who are the people who foster and maintain that American civilization of which I hear so much, but which I have not yet known? I have seen a multitude of Irish, Italians, Poles, Russians, Chinese, and other human elements which make up the community in which I am living, but where are the Americans? It seemed to me that in a cosmopolitan city like New York it was well-nigh impossible for a poor foreigner like me to come into helpful contact with its real American families. Therefore I would leave the great city and seek the smaller centers of population, where men came in friendly touch with one another, daily. It had been made clear to me that a purely commercial career could not satisfy me, that I had a deep longing for something more in the life of America than the mere loaves and fishes, therefore *that* something would I seek.

But, as has been already stated, at the end of my year-and-a-half's labors in New York, I found myself almost penniless. I had not enough money to carry me two hundred miles from that city. Whatever my *theory* of the "loaves and fishes" may have been, the *fact* was that I sorely needed them.

It so happened that the most intimate friend I had in America at the time was a young man, a graduate of the Syrian Protestant College in Beyrout, who was engaged by the Presbyterian churches of Pittsburg as a missionary among the Syrians in that city. Amin sent me a most urgent invitation and money enough to come to him. He thought his salary would keep us both, until we had matured our plans for the future. We were "to live and die together!"

Fortune smiled also from another direction. Several Syrian silk-merchants in New York, learning that I was about to leave the colony and that I was in straitened financial circumstances, offered to give me all the silk goods I might want to sell in my travels, "to keep me alive until I found a more congenial occupation,"—for which goods I was to pay at my convenience. The selling of silk, or anything else, was really hateful to me, but urgent necessity compelled me to carry with me a small quantity of the fabrics. The Syrian missionary in New York introduced me to the noted Presbyterian divine, Dr. David Gregg, of Brooklyn, who gave me a letter of recommendation. In compliance with wise advice I went also to Dr. Henry van Dyke, then pastor of the Brick Presbyterian Church, and requested his indorsement of Dr. Gregg's letter. Dr. van Dyke met me very cordially, but felt some hesitancy about giving a recommendation to one who was an entire stranger to him. But I said to him, in my broken English, not to be afraid because *"I was very good man,"* at which I saw him turn his face from me and smile. Reaching to the bookcase behind him he took out a book of a very strange character and asked me whether I could read that. I said "No. This must be Babylon writing." Shaking with laughter, he said, "It is shorthand." He wrote on my letter, "I join in Dr. Gregg's wish for Mr. Rihbany's success," and so forth, and dismissed me with a "God bless you."

Armed with those weighty documents, on the strength of which a man of stronger commercial instincts than I possessed might have done much business, I started out of New York. Upon my arrival at the Pennsylvania Railroad station to take my first railway trip in America, the luxurious coaches seemed forbidden to me. Recalling to mind the rough and dingy "third-class" car in which I was shipped from Marseilles to Havre, I thought certainly the plush-seated, mahogany-finished coaches which stood before me were not for penniless foreigners such as I was. Failing to

find the humble conveyance I was looking for, I asked a uniformed man, "Which the train to Pittsburg?" Pointing to the
train which I had inspected three times, he said, "This." Still
afraid of getting into the wrong car, I gazed at the man, who,
perceiving my perplexed condition, took me by the arm to
the door of one of those costly coaches and said, "Get in
here." I immediately obeyed, and the moving palace carried
me to Pittsburg, where my friend Amin and I were to seek as
our fortune the best things in the life of America.

In Pittsburg, where I sojourned for about two months,
Amin and I, like our countrymen of the primitive church in
Jerusalem, "had all things common." We abrogated the law
of private property between us altogether. Whether of
books, clothing, money, or even letters, there was no "This
is mine" and "This is thine"; all that we possessed was *ours*.
Oriental sentimentalism and brotherly feelings reached
their height with us when we vowed that "so long as we
both shall live, we will have a common purse and share to
the utmost each other's joys and sorrows." In our sharing
the one bed and eating our meals at a restaurant on one
"twenty-one-meal ticket" there was nothing particularly interesting to the public. But when we wore one another's
clothes, being different in size, we attracted some attention.

Our plan for the future was that we would enter college
together at the earliest possible date. Amin, as I have already said, was a graduate of the Syrian Protestant College
of Beyrout, Syria, but he was wise enough to suppose that
there were "more things in heaven and earth" than he had
yet learned, and that a course of study in the higher branches
of knowledge in one of the leading universities of this country would not, in his case, be superfluous. To secure funds
for this worthy purpose we decided to travel in these States,
and, wherever possible, lecture before churches and societies on the Holy Land, sell goods, seek financial aid by
whatever other honorable means, and, as soon as our financial circumstances warranted, apply for admission at that
great university which happened at the time to be nearest to
us. My friend, who had a very fair knowledge of the English
language, was to be the senior member of the firm. He was

to address the large assemblies on Sundays and other occasions, and I, who had never spoken English in public, was to screw my courage to the sticking-point and address small groups, in parlors and at prayer-meetings. Our choice of a vocation was to be made while in college, with the assistance of our professors.

But our fine plan was ere long destined to fail, and our fraternal vow to be broken. We started out on our "lecturing" tour in the summer, when the activities of the churches are at their lowest ebb. We encountered the absorbing excitement of the World's Fair, which was in progress at Chicago, and plunged into the memorable financial panic of 1893. The public mind was not in tune for lectures on the Holy Land, or any other land, and there was very little money available in the hands of the public to invest in Oriental silks. And what I felt was the severest trial to me was that my beloved friend, Amin, proved decidedly "infirm of purpose." The least difficulty discouraged him. He was a complete failure as a public speaker, and whenever he could dispose of a piece of silk, he sold it at cost and spent the money in defraying his expenses. Late that summer, utterly crushed by the many difficulties which beset our way, he left me, for aye, and joined some members of his family who were at the World's Fair.

I was left alone battling against a sea of trouble. However, I made a resolution which never was broken, namely, that, while I longed passionately for that unaffected, juvenile warmth of Syrian friendship, I would enter into no new partnership of any sort with any one of my countrymen. I thought I could hear the same voice which said to my namesake, Abraham, "Get thee out of thy country, and from thy kindred, and from thy father's house, into the land that I will show thee." I renewed my resolution to do my utmost to secure a college education, or in some other way relate myself to the higher life of America.

Shortly after the departure of my friend Amin, my career as a "silk-seller," which had by no means been an ideal success, came to an end. I certainly lacked to a very large extent the sagacity of the merchant. I did not believe in letting the customer "look out for herself"; I deemed it my duty to guard her interests with scrupulous care. I would point out to the prospective purchaser all the flaws in a piece of silk, in advance, believing that the excellencies were too obvious to be detailed. Whenever I was asked whether the goods were all handmade, I would answer that while I was morally certain that they were, "I could not swear to it," because I had never seen the process with my own eyes. Such conduct was not due to the fact that my honesty never was accustomed to failing, but to my theory that the business I was in was mean enough without lying about it. Consequently, the high prices of the goods, coupled with my uncalled-for conscientiousness, were by no means conducive to winning the confidence of would-be purchasers and to doing a "rushing business." I returned the goods to the merchant who had been my source of supply in silks during my business career, and decided to pursue my life's ideal as a "lecturer."

CHAPTER 11

LIGHTS AND SHADOWS

My struggles with the English language (which have not yet ceased) were at times very hard. It is not at all difficult for me to realize the agonizing inward struggles of a person who has lost the power of speech. When I was first compelled to set aside my mother-tongue and use English exclusively as my medium of expression, the sphere of my life seemed to shrink to a very small disk. My pretentious purpose of suddenly becoming a lecturer on Oriental customs, in a language in which practically I had never conversed, might have seemed to any one who knew me like an act of faith in the miraculous gift of tongues. My youthful desire was not only to inform but to *move* my hearers. Consequently, my groping before an audience for suitable diction within the narrow limits of my uncertain vocabulary was often pitiable.

The exceptions in English grammar seemed to be more than the rules. The difference between the conventional and the actual sounds of such words as "victuals" and "colonel" seemed to me to be perfectly scandalous. The letter *c* is certainly a superfluity in the English language; it is never anything else but either *k* or *s*. In my native language, the Arabic, the accent is always put as near the end of the word as possible; in the English, as near the beginning as possible. Therefore, in using my adopted tongue, I was tossed between the two extremes and very often "split the difference" by taking a middle course. The sounds of the letters, *v, p,* and the hard *g,* are not represented in the Arabic. They are symbolized in transliteration by the equivalents of *f, b,* and *k.* On numerous occasions, therefore, and especially when I waxed eloquent, my tongue would mix these sounds hopelessly, to the amused surprise of my hearers. I would say "coal" when I meant "goal," "pig man" for "big man," "buy" for "pie," "ferry" for "very," and *vice versa.* For some time I had, of course, to think in Arabic and try to translate my thoughts *literally* into English, which practice caused me many troubles, especially in the use of the connectives. On one occasion, when an American gentleman told me that he was a Presbyterian, and I, rejoicing to claim fellowship with him, sought to say what should have been, "We are brethren in Christ," I said. "We are brothers, by Jesus." My Presbyterian friend put his finger on his lip in pious fashion, and, with elevated brows and a most sympathetic smile, said, "That is swearing!"

But in my early struggles with English, I derived much negative consolation from the mistakes Americans made in pronouncing my name. None of them could pronounce it correctly—Rih-ba'-ny—without my assistance. I have been called Rib'-beny, Richbany, Ribary, Laborny, Rabonie, and many other names. An enterprising Sunday School superintendent in the Presbyterian Church at Mansfield, Ohio, introduced me to his school by saying, "Now we have the pleasure of listening to Mr. Rehoboam!" The prefixing of "Mr." to the name of the scion of King Solomon seemed to me to annihilate time and space, and showed me plainly how the past might be brought forward and made to serve the present.

But my struggles with the technicalities of language were not the only pains of my second birth into the new environment. The social readjustments were even more difficult to effect. Coming into the house in Syria, a guest removes his shoes from his feet at the door, but keeps his fez or turban on. It was no easy matter, therefore, for me, on going into an American home, to realize instantly which extremity to uncover.

The poetic Oriental mind extends hospitality in a very warm and dramatic manner. The would-be guest, although able and willing to accept an invitation to dinner, expects to be urged repeatedly by the would-be host, to have all his feigned objections overruled, to be even pulled bodily into the house before he gives his consent. By following such tactics in this country, I lost many a precious privilege. The brevity of the American invitation distressed me greatly. Whenever I was told, "We should be much pleased to have you come in and have dinner with us, if you can," I would answer, "No, thank you; I cannot possibly come," when I had it in mind all the time that I would gladly accept if they would only urge me. But they would let me go! They would take me at my word (as they should not do, I thought, in such matters), to my great disappointment. It was not very long, however, before I became on this point thoroughly Americanized. However, eating butter on bread, dessert with every meal, and sitting in rocking-chairs seemed to me to be riotous luxuries. It took me about three years to become accustomed to these seeming superfluities. It would require six now to make me give them up.

The prominence of woman in domestic and social affairs seemed to me, when I first came in close touch with American society, a strange and unnatural phenomenon. While in Syria, contrary to the view which generally prevails in this country, the woman is not *considered* a slave by the man, yet in all important domestic and social matters she is looked upon as only his *silent* partner. The American woman is by

no means silent; she finds it neither convenient nor necessary to assume such an attitude.

The first opportunity I had of making close observation
of the social position of the American woman was at the
home of a Methodist minister where I proved sensible and
fortunate enough to accept "without controversy" an invitation to dinner. His wife presided at the table with so much
grace and dignity that my astonishment at the supreme authority she exercised on the occasion was deeply tinged
with respect. How harmonious the husband and wife
seemed! What mutual regard! What delicacy of behavior
toward each other! But I could not avoid asking, subjec-
tively, "Is all this really genuine? Does this man treat his
wife in this manner always, or only when they have company? Why, my host seems to be in the hands of his wife
like the clay in the hands of the potter! Why should a woman
be given so much latitude?" and so forth.

When, later in the evening, upon retiring, the lady said to
her husband, "Good-night, dear," and *kissed him in my presence*, the act seemed to me distressingly unseemly. It is no
longer distressing to me.

It should not be counted against an Oriental that he is unable in a very short period of time to invest such phases of
conduct with high idealism. If his instincts are normal, intimate associations with the better class of Americans cannot
fail to change his sentiments and clarify his vision. Not
many years will be required to reveal to him the elevating
beauty of a woman's being the queen of her home, with her
husband as a knight-errant by her side; to teach him that
America, as the heir to the noblest traditions of northwestern Europe, has discovered that which neither the Oriental
peoples, ancient Egypt, Greece, nor Rome succeeded in discovering, namely, that true civilization can arise only from
a mutual regard of the equal rights, and, within the family
circle, the mutual love of man, woman, and child.

All such discipline, however, was not to be compared
with the economic difficulties which beset my way, put my
optimism to the severest test, and seriously threatened my

stoutest resolutions. In my travels westward, the expressions, "These are very hard times," "The summer is a dull season for the churches," "Not many people care for lectures this time of year," tortured my hearing everywhere. It was so difficult for me to secure money enough to keep soul and body together. In Oil City, Pennsylvania, I longed for the first time for the "flesh-pots of Egypt" and wished that I had never left Syria. In my search for a cheap lodging-place, I was directed by a police officer to an old house which seemed to me the symbol of desolation. An elderly lady, who appeared very economical in smiling, "showed me into my room" and disappeared. As my weary arm dropped the valise inside the door, every sustaining power in me seemed to give way. Sobs and tears poured forth simultaneously with, "Why did I ever leave Syria?" "Why did I not stay in New York?" "Is this what America has for me?" and other questions with which I besieged the deaf ears of a lonely world. The fact that my hostess served no meals afforded me an excellent excuse to ask her to direct me to a "real" boarding-house. She did so, and I transferred my headquarters to a more cheery dwelling, where the landlady smiled graciously and generously, and the presence of fellow guests helped to lighten my burdens.

The veiling of the future from mortal eyes is, I believe, a divine provision whose purpose seems to be to tap the springs of heroism in human nature and to equip the soul with the wings of hope. Nevertheless, this blessed mystery has its drawbacks. Prolonged uncertainty of the future in those days of loneliness and poverty threatened to sink the goal of life below the horizon and make of me a wanderer in a strange land. The alternation of life between the two extremes, feast and famine, is never conducive to connected planning and constancy of endeavor.

At Columbus, Ohio, I spent a whole week in strenuous but utterly fruitless endeavor to secure opportunities to earn some money. Having had to pay in advance for my week's keep at a very frugal boarding-house, I had only ten cents left, which I put in the "collection plate," at a Salvation Army meeting. To be penniless was not entirely new to me, but as the week drew to a close, the question where I was going to secure money enough with which to leave Columbus became terribly oppressive. There was one more venture for me to make. I had the name of a Methodist minister, the Rev. John C. Jackson, pastor of the Third Avenue Methodist Episcopal Church, whom I had not yet seen during my sojourn in the capital of Ohio. My courageous plan was to call on this clergyman and request him either to give me the chance to lecture in his church for a small financial compensation or to lend me money enough to enable me to leave Columbus. The distance from my boarding-house to his residence measured, if I may trust my memory, twenty-four blocks, which I walked in what seemed to me the hottest day in the calendar of the years.

My general appearance when I arrived at the parsonage was not exactly what I should call a clear title to confidence and the securing of credit. Nevertheless, I made my application with a creditable show of firmness, placing in the hands of the clergyman, who was just recovering from a long illness, my letters of recommendation. He disposed of my request to lecture in his church by saying, "There is no possible chance for the present." When I applied for a loan of five dollars, his pale face lighted up with a short-lived smile as he asked, "Do you expect you will get it?" "Y-e-s," I answered, "and to return it, also." "When would you return it?" he asked again. Falling back upon the Biblical language of my kinsmen, I said, "If God prolong my life and prosper me, I will pay you." Assuming the attitude of perplexed charity, Mr. Jackson said, "I do not know whether you are the man to whom these letters pertain, nor, if you *are* the man, how you secured them in the first place; but I am going to try you. Here is five dollars." "Certainly God has not left this world," I said inwardly, as I received the money from the good man's hand. It was only a week thence when God did prosper me just enough so that I was able to return to Mr. Jackson his money and I received a letter from him (which I still treasure) thanking me for my "promptness" and wishing me all kinds of success.

The Americanization of Edward Bok
Edward Bok

Edward Bok was born in Den Helder, the Netherlands, on October 9, 1863. As the descendant of an admiral of the Dutch Navy and a chief justice of the Dutch Supreme Court, one might speculate that Edward Bok could have had a successful political career in his homeland. However, a reversal of fortune forced Bok's family to leave for America in 1869, with hopes of building a new life.

The Boks settled in Brooklyn, New York, soon after their arrival. Fellow schoolboys nicknamed him "Dutchy," but Edward set out to learn English to become distinctly American. To help support his family, Bok sold lemonade on the Coney Island car line, and took a job as a newspaper carrier. At the age of thirteen, Bok dropped out of school and went to work for the Western Union Telegraph Company. Edward gained notoriety because of his impressive collection of the letters and autographs of many famous people, which he had started on a whim. Consequently, even at a young age, Bok had many connections. One such friend knew Henry Holt, a publisher, who promoted Bok to stenographer. In the evening Bok edited *The Brooklyn Magazine.* His success there garnered him the position of advertising manager at *Scribner's Magazine.* Once in the ranks, Bok rose quickly. In 1886 he established the Bok Syndicate Press, which sold the writings of prominent authors. The syndicate also published a popular women's page for newspapers, which came to be known as the "Bok page." Bok's father-in-law, Cyrus Curtis, the publisher and owner of *The Ladies' Home Journal*, named Bok editor in 1889.

Bok's career at *LHJ* was remarkable on many accounts. His magazine advised women on politics, social welfare, suffrage, and an often omitted topic in popular publications at the time: health. Unreliable medicine advertisements were not published in the pages of the *LHJ*, for example, and taboo discussions concerning sex and venereal disease were printed with the hopes of educating American society. Despite these advances, Bok was reported to be a strict Victorian, who never relinquished his personal view that women should only aspire to become homemakers, mothers, and wives.

After his retirement in 1919, Bok wrote his autobiography, *The Americanization of Edward Bok*, which won the Pulitzer Prize in 1921. Edward Bok's other writings include *Two Persons* (1922), *A Man from Maine* (1923), and *Dollars Only* (1926). During his retirement, he donated money to the Philadelphia orchestra and other charities, as well as establishing the Harvard Advertising Awards and the American Peace Award. Bok died of heart failure on January 9, 1930.

Though Edward Bok was thoroughly "Americanized," he did not forget his Dutch heritage. In the chapters "Where America Fell Short with Me" and "What I Owe to America," a successful editor and philanthropist reflects on the nation that changed the course of his life.

CHAPTER 38

WHERE AMERICA FELL SHORT WITH ME

When I came to the United States as a lad of six, the most needful lesson for me, as a boy, was the necessity for thrift. I had been taught in my home across the sea that thrift was one of the fundamentals in a successful life.

My family had come from a land (the Netherlands) noted for its thrift; but we had been in the United States only a few days before the realization came home strongly to my father and mother that they had brought their children to a land of waste.

Where the Dutchman saved, the American wasted. There was waste, and the most prodigal waste, on every hand. In every street-car and on every ferry-boat the floors and seats were littered with newspapers that had been read and thrown away or left behind. If I went to a grocery store to buy a peck of potatoes, and a potato rolled off the heaping measure, the groceryman, instead of picking it up, kicked it into the gutter for the wheels of his wagon to run over. The butcher's waste filled my mother's soul with dismay. If I bought a scuttle of coal at the corner grocery, the coal that missed the scuttle, instead of being shovelled up and put back into the bin, was swept into the street. My young eyes quickly saw this; in the evening I gathered up the coal thus swept away, and during the course of a week I collected a scuttleful. The first time my mother saw the garbage pail of a family almost as poor as our own, with the wife and husband constantly complaining that they could not get along, she could scarcely believe her eyes. A half pan of hominy of the preceding day's breakfast lay in the pail next to a third of a loaf of bread. In later years, when I saw, daily, a scow loaded with the garbage of Brooklyn householders being towed through New York harbor out to sea, it was an easy calculation that what was thrown away in a week's time from Brooklyn homes would feed the poor of the Netherlands.

At school, I quickly learned that to "save money" was to be "stingy"; as a young man, I soon found that the American disliked the word "economy," and on every hand as plenty grew spending grew. There was literally nothing in American life to teach me thrift or economy; everything to teach me to spend and to waste.

I saw men who had earned good salaries in their prime, reach the years of incapacity as dependents. I saw families on every hand either living quite up to their means or beyond them; rarely within them. The more a man earned, the more he—or his wife—spent. I saw fathers and mothers and their children dressed beyond their incomes. The proportion of families who ran into debt was far greater than those who saved. When a panic came, the families "pulled in"; when the panic was over, they "let out." But the end of one year found them precisely where they were at the close of the previous year, unless they were deeper in debt.

It was in this atmosphere of prodigal expenditure and culpable waste that I was to practise thrift: a fundamental in life! And it is into this atmosphere that the foreign-born comes now, with every inducement to spend and no encouragement to save. For as it was in the days of my boyhood, so it is to-day—only worse. One need only go over the experiences of the past two years, to compare the receipts of merchants who cater to the working-classes and the statements of savings-banks throughout the country, to read the story of how the foreign-born are learning the habit of criminal wastefulness as taught them by the American.

Is it any wonder, then, that in this, one of the essentials in life and in all success, America fell short with me, as it is continuing to fall short with every foreign-born who comes to its shores?

As a Dutch boy, one of the cardinal truths taught me was that whatever was worth doing was worth doing well: that next to honesty came thoroughness as a factor in success. It was not enough that anything should be done: it was not done at all if it was not done well. I came to America to be taught exactly the opposite. The two infernal Americanisms "That's good enough" and "That will do" were early taught me, together with the maxim of quantity rather than quality.

It was not the boy at school who could write the words in his copy-book best who received the praise of the teacher; it was the boy who could write the largest number of words in a given time. The acid test in arithmetic was not the mastery of the method, but the number of minutes required to work out an example. If a boy abbreviated the month January to "Jan." and the word Company to "Co." he received a hundred per cent mark, as did the boy who spelled out the words and who could not make the teacher see that "Co." did not spell "Company."

As I grew into young manhood, and went into business, I found on every hand that quantity counted for more than quality. The emphasis was almost always placed on how much work one could do in a day, rather than upon how well the work was done. Thoroughness was at a discount on every hand; production at a premium. It made no difference in what direction I went, the result was the same: the cry was always for quantity, quantity! And into this atmosphere of almost utter disregard for quality I brought my ideas of Dutch thoroughness and my conviction that doing well whatever I did was to count as a cardinal principle in life.

During my years of editorship, save in one or two conspicuous instances, I was never able to assign to an American writer, work which called for painstaking research. In every instance, the work came back to me either incorrect in statement, or otherwise obviously lacking in careful preparation.

One of the most successful departments I ever conducted in *The Ladies' Home Journal* called for infinite reading and patient digging, with the actual results sometimes almost negligible. I made a study of my associates by turning the department over to one after another, and always with the same result: absolute lack of a capacity for patient research. As one of my editors, typically American, said to me: "It isn't worth all the trouble that you put into it." Yet no single department ever repaid the searcher more for his pains. Save for assistance derived from a single person, I had to do the work myself for all the years that the department continued. It was apparently impossible for the American to work with sufficient patience and care to achieve a result.

We all have our pet notions as to the particular evil which is "the curse of America," but I always think that Theodore Roosevelt came closest to the real curse when he classed it as a lack of thoroughness.

Here again, in one of the most important matters in life, did America fall short with me; and, what is more important, she is falling short with every foreigner that comes to her shores.

In the matter of education, America fell far short in what should be the strongest of all her institutions: the public school. A more inadequate, incompetent method of teaching, as I look back over my seven years of attendance at three different public schools, it is difficult to conceive. If there is one thing that I, as a foreign-born child, should have been carefully taught, it is the English language. The individual effort to teach this, if effort there was, and I remember none, was negligible. It was left for my father to teach me, or for me to dig it out for myself. There was absolutely no indication on the part of teacher or principal of responsibility for seeing that a foreign-born boy should acquire the English language correctly. I was taught as if I were American-born, and, of course, I was left dangling in the air, with no conception of what I was trying to do.

My father worked with me evening after evening; I plunged my young mind deep into the bewildering confusions of the language—and no one realizes the confusions of the English language as does the foreign-born—and got what I could through these joint efforts. But I gained nothing from the much-vaunted public-school system which the United States had borrowed from my own country, and then had rendered incompetent—either by a sheer disregard for the thoroughness that makes the Dutch public schools the admiration of the world, or by too close a regard for politics.

Thus, in her most important institution to the foreign-born, America fell short. And while I am ready to believe that the public school may have increased in efficiency since that day, it is, indeed, a question for the American to ponder, just how far the system is efficient for the education of the child who comes to its school without a knowledge of the first word in the English language. Without a detailed knowledge of the subject, I know enough of conditions in the average public school to-day to warrant at least the suspicion that Americans would not be particularly proud of the system, and of what it gives for which annually they pay millions of dollars in taxes.

I am aware in making this statement that I shall be met with convincing instances of intelligent effort being made with the foreign-born children in special classes. No one has a higher respect for those efforts than I have—few, other than educators, know of them better than I do, since I did not make my five-year study of the American public school system for naught. But I am not referring to the exceptional instance here and there. I merely ask of the American, interested as he is or should be in the Americanization of the strangers within his gates, how far the public school system, as a whole, urban and rural, adapts itself, with any true efficiency, to the foreign-born child. I venture to color his opinion in no wise; I simply ask that he will inquire and ascertain for himself, as he should do if he is interested in the future welfare of his country and his institutions; for what happens in America in the years to come depends, in large measure, on what is happening to-day in the public schools of this country.

As a Dutch boy I was taught a wholesome respect for law and for authority. The fact was impressed upon me that laws of themselves were futile unless the people for whom they were made respected them, and obeyed them in spirit more even than in the letter. I came to America to feel, on every hand, that exactly the opposite was true. Laws were passed, but were not enforced; the spirit to enforce them was lacking in the people. There was little respect for the law; there was scarcely any for those appointed to enforce it.

The nearest that a boy gets to the law is through the policeman. In the Netherlands a boy is taught that a policeman is for the protection of life and property; that he is the natural friend of every boy and man who behaves himself. The Dutch boy and the policeman are, naturally, friendly in their relations. I came to America to bè told that a policeman is a boy's natural enemy; that he is eager to arrest him if he can find the slightest reason for doing so. A policeman, I was informed, was a being to hold in fear, not in respect.

He was to be avoided, not to be made friends with. The result was that, as did all boys, I came to regard the policeman on our beat as a distinct enemy. His presence meant that we should "stiffen up"; his disappearance was the signal for us to "let loose."

So long as one was not caught, it did not matter. I heard mothers tell their little children that if they did not behave themselves, the policeman would put them into a bag and carry them off, or cut their ears off. Of course, the policeman became to them an object of terror; the law he represented, a cruel thing that stood for punishment. Not a note of respect did I ever hear for the law in my boyhood days. A law was something to be broken, to be evaded, to call down upon others as a source of punishment, but never to be regarded in the light of a safeguard.

And as I grew into manhood, the newspapers rang on every side with disrespect for those in authority. Under the special dispensation of the liberty of the press, which was construed into the license of the press, no man was too high to escape editorial vituperation if his politics did not happen to suit the management, or if his action ran counter to what the proprietors believed it should be. It was not criticism of his acts, it was personal attack upon the official; whether supervisor, mayor, governor, or president, it mattered not.

It is a very unfortunate impression that this American lack of respect for those in authority makes upon the foreign-born mind. It is difficult for the foreigner to square up the arrest and deportation of a man who, through an incendiary address, seeks to overthrow governmental authority, with the ignoring of an expression of exactly the same sentiments by the editor of his next morning's newspaper. In other words, the man who writes is immune, but the man who reads, imbibes, and translates the editor's words into action is immediately marked as a culprit, and America will not harbor him. But why harbor the original cause? Is the man who speaks with type less dangerous than he who speaks with his mouth or with a bomb?

* * *

At the most vital part of my life, when I was to become an American citizen and exercise the right of suffrage, America fell entirely short. It reached out not even the suggestion of a hand.

When the Presidential Conventions had been held in the year I reached my legal majority, and I knew I could vote, I endeavored to find out whether, being foreign-born, I was entitled to the suffrage. No one could tell me; and not until I had visited six different municipal departments, being referred from one to another, was it explained that, through my father's naturalization, I became, automatically, as his son, an American citizen. I decided to read up on the platforms of the Republican and Democratic parties, but I could not secure copies anywhere, although a week had passed since they had been adopted in convention.

I was told the newspapers had printed them. It occurred to me there must be many others besides myself who were anxious to secure the platforms of the two parties in some more convenient form. With the eye of necessity ever upon a chance to earn an honest penny, I went to a newspaper office, cut out from its files the two platforms, had them printed in a small pocket edition, sold one edition to the American News Company and another to the News Company controlling the Elevated Railroad bookstands in New York City, where they sold at ten cents each. So great was the demand which I had only partially guessed, that within three weeks I had sold such huge editions of the little books that I had cleared over a thousand dollars.

But it seemed to me strange that it should depend on a foreign-born American to supply an eager public with what should have been supplied through the agency of the political parties or through some educational source.

I now tried to find out what a vote actually meant. It must be recalled that I was only twenty-one years old, with scant education, and with no civic agency offering me the information I was seeking. I went to the headquarters of each of the political parties and put my query. I was regarded with puzzled looks.

"What does it mean to vote?" asked one chairman.

"Why, on Election Day you go up to the ballot-box and put your ballot in, and that's all there is to it."

But I knew very well that that was not all there was to it, and was determined to find out the significance of the franchise. I met with dense ignorance on every hand. I went to the Brooklyn Library, and was frankly told by the librarian that he did not know of a book that would tell me what I wanted to know. This was in 1884.

As the campaign increased in intensity, I found myself a desired person in the eyes of the local campaign managers, but not one of them could tell me the significance and meaning of the privilege I was for the first time to exercise.

Finally, I spent an evening with Seth Low, and, of course, got the desired information.

But fancy the quest I had been compelled to make to acquire the simple information that should have been placed in my hands or made readily accessible to me. And how many foreign-born would take equal pains to ascertain what I was determined to find out?

Surely America fell short here at the moment most sacred to me: that of my first vote!

Is it any easier to-day for the foreign citizen to acquire this information when he approaches his first vote? I wonder! Not that I do not believe there are agencies for this purpose. You know there are, and so do I. But how about the foreign-born? Does he know it? Is it not perhaps like the owner of the bulldog who assured the friend calling on him that it never attacked friends of the family? "Yes," said the friend, "that's all right. You know and I know that I am a friend of the family; but does the dog know?"

Is it to-day made known to the foreign-born, about to exercise his privilege of suffrage for the first time, where he can be told what that privilege means: is the means to know made readily accessible to him: is it, in fact, as it should be, brought to him?

It was not to me; is it to him?

One fundamental trouble with the present desire for Americanization is that the American is anxious to Americanize two classes—if he is a reformer, the foreign-born; if he is an employer, his employees. It never occurs to him that he himself may be in need of Americanization. He seems to take it for granted that because he is American-born, he is an American in spirit and has a right understanding of American ideals. But that, by no means, always follows. There are thousands of the American-born who need Americanization just as much as do the foreign-born. There are hundreds of American employers who know far less of American ideals than do some of their employees. In fact, there are those actually engaged to-day in the work of Americanization, men at the top of the movement, who sadly need a better conception of true Americanism.

An excellent illustration of this came to my knowledge when I attended a large Americanization Conference in Washington. One of the principal speakers was an educator of high standing and considerable influence in one of the most important sections of the United States. In a speech setting forth his ideas of Americanization, he dwelt with much emphasis and at considerable length upon instilling into the mind of the foreign-born the highest respect for American institutions.

After the Conference he asked me whether he could see me that afternoon at my hotel; he wanted to talk about contributing to the magazine. When he came, before approaching the object of his talk, he launched out on a tirade against the President of the United States; the weakness of the Cabinet, the inefficiency of the Congress, and the stupidity of the Senate. If words could have killed, there would have not remained a single living member of the Administration at Washington.

After fifteen minutes of this, I reminded him of his speech and the emphasis which he had placed upon the necessity of inculcating in the foreign-born respect for American institutions.

Yet this man was a power in his community, a strong influence upon others; he believed he could Americanize others, when he himself, according to his own statements, lacked the fundamental principle of Americanization. What is true of this man is, in lesser or greater degree, true of hundreds of others. Their Americanization consists of lip-service; the real spirit, the only factor which counts in the successful teaching of any doctrine, is absolutely missing. We certainly cannot teach anything approaching a true Americanism until we ourselves feel and believe and practise in our own lives what we are teaching to others. No law, no lip-service, no effort, however well-intentioned, will amount to anything worth while in inculcating the true American spirit in our foreign-born citizens until we are sure that the American spirit is understood by ourselves and is warp and woof of our own being.

To the American, part and parcel of his country, these particulars in which his country falls short with the foreign-born are, perhaps, not so evident; they may even seem not so very important. But to the foreign-born they seem distinct lacks; they loom large; they form serious handicaps which, in many cases, are never surmounted; they are a menace to that Americanization which is, to-day, more than ever our fondest dream, and which we now realize more keenly than before is our most vital need.

It is for this reason that I have put them down here as a concrete instance of where and how America fell short in my own Americanization, and, what is far more serious to me, where she is falling short in her Americanization of thousands of other foreign-born.

"Yet you succeeded," it will be argued.

That may be; but you, on the other hand, must admit that I did not succeed by reason of these shortcomings: it was in spite of them, by overcoming them—a result that all might not achieve.

CHAPTER 39

WHAT I OWE TO AMERICA

Whatever shortcomings I may have found during my fifty-year period of Americanization; however America may have failed to help my transition from a foreigner into an American, I owe to her the most priceless gift that any nation can offer, and that is opportunity.

As the world stands to-day, no nation offers opportunity in the degree that America does to the foreign-born. Russia may, in the future, as I like to believe she will, prove a second United States of America in this respect. She has the same limitless area; her people the same potentialities. But, as things are to-day, the United States offers, as does no other nation, a limitless opportunity: here a man can go as far as his abilities will carry him. It may be that the foreign-born, as in my own case, must hold on to some of the ideals and ideas of the land of his birth; it may be that he must develop and mould his character by overcoming the habits resulting from national shortcomings. But into the best that the foreign-born can retain, America can graft such a wealth of inspiration, so high a national idealism, so great an opportunity for the highest endeavor, as to make him the fortunate man of the earth to-day.

He can go where he will: no traditions hamper him; no limitations are set except those within himself. The larger the area he chooses in which to work, the larger the vision he demonstrates, the more eager the people are to give support to his undertakings if they are convinced that he has their best welfare as his goal. There is no public confidence equal to that of the American public, once it is obtained. It is fickle, of course, as are all publics, but fickle only toward the man who cannot maintain an achieved success.

A man in America cannot complacently lean back upon victories won, as he can in the older European countries, and depend upon the glamour of the past to sustain him or the momentum of success to carry him. Probably the most alert public in the world, it requires of its leaders that they be alert. Its appetite for variety is insatiable, but its appreciation, when given, is full-handed and whole-hearted. The American public never holds back from the man to whom it gives; it never bestows in a niggardly way; it gives all or nothing.

What is not generally understood of the American people is their wonderful idealism. Nothing so completely surprises the foreign-born as the discovery of this trait in the American character. The impression is current in European countries—perhaps less generally since the war—that America is given over solely to a worship of the American dollar. While between nations as between individuals, comparisons are valueless, it may not be amiss to say, from personal knowledge, that the Dutch worship the gulden infinitely more than do the Americans the dollar.

I do not claim that the American is always conscious of this idealism; often he is not. But let a great convulsion touching moral questions occur, and the result always shows how close to the surface is his idealism. And the fact that so frequently he puts over it a thick veneer of materialism does not affect its quality. The truest approach, the only approach in fact, to the American character is, as Sir James Bryce has so well said, through its idealism.

It is this quality which gives the truest inspiration to the foreign-born in his endeavor to serve the people of his adopted country. He is mentally sluggish, indeed, who does not discover that America will make good with him if he makes good with her.

But he must play fair. It is essentially the straight game that the true American plays, and he insists that you shall play it too. Evidence there is, of course, to the contrary in American life, experiences that seem to give ground for the belief that the man succeeds who is not scrupulous in playing his cards. But never is this true in the long run. Sooner or later—sometimes, unfortunately, later than sooner—the public discovers the trickery. In no other country in the world is the moral conception so clear and true as in America, and no people will give a larger and more permanent reward to the man whose effort for that public has its roots in honor and truth.

"The sky is the limit" to the foreign-born who comes to America endowed with honest endeavor, ceaseless industry, and the ability to carry through. In any honest endeavor, the way is wide open to the will to succeed. Every path beckons, every vista invites, every talent is called forth, and every efficient effort finds its due reward. In no land is the way so clear and so free.

How good an American has the process of Americanization made me? That I cannot say. Who *can* say that of himself? But when I look around me at the American-born I have come to know as my close friends, I wonder whether, after all, the foreign-born does not make in some sense a better American—whether he is not able to get a truer perspective; whether his is not the deeper desire to see America greater; whether he is not less content to let its faulty institutions be as they are; whether in seeing faults more clearly he does not make a more decided effort to have America reach those ideals or those fundamentals of his own land which he feels are in his nature, and the best of which he is anxious to graft into the character of his adopted land?

It is naturally with a feeling of deep satisfaction that I remember two Presidents of the United States considered me a sufficiently typical American to wish to send me to my native land as the accredited minister of my adopted country. And yet when I analyze the reasons for my choice in both these instances, I derive a deeper satisfaction from the fact that my strong desire to work in America for America led me to ask to be permitted to remain here.

It is this strong impulse that my Americanization has made the driving power of my life. And I ask no greater privilege than to be allowed to live to see my potential America become actual: the America that I like to think of as the America of Abraham Lincoln and of Theodore

Roosevelt—not faultless, but less faulty. It is a part in trying to shape that America, and an opportunity to work in that America when it comes, that I ask in return for what I owe to her. A greater privilege no man could have.

Up Stream
Ludwig Lewisohn

Ludwig Lewisohn (1883–1955) was a prominent if embattled man of letters of the 1920s and 1930s. As an outspoken critic of Puritanism, he exerted a significant pressure on the discussion of literature and morality, and established himself as one of the leading authors of immigrant experience, first in his autobiographical volumes, *Up Stream* (1922) and *Mid-Channel* (1930), and in his excellent novel *The Island Within* (1928). A vigorous antagonist of anti-Semitism, he became a passionate Zionist when the nationalist movement began to make its presence felt in the late 1920s.

Lewisohn arrived in South Carolina in 1890 at the age of seven. Because of a scandal involving the business dealings of his father, Jacques Lewisohn, his German-Jewish family had left their comfortable life of cultural assimilation in Berlin. The valedictorian of his Charleston high school class, Lewisohn received further distinction at Charleston College, graduating with honors and an M.A. Throughout his adolescence, Lewisohn had participated in the Methodist church, but was refused a position with a church-related military academy because of his Jewish origins.

As a result of this insult, Lewisohn pursued a doctorate in English literature at Columbia where he was also dismayed to encounter anti-Semitism. His professors warned, not altogether kindly, that he should expect further disregard in the future. Leaving his dissertation unfinished, he dabbled somewhat unsuccessfully in the world of publishing and journalism. By 1908, he had moved back to Charleston, but returned to New York with a successful novel, *The Broken Snare,* and wife, Mary, twenty years his senior.

In 1910, Lewisohn was offered a lectureship in the German department at the University of Wisconsin, and a year later moved to Ohio State for a more secure position. While it rankled him that he was still unable to find a position as a professor of English literature, his credentials as a German literature critic and translator grew more distinguished, and he published several books on drama and German literature. In 1917, anti-German sentiment during the First World War led Lewisohn to terminate his academic career, unwilling and unable to compromise with an academic atmosphere he saw as barbaric and anti-intellectual.

Lewisohn joined the staff of *The Nation* as a drama critic in 1919, a position that enabled him to champion the avant garde as well as Yiddish and African-American theater, along with the works of the European modernists. He was closely aligned with such writers as Theodore Dreiser, Sinclair Lewis, Edgar Lee Masters, and H. L. Mencken, who gave *Up Stream* a glowing review, though, in general, the reception was mixed.

Lewisohn continued to make his living as an author and critic, publishing several novels, including the notorious *Case of Mr. Crump* (1931), and literary and cultural studies, most notably *Expression in America* (1932), the first full-scale psychoanalytic treatment of American literature.

He became the editor of the Zionist Organization of America's journal, *New Palestine* (1944), and joined the faculty of the newly formed Brandeis University (1948), in which capacity he was finally given the chance to teach Shakespeare. He held a chair in comparative literature there until his death in 1955.

In the following chapter entitled "The American Discovers Exile" taken from *Up Stream*, Ludwig Lewisohn describes a troubled arrival in New York City as a student at Columbia University. Through his experiences at Columbia, Lewisohn learns how feelings of exile are caused where discrimination exists.

CHAPTER 5

THE AMERICAN DISCOVERS EXILE.

I.

In those days the steamers from the South landed at piers on the North River. I was too deeply preoccupied with that first, tremendous, lonely plunge into the world to watch the harbor or the sky-line of New York. I stood on deck, grasping my valise tightly, holding my hat. The sharp wind was full of scurries of rain. It was almost dark when we passengers trickled across the plank into the appalling mud of the streets. The lower West side is, I still think, the dismallest port of the city. On that day, coming from the bland and familiar South and from a life that touched reality so feebly, it seemed brutal, ferocious, stark. . . . An indifferent acquaintance met me and hustled me to the nearest station of the Ninth Avenue "L." We climbed the iron staircase, scrambled for tickets and were jammed into a car. It was the evening rush hour and we had barely standing room. The train rattled on its way to Harlem. At One Hundred and Sixteenth Street we slid down in the elevator to the street, frantically dodged people and vehicles across Eighth Avenue, turned south and west and stood presently before one of a row of three story houses wedged in between huge, dark buildings. My guide introduced me to the boarding-house keeper, a hard-featured, heavily rouged woman who seemed in pain and in a hurry. They led me to a hall bedroom on the third floor, lit a whirring gas-jet and, in another minute, were gone. I put down my valise and took off my overcoat and stood still, quite still, between the bed and the chiffonier. I could touch one with either hand. I was in New York. I was alone.

At such moments one's intentions to conquer the world avail little. Especially if one is twenty. I heard the far away roar of New York like the roar of a sinister and soulless machine that drags men in and crunches them between its implacable wheels. It seemed to me that I would never be able to face it. I huddled in that small, cold room in an old traveling robe of my father's and bit my lips. But I had the manhood not to write home in that mood. Indeed my old stoicism had not deserted me and my parents never learned of the grinding misery of my first weeks in New York.

In the morning the October sun shone. At breakfast the landlady seemed not nearly so menacing. I may add at once that she was an intelligent and courageous woman who had suffered much and undeservedly and that we became great friends. She gave me on that first day what simple directions I needed. I left the house, walked to the corner and turned my face toward the west. Morningside Heights with its many poplars rose sheer against a sparkling autumn sky. The beauty of it seemed much colder to me that day than it does now. But it was beauty—something to dwell with, to calm and to console the mind. I took heart at once and climbed the heights and presently came upon the approach to the University library. The river shone still farther to the west, with the russet palisades beyond. But I hastened across the quadrangle, eager for some human contact in this new world full of cold power and forbidding brilliance.

Professor Brent of the department of English, with whom I had had some correspondence, received me with a winning kindliness. We had a talk the other day and I observed him and remembered the old days. He has grown grayer. Otherwise he is the same—the lank, unathletic but not graceless form, the oblong head lengthened by a pointed beard, the pleasant, humorous but powerful glance, the easy pose, tilted back in his chair, the eternal cigarette between his long, bony, sensitive fingers. A scholarly and poetic figure, languid enough, but capable of a steady tenacity at the urge of some noble passion of the mind. That he was a trenchant and intrepid thinker I always knew. How magnificently he would stand the ultimate intellectual test of this, or perhaps, any age, I was to learn much later. . . . He introduced me to Brewer, secretary of the department, a pale, hesitant, chill-eyed New Englander with a thin strain of rhetorical skill and literary taste.

German was to be my second "minor," largely because it would be easy and would give me more time for my English studies. And so I went to present myself to Professor Richard who had also written me a pleasant letter. I found him tall, erect, frugal and incisive of speech, a spirit of great rectitude, of a purity almost too intense to grasp the concrete forces and passions of the fevered world; clear, high-souled, a little passionless, but all that without effort or priggishness. His intellectual and artistic sympathies were, of course, limited. But within its limits his was an admirable and a manly mind.

The qualities of Brent and Richard did not, of course, reveal themselves to me at once. Nor, indeed, for long thereafter and then in private interviews and at club-meetings. The lectures of these excellent professors were dull and dispiriting to me. I found in them no living sustenance of any sort. For years I sought to grasp the reasons for this fact. I do not think I grasped them wholly until I myself began to lecture to graduate students and to have such students in my own seminar. I came to the university with the reading I have described. I knew all the books that once was required to know in the various lecture courses. What I wanted was ideas, interpretative, critical, aesthetic, philosophical, with which to vivify, to organize, to deepen my knowledge, on which to nourish and develop my intellectual self. And my friends, the professors, ladled out information. Poor men, how could they help it? I thought in those days that all graduate students knew what I and a small group of my friends knew. I am aware now of the literally incredible ignorance of the average bachelors of our colleges. . . . I cannot, of course, absolve the professors entirely, though only the rigorous veracity that gives its meaning to this narrative can force me to admit even so much of friends who have stood by me so long and so wholeheartedly as Brent and Richard. They did not give themselves enough, nor freely enough. They did not realize that, the elementary tools of knowledge once gained, there is but one thing that can teach men and that is the play of a large and an incisive personality. In a word, I was an ardent disciple and I found no master. So I drifted and occasionally "cut" lectures and wrote my reports and passed creditable examinations without doing a page of the required reading. I had done it all! I read for myself in entirely new directions—books that changed the whole tenor of my inner life—and struggled to make a living and wrote verses and walked and talked and sat in bar-rooms and cheap eating-houses with my friend Ellard— my friend of friends, whom I found at this time and who is still *animae dimidium meae*.

II.

It was a grey, windy November forenoon that we first talked on the steps of Fayerwether Hall. He was tall and lank and thin to emaciation. An almost ragged overcoat fluttered behind him, a shapeless, discolored hat tilted a little on his head. His delicate nostrils seemed always about to quiver, his lips to be set in a half-petulant, half-scornful determination. From under the hat shone two of the most eloquent eyes—fiery and penetrating, gloomy and full of laughter in turn—that were ever set in a human head. He spoke with large, loose, expressive gestures and with a strange, abrupt way of ending his sentences. I felt drawn to him at once. Freedom and nobility seemed to clothe him and a stoic wildness. A young eagle with plumage ruffled by the storm. . . . ! I asked him, I don't know why, whether he wrote verse. And when he said that he did I knew instinctively that his verses were better than mine, far better, and curiously enough I was not sorry but glad and, in a way, elated. I cannot tell at this distance of time how rapidly our friendship ripened, but I know that we soon saw a great deal of each other.

He lived in a small, crowded room up four flights of stairs. A large kerosene lamp stood on his study table. A sharp, triangular shadow lay steadily across bed and wall. He was tormented by poverty and love and by the intellectual bleakness that was all about us. For two years he had been at Bonn and though by blood a New England Brahmin of the purest strain, the sunny comradeship and spiritual freedom of the Rhineland city had entered into his very being. I see him standing there in the blue cloud of our cigarette-smoke chanting me his verses. I had never met a poet before and poetry meant everything to me in those days. A lovely or a noble line, a sonorous or a troubling turn of rhythm could enchant me for days. So that I was wholly carried away by my friend and his poems. And we both felt ourselves to be in some sort exiles and wandered the streets as the fall deepened into winter, engaged in infinite talk. We watched as evening came the bursting of the fiery blooms of light over the city and again, late at night, met in some eating-house or bar-room on Amsterdam Avenue where the belated, frozen car men watched us with heavy curiosity. We found ourselves then, as we have found ourselves ever since, in complete harmony as to the deeper things in life. That that harmony has become, if anything, more entire during the past seven crucial years of the world's history, I account as one of the few sustaining factors in my life and to it I attach, not foolishly I think, an almost mystical significance. . . .

I have been re-reading his poetry. I can detach it quite coldly now from the romance of our early comradeship, from the comforts of our maturer friendship. Nor am I as easily stirred as I was once. It is inferior to no poetry that has been written on this continent. At its best it is at least equal to the noblest passages of Emerson and it is far less fragmentary, far more sustained upon an extraordinary level of intellectual incisiveness, moral freedom and untraditional beauty. And there are many lines and passages that in their imagination and passion and wisdom cleave so deeply to the tragic core of life that they might bring tears to the eyes of grave and disillusioned men. . . . What has it availed him? His volumes scarcely sell; the manuscript of his third one is being hawked about from publisher to publisher. His verse is handicapped by its intellectual severity and its disdain of fashion—the poetic fashion of either yesterday or to-day. But it has the accent of greatness and that is bound to tell in the long run.

Other friendships there were for me at the university, pleasant enough at that time, but all impermanent save one more. I still count George Fredericks, sober-minded, virile, generous, among my chosen comrades. And I still think, with much kindness, of G. now a college professor in the East, a fine, pure spirit, a New Englander like Ellard, but unlike him striving quite in vain to transcend the moral and intellectual parochialism of his section and his blood. But, indeed, I sought no companionship, taking only such as came my way. For mean anxieties soon beset me as my slender borrowings came to an end and I tramped the streets in search of tutoring. A crowd of queer and colorful and comic scenes—sorrowful and humiliating enough at that time—floats into my mind. In a gorgeous palace near Central Park the footman eyed me contemptuously and an elderly woman tried to hire me to conduct her evidently rowdy boys to and from school. I refused curtly to do a nurse-maid's work. But walking across the rich carpet to the door I heard my torn shoes make a squdgy sound and almost repented. In another elaborate establishment I gave, in a very ready-made Louis XV room a single lesson to the young daughter of the house. Next day a note came dispensing with my services. I wasn't surprised. The girl was pretty and I was hungry for charm and love and she had evidently not disliked me. . . . At last I got a couple of boys to tutor (one a deaf-mute) and lessons in scientific German to give to the staff of one of the city institutions. Two evenings a week I was ferried across Hellgate in the icy wind to give this instruction. It was a bleak and tiresome business, but it paid room and board and tobacco and an occasional glass of beer.

III.

Meanwhile I read the nights away. Fascinating hints had come to me in Queenshaven, despite my whole-souled absorption in English literature, of certain modern German plays and poems and novels which seemed, by all reports, to differ wonderfully from both Schiller and Heine, the two German poets whom I knew best, and also from such popular mid-century writers as Scheffel and Heyse. But very few German books ever made their way to Queenshaven. Here, in the University library, I found them all and I read them all.

I read them with joy, with a sense of liberation, with a feeling that no other books in the world had ever given me. I struggled against that feeling; I seemed to myself almost disloyal to the modern English masters, to the very speech that I loved and which I hoped to write notably some day. But a conviction came upon me after some months with irresistible force. All or nearly all English books since Fielding were literature. This was life. All or nearly all the English literature by which our generation lives is, in substance, rigidly bounded within certain intellectual and ethical categories. This was freedom. I now understood my old, instinctive love for the prosemen of the eighteenth century. They had the sense for life—a life remote from ours, to be sure—but their sense of it was manly and incorruptible. In Wordsworth and in Tennyson I found substantially the same elevated sentiments. Except in the narrow field of the religious emotions, they and their contemporaries had no sense for reality at all, only for pseudo-nobility. And in English fiction, in 1904, all the people really held the same elevated sentiments, sentiments which were mostly false and unnecessary, and of course couldn't and didn't live up to them. They were all like poor Byron who half believed that one ought to be a Christian and a church-going householder and who was romantically desperate over his own wicked nature. Or they were like the slim, pale-eyed son of my old Sunday school superintendent. The lad had an excellent tenor voice and joined a small opera company. On one of his visits home he said to me with a troubled look in his eyes: "I don't see why I should be this way. My father's such a good man." . . . Of course I'm stating the case crassly and unjustly as one always does and must for the sake of emphasis. And, of course, I shall be held, whatever I say, to be approving a drifting with the passions of human life—like that of Burns—instead of an understanding and use and mastery of them. But it will not be denied by any really honest and penetrating thinker that English literature from Fielding until quite recently was curiously remote from life, curiously helpless and unhelpful and yet arrogant in the face of it. Such books as Moore's Esther Waters, which I hadn't read, and Wells' The Passionate Friends, which hadn't yet been written, have introduced into English letters an entirely new element of spiritual veracity and moral freedom. And these were the qualities which I found so pervasively and overwhelmingly present (yet with no lack of beauty and music in structure and style) in modern German literature. If in these books there was a noble sentiment it was there because it had grown inevitably from the sweat and tears, the yearning and the aspiration of our mortal fate—it was never set down because it was a correct sentiment to which human nature must be made to conform. I understood very fully now the saying of that character in one of Henry James' stories: "When I read a novel, it's usually a French one. You get so much more life for your money." I read French books, too. But compared to the German ones they seemed, as they are, rather hard and monotonous and lacking in spiritual delicacy. . . . Someone gave me a copy of Hans Benzmann's anthology of the modern German lyric. I found there an immediate rendering of life into art, not mere isolated elements of it selected according to a tradition of pseudo-nobility and then fixed in the forms of post-Renaissance culture. The pangs and aspirations of my own heart—and of all hearts, if men would but be honest among us—were here, the haunting echoes of my inner life, the deep things, the true things of which I had been ashamed and which I had tried to transmute into the correct sentiments of my Anglo-American environment—I found them all in the lyrical charm of these poets, in their music, which is the very music

of the mind, in their words, which are the very words of life.
They spoke my thoughts, they felt my conflicts; they dared
to be themselves—these modern men and women who were
impassioned and troubled like myself, who had not snared
the universe in barren formulae, but who were seekers and
strivers! They didn't know the whole duty of man; they didn't
try to huddle out of sight the eternal things that make us
what we are; they hadn't reduced the moral and spiritual life
of the race to a series of gestures of more than Egyptian
rigidity. They made me free; they set me on the road of trying to be not what was thought correct without reference to
reality, but what I was naturally meant to be. They taught
me, not directly, but by the luminous implications of their
works, the complete spiritual unveracity in which I had
been living and in which most of my Anglo-American
friends seemed to be living. . . . This whole process was, of
course, very gradual on its practical or outer side. Within
me, too, the old ready-made formulae would often arise to
inhibit or torment me. And from this conflict and turbidness
of feeling and vision there sprang some grave errors of action. But that was because my freedom was not yet a rational freedom, nor one corrected by a power of rational
experience. My youth had been passed amid so much false-
ness that my mastery of fact was quite inadequate for the
practice of a real moral freedom. I had no way at all of seeing things as they really are, no power of measuring the origin and direction of the forces that rule men and the world.
I was like someone to whom is offered the freedom of a
great library, but who had been deliberately mistaught the
meaning of the symbols in which the books are written. I
knew that it was my duty now to read for myself. I didn't
know how to read. I am struggling to express a difficult and
momentous truth: The young creators of new values come
to grief so often not because their values are wrong, nor because their rebellion is not of the very breath of the world's
better life. They come to grief because they have no mastery
of fact, because they carry with them the false old interpretations and conventional idealizations of man, and nature,

and human life. . . . Nevertheless the world now opened itself to me in a new guise. I had been accustomed, as I had been taught, to approve and to disapprove. Now for the first time I watched life honestly and lost myself in it and became part of it with my soul and my sympathies, detached only in the citadel of the analytic and recording, never more of the judging mind. I became aware of faces—the faces of people on the streets, in the cars, in the subway. And I no longer thought of people as good and bad or desirable or undesirable, but I saw in all faces the struggle and the passion and the sorrow, sometimes ugly, unheroic enough always by the old, foolish tests, but full of endless fascination. . . .

To a modern Continental, French or German or Italian, this whole matter will seem primitive and absurd. He may be sure that I am touching on the central weakness of the Anglo-American mind—its moral illusionism. That mind is generally quite sincere. It really arranges its own impulses and the impulses of other men in a rigid hierarchy of fixed norms. It has surrendered the right and the power of examining the contents of such concepts as "right," "wrong," "pure," "democracy," "liberty," "progress," or of bringing these conventionalized gestures of the mind to the test of experience. It has not, indeed, ever naively experienced anything. For it holds the examination of an experience in itself, and without reference to an anterior and quite rigid norm to be a "sin." It hides the edges of the sea of life with a board-walk of ethical concepts and sits there, hoping that no one will hear the thunder of the surf of human passions on the rocks below. . . .

IV.

A face, a voice, a gesture that seemed strange and unheard of arose before me and I was stricken by a blind and morbid passion. All the repressions of my tormented adolescence, all the false inhibitions in thought and deed now went toward the nourishing of this hectic bloom. It was winter. A white and silent winter. Playing with curious fancies we called our passion roses in the snow. I committed every extravagance and every folly. I knew nothing of life, nothing of human nature. I knew ethical formulae which, obviously, didn't apply—that were, at best, vicious half-truths. Thus all the defences of my soul broke down. I had never been taught a sane self-direction. The repetition of tribal charms which were quite external had been deemed a sufficient safeguard. Happily, though my passion was morbid enough and caused me untold suffering, it was blended with the love of letters and with a keen though unwholesome romance. There was nothing in it of baseness, nothing of degradation. I am not proud of it but I am not ashamed of it. I look back upon it and it blends, in strange tones, into the inevitable music of life—neither good nor evil, neither right nor wrong. We are both married now and meet in pleasant friendship and remember half-humorously that long ago— so long ago, it seems a fairy-tale—we caused each other delights and pangs and tears. . . .

But if I had a son I should say to him: "Dismiss from your mind all the cant you hear on the subject of sex. The passion of love is the central passion of human life. It should be humanized; it should be made beautiful. It should never be debased by a sense that it is in itself sinful, for that is to make the whole of life sinful and to corrupt our human experience at its very source. Love is not to be condemned and so degraded, but to be exercised and mastered. If you are of a cool temper and continence leaves your mind serene and your imagination unbesmirched, very well. But let not your soul, if it is ardent, become contaminated and disordered by false shames and a false sense of sin. Love in itself is the source of loveliness and wisdom if it is gratified without falsehood and without abandoning the sterner elements of life. Natural things are made sinful only by a mistaken notion that they are so. Account love, then, as inevitable and lovely, but remain master of your soul and of yourself and of the larger purposes which you were born to fulfill."

To me, as to every American youth, it had been said: "Passion, except within marriage, is the most degrading of sins. Within marriage it is forgiven but never mentioned as being, even there, unmentionable. This is the law." Meantime all the men and youths I knew slunk into the dark alleys of Queenshaven whither I did not follow them. And curiously, in that very act, they still believed the follies they proclaimed. They were simply moral men sinning against their own convictions. That astonishing ethical dualism of the English mind—(so truly and so moderately set forth by George Gissing in the memorable twentieth chapter of the third book of The Private Papers of Henry Ryecroft)—that ethical duality of conscience I hold the chief and most corrupting danger of our life as a people. It must be fought without ceasing and without mercy. . . .

Of that duality there was nothing in my being. I was bound or I was free. But having been a slave so long I ran amuck in my freedom and in the recoil came almost to utter grief. I was saved and made steadfast only by the thought of those two watchers in the distant South. However absorbed in that most passionate adventure, I never missed an opportunity of going home at Christmas or even at Easter—planned for it, saved for it, and always my mother's hand in mine and her eyes upon me made me well again.

Also I could now conquer many moods and free myself from them by fixing them in art. My verse was no longer the echo of a sonorous tradition. It grew no longer out of the love of poetry but out of the pain of life. And from my modern Germans as well as from a new and powerful movement in our English verse I learned to write directly and truly. Somehow, in Queenshaven, I had missed a poem which is not, of course, the greatest, but assuredly the most important English poem of the third quarter of the nineteenth century: Meredith's Modern Love. The application of English poetic art to the actual, the contemporary and the real had there been inaugurated. In addition I now read Henley and Housman's A Shropshire Lad and The Love Sonnets of Proteus and, above all, I found the two-volume edition of the poems of Arthur Symons. Granting the hostile critic his monotony of mood (but is not Shelley's mood quite as monotonous in a different spiritual key?), and his morbidness (though what is morbidness, after all?) and there remains in his work the creation of a new style, a new method, a new power. The conventional taste of his generation still lags behind his method, but in it is one of the essential forces of the future of English poetry.

V.

The various experiences which I have set down so briefly extended over two years. At the end of the first year I duly took my master's degree and applied for a fellowship. Among the group of students to which I belonged it was taken for granted that, since Ellard had completed his studies for the doctorate, I would undoubtedly be chosen. I record this, heaven knows, not from motives of vanity but as part of the subtler purpose of this story. The faculty elected my friend G. I went, with a heavy heart, to interview Professor Brewer, not to push my claims to anything, but because I was at my wits' end. I dreaded another year of tutoring and of living wretchedly from hand to mouth, without proper clothes, without books. Brewer leaned back in his chair, pipe in hand, with a cool and kindly smile. "It seemed to us," he stuttered, "that the university hadn't had its full influence on you." He suggested their disappointment in me and, by the subtlest of stresses, their sorrow over this disappointment. I said that I had been struggling for a livelihood and that, nevertheless, my examinations had uniformly received high grades and my papers, quite as uniformly, the public approval of Brent and himself. He avoided a direct answer by explaining that the department had recommended me for a scholarship for the following year. The truth is, I think, that Brewer, excessively mediocre as he was, had a very keen tribal instinct of the self-protective sort and felt in me—what I was hardly yet consciously—the implacable foe of the New England dominance over our national life. I wasn't unaware of his hostility, but I had no way of provoking a franker explanation.

I forgot my troubles in three beautiful months at home— three months seemed so long then—or, rather, I crowded these troubles from my field of consciousness. I wouldn't even permit the fact that I wasn't elected to a scholarship to depress me. Brewer wrote a letter of regret and encouragement that was very kindly in tone. The pleasant implication of that letter was, of course, a spiritual falsehood of the crassest. He knew then precisely what he knew and finally told me ten months later. But his kind has a dread of the bleak weather of the world of truth, and approaches it gingerly, gradually, with a mincing gait. He, poor man, was probably unconscious of all that. In him, as in all like him, the corruption of the mental life is such that the boundaries between the true and the false are wholly obliterated.

In the passionate crises of the second year I often walked as in a dream. And I was encouraged by the fact that the department arranged a loan for my tuition. In truth, I was deeply touched by so unusual a kindness and I feel sure that the suggestion came from Brent. If so, Brewer again did me a fatal injury by not preventing that kindness. For he had then, I must emphasize, the knowledge he communicated to me later—the knowledge that held the grim upshot of my university career.

Spring came and with it the scramble for jobs among the second year men. My friends were called in to conferences with Brewer; I was not. They discussed vacancies, chances here and there. It wasn't the chagrin that hurt so; it wasn't any fear for myself. After all I was only twenty-two and I was careless of material things. I thought of my father and my mother in the cruel sunshine of Queenshaven. Their hope and dream and consolation were at stake. I could see them, not only by day, but in the evening, beside their solitary lamps, looking up from their quiet books, thinking of me and of the future. . . . I remembered how my father had believed in certain implications of American democracy. I remembered . . . I was but a lad, after all. I couldn't face Brewer's cool and careless smile. I wrote him a letter—a letter which, in its very earnestness and passionate veracity must have struck like a discord upon the careful arrangements of his safe and proper nature. For in it I spoke of grave things gravely, not jestingly, as one should to be a New England gentleman: I spoke of need and aspiration and justice. His answer lies before me now and I copy that astonishingly smooth and chilly document verbatim: "It is very sensible of you to look so carefully into your plans at this juncture, because I do not at all believe in the wisdom of your scheme. A recent experience has shown me how terribly hard it is for a man of Jewish birth to get a good position. I had always suspected that it was a matter worth considering, but I had not known how wide-spread and strong it was. While we shall be glad to do anything we can for you, therefore, I cannot help feeling that the chances are going to be greatly against you."

I sat in my boarding-house room playing with this letter. I seemed to have no feeling at all for the moment. By the light of a sunbeam that fell in I saw that the picture of my parents on the mantelpiece was very dusty. I got up and wiped the dust off carefully. Gradually an eerie, lost feeling came over me. I took my hat and walked out and up Amsterdam Avenue, farther and farther to High Bridge and stood on the bridge and watched the swift, tiny tandems on the Speedway below and the skiffs gliding up and down the Harlem River. A numbness held my soul and mutely I watched life, like a dream pageant, float by me. . . . I ate nothing till evening when I went into a bakery and, catching sight of myself in a mirror, noted with dull objectivity my dark hair, my melancholy eyes, my unmistakably Semitic nose. . . . An outcast. . . . A sentence arose in my mind which I have remembered and used ever since. So long as there is discrimination, there is exile. And for the first time in my life my heart turned with grief and remorse to the thought of my brethren in exile all over the world. . . .

VI.

The subconscious self has a tough instinct of self-preservation. It thrusts from the field of vision, as Freud has shown, the painful and the hostile things of life. Thus I had forgotten, except at moments of searching reflection, the social fate of my father and mother, my failure to be elected to the fraternity at college, and other subtler hints and warn-

ings. I had believed the assertion and made it myself that
equality of opportunity was implicit in the very spiritual
foundations of the Republic. This is what I wanted to believe, what I needed to believe in order to go about the business of my life at all. I had listened with a correct American
scorn to stories of how some distant kinsman in Germany,
many years ago, had had to receive Christian baptism in order to enter the consular service of his country. At one blow
now all these delusions were swept away and the facts stood
out in the sharp light of my dismay. Discrimination there
was everywhere. But a definite and public discrimination
is, at least, an enemy in the open. In pre-war Germany, for
instance, no Jew could be prevented from entering the academic profession. Unless he was very brilliant and productive his promotion was less rapid than that of his Gentile
colleagues. He knew that and reckoned with it. He knew,
too, for instance, that he could not become senior professor
of German at Berlin (only associate professor like the late
R. M. Meyer), nor Kultusminister, but he could become a
full professor of Latin or philosophy, and, of course, of all
the sciences. I am not defending these restrictions and I
think the argument for them—that the German state was
based upon an ethnic homogeneity which corresponds to a
spiritual oneness—quite specious. I am contrasting these
conditions with our own. We boast our equality and freedom and call it Americanism and speak of other countries
with disdain. And so one is unwarned, encouraged and
flung into the street. With exquisite courtesy, I admit. And
the consciousness of that personal courtesy soothes the
minds of our Gentile friends. . . . It will be replied that there
are a number of Jewish scholars in American colleges and
universities. There are. The older men got in because nativistic anti-Semitism was not nearly as strong twenty-five
years ago as it is to-day. Faint remnants of the ideals of the
early Republic still lingered in American life. But in regard
to the younger men I dare to assert that in each case they
were appointed through personal friendship, family or financial prestige or some other abnormal relenting of the
iron prejudice which is the rule. But that prejudice has not,

to my knowledge, relented in a single instance in regard to the teaching of English. So that our guardianship of the native tongue is far fiercer than it is in an, after all, racially homogeneous state like Germany. Presidents, deans and departmental heads deny this fact or gloss it over in public. Among themselves it is admitted as a matter of course.

I have not touched the deeper and finer issues, though I have written in vain if they are not clear. My purest energy and passion, my best human aspirations have been dedicated from my earliest years to a given end. It was far more than a question of bread and butter, though it was that too. I didn't know how to go on living a reasonable and reasonably harmonious inner life. I could take no refuge in the spirit and traditions of my own people. I knew little of them. My psychical life was Aryan through and through. Slowly, in the course of the years, I have discovered traits in me which I sometimes call Jewish. But that interpretation is open to grave doubt. I can, in reality, find no difference between my own inner life of thought and impulse and that of my very close friends whether American or German. So that the picture of a young man disappointed because he can't get the kind of a job he wants, doesn't exhaust, barely indeed touches the dilemma. I didn't know what to do with my life or with myself.

In this matter of freedom and equality and democratic justice, then, I found in my Anglo-American world precisely that same strange dualism of conscience which I had discovered there in the life of sex. The Brewers in the academic world do truly believe that our society is free and democratic. When they proclaim that belief at public banquets a genuine emotion fills their hearts. Just as a genuine emotion filled the hearts of my Southern friends (who used Mulatto harlots) when in the interest of purity and the home they refused to sanction the enactment of any divorce law in their native state.

I do not wish to speak bitterly or flippantly. I am approaching the analysis of thoughts and events beside which my personal fate is less than nothing. And I need but think of my Queenshaven youth or of some passage of Milton or

Arnold, or of those tried friendships that are so large a part of the unalterable good of life, or of the bright hair and gray English eyes of my own wife to know that I can never speak as an enemy of the Anglo-Saxon race. But unless that race abandons its duality of conscience, unless it learns to honor and practice a stricter spiritual veracity, it will either destroy civilization through disasters yet unheard of or sink into a memory and into the shadow of a name.

Caste and Outcast
Dhan Ghopal Mukerji

Dhan Ghopal Mukerji was born into the Brahmin, or priest, caste on the outskirts of Calcutta, India, in 1890. As members of the highest caste, Mukerji's family was educated, although, as he explains in *Caste and Outcast* (1923), his mother, Bhuban Goswami Mukerji, could not read or write. Bhuban displayed her intellect and social standing instead with an extraordinary ability to tell epic Hindu religious tales; and memorizing these stories was Mukerji's first form of education. Mukerji also gained a traditional sense of English language and literature while attending a Presbyterian school at the age of ten. Both cultural legacies prepared Mukerji for a life of letters in America that he did not foresee while under the care of his parents. To continue a long lineage of Brahmin priests and appease his father, Kissori, Mukerji entered the Hindu priesthood at the age of fourteen and set out to make the customary two-year pilgrimage of beggary. This spiritual journey ended with Mukerji's decision to forsake this ancestral occupation and attend the University of Calcutta in 1908. Through British contacts, Mukerji moved to Japan a year later and studied engineering at Tokyo University. Unhappy with his education in Asia, Mukerji sailed for the United States in 1910 and expected to attend school there.

Arriving in San Francisco, Mukerji spent his last borrowed dollar to enter the University of California,

Berkeley, but he eventually left due to financial concerns in 1913. To earn money, Mukerji worked as a laborer in factories, and joined the Industrial Workers of the World, a socialist group. Mukerji eventually completed a Ph.D. in metaphysics at Stanford University in 1914, and began lecturing in comparative literature following graduation. He also gave lecture tours on Indian language and life to men's and women's clubs throughout the country. Throughout his education and teaching career, however, Mukerji harbored a deep desire to become an author. In 1914, he published the play *Chintamini*, and in 1916–17, he published two books of poetry entitled *Rajani: Songs of the Night* and *Sandhya: Songs of Twilight* to little critical attention. In 1918, Mukerji married an American woman, Ethal Ray Dugan of Norristown, Pennsylvania, a teacher, and he traveled with her to India.

Although he began his literary career writing for an adult audience, Mukerji is most famous for his children's books that often tell moral tales through interactions between humans, animals, and nature. Beginning with the publication of *Kari the Elephant* in 1922, Mukerji wrote six critically acclaimed juvenile books, including *Chief of the Herd* (1929) and *Gay-Neck, the Story of a Pigeon*, which won a Newbery Medal for children's literature in 1928. With these works, Mukerji attempted to render the "inmost things" of Hindu life with the English language. Reviewers such as Helen Ferris of *Bookman* (1928) and Dudley Cammett Lunt of the *New York Herald Tribune* (1929) commended Mukerji not for this attempt but for "beautiful language," "unusual style," and "sensitivity" to nature. Before his death in 1936, Mukerji reached out again to an adult audience with the publication of *Caste and Outcast*, his autobiography, and the nonfiction works of Indian history and culture *A Son of Mother India Answers* (1928) and *Visit India with Me* (1929). This prolific author died by suicide after a prolonged mental breakdown in New York City

In *Caste and Outcast*, Dhan Ghopal Mukerji emphasizes that spirituality is a daily part of life in India afforded to all members of society, however oppressed.
The chapter "What is the Answer?" questions how this
Indian sense of spirituality can survive in a free but capi-
talistic America.

CHAPTER 5

WHAT IS THE ANSWER?

When I reached San Francisco I found that the college
had opened already. I paid my fees there and found a
good job under a Negro woman, waiting on tables, washing
dishes, keeping the house clean. My zest for anarchism was
coming to an end. I began to see that there was nothing to
do but to find a new philosophy, something that had little
concern with the material future of mankind. It was during
this period that I began to rediscover India.

We had reached the fall of the year nineteen hundred and
twelve. Things, both political and otherwise, were ferment-
ing in India. Batches of Indian students began to come to
America for wisdom and knowledge and the more I saw
these men coming, the more I grew convinced that they
were coming through a desert to slake their thirst with the
waters of a mirage.

By now I had drunk the dregs of the Western civilization.
I found it had its vulgarity, its bitter indifference, its colos-
sal frauds. It has made just as many mistakes as India has in
her time. And yet there was something constructive in both
of these civilizations.

All these Indian students I met were nationalists. They
wanted to free India. As if a politically free India meant an
India traditionally and uniquely herself! Bitter quarrels ensued between myself and many of these Indians. These people thought that if India had factories and a government as

well as an army and navy of her own, she would be one of the civilized countries of the earth.

Take the typical Indian revolutionist. Many people remember him in San Francisco. He wanted to cut the throat of every English official just as he wanted to cut the throat of every Indian traitor. He meditated such a gigantic slaughter that he seemed to me like an epic poet of death. He contemplated vast holocausts as magnificent offerings to the god of Patriotism. He devised ingenious plans to blow up garrisons of English soldiers as a disinfectant and a preventive of political hells, and once in a while he would grow lyrical about the joy of belonging to a free people. He imagined very suave massacres, and delicate assassinations.

One day I told him, "Look here, why should we supersede British massacres by our own, except that our own may be a little more radical? Theirs are only practical and utilitarian."

He said, "Their massacres are continuous. Ours would be only momentary and purely unavoidable. There is economy in killing. If by killing a few hundred English you could create a free India, then it must be done. I am looking at it from the standpoint of economy."

"That is what wearies me so much," I answered. "Your economy is so scientific, your massacres are so hygienic, that I have no more interest in them than I have in conic sections. All your assassinations are mathematical and well founded in fact and if they really came off they would be more cruel than the massacre of St. Bartholomew or the Russian pogroms. These at least had a religion and a ritual to make them bearable."

To this he said, "You talk like a slave. Not only have the British conquered us, but they charge that rebellion is unholy, and a destructive profanity. If you could see their soulless railroads piercing through the sacred places throughout India, tunnelling the Himalayas like a monster driving its tentacles into the vitals of your body and sucking out your life blood! If you only realized and imagined these things vividly you would not be sitting here talking like a fool."

"It is true that this industrialization of Asia is terrible,"

I admitted. "It is sucking out the life blood of Asia, but your quarrel is not with the British nation, but with Western capitalism."

He shook his head and said, "No, if we had our own people exploiting the natural resources of our country, and if we had our own army and navy, we would be spending our money in our own country. Our money wouldn't be spent in England and Europe as it is spent by giving salaries to European officials. Think of it! If our dividends were paid to Indians in India, how much better off our country would be."

So he wanted to overcome imperialism by a nationalism just as crude and as greedy. I told him so, and added, "I do not like to interpret you this way."

"I don't care how you interpret me," he answered. "Your interpretations are tainted with pro-Western bias. You are a slave."

"But why," I asked him, "don't we think in terms of two classes, the possessing class and the dispossessed classes, throughout the world? These two marching against each other are to my mind the forces of the conflict. I cannot make out much difference between imperialism and nationalism."

To this his rejoinder was that I talked like a soulless Socialist.

"I am not a Socialist," I said. "I hate Socialism. Socialists only want to create a new authority in the place of an old one. What I want is to create a sense of freedom in people's souls. Then all will be well."

"How dare you talk about souls when the bodies are starving to death? How dare you insult a man dying for lack of food with your talk of philosophy?"

"Yes," I agreed, "you are right, but one must talk of souls after the body is fed. It is the most important thing according to our ancestors."

He was becoming more and more provoked with me and now sneered, "What do you know about your ancestors?"

I tried then another way and asked, "Tell me, how can I serve my country?"

He answered, "By holding your tongue."

However, I saw all kinds and shades of opinions regard-

ing nationalism in India. The most pathetic one that I came across was the following from another Hindu. I shall call him Nanda.

I said to Nanda, who was a recent arrival from India at that time: "Look here, I have been living in the West nearly three years now, and I am quite convinced that I have nothing to learn from the West. What we have to do is to go back to the belief of our ancestors that there is nothing wrong with this world. Whatever is wrong with the world is wrong with us first. So as we purify our own hearts and become holy men ourselves, the problem of the world will be solved. We must become like the gods. Then we shall want nothing because we have overcome our sense of want within ourselves. If we control our appetites by our soul, we will have very little to fight for and against. By changing ourselves we automatically change the world.

"You remember when Buddha walked by the harlot's house, the house became purified because a spiritual human being walked by it. So I think, Nanda, that the road open to us is not the way of the college, but the way of the spirit. And I do think in this matter our country can teach the West."

Nanda replied, "I agree with you that we have a spiritual wealth which is more important than our material wealth. The material wealth that we have underground in India combined with the cheap labor that lives above the ground is the thing that attracts Western exploitation. Western capitalism finds in those two factors enough inducement to come to India and to tear up the whole system of personal relationship founded on domestic industry, substituting in its place this terrible Western 'civilization.' Peasants are driven from their fields where they worked eight hours a day to other people's factories where they work twelve hours a day. When a peasant breaks the ground he sings, when he works in a factory he spits and swears."

And I added, "In order to overcome this great industrialization of the East by the West, we must overcome ourselves first. If we want to fight this gregarious gluttony which the

West brings to us, we must overcome our own gluttony. If we free ourselves from ourselves first, we will be able to save Asia from the West, I think, almost automatically."

"Well," said Nanda, "that is true. India has material resources and untold riches, and think of her subjective background of spiritual wealth. If the West could only tap this wealth! But how to give it, that is the problem. If we come to the West and say, 'We have spiritual wealth—take it from us,' the West will say, 'How can you be spiritual when you are a conquered race? Races that are truly spiritual have their own economic system and are masters of everything.' How are we going to meet this question of the West?"

I said, "I don't know. Do you?"

Nanda said, "The West will never accept the spirituality of the East until by force we free our country from any Western domination. In order to give the spirituality of India to the modern barbarism of Europe we must beat them at their own game. We must go through the necessary step of nationalism and nationality. Until we have a victorious India free from all foreign control and domination no proud Western nation will ever care to listen to our spiritual talk."

That afternoon with the thought of Nanda in my mind I went over to visit Jerry. What Nanda said troubled me. Must the East also be hooliganized in order to give the West its spiritual truth? Was it necessary?

At this time Leo and Jerry and Frank were living together and from San Francisco Frank was editing his Socialist weekly. He had shaved off his beard, and now that I did not need his money, with some saving, he had managed to buy for himself and the other two, new suits of clothes. When I came in they were all sitting together and talking.

Frank asked me, "Dhan, how long have you owned that grey suit?"

I said, "Two years."

"Well, when next week's salary comes I will go and buy you a new suit," Frank said; but Leo objected, urging immediate action.

"They will let you have it on credit," he said, "and you can pay them next week. Dhan looks like the devil in that suit, it looks like the national flag of India. I can recognize it from any distance."

So we went to the tailor's and they gave me a ready-made suit. These were the first new clothes that I had worn in nearly three years. I was so proud of them that I felt hurt because people didn't look at me. They always used to look at me when I came in with the other suit.

We adjourned to a pinochle joint, and discussed philosophy. I told Jerry what had passed between me and Nanda.

Frank said, "You know, Nanda must be a brilliant fellow!"

"I don't like it," said Leo. "These brilliant Indians, in order to overcome the intellectualism of the West, are creating a rival intellectualism of their own. I can quite imagine Gladstone or rather Lord Salisbury saying solemnly, 'We are forced to conquer the world in order to give it the benefit of the spirituality of our nation. England must take over miles of "undesirable territory" in order to give other nations her spiritual institutions, her moral wealth, and her Shakespeare. These Indians ought to know better than to tell us that they have to conquer us first in order to give us their spiritual wealth.' "

Suddenly Leo turned his gaze on me and asked, "Do you notice how the Western ruler is conquering India mentally? You are thinking in his terms!"

"That is true," said Frank, "but I think there is an aim to this whole thing. You know the Jewish history. The Jews are an oriental people. If I remember their book clearly, the greatest events came to them when they were either in exile or in captivity. Their important prophets arose when they were persecuted, and their greatest prophet came when they were groaning under the Roman rule.

"There is a curious thing. When Jesus was asked whether the Jews should pay taxes to Caesar, he said, 'Give unto Caesar what is Caesar's.' By this he meant to say to the Jews that it was easy to placate their Roman lords by sacrificing a few ounces of matter, gold or silver, which had no importance. But it was their relation to God which was of real value.

"Now I think," Frank continued, "that the Indian should

look at it in that way. He must not try to overcome Western
materialism with a rival materialism of his own. The Indian
who is an oriental must give an answer like Christ's—'I am
so busy with my spiritual business that I have no time to pay
attention to you who are demanding something material.'
And it is not a humiliation to belong to a conquered race.
The people that are most humiliated in this Indian-British
transaction are the British. They are damning their souls by
exploiting a race in the name of British liberty. They are
selling liberty as a prostitute sells her body.

"The Indian, on the contrary, is selling very little, so if I
were to choose between the conquered or the conqueror I
would prefer to be the conquered. At least your soul is
saved. Give your spirituality to the British as Christ gave
his to the Romans. And it is because you are conquered that
you are spiritually sound. If you were not conquered you
would not be spiritual."

I looked at Jerry because I knew that he did not have
Frank's systematic way of thinking, but he had a mind
which like the lightning cleaved the sky.

Jerry said, after a long pause, "It is all so unnecessary.
You may have a free country, but it does not follow that you
have a free soul. To give a man a vote in a so-called free
country is like giving a lantern to a blind man. What use is
it? We are in this world to destroy our blindness and then see
the light. And these fools come and want to make a ghastly
mockery of blindness by giving it a vote. Because every
blind voter has a vote which is his lantern, it does not necessarily follow that he will find the road to freedom. By
stringing blind men to blind men, you do not create vision.
The sophistry of these Indians is very brilliant, and like all
sophistry has its uses, but it always misleads the young, and
the young love to be deceived."

And Leo asked, "And the old, Jerry?"

"The old live by deceiving the young. The men work; the
women work and spend. Every folly thus is balanced with
irony, and every irony in turn begets its folly. This is the description of that brilliant chaos we call the universe."

"But, Jerry," I said, "what is the answer to all this?"

"There is an answer somewhere, but he who has found it, as some of your old Indian sages have done, knows that the little chalice of the human world cannot hold it."

A Daughter of the Samurai
Etsu Sugimoto

At the time of Etsu Sugimoto's birth in 1874 (born Et-
suko Inagaki), the place of the shoguns as Japan's most
powerful political and social leaders was seriously di-
minished under emperor Meiji (1868–1912). Through
Meiji's reforms to break the "old order" of samurai rule
(called the Meiji Restoration), Japan would become
an industrialized and westernized player in world politics. The young Sugimoto did not immediately feel the
strain of these changes from the snowy and remote province of her childhood (then called Echigo). There, she
was educated in silent self-discipline, duty, and honor
according to the *bushido* (warrior way of life) of her
ancestors, training as a Buddhist priestess and future
samurai's wife. Later, Sugimoto would remember the
seclusion of her childhood with nostalgia for a lost way
of life.

Strangely, it was Sugimoto's conservative father who
created the impetus for her emigration. Betrothed at the
age of thirteen to a Japanese businessman in America
(Matsuo), she attended an English school in Tokyo to
prepare for her marriage in 1901. Like many *issei*, or
first-generation Japanese in America at this time, Etsu
and Matsuo fully expected to return to their homeland as
richer, better-skilled citizens. Sugimoto was taken with
the education available in America for women, however,
and much to the disapproval of her parents, she wore
western dress, converted to Christianity, and remained

in the United States until her death in 1950. This experience is quite unlike the majority of other *issei* immigrants who toiled as laborers for low wages, only to be denied land-owning rights or citizenship by anti-Asian legislation across the country. These *issei* returned to Japan.

Sugimoto wrote her most successful work, *A Daughter of the Samurai*, while teaching Japanese language and culture at Columbia University in 1926. Although it was a popular nonfiction book before World War II, some postwar critics viewed it as an apology for American racism and imperialism. In addition to *A Daughter of the Samurai*, Sugimoto wrote three other works based on her heritage, *The Daughter of the Narikin* (1932), *A Daughter of the Nohfu* (1935), and *Grandmother O-Kyo* (1940). As an affluent, active member of American society, Sugimoto never fully reconciled the samurai teachings of her youth with the liberty of her immigration. In this section from her autobiography, Etsu Sugimoto records the inner conflicts she experienced as both a Japanese and an American woman.

CHAPTER 20

NEIGHBOURS

When I came to America I expected to learn many things, but I had no thought that I was going to learn anything about Japan. Yet our neighbours, by their questions and remarks, were teaching me every day new ways of looking at my own country.

My closest friend was the daughter of a retired statesman, the General, we called him, who lived just across the steep little ravine which divided our grounds from his. Our side was bordered by a hedge of purple lilacs, broken, opposite the path to the well, by a rustic drawbridge. One autumn afternoon I was sitting on the shady step of the bridge with a many-stamped package in my lap, watching for the postman. Just about that hour his funny little wagon, looking, with its open side-doors, like a high, stiff *kago*, would be passing on its return trip down the hill, and I was anxious to hurry off my package of white cotton brocade and ribbons of various patterns and colours—the most prized gifts I could send to Japan.

Suddenly I heard a gay voice behind me reciting in a high sing-song:

> Open your mouth and shut your eyes
> And I'll give you something to make you wise.

I looked up at a charming picture. My bright-eyed friend, in a white dress and big lacy hat, was standing on the bridge, holding in her cupped hands three or four grape leaves pinned together with thorns. On this rustic plate were piled some bunches of luscious purple grapes.

"Oh, how pretty!" I exclaimed. "That is just the way Japanese serve fruit."

"And this is the way they carry flowers," she said, putting down the grapes on the step and releasing a big bunch of long-stemmed tiger lilies from under her arm. "Why do Japanese always carry flowers upside-down?"

I laughed and said, "It looked very odd to me, when I first came, to see everybody carrying flowers with the tops up. Why do you?"

"Why—why—they look prettier so; and that's the way they grow."

That was true, and yet I had never before thought of any one's caring for the appearance of flowers that were being carried. We Japanese have a way of considering a thing invisible until it is settled in its proper place.

"Japanese seldom carry flowers," I said, "except to the temple or to graves. We get flowers for the house from flower-venders who go from door to door with baskets swung from shoulder poles, but we do not send flowers as gifts; and we *never* wear them."

"Why?" asked Miss Helen.

"Because they wither and fade. And so, to send flowers to a sick friend would be the worst omen in the world."

"Oh, what a lot of pleasure your poor invalids in hospitals are losing!" said Miss Helen. "And Japan is the land of flowers!"

Surprised and thoughtful, I sat silent; but in a moment was aroused by a question. "What were you thinking of when I came—sitting here so quietly with that big bundle on your lap? You looked like a lovely, dainty, picturesque little peddler."

"My thoughts were very unlike those of a peddler," I replied. "As I sat here watching the dangling end of the bridge chain I was thinking of a Japanese lover of long ago who crossed a drawbridge ninety-nine times to win his ladylove, and the one hundredth time, in a blinding snowstorm, he failed to see that it was lifted, and so fell to his death in the moat below."

"How tragic!" exclaimed Miss Helen. "What did the poor lady do?"

"It was her fault," I said. "She was vain and ambitious, and when she saw a chance to win the love of a high official at court, she changed her mind about her lover and commanded her attendants not to lower the bridge the day he expected to come triumphant."

"You don't mean that the cold-blooded creature actually planned his death?"

"It was the storm that caused his death," I said. "She was fickle, but not wicked. She thought that when he found the bridge lifted he would know her answer and go away."

"Well, sometimes our girls over here are fickle enough, dear knows," said Miss Helen, "but no American woman would ever do a thing like that. She was actually a murderess."

I was shocked at such a practical way of looking at my romantic tale, and hastened to add that remorseful Lady Komachi became a nun and spent her life in making pilgrimages to various temples to pray for the dead. At last she partially lost her mind, and, as a wandering beggar, lived and died among the humble villagers on the slopes of

Mount Fuji. "Her fate is held up by priests," I concluded, "as a warning to all fickle-minded maidens."

"Well," said Miss Helen, drawing a deep breath, "I think she paid pretty dearly for her foolishness, don't you?"

"Why—well, perhaps," I replied, rather surprised at the question, "but we are taught that if a woman so loses her gentle modesty that she can treat with scorn and disrespect the plea of a loyal lover, she is no longer a worthy woman."

"Suppose a man jilts a maid, what then?" quickly asked Miss Helen. "Is he no longer considered a worthy man?"

I did not know how to reply. Instinctively I upheld to myself the teachings of my childhood that man is the protector and guide and woman the helper—the self-respecting, but nevertheless, uncritical, dutiful helper. Often afterward Miss Helen and I had heart-to-heart talks in which her questions and remarks surprised and sometimes disturbed me. Many of our customs I had taken for granted, accepting the ways of our ancestors without any thought except that thus they had been and still were. When I began to question myself about things which had always seemed simple and right because they were in accordance with laws made by our wise rulers, sometimes I was puzzled and sometimes I was frightened.

"I am afraid that I am growing very bold and man-like," I would think to myself, "but God gave me a brain to use, else why do I have it?" All my childhood I had hidden my deepest feelings. Now again it was the same. My American mother would have understood, but I did not know; and so, repressing all outward signs, I puzzled my way alone, in search of higher ideals—not for myself, but for Japan.

Miss Helen's father was ninety years old when I knew him. He was a wonderful man, tall, with broad shoulders just a trifle stooped and with thick iron-gray hair and bushy eyebrows. A strong face he had, but gentle and humorous when he talked. I looked upon him as an encyclopedia of American history. I had always loved the study of history, in childhood and at school, but I had learned little of the details of America's part in the world; and would sit with the General and his invalid wife listening by the hour while he told stories of early American life. Knowing that incidents of personal history especially appealed to me, he once told me that his own large estate was bought by his father from an Indian chief in exchange for one chair, a gun, and a pouch of tobacco; and that Mother's large home was once an Indian village of bark tents and was purchased for half-a-dozen split-seated kitchen chairs. These incidents seemed to me almost pre-historic; for I had never known any one whose home did not date back into a far past.

When America was a still youthful nation the General had represented his country as a diplomat in Europe, and, with his beautiful young wife, had taken part in the foreign social life in Paris and later in Washington. My first glimpse of American life abroad, I received through the word pictures of this gracious lady, and through her experiences I began to understand, with sympathy, something of the problem in Japan of Americans trying to understand the Japanese, which heretofore I had looked upon only as the problem of Japanese trying to understand Americans.

From childhood until I met the General the word "ancient" had commanded my reverence. I had been conscious that the Inagaki family tree was rooted in a history centuries old, and that our plots in the cemetery were the oldest in Nagaoka. It had seemed an unquestioned necessity that we should follow the same customs that our ancestors had observed for hundreds of years, and it was my pride that they were the customs of a dynasty which was among the very oldest in the world.

After I became acquainted with the General and heard him talk of the wonderful development of a nation much younger than my own family tree, the word "ancient" lost some of its value. Even the General's own lifetime—the years of only one man's life—represented such a marvellous advance in national growth that sometimes I looked upon him almost with awe, wondering how much real value should be attached to antiquity. "Perhaps," I sometimes said to myself, "it would be better not to look back with such pride to a glorious past; but instead, to look forward to a glorious future. One means quiet satisfaction; the other, ambitious work."

One evening, after Matsuo and I had been over to call on the General, Miss Helen walked back with us across the drawbridge. Matsuo went on to join Mother on the porch, and Miss Helen and I sat down on the step of the bridge, as we often did, to talk.

"When Father told that story about Molly Pitcher," said Miss Helen, "I wondered if you were thinking about Japanese women."

"Why?" I asked.

"Well," she replied hesitatingly, "several times I've heard you say that American women are like Japanese. I don't see that Molly Pitcher is much of a Japanese specimen."

"Oh, you don't know Japanese history," I exclaimed. "We have many women heroes in Japan."

"Yes, of course," said Miss Helen quickly. "In every country there are heroic women who rise to noble sacrifice on occasion. But they are exceptions. Books and travellers all speak of Japanese women as being quiet, soft-spoken, gentle, and meek. That picture doesn't apply to the American type of women."

"The training is different," I said, "but I think that at heart they are much the same."

"Well," said Miss Helen, "when it becomes the fashion for us to wear our hearts on our sleeves, perhaps we will appear gentle and meek. But," she added as she rose to go, "I don't believe that Japanese men think as you do. To-night, when I spoke of the book on Japan that I have been reading, and said that I believed the author was right when he declared that 'for modesty and gentle worth, Japanese women lead the world,' your husband smiled and said, 'Thank you,' as if he thought so too."

"Miss Helen," I said earnestly, "although our women are pictured as gentle and meek, and although Japanese men will not contradict it, nevertheless it is true that, beneath all the gentle meekness, Japanese women are like— like—volcanoes."

Miss Helen laughed.

"You are the only Japanese woman that I ever saw—
except at the Exposition," she said, "and I cannot imagine
your being like a volcano. However, I'll give in to your superior knowledge. You have had Molly Pitchers among
your women, and flirts—that Lady What's-her-name whom
you told me about the other day: she *was* a flirt, with a
vengeance!—and now you say that you have volcanoes.
Your demure-appearing countrywomen seem to have surprising possibilities. The next time I come over I'm going
to challenge you to give me a specimen of a Japanese genuine woman's-rights woman."

"That is easy," I said, laughing in my turn. "A genuine
woman's-rights woman is not one who *wants* her rights, but
one who *has* them. And if that means the right to do men's
work, I can easily give you a specimen. We have a whole island of women who do men's work from planting rice to
making laws."

"What do the men do?"

"Cook, keep house, take care of the children, and do the
family washing."

"You don't mean it!" exclaimed Miss Helen, and she sat
down again.

But I did mean it, and I told her of Hachijo, a little island
about a hundred miles off the coast of Japan, where the
women, tall, handsome, and straight, with their splendid
hair coiled in an odd knot on top of the head, and wearing
long, loose gowns bound by a narrow sash tied in front,
work in the ricefields, make oil from camellia seeds, spin
and weave a peculiar yellow silk which they carry in bundles on their heads over the mountains, at the same time
driving tiny oxen, not much larger than dogs, also laden
with rolls of silk to be sent to the mainland to be sold. And in
addition to all this they make some of the best laws we have
and see that they are properly carried out. In the meantime,
the older men of the community, with babies strapped to
their backs, go on errands or stand on the street gossiping
and swaying to a sing-song lullaby; and the younger ones
wash sweet potatoes, cut vegetables, and cook dinner; or, in

big aprons and with sleeves looped back, splash, rub, and wring out clothes at the edge of a stream.

The beginning of this unusual state of things dates back several centuries, to a time when the husbands and sons were forced to go to another island about forty miles away, for fishing, very little of which could be done near Hachijo. When silk proved more profitable than fish, the men returned to the island, but the Government was in capable hands which have never given up their hold.

I told all this to Miss Helen, and closed by saying, "A subject for your meditation is the fact that with these women rulers, both men and women are healthy and happy; and the social life there is more strictly moral than it is in any other community of equal intelligence in Japan."

"You had better join the Equal Suffrage party," said Miss Helen, "and go on the lecture platform with that story. It has a list toward moral uplift and might win voters for the cause. Well," and again she rose to go, "your women are such unexpected creatures that I am more than ever convinced that American women are not like Japanese. We talk so much and are so noisily interested in public affairs that we are expected to do almost anything. Whatever happens, we cannot surprise the world. But for one of your timid, shrinking kind suddenly to burst out into a bold, strong act, like lifting drawbridges and that sort of thing, completely upsets our pre-conceived ideas. And then to hear of its being quietly but effectively done *en masse*, like those island women, is rather—disconcerting."

She ran over the bridge, calling back, "Anyway, although you are the sweetest little lady that ever walked on sandals, you haven't convinced me. American women are *not* like Japanese women—more's the pity!"

With this absurd compliment from my extravagantly partial friend ringing in my ears, I started to walk toward the porch, when suddenly a voice called from the dusky shadows across the bridge, "Oh, I didn't think of Mrs. Newton! I'll give up. *She* is like a Japanese woman. Good-night."

I smiled as I walked on toward the porch, for I was thinking of something Mother had told me that very morning about Mrs. Newton. She was our nearest neighbour on the opposite side of our place from Miss Helen's home, and I knew her very well. She was a gentle woman, soft-voiced and shy, who loved birds and had little box-houses for them in her trees. I understood why Miss Helen should say that she was like a Japanese woman, but I had never thought that she was. Her ideas were so very sensible and practical; and she allowed her husband to be too attentive to her. He carried her cloak and umbrella for her; and once, in the carriage, I saw him lean over and fasten her slipper strap.

What Mother had told me was that, a few days before, Mrs. Newton was sitting by the window sewing, when she heard a frightened chirping and saw a large snake reaching up the trunk of a tree to one of her bird-boxes on a low branch. She dropped her sewing, and running to a drawer where her husband kept a gun, she shot through the open window, right into the snake's head, and her little bird family was saved.

"How could she do it?" I said to Mother. "I never would have believed that frail, delicate Mrs. Newton would dare even *touch* a gun. She is afraid of every dog on the street, and she starts and flushes if you speak to her unexpectedly. And then, anyway, how could she ever *hit* it?"

Mother smiled.

"Mrs. Newton can do many things that you don't know about," she said. "When she was first married she lived for several years on a lonely ranch out West. One stormy night, when her husband was gone, she strapped that same gun around her waist and walked six miles through darkness and danger to bring help to an injured workman."

I recalled Mrs. Newton's soft voice and gentle, almost timid manner. "After all," I said to myself, "she *is* like a Japanese woman!"

From Immigrant to Inventor
Michael Pupin

Pulitzer prize–winning author and inventor Michael
Pupin was born in 1858 in the village of Idvor, Hungary.
From the beginning of his life, his mother taught him
the importance of education. As he outgrew school in
Idvor, switching to a higher-level school in nearby
Panchevo, Pupin's desire to learn more surpassed even
his mother's ambitions. In *From Immigrant to Inventor*,
Pupin recalls one instance when he excitedly told his
family about Ben Franklin's research with electricity
and thunderstorms only to have them pointedly remind
him that thunder was caused by St. Elijah's cart rolling
through the sky. When Pupin went to study in Prague,
experiences with ethnic prejudice convinced him that
only in America would he find complete freedom to
learn all that he wanted to know. He arrived in New York
in 1874.

Pupin worked at odd jobs while obtaining education
and a knowledge of English. He attended classes at Cooper
Union, where his interest in science flourished. He entered Columbia University on a full scholarship in 1879,
and immersed himself in becoming an American through
studies as well as athletics. Pupin was popular and academically successful, graduating a day after he received
his American citizenship. He then went on to Cambridge
University on a fellowship to study physics. At Cambridge and at the University of Berlin, Pupin's growth
was nurtured by some of the scientific world leaders, in-

cluding Herman von Helmholtz, Frankland Faraday, and Heinrich Hertz. Pupin returned to Columbia to teach in 1889, and his electrical studies there led to several important patented inventions. His first well-known invention shortened the time needed for an x-ray photograph, so that the technology could be used diagnostically for more people in a shorter period of time. His work on the inductance coil, also known as the "Pupin coil," allowed long-distance telecommunication. His last invention was the electrical resonator, which clarified sound transmission for radio and television.

Though his major impact was on the field of science, Pupin left his mark on literature as well. *From Immigrant to Inventor*, his successful autobiography, was published in 1923 and reprinted eleven times from 1923 to 1926, winning the Pulitzer Prize in 1924. Pupin's appointments included the presidency of the American Association for the Advancement of Science from 1925 to 1926. During World War I, as a result of propaganda and financial support for Serbia, he was appointed Honorary Consul General of New York and received the Order of the White Eagle. After several years of poor health, Pupin died in New York City in 1935.

Some of Pupin's most joyous moments in *From Immigrant to Inventor* were experienced in his undergraduate years at Columbia. Having achieved his long-cherished dream of being accepted to college, Pupin embraced the opportunities for friendship and learning he found there. In the chapter "From Greenhorn to Citizenship," Pupin's hard hours of work and study began to pay off.

FROM GREENHORN TO CITIZENSHIP

. . . .Several incidents in my college career bear upon the interesting feature of athletics in American college life, and I shall describe them later even at the risk of appearing egotistical. This feature is characteristically American and is quite unknown on the continent of Europe.

Eight hours each day I devoted to study: three in the morning to Greek, three in the afternoon to Latin, and two in the evening to other studies. It was a most profitable summer outing of over three months, and it cost me only thirty dollars; the rest was paid in sawing and splitting of kindling-wood. Whenever I read now about the Kaiser's activities at Doorn, I think of my summer activities in 1879, and I wonder who in the world suggested my scheme to William Hohenzollern!

During the last week of September of that year I presented myself at Columbia for entrance examinations. They were oral, and were conducted by the professors themselves and not by junior instructors. The first two books of the Iliad, excepting the catalogue of ships, and four orations of Cicero, I knew by heart. My leisure time at my Passaic River "villa" had permitted me these pleasant mental gymnastics; I wanted to show off before Bilharz with my Greek and Latin quotations; to say nothing of the wonderful mental exhilaration which a young student gets from reading aloud and memorizing the words of Homer and of Cicero. The professors were greatly surprised and asked me why I had taken so much trouble. I told them that it was no trouble, because Serbs delight in memorizing beautiful lines. The Serbs of Montenegro, for instance, know by heart most of the lines which their great poet Nyegosh ever wrote, and particularly his great epic "The Mountain Glory." I told them also of illiterate Baba Batikin, the minstrel of my native village, who knew most of the old Serbian ballads by heart. Besides, I assured the professors, I wanted to do in Greek and Latin as well as I possibly could, so as to gain free tuition. For the other studies I was not afraid, I told them, and they assured me that my chances for free tuition were certainly good. The other examinations gave me no trouble, thanks to my training with Bilharz and with the lecturers in the evening classes at Cooper Union. A note from the Registrar's office informed me a few days later that I was enrolled as a student in Columbia College with freedom from all tuition fees. There was no person in the United States on that glorious day happier than I!

The college atmosphere which I found at Columbia at that time gave me a new sensation. I did not understand it at first and misinterpreted many things. The few days preceding the opening of the college sessions I spent chasing around for a boarding-house, while my classmates were hanging around the college buildings, making arrangements to join this or that fraternity, and also solidifying the line of defense of the freshmen against the hostile sophomores. There was a lively process of organization going on under the leadership of groups of boys who came from the same preparatory schools. These groups led and the others were expected to follow without a murmur. Insubordination or even indifference was condemned as lack of college spirit. This spirit was necessary among the freshmen particularly, because, as I was informed later, there was a great common danger—the sophomores! I saw some of this feverish activity going on, but did not understand its meaning and hence remained outside of it, as if I were a stranger and not a member of the freshman class, which I heard described, by the freshmen themselves, as the best freshman class in the history of Columbia. The sophomores denied this in a most provoking manner; hence the hostility. Nobody paid any attention to me; nobody knew me, because I did not come from any of the preparatory schools which prepared boys for Columbia. One day I saw on the campus two huge waves of lively youngsters beating against each other just like inrolling waves of the sea lifting on their backs the returning waves which had been reflected from the cliffs of the shore. The freshmen were defending a cane against fierce attacks of the sophomores. It was the historic Columbia cane rush, I was told by Michael, the college janitor, who stood alongside of me as I looked on. It was not a real fight resulting in broken noses or blackened eyes, but just a most vigorous push-and-pull contest, the sophomores trying to take possession of a cane which a strong freshman, surrounded by a stalwart body-guard of freshmen, was holding and guarding just as a guard of fanatic monks would defend the sacred relics of a great saint. This freshmen group was the centre of the scrimmage and it stood there like a high rock in the midst of an angry sea. Coats and shirts were torn off the backs of the brave fighters, some attacking and others defending the central group, but not a single ugly swear-word was heard nor did I see a single sign of intentional bloodshed. Members of the junior and senior classes watched as umpires. Michael, the janitor, who knew everybody on the college campus as a shepherd knows his sheep, was not quite certain about my identity. He asked me whether I was a freshman, and when I said "yes," he asked me why in the world I was not in the rush, defending the freshmen body-guard. He looked so anxious and worried that I felt sure of being guilty of some serious offense against old Columbia traditions. I immediately took off my coat and stiff shirt and plunged into the surging waves of sophomores and freshmen and had almost reached the central body-guard of freshmen, eager to join in its defense, when a sophomore, named Frank Henry, grabbed me and pulled me back, telling me that I had no business to cross the line of umpires at that late moment. I did not know the rules of the game and shoved him aside and we clinched. He was the strongest man in Columbia College, as I learned later, but my kindling-wood operations on the banks of the Passaic River had made me a stiff opponent. We wrestled and wrestled and would have wrestled till sunset like Prince Marco and the Arab Moussa Kessedjia in the old Serbian ballads, if the umpires had not proclaimed the cane rush a draw. The main show being over, the side show which Henry and I were keeping up had no further useful purpose to serve, and we stopped and shook hands. He was glad to stop, he admitted, and so was I, but he told my classmates that "if that terrible Turk had been selected a member of the freshmen body-guard the result of the cane rush might have been different." I told him that I was a Serb, and not a Turk, and he apologized, saying that he could never draw very fine distinctions between the various races in the Balkans. "But, whatever race you are," said he, "you will be a good fellow if you will learn to *play the game*." Splendid advice from a college boy! *"Play the game,"* what a wonderful phrase! I studied it long, and the more I thought about it the more I was convinced that one aspect of the history of this country with all its traditions is summed up in these three words. No foreigner can understand this country who does not know the full meaning of this phrase, which I first heard from a Columbia College youngster. No foreign language can so translate the phrase as to reproduce its brevity and at the same time convey its full meaning. But, when I heard it, I thought of the bootblacks and newsboys who, five years previously, had acted as umpires when I defended my right to wear a red fez. To "play the game" according to the best traditions of the land which offered me all of its opportunities was always my idea of Americanization. But how many immigrants to this land can be made to understand this?

Some little time after this incident I was approached by the captain of the freshman crew, who asked me to join his crew. I remembered young Lukanitch's opinion about oarsmanship at Columbia, and I was sorely tempted. But, unfortunately, I had only three hundred and eleven dollars when I started my college career, and I knew that if I was to retain my free tuition by high standing in scholarship and also earn further money for my living expenses I should have no time for other activities. "Study, work for a living, no participation in college activities outside of the recitation-room! Do you call that college training?" asked the captain of the freshman crew, looking perfectly surprised at my story, which, being the son of wealthy parents, he did not understand. I admitted that it was not, in the full sense of the word, but that I was not in a position to avail myself of all the opportunities which Columbia offered me, and that, in fact, I had already obtained a great deal more than an immigrant could reasonably have expected. I touched his sympathetic chord, and I felt that I had made a new friend. The result of this interview was that my classmates refrained from asking me to join any of the college activities for fear that my inability to comply with their request might make me feel badly. I had their sympathy, but I missed their fellowship, and therefore I missed in my freshman year much of that splendid training outside of the classroom which an American college offers to its students.

At the end of the freshman year I gained two prizes of one hundred dollars each, one in Greek and the other in mathematics. They were won in stiff competitive examinations and meant a considerable scholastic success, but, nevertheless, they excited little interest among my classmates. Results of examinations were considered a personal matter of the individual student himself and not of his fellow classmen. The prizes were practically the only money upon which I could rely to help carry me through my second year. The estimated budget for that year, however, was not fully provided for, and I looked for a job for the long summer vacation. I did not want a job in the city. My kindling-wood activity of the preceding summer suited me better, and after some consultation with my friend Christopher, the kindling-wood peddler of Rutherfurd Park, I decided to accept a job on a contract of his to mow hay during that summer in the various sections of the Hackensack lowlands. No Columbia athlete ever had a better opportunity to develop his back and biceps than I had during that summer. I made good use of it, and earned seventy-five dollars net.

When my sophomore year began I awaited the cane rush which, according to old Columbia custom, took place between the sophomores and the freshmen at the beginning of each academic year, and I was prepared for it; I knew also what it meant to "play the game." This time my class had to do the attacking and I helped with a vengeance. The muscles which had been hardened in the Hackensack meadows proved most effective and the result was that shortly I had the freshmen's cane on the ground, and was lying flat over it, covering it with my chest. The pressure of a score of freshmen and sophomores piled up on top of me threatened to squeeze the cane through my chest bone, which already, I imagined, was pressing against my lungs, my difficult breathing leading me to think that my last hour had come. Fortunately, the umpires cleared away the lively heap of struggling boys on top of me, and I breathed freely again. Some freshmen were found stretched alongside of me with their hands holding on to the stick. An equal number of sophomores held on, and, consequently, the umpires declared the rush a draw. Nobody was anxious to have another rush, and it was proposed by the freshmen to settle the question of class superiority by a wrestling-match, two best out of three falls, catch as catch can. They had a big fellow who had some fame as a wrestler of great strength, and they issued a defiant challenge to the sophomores. My classmates held a meeting in order to pick a match for the freshman giant, but nobody seemed to be quite up to the job. Finally I volunteered, declaring that I was not afraid to tackle the freshman giant. "Do you expect to down him with Greek verses and mathematical formulæ?" shouted some of my classmates, who had grave doubts about the muscle and the wrestling ability of a fellow who had won Greek and mathematical prizes. They knew nothing about my strenuous mowing in the Hackensack meadows during three long months of that summer. The captain of the class crew approached me, felt my biceps, my chest, and my back, and shouted, "All right!" the wrestling-match came off, and the freshman giant had no show with a boy who had learned the art of wrestling on the pasture-lands of Idvor, and had held his own against experienced mowers in the Hackensack meadows. The victory was quick and complete, and my classmates carried me in triumph to Fritz's saloon, not far from the college, where many a toast was drunk to "Michael the Serbian." From that day on my classmates called me by my first name and took me up as if I had been a distinguished descendant of Alexander Hamilton himself. My scholastic victory in Greek and mathematics meant nothing to my classmates, because it was a purely personal matter, but my athletic victory meant everything, because it was a victory of my whole class. Had I won my scholastic victory in competition with a representative from another college, then the matter would have had an entirely different aspect. *Esprit de corps* is one of those splendid things which American college life cultivates, and I had the good fortune to reap many benefits from it. He who pays no attention to this *esprit de corps* in an American college runs the risk of being dubbed a "greasy grind."

The sophomore year opened auspiciously. Eight of my classmates formed a class, the Octagon, and invited me to coach them in Greek and in mathematics, twice a week. The captain of the class crew was a member of it. I suspected that he remembered my reasons for refusing to join the freshman crew and wanted to help. The Octagon class was a great help in more ways than one. I gave instruction in wrestling also to several classmates, in exchange for instruction in boxing. This was my physical exercise, and it was a strenuous one. Devereux Emmet, a descendant of the great Irish patriot, was one of these exchange instructors; he could stand any amount of punishment in our boxing bouts, which impressed upon my mind the truth of the saying that "blood will tell." Before the sophomore year was over my classmates acknowledged me not only a champion in Greek and in mathematics but also a champion in wrestling and boxing. The combination was somewhat unusual and legends began to be spun about it, but they did not turn my head, nor lull me to sleep, not even when they led to my election as class president for the junior year. This was indeed a great compliment, for, because of the junior promenade, the dance given annually by the junior class, it was customary to elect for that year a class president who was socially very prominent. A distinguished classmate, a descendant of the three great American names, and a shining light in New York's younger social set, was my chief opponent and I begged to withdraw in his favor; a descendant of Hamilton inspired awe. But my opponent would not listen to it. He was a member of the most select fraternity and not at all unpopular, but many of my classmates objected to him, although he was the grandson of a still living former Secretary of State and chairman of the board of trustees of Columbia College. They thought that he paid too much attention to the fashionplates of London, and dressed too fashionably. There were other Columbia boys at that time who, I thought, dressed just as fashionably, and yet they were very popular; but they were fine athletes, whereas my

opponent was believed to rely too much upon the history
of his long name and upon his splendid appearance. He
certainly was a fine example of classical repose; his classmates, however, admired action. He was like a young Alci-
biades in breeding, looks, and pose, but not in action.

Some of the old American colleges have been accused
from time to time of encouraging snobbery and a spirit of
aristocracy which is not in harmony with American ideas of
democracy. My personal experience as student at Columbia
gives competency to my opinion upon that subject. Snobs
will be found in every country and clime, but there were
fewer snobs at Columbia in those days than in many other
much less exalted places, although Columbia at that time
was accused of being a nest of dudes and snobs. This was
one of the arguments advanced by those friends of mine at
the Adelphi Academy who tried to persuade me to go to
Princeton or Yale. The spirit of aristocracy was there, but it
was an aristocracy of the same kind as existed in my native
peasant village. It was a spirit of unconscious reverence for
the best American traditions. I say "unconscious," and by
that I mean absence of noisy chauvinism and of that racial
intolerance by which the Teutonism of Austria and the Magyarism of Hungary had driven me away from Prague and
from Panchevo. A name with a fine American tradition back
of it attracted much attention, but it was only a letter of
recommendation. He who was found wanting in his make-
up and in his conduct when weighed by the best Columbia College traditions—and they were a part of American
traditions—had a lonely time during his college career, in
spite of his illustrious name or his family's great wealth.
Foreign-born students, like Cubans and South Americans,
met with a respectful indifference so long as they remained
foreigners. Needless to say, many of them adopted rapidly
the attractive ways of the Columbia boys. But nobody
would have resented it, or even paid any attention to it, if
they had retained their foreign ways. A hopeless fellow became a member of that very small class of students known
at that time as "muckers." They complained bitterly of
snobbery and of aristocracy. I do not believe that either the

spirit of plutocracy, or of socialism and communism, or of any other un-American current of thought could ever start from an American college like Columbia of those days, and bore its way into American life. That type of aristocracy which made the American college immune from contagion by un-American influence existed; it was very exacting, and it was much encouraged. But when American college boys, accused of bowing to the spirit of aristocracy, have among them a Hamilton, a Livingston, a DeWitt, and several descendants of Jay, and yet elect for class president the penniless son of a Serbian peasant village, because they admire his mental and physical efforts to learn and to comply with Columbia's traditions, one can rest assured that the spirit of American democracy was very much alive in those college boys.

My success with the Octagon class established my reputation as a doctor for "lame ducks." This was the name of those students who failed in their college examinations, usually examinations in Greek, Latin, and mathematics. Lame ducks needed a special treatment, called *coaching*. I became quite an expert in it, and presently I saw a flock of lame ducks gathering around me, offering liberal rewards for a speedy cure. My summer vacations no longer called me to the Passaic River to cut kindling-wood, nor to the Hackensack meadows to strain my back to the utmost trying to keep up with experienced mowers. Coaching lame ducks was incomparably more remunerative and also left me with plenty of leisure time for tennis, horseback riding, or swimming and diving contests. During the college sessions I usually had in charge several bad cases of academic lameness, cases that could not be cured during the summer vacations, but had to be carefully nursed throughout the whole academic year. Financially I fared better than most of my young professors, and I saved, looking ahead for the realization of a pet dream of mine. My coaching experience was remunerative not only from the material but also from the cultural side; it brought me in touch with some of the best exponents of New York's social life, where I found a hearty welcome, a friendly sympathy, and many lessons which I considered as among the most valuable acquisitions in my college life. One of them deserves special mention here.

Lewis Morris Rutherfurd, a trustee of Columbia College, was at that time the head of the famous Rutherfurd family. He was a gentleman of leisure and devoted himself to science and particularly to photographic astronomy, just as did his famous friend, Doctor John William Draper, the author of the "History of the Intellectual Development of Europe." Rutherfurd was a pioneer worker in this field of astronomy, and his photographs of the moon and of the stars were always regarded by the scientists of the world as most valuable contributions to astronomy. The historic Rutherfurd mansion, with its astronomical observatory, was on Eleventh Street and Second Avenue. Rutherfurd's sons, Lewis and Winthrop, were my fellow students at Columbia; Lewis was a year ahead of me and Winthrop was a year below me. Through their cousin, a chum and classmate of mine, I became acquainted with them. No handsomer boys ever sat in Hamilton Hall: tall, athletic, and graceful, just like two splendid products of the physical culture of classical Greece. One of them held the American championship in racquets, and the Long Island hunt clubs counted them among their best steeplechase riders. Lewis just squeezed his way through college, but Winthrop, owing to circumstances beyond his control, threatened to drop by the academic roadside; the load of some seven conditions was too heavy and too discouraging.

My chum, Winthrop's cousin mentioned above, was a brilliant raconteur, and he used to spin out with wonderful skill many a funny tale about my coaching experiences, describing in a grotesque manner how an audacious youngster, straying over here from a Serbian peasant village, was bullying young aristocrats of New York, and how these aristocrats were submitting to it like little lambs. Rutherfurd, senior, who was my chum's uncle, heard some of these humorous tales. He enjoyed them hugely, and they suggested to him a scheme for diminishing somewhat his son's heavy load of conditions. He and his family were to spend the summer of 1882 in Europe, and he suggested that Winthrop and I go to his country place, where we could rule supreme and spend the summer preparing for Winthrop's autumn examinations. Winthrop consented, in order to please his family, and he agreed to the definite programme of work which I prescribed. Rutherfurd, senior, was anxious that Winthrop should breathe the atmosphere of Columbia College for four years, even if he should not get the full benefit of the college curriculum. He had a view of college education which was somewhat novel to me and made me understand more clearly the question which the captain of the freshman crew had addressed to me in my freshman year: "Study, work for a living, no participation in college activities outside of the recitation rooms! Do you call that college training?" But I shall return to this a little later.

"Winthrop is very fond of you," said Rutherfurd, senior, before he sailed for Europe, "and if you fail to pull him through, that will be the end of his college career. Your job is a difficult one, almost hopeless, but if you should succeed you would place me under a very great obligation." I was already under great obligations to him, for he had disclosed a view of the world of intellect before my eyes such as nobody else ever had. New York never produced a finer type of gentleman and scholar than was Lewis Rutherfurd. His personality impressed me as Henry Ward Beecher's had, and I could easily have persuaded myself that he was the reincarnation of Benjamin Franklin. I vowed to spare no effort in my attempts to "place" him "under a very great obligation."

Winthrop co-operated at first. But Winthrop's friends at the Racquet Club, at the Rockaway Hunt Club, and at Newport were puzzled, and they inquired what strange influences kept Winthrop in monastic seclusion at the Rutherfurd Stuyvesant estate in the backwoods of New Jersey. Besides, a stableful of steeplechasers, which had won many prizes, stood idle and looked in vain for their master, Winthrop, to train them. Even the servants on the estate looked puzzled and could not decipher the mysterious change that had come over their young autocrat. A foreign-born youngster, a namesake of Michael, the Irish gardener on the estate, seemed to be supreme in authority, and that puzzled the servants still more. Winthrop was making great scholastic efforts, in order to please his distinguished father, but he was a high-strung youth and after a while his behavior began to suggest the fretting of a thoroughbred protesting against the bit handled by the heavy touch of an unskilled trainer. I saw a crisis approaching, and it finally came. Winthrop suddenly refused to do another stroke of work unless the programme of work was greatly modified to permit him to make occasional trips to the Racquet Club, to the Rockaway Hunt Club, and to Newport. I knew what that meant, and promptly refused; a hot discussion followed, and some harsh words were spoken, resulting in a challenge by Winthrop; I accepted and agreed that the best man was to have his way during the remainder of the summer. Winthrop, the great racquet player of America, the famous steeplechase rider of Long Island, and the young aristocrat, kept his word, and responded eagerly to my calls for additional scholastic efforts. He was a noble, handsome, and manly American youth whose friendship I was proud to possess.

In the autumn Winthrop got rid of most of his conditions, proceeded with his class, and eventually graduated from Columbia in 1884. My imaginative chum, Winthrop's cousin, composed a great tale describing this incident and called it: "A Serbian Peasant versus an American Aristocrat." Those who had the good fortune to enjoy the humor of this tale (and among them was F. Marion Crawford, the novelist and cousin of my chum) pronounced it a great literary accomplishment, and they all agreed that Winthrop was the real hero of the story; he had played the game like a thoroughbred. Mr. Rutherfurd, senior, enjoyed the tale as much as anybody, and he was delighted with the result of our summer work. Winthrop's behavior did not surprise him, because, he assured me, Winthrop played the game as every American gentleman's son would have played it. "Every one of your classmates," exclaimed this trustee of Columbia College, "would have done the same thing; or he would be unworthy of a Columbia degree." The first function of the American college, according to him, was to train its students in the principles of conduct becoming an American who is loyal to the best traditions of his country.

My senior year opened even more auspiciously than my sophomore or my junior year had. Lewis Rutherfurd, trustee of Columbia College, gentleman and scholar, and famous scientist, became my mentor. Winthrop's success was to place him under very great obligations to me, he had said before he sailed for Europe in the spring, and after his return his actions proved that he had meant even more than he had said. A father could not have been more solicitous about my future plans than he was, and his advice indicated that he understood my case much better than I did myself. At the beginning of my senior year I was still undecided as to what I was to do after graduation, and I began to feel anxious; my mentor's advice was most welcome, and it certainly was one of the determining factors of my future plans.

In my preceding account of my preparations for college and of my life in college there is much which sounds like a glorification of muscle and of the fighting spirit. I feel almost like apologizing for it, but do I really owe an apology? My whole life up to this point of my story was steered by conditions which demanded muscle and the fighting spirit. To pass six weeks during each one of several summers as herdsman's assistant in company with twelve other lively Serb youngsters as fellow assistants, meant violent competitions in wrestling, swimming, herdsman's hockey, and other strenuous games for hours and hours each day, and one's position in this lively community depended entirely upon muscle and the fighting spirit. Magyarism in Panchevo and Teutonism in Prague produced a reaction which appealed to muscle and to the fighting spirit, which finally drove me to the land of Lincoln. Muscle and the fighting spirit of the bootblacks and newsboys on Broadway met me on the very first day when I ventured to pass beyond the narrow confines of Castle Garden, in order to catch my first glimpse of the great American metropolis. No sooner had I finished serving my apprenticeship as green-

horn, and advanced to a higher civic level, than I encountered again muscle and the fighting spirit of the college
boys. In the beginning of my college career I found very little difference between the pasture-lands of my native village and the campus of the American college. The spirit of
playfulness and the ferment of life in the hearts of youth
were the same in both, and were manifested in the same
way, namely, in athletics which encourage a glorification of
muscle and of the fighting spirit. This was most fortunate
for me, because it offered me a wide avenue by which I
could enter with perfect ease into that wonderful activity
called college life. Other avenues existed, but to a Serbian
youth who but a few years before had been a herdsman's assistant these other avenues were practically closed. I have
described the avenue which was open to me, but with no
intention to indulge in an egotistical glorification of that
avenue.

Rutherfurd, my mentor, scholar, scientist, and trustee of
Columbia College, did not believe as some people do that
athletics would ever cause our colleges to degenerate into
gladiatorial schools. Athletics in the form of wrestling and
boxing did not interfere in the least with my scholarship.
Healthy young people and healthy young nations are prone
to worship the heroic element in human life, thought trustee
Rutherfurd, and, according to him, the Greeks, by the art of
physical culture, prevented this exuberance of youth from
degenerating into brutality. He was longing forty years ago,
and I am still longing today, for the time when American
colleges will have a four years' course in physical culture,
conducted by medical and athletic experts. His sons, he
thought, practised this art by their devotion to the game of
racquets and of steeplechase riding. They were splendid
athletes, but nevertheless they were mellow-hearted and
gentle youths. The fact that their scholarship was not high
did not disturb their learned father, because much of his
own scholarship and scientific learning, he told me, had
been acquired long after he had graduated from Williams
College.

Many of my fellow students were, just like myself, very

fond of athletics and of other activities outside of the college curriculum, and yet we were enthusiastic students of Greek literature, of history and economics, of constitutional history of the United States, and of English literature. But here was the secret: Professor Merriam was a wonderful expounder of the great achievements of Greek civilization; Professor Monroe Smith made every one of us feel that history was in indispensable part of our daily life; Professor Richmond Mayo-Smith made us believe that political economy was one of the most important subjects in the world; and Professor Burgess' lectures on the Constitutional History of the United States made us all imagine that we understood the spirit of 1776 just as well as Hamilton did. These professors were the great scholars of Columbia College when I was a student there, and they had most attractive personalities too. The personality of the professors, like that of the famous Van Amringe, and their learning, like that of the venerable President Barnard, were the best safeguards for students who showed a tendency to devote themselves too much to the worship of muscle and the fighting spirit, and of activities outside of the college curriculum. Fill your professorial chairs in colleges with men of broad learning, and of commanding personality, and do not worry about the alleged evil influences of athletics, and of other college activities outside of the recitation-room. That was the recommendation of trustee Rutherfurd forty years ago; to-day I add: the college needs great professors just as much as the various research departments of a university need them; perhaps even more.

Literary societies, college journalism, glee-club practice, and exercises in the dramatic art consumed, when I was a college student, just as much of the college student's time as athletics did. They and athletics constituted the outside college activities. The recitation-room brought the student into touch with the personalities of the professors; college activities outside of the recitation-room, whether they were athletics or anything else, brought the student into touch with the personalities of his fellow students. Each one of these influences had, according to the experiences of my college life, its own great value, and contributed its distinct share to what is usually called the character-forming of the college student, but what Rutherfurd, the Columbia College trustee, called training in the principles of conduct becoming an American who is loyal to the best traditions of his country. Neither one nor the other influence can be weakened without crippling seriously that great object which trustee Rutherfurd called "the historical mission of the American college."

There was another educational activity which should be mentioned here. My regular attendance at Plymouth Church I considered one of my most important college activities outside of the recitation-room. Beecher's sermons and Booth's interpretations of Shakespeare were sources of stirring inspiration. They occupied a very high place among my spiritual guides. Beecher, Booth, and several other men of genius who were active in New York in those days were, as far as my college training was concerned, members of the Columbia College faculty. This is what I probably meant when I said to my friends at the Adelphi Academy that "Columbia College in the City of New York" was the port for which I was sailing and that Beecher's church in Brooklyn was a component part of Columbia College. Taking college activities in this broader sense I always believed that the spiritual, intellectual, and artistic activities in the city of New York were component parts of Columbia College; they certainly contributed much to the fulness of my college life. I often wondered whether this was in the minds of those who framed the official name "Columbia College in the City of New York," when the old name "King's College" was abandoned in 1787.

I have nearly finished the story of my college career, and I am aware that it is silent on a subject which was always dear to my heart; that subject is science. A young lad who was stimulated so much by the lives of the men represented in the Cooper Union library painting, entitled "Men of Progress"; by the splendid scientific exhibits in Philadelphia in 1876; by Jim's boiler-room demonstrations supplemented by Cooper Union lectures on heat; by Tyndall's and Hunt's poetic descriptions of scientific achievements; and above all by his own visions concerning physical phenomena on the pasture-lands of his native village—that lad goes through college, and the story of his college career is nearly closed without saying anything about his scientific studies at Columbia College! That certainly looks strange, and suggests the inference that after all Bilharz had finally succeeded in tearing me away completely from what he called the worship of scientific materialism. Bilharz did not succeed in that, but what he actually did is worth relating here.

After my departure from Cortlandt Street, Bilharz felt quite lonesome and tried to get companionship and consolation from a Tyrolean zither which he managed well in spite of his stiff fingers. Knowing my fondness for Homer's heroic verse and for the lyric verse in the chorus of Greek dramas, he practised reciting them with zither accompaniment. He thus initiated most successfully a Serbian guslar's recitations of old Serbian ballads, accompanied by the single-string instrument, called *gusle*. In recognition of the success of his clever scheme, which, I was sure, he had devised for my special benefit, I called him the Greek guslar. He who has seen huge multitudes of Serbs assembled around a blind guslar in the midst of some great festive gathering, listening by the hour in spellbound silence to his recitations, will understand how Bilharz managed to attract me to many a neighborhood gathering on the top loft of the Cortlandt Street factory. Every time I listened to the zither accompanying his chanting of familiar Greek verses I imagined that Baba Batikin's spirit was transferred from the little peasant village of Idvor to the great metropolis of America! Whenever I told him that, he seemed to be immensely pleased, because the life of a blind guslar appealed to him much. Professor Merriam was certainly a great Greek scholar, but Bilharz was a great Greek guslar, and when he chanted the verses of the Iliad with zither accompaniment I was tempted to imagine that he was a reincarnation of Homer. Between Bilharz and Merriam I could not help devoting much of my time in college to the study of Greek. I have never regretted it, but I do regret that the academic halls of the American colleges of to-day do not resound any more with that solemn Greek rhythm which I first heard on the top loft of the Cortlandt Street factory. Bilharz disappeared from Cortlandt Street a short time before I graduated, and he left me his zither as a souvenir, and also an old edition of Homer's Iliad by the famous German philologist Dindorf. I have not seen him since that time, but I shall never forget him. He was the first to call my attention to an old and magnificent civilization, the spiritual beauty of which appealed to my young imagination with increasing force as my knowledge of it increased. I often recall his almost fanatical dislike of mechanisms, and wonder what he would say to-day if he heard the pianola, the phonograph, and some of the distortions of radio broadcasting, to say nothing of the dramatic atrocities of the kinematograph!

On the other hand, the growth of my understanding from the first day of my landing at Castle Garden was due to my feeding upon the spiritual food offered to me daily by a civilization in which I was living, and which I wished to understand but did not understand. My preparation for college lifted here and there the mist which prevented my vision from seeing the clear outline of American civilization. Columbia College brought me into touch with the college life of American boys and with men of great learning and wonderful personalities, and they helped me to dispel every particle of that mist, and there in the clear sunshine of their learning I saw the whole image of what I believed to be American civilization: a beautiful daughter of a beautiful mother, which is the Anglo-Saxon civilization. The memory of this vision always recalled to my mind the ode of Horace which opens with the line:

O matre pulchra filia pulchrior!

The study and the contemplation of these two civilizations, the ancient civilization of Greece and the new civilization of the Anglo-Saxons, which appealed to me as the two greatest civilizations of human history, made every other study in my college curriculum appear insignificant, although I gained several prizes in the exact sciences, and although I never gave up the idea that my future work would be in the field of science.

But there is another and perhaps the most potent reason why science figures so little in the preceding part of the story of my college career. Instruction in the exact sciences in those days was most elementary, not only at Columbia College but also in most American colleges. For instance, laboratory work in physics and in chemistry was not a part of the Columbia College curriculum, and the lecture-room told me less about physics than I had known from my studies of Tyndall's popular publications and from the Cooper Union instruction before I entered college. The question "What is Light?" I brought with me from the pasture-lands of my native village, and the professor of physics at Columbia College offered no answer to it except to refer to vibrations in an ether, the physical properties of which he admitted he could not satisfactorily describe. On this point he did not seem to be much wiser than my humble teacher Kos in Panchevo. My mentor, Rutherfurd, was always interested in this question, as in many other advanced questions in science, and he took much delight in discussing them with me. He was the first to inform me that the great question, "What is Light?" would probably be answered when we understood more clearly a new electrical theory advanced by a Scotch physicist, Maxwell by name, who was a pupil of the great Faraday.

One day toward the end of my senior year I told my mentor, Rutherfurd, of a lecture-room experiment performed by Rood, his friend, at that time professor of physics at Columbia College. This experiment was the first announcement to me that Faraday was one of the great discoverers in electrical science. The experiment was simplicity itself, and consisted of a loose coil of copper wire, held in the left hand of the lecturing professor, the terminals of the coil being connected to a galvanometer supported on the wall of the lecture-room, so that its needle could be seen by every student in the room. When Rood, like a magician manipulating a wand, moved with his right hand a small magnet toward the coil, the distant galvanometer needle, impelled by a force which up to that time was a mystery to me, swung violently in one direction, and when the magnet was moved away from the coil the galvanometer needle swung just as violently in the opposite direction. When one terminal, only, of the coil was connected to the galvanometer, and thus the electric circuit of the coil was broken, the motion of the magnet produced no effect. *"This is Faraday's discovery of Electromagnetic Induction,"* said Rood with a deep sigh, and ended the lecture without any further comment, as if he wished to give me a chance to think it over before he added additional information. Rutherfurd knew Rood's picturesque mannerism, and my description of the experiment amused him. He suggested that the good professor was very fond of mystifying his students. I certainly was much mystified and did not wait for the next lecture to clear the mystery, but spent all day and most of the night reading about Faraday's wonderful discovery. It was made over fifty years before that time, but I had never known anything about it, although Edison's dynamos in his New York Pearl Street station had been supplying for over a year thousands of customers with electric power for incandescent lighting. Columbia College was not one of these customers for a long time after my graduation. When I finished my description of the experiment, and assured Rutherfurd that it was the most thrilling physical phenomenon that I had ever seen, and that I had remained awake almost all night after seeing it, he looked pleased, and informed me that this very phenomenon was the basis of Maxwell's new Electrical Theory.

That was the experiment which helped me to decide a very weighty question. Professor Rood had informed me that in recognition of my high standing in science as well as in letters I could choose either of two graduate fellowships, one in letters or one in science, each worth five hundred dollars a year. Either would have meant an additional three years of graduate study at Columbia. I was much tempted to turn to letters and continue my work with Merriam, the idol of all Columbia College students, including myself, who had felt the wonderful charm of his personality and of his profound and at the same time most picturesque classical scholarship. But the magic experiment which had told me the first story of Faraday's great discoveries, and had aroused my dormant enthusiasm for physics, caused me to bid good-by to Merriam and turn to science, my first love. Nevertheless, I did not accept the fellowship in science and stay three years longer at Columbia; I preferred to take up the study of Faraday and of Maxwell in the United Kingdom, where these two great physicists were born and where they had made their great discoveries. Trustee Rutherfurd and his young nephew, my chum and classmate, John Armstrong Chanler, applauded my decision, and promised to assist me in my undertaking whenever assistance should be needed. Rutherfurd assured me that I should certainly succeed as well in my scientific studies in European universities as I had succeeded in my general cultural studies at Columbia College, if the revelations of the new world of physics, certainly in store for me, could arouse in me the same enthusiasm which had been aroused by the revelations of that new spirit and that new current of thought which had given birth to the American civilization. That this enthusiasm would not be wanting was amply demonstrated, he said, by the effect which Faraday's fundamental experiment had produced in my imagination.

Professor Burgess, my teacher in constitutional history, had assured me, toward the end of the senior year, that I was fully prepared for American citizenship, and I had applied for my naturalization papers. I received them on the day before I was graduated. Two ceremonies which are recorded in my life as two red-letter days took place on two successive days; it is instructive to give here a brief comparison between them. The ceremony which made me a citizen of the United States took place in a dingy little office in one of the municipal buildings in City Hall Park. I received my diploma of Bachelor of Arts in the famous old Academy of Music on Fourteenth Street on the following day. There was nobody in the naturalization office to witness the naturalization ceremony except myself and a plain little clerk. The graduation ceremonies in the Academy of Music were presided over by the venerable President Barnard; his luxuriant snowy-white locks and long beard, and his luminous intelligence beaming from every feature of his wonderful face, gave him the appearance of Moses, as Michael Angelo represents him; and the academy was crowded with a distinguished and brilliant audience. The little clerk in the office handed me my naturalization papers in an offhand manner, thinking, apparently, of nothing but the fee due from me. President Barnard, knowing of my high standing in the graduating class and of my many struggles to get there, beamed with joy when he handed me my diploma amidst the applause of my numerous friends in the audience. When I left the naturalization office, carrying my precious multicolored and very ornate naturalization papers, the crowd in City Hall Park was moving about as though nothing had happened; but when I stepped down from the academy stage, with my Columbia diploma in hand, my old friend Doctor Shepard handed me a basket of roses with the best wishes of his family and of Henry Ward Beecher; Mr. and Mrs. Lukanitch were there, and the old lady kissed me, shedding tears copiously and assuring me that if my mother were there to see how well I looked in my academic silk gown she also would have shed many a tear of joy; numerous other friends were there and made much fuss over me, but all those things served only to increase the painful contrast between the gay commencement ceremonies and the prosy procedure of my naturalization on the preceding day. One ceremony made me only a Bachelor of Arts. The other made me a citizen of the United States. Which of the two should have been more solemn?

There was a picture which I had conjured up in my imagination when first I walked one day from the Cortlandt Street factory to Wall Street to see the site of old Federal Hall. The picture was that of Chancellor Livingston administering the constitutional oath of office to President Washington. To me it was a picture of the most solemn historical act which New

York or any other place in the world ever had witnessed. When the little clerk in the naturalization office handed me my naturalization papers, and called upon me in a perfunctory way to promise that I would always be loyal to the Constitution of the United States, the picture of that historical scene in Federal Hall suddenly reappeared to me, and a strange mental exaltation made my voice tremble as I responded: "I will, so help me God!" The little clerk noticed my emotion, but did not understand it, because he did not know of my long-continued efforts throughout a period of nine years to prepare myself for citizenship of the United States.

As I sat on the deck of the ship which was taking me to the universities of Europe, and watched its eagerness to get away from the busy harbor of New York, I thought of the day when, nine years before, I had arrived on the immigrant ship. I said to myself: "Michael Pupin, the most valuable asset which you carried into New York harbor nine years ago was your knowledge of, and profound respect and admiration for, the best traditions of your race . . . the most valuable asset which you are now taking with you from New York harbor is your knowledge of, and profound respect and admiration for, the best traditions of your adopted country."

The Soul of an Immigrant
Constantine Panunzio

In 1885, Constantine Panunzio was born in Molfetta, a village in southern Italy. He was named after his deceased grandfather, both a doctor and a lawyer who was admired throughout Molfetta for his professional skills and patriotism. Panunzio's grandmother swore that she would make little Constantine into an exact replica of his grandfather. Thus, when Panunzio began school, he was already burdened with the knowledge that he must enter a profession. Even at that early age, Panunzio already had a different occupation in mind: he wanted to become a sailor. Despite his father's best efforts to the contrary, Panunzio dropped out of *gimnasio* in 1897, signed up as a "stub," or sailor boy with the schooner *Angelo*, and sailed around Italy for two years. Although Panunzio was curious to see America, his immigration was unintentional. During a long voyage to Montevideo, the young sailor became homesick, abandoned his shipmates in Boston, and planned to remain in the United States only until he could afford a return passage home to Italy. The date of Panunzio's arrival was July 4, 1902.

Without knowing any English, Panunzio first looked for manual labor among recent Italian immigrants in Boston. Panunzio found it difficult, however, to make a livable income under the *padrone* system enforced by dominant figures in the Italian-American community. Left unpaid by bosses time and time again, Panunzio learned English and sought better employment. Once outside of the *padrone* system, Panunzio's sympathy for the plight of fellow immigrants grew, and the one-time sailor became inspired by social advocates at a Methodist mission. Just before World War I, Panunzio converted to Methodism, became ordained as a minister, and worked in several eastern cities as a mediator between Italian immigrants and their predecessors. Following this conversion experience, Panunzio never strayed from the conviction that good Americans could help immigrants assimilate. He hypothesized that the idea of the "alien" was born because people from the crowded immigrant ghettos were not offered the education that would encourage them to be useful citizens. To heighten awareness of such injustices inflicted upon immigrants in America, Panunzio published *The Deportation Cases of 1919–1920,* an account of actual government decisions to deport immigrants due to their ethnicity. Further Congressional actions to bar entrance to the United States following 1920 compelled Panunzio to write his personal story, *The Soul of an Immigrant.* Because Panunzio expressed a deep sense of patriotism and loyalty to the United States in *The Soul of an Immigrant,* he was honored at the 1939–40 New York World's Fair as a foreign-born citizen who had made outstanding contributions to American culture. Panunzio went on to become a professor of sociology at the University of California. He died in 1964.

In the following chapters Constantine Panunzio returns to Italy, not just as a long-lost son, but as an American soldier in World War I, to experience at once two compelling forces: his new identity and his old way of life.

Be it weakness, it deserves some praise,
We love the play-place of our early days.
The scene is touching and the heart is stone
That feels not at that sight, and feels at none.
. . . .

This fond attachment to the well-known place
Whence first we started into life's long race,
Maintains its hold with unfailing sway,
We feel it e'en in age and our latest day.

WILLIAM COWPER.

CHAPTER 19

HOME!

Fifteen years had now passed since landing in this country. During all this time my people had never ceased to entreat me to return, and I had ever kept before me the dream of going back, at least for a brief visit. I had planned each year to do so, but never had enough money to make the trip. That I had worked faithfully and continuously no one could question; many times not eight or ten hours a day, but fourteen and sixteen; and I had even done night work in order to make both ends meet. I had driven myself so hard and so incessantly that vigor and health were fast slipping away. Again and again I was forced to count the pennies, wondering what further sacrifices I could possibly make that I might have just enough for a visit home. There were times when a longing for the sight of my people was almost unbearable. All that I had gone through in America would make itself felt with a tremendous accumulative power. I could again see my meager earnings being taken away from me; I could feel anew the bitter insults, the unfavorable discrimination, the ridicule, the prejudice; I could see again the prison walls within which I had been enclosed; I could experience again the pangs of hunger, the shivering cold, the hateful persecutions, the awful, terrible loneliness. My soul would almost cry out in madness for just a glimpse of those I loved and had "lost a while." With a wide ocean lying between, and with no money with which to go *and return to America*, my dream of seeing my people again was fast vanishing.

"And return to America," I said. For now I was of America. Sometimes I would wonder just how I would feel if I were suddenly placed among my relatives in Italy. Would I, after all, feel at home even for a day? Would I want to remain in Italy, should the opportunity arise, and enter some form of public life there? I did not know.

Then came the World War and thoughts something like these ran through my mind. Suppose that Italy should side with one of the powers and America with another, just where would I stand, just where would my loyalty lie? The answer came in an unforeseen manner. One day I chanced to be in Plymouth, Massachusetts. Naturally I went to visit Plymouth Rock with a group of friends. I was standing upon the Rock when patriotic emotions which I had never experienced before gripped me and a sudden revelation of all that America had stood for throughout its history and what it had meant to me, dawned upon me in a forceful manner. With the least possibility of harm coming to America, it was borne in upon my consciousness what she now meant to me. America in all her fullness was the very life of me. Later America entered the War. One evening I was walking through the Common when I looked up and there, high above my head, on the roof of one of the highest buildings facing the historical grounds, and shot through with a radiant light, I saw the Stars and Stripes, refulgent and glorious in her streaming. Again an inexplicable something gripped the very soul of me and I worshipped as if at a shrine. Where would my loyalty lie? No answer! I have often wondered since then whether native-born Americans ever feel anything like what I felt on those two occasions.

And it was that very vision that, by a series of unforeseen circumstances, was to lead me back to my native Italy. Even before America declared war, I offered myself to the Government for military service. When enlistments began, I

twice volunteered in the hope that, notwithstanding my de-
fective eye, I might get into the ranks before the authorities
should become too particular. It was one of the most disap-
pointing experiences of my life to be rejected. I still sought
a possible way of serving this country in the war. Finally, as
a last resort, I enlisted for service with the Y. M. C. A. and
went to France. I had been there about a month and a half
when I was ordered to go to Italy, with the first Y.M.C.A.
party, five in all, sent to that country.

Headed by that man of magnificent spirit, Doctor John S.
Nollen, formerly president of Lake Forest University, on
January 3, 1918, we crossed the French-Italian border at
Modane. As the train slowly wound its way down into the
valley, the cold, ugly fogs of northern France gave way to
the radiant sunshine of Italy. The warm sun rays were flood-
ing the plains below. The mountains, snow-capped, stood
out clear-cut as diamonds, as if God had made them that
very morning. Italy was wonderful; Italy of my childhood.
A flood of emotion surged through my being, warm as the
sun rays, pure as the summit snows. For a time I closed my
eyes; I could not bear the glory of the sight; at last I was in
my native Italy! Donizetti's famous lines and strains of music came to my mind:

> Oh, Italia, Italia beloved,
> Land of beauty, and sunlight and song!—
> Tho' afar from thy bright skies removed,
> Still our fond hearts for thee ever long!

It was my good fortune to visit my people soon after my
arrival in Italy. There was an important errand to be done in
connection with the American Aviators who were then located at Foggia, and I was detailed to do it. Naturally, since
I was so near, I seized the opportunity to visit my native
town which I had not seen for these many years.

On my way from Naples to Foggia, while passing through
that delightful country which Horace so beautifully painted
centuries ago, I sat reading a book about that section of Italy
and meditating. Into my compartment came a man with

a valise, who from his appearance I recognized as a late comer from America. Seeing me in the American uniform, he at once opened a conversation in what he would have called English. He told me he had just returned from far-off America, how many years he had been there, what a good country it was, how much money he had made, and so on. I do not know whether he thought I questioned his statements, or that I did not understand his wretched English, but whatever the reason, he proceeded to furnish proofs of his long residence in America. First he showed me a dollar bill, much the worse for wear; then a watch, an "Ingersoll," and a cheap chain. Finally, he opened his valise and showed me several presents which he was taking to his relatives, among others a much-prized "Big Ben" which he was taking to his aged mother.

We came to a small station and the man left with profuse farewells. Into the compartment came a group of five beautiful Italian young women. They were carrying books and from the conversation which I overheard, it was plain they were going to a larger village to attend high school. As they went on with their conversation, I once more took up my reading, occasionally overhearing snatches of what they were saying. Finally, I became conscious that their remarks were directed toward "that nice young American" who was reading all by himself, and of course, they thought, not understanding a word they were saying. One of the girls had a beautiful orange, hanging from a long stem with four or five leaves on it. From its freshness, it was clear that the orange had just been plucked from a tree. Their conversation continued to center round "that nice young American" and his country, America. One of them said, "Wouldn't it be nice to go to America with him?" To this all agreed. Gradually they began to joke with each other as to who would be *the one* to go. All this time, of course, I gave no indication that I understood a word they were saying. Finally, one suggested that the girl who had the orange should have the preference. And she was as beautiful a specimen of womanhood as Italy knows how to produce. They suggested that if she would only offer me her orange I would surely take her to

America with me. She blushed, and to ward off the attack which was now centering upon her, she said: "No, I won't give him the orange, even to go to America," but she added: "Well, I might give him the stem and the leaves." This was more than I could resist. So rising and walking up to her, I made my best bow and said in as good Italian as I could command: "Thank you, gracious (graziosa) young lady, I will take you to America for the stem and the leaves." The screams, the laughter, the blushes which followed can easily be imagined, but just then the train pulled into the station to which the young women were going, and they precipitately left the compartment pell-mell amid laughter and shouts which attracted the attention of all. I stood by the window and waved them a good-by.

The train wound its way down the mountainous path and was soon at Foggia. I did the errand which had brought me there, and soon was speeding toward my native Molfetta. I had in the meantime sent a telegram to Aunt Rose stating that I would arrive on a certain train. The time consumed by that journey from Foggia to Molfetta seemed like ages. The trainman came into my compartment to talk about America. But I led him to talk about that section of Italy. He told me of its history, its general contour, the location of the various cities and villages, not knowing that I knew all about it. Then he entered upon an account of the advance that Italy, and especially Puglia, had made in recent years; the opening up of new railroads, the making of double track lines, the building of an aqueduct stretching for miles from the mountainous regions near Foggia through the whole length of the province, the building of electric plants, the industrial expansion of Bari, all of which was exceedingly interesting to me.

At about nine o'clock in the evening the conductor passed through the corridor and shouted "Molfetta." I took my suitcase and dismounted. No sooner had I left the train than I heard a voice in the distance shout, like an unexpected call of anguish in the night: "Costantino." No one was on the platform. The police guard was keeping every one back in the street. He scrutinized me in a special way, examined my papers, and let me pass. I pressed through a number of people who were crowding around the gate and the next moment I was in his arms. It was my good Uncle Carlo. "Zio" (uncle) I said, as he pressed me close to him and passed his hand gently over my face. "It is eighteen years almost to a day since you saw me off at this very station. I thought I should never see you again."

He took my suitcase from my hand and locking his arm with mine, led me on, as if feeling a special paternal pride. We walked in almost complete silence. It was one of those moonlight nights of Southern Italy, when the sky is so infinitely clear and the air so balmy as to make one forget that winter ever existed. The long dark shadows of the low, flat buildings covered the narrow streets, the slender ash trees near the station and in the Villa Garibaldi, which we passed, were standing like silent sentinels as of yore. In the distance I could see the Campanile rising above the Cathedral. All was at peace. But all was changed. The shadows, the streets, the houses, the trees, the public buildings were all the same,—and yet so changed. Why did they look so small? What are these? Are they the same houses which had towered so high above my head when a boy? Are these the same streets which had seemed so spacious and which it had taken my little legs so long to traverse? Are these the same "portoni" which had seemed to my child eyes as gates to fairy castles? Are these the same trees which once had reached the very zenith of my childhood skies? Why are things so shrunken, so small? Is the Molfetta of my boyhood days after all a toy thing?

Such thoughts crowded one after another in rapid succession through my mind as I walked along by the side of Uncle Carlo. At last we reached the very house in which, with grandmother, I had spent most of my childhood and boyhood days. At the door was Aunt Rose, quivering with emotion. She, more than all the others, had been the faithful one in writing to me, in keeping in touch with all my doings in far-away America; the one who had again and again pleaded with me to return, and had offered to send me the money to do so, if I only would. Now in a moment she gave vent to all the pent-up feelings of the years. The first words she uttered, as her arms pressed me close and her warm kisses and warmer tears touched my face were: "I thank Thee, God. I have seen him. Now I am ready to die." In the next few moments she lived over all the years since we had seen each other. Much that followed is too sacred to narrate. I was thankful that I had arrived at night, and so late that I had avoided the conspicuous attention which my uniform would have given me, and had escaped meeting the large group of friends and relatives all at once.

That night I slept in the very bed in which I had lain as a boy, with the same old posts and the same quaint canopy covering it as of old. But now it was not quite long enough for my outstretched body. I slept and I did not sleep. It seemed as if I could see my uncle going toward the balcony to fill my Santa Claus boot, as on that night long ago when I had first learned that Uncle Carlo was Santa, and I had loved him all the more. The next morning, long before I had risen, my little nephews and nieces—and it seemed their name was legion—who had learned of my arrival, tip-toed into the room in which they thought I was asleep, to view their long-lost uncle of whom they had heard so much and who had become the household saint of the whole family. One after another they ran back to their parents with descriptions of him—how he looked, how long he was, that his feet almost stuck out from the foot of the bed, that he was almost bald, had no mustaches, and had a big nose. When the reports they had carried to their parents came back to me, I had all I could do to recognize myself. As soon as the long line of nephews and nieces had come to an end, even as I was having a moment to rise and dress, in began to file an equally long line of sisters, uncles and aunts, and I even had to wash the shaving lather from my face to do my duty by one of my sisters, Agata, the jolliest of them all. In the meantime, that dear old aunt of mine, Aunt Rose, stood by with her bosom heaving, witnessing the whole proceeding like a sentinel, and taking a maternal pride in what was going on.

I had scarcely had time to dress, when a "banquet" was

ready for the "distinguished" guest. I wondered how they got so many relatives into so small a space. I was not surprised that they had sent all the children off to play. After the dinner party, my uncle took me out to see the town and to show me off to it. We went to see my old nurse and the old shoemaker who had made all my shoes in my youth; we called upon some former pupils of my father, now grown men and established in business. I had now and then to accept a kiss on each cheek, which, strange to say, was not quite as pleasing to me as it should have been. I had been in America, where kisses are reserved for a special kind of creatures. We went to the mole and the harbor, both of which had seemed so enormous to me in my youth, but now were little toy things; we passed through the Villa Garibaldi, a small round patch as compared to its past splendors. The clock tower above the West gate had been torn down. Everything seemed to have shrunken to miniature size, while my boyhood friends had grown to be men, and some were gone. The "big" city of my boyhood days was no more.

My relatives and friends asked all kinds of questions about America; what the climate and the country were like; what the living conditions were there; was it true that money was in great abundance; what were the chances of good employment? They asked no questions about the government and the general life of the country. I spoke of the good things, but was too jealous of America to tell them all I knew of the life of the immigrant there, or even to hint at some of the things that I myself had gone through. They would have been shocked beyond expression to have learned that the son of Don Coli had suffered such things as I have narrated in the preceding pages. When they asked my advice about their going to America, I could not honestly counsel them to do so. I was not unmindful of the practical misery in which most of the poorer classes live in Italy, but even misery is more easily endured in one's own country. When I gave evasive answers or was silent in the face of their persistent questionings, they were astonished. They wondered why I would not remain in Italy then? I shrugged my shoulders, Italian style, and passed to the next question.

That night I again returned to the home of my childhood and was glad that my relatives were considerate enough to leave me in the quiet of that home with my good aunt and uncle. With them I renewed my play life. We played hide-and-go-seek as of old; I played stealing almonds and figs as once I used to do in earnest; I looked over all my little books and mementoes, closely guarded by Aunt Rose through all the years; I examined my little ships, some of which hung on the walls; I sat in uncle's lap and put on his nose those funny old glasses he used to wear when he would read to me those fascinating sea tales.

But through it all I was conscious, and so were they, that a great change had taken place, deeper and more significant by far than any mere physical change. There were changes in training, in outlook, in habits, in motives, which separated us forever. Aunt Rose pleaded with me to promise that I would remain with her, that at least I would remain in Italy as long as she lived. She told me that the tract of land and the "casino" on it, which she had kept for me all these years, was still mine and that I could have it for the mere staying and the mere taking. She said that she would be so happy if I would only stay with her until she died, "only a few years more." I remained silent, though not unmoved, comforting her with a word now and then. "I will come again, aunt," I said. "I will come again." She understood! I was no more of this fair clime—no more!

> Oh, it's home again, and home again, America for me!
> I want a ship that's westward bound, to plough the
>   rolling sea,
> To the blesséd Land of Room Enough beyond the ocean
>   bars,
> Where the air is full of sunlight, and the flag is full of
>   stars!

CHAPTER 20

MY FINAL CHOICE

The next morning I left Molfetta, and save for a visit of a few hours' duration which I made later, I returned to it no more. In forty-eight hours I had passed from the peaceful scenes and the reminiscences of my childhood into the throbbing activities of the most bloody war in human history. It was while in the midst of these scenes and on my own native soil, that my supreme choice was made.

I was assigned the task of projecting the work of the "Y" at the Italian front, and by a series of strange circumstances I had the privilege of close contact with some of Italy's most eminent men, both in military and civil life, and was permitted to render to Italy, in the name of my adopted country, a distinct, even though a humble, service. At Mogliano, Veneto, not far from Venice, was then located the Headquarters of the famous Third Army. Under the command of the far-famed Duca d'Aosta, this army had accomplished a prodigious feat in checking the Austrian advance in the fall of 1917, and had thereby saved Italy from further invasion and ravage. As it was only about two months since the terrible defeat of "Caporetto" had taken place, the lines of the Italian forces were just beginning to take definite shape. Under the newly appointed Commander in Chief, General Diaz, a general work of reconstruction was going on. As the Third Army had suffered most severely in the recent retreat, we decided to begin our work with it and to do what we could to help the authorities build up the "morale" of the men. We therefore located our first headquarters near the command of the Third Army at Mogliano.

It was my privilege, in an entirely unforeseen way, to raise the first Stars and Stripes which, to my knowledge, ever flew near the lines of the Italian army. We had been at the front about a week, when we realized the need of having our national colors flying above our headquarters. The only persons representing the United States who had up to this time made their way to the Italian front were a small group of ambulance drivers, who had taken the famous Poets' Ambulances to the relief of the Italian forces. We inquired of them about a flag, but they did not have one themselves, so could not supply us with one. We made inquiries at several places, we sent to Venice, to Padua, to Milan, but from everywhere came the answer that no Stars and Stripes were to be found. It would take three or four weeks, we were told, to have one made. Finally one day I made it known to my fellow-workers that since leaving the United States I had carried, carefully folded against my heart, a small silk flag, about eighteen by twenty-four inches in size. We decided that since we could not get any other for the present we would raise this one; and we did. We had our little ceremony and it was my privilege to put it out upon our balcony, where it remained until we had displaced it with a larger one. Later I carried that little flag, attached to my car, to the remotest spots on the firing lines and even down into Sicily, in places where it had never been seen before, I was told, and may never be seen again. Wherever it went it carried new hope and inspiration. And so it happened that it was given to an adopted American to unfurl the first American colors on the lines of his own native country during the Great War.

It was given to me to perform a still greater duty; that of carrying to the discouraged soldiers of my native country, and later to the people in the remotest spots of the interior the message of hope and encouragement from far-off America. This, too, was purely an accident. On the first Sunday we were at the front, a new Italian Casa del Soldato, or soldier's hut, was to be opened. The famous priest and patriot, Padre Semeria, was to deliver the address. On the preceding Friday it was announced that on account of illness Padre Semeria could not be present. Doctor Nollen, our chief for the whole of Italy, happened to be at the front when the news reached us, and he casually suggested to the chaplain who was in charge of the opening, that he should ask me to make a few remarks about America's participation in the war. So I was requested to speak at the opening of this first Casa del Soldato in the newly formed lines. I hesitated at first, chiefly because my practice in Italian public speaking had been somewhat limited, and I did not wish to mar the coming festivities by making a bad impression or by failing to interpret in adequate terms the ideals and the aims of America's participation in the war. However, the request was so urgent that it seemed my duty to do the best I could.

The Casa to be opened was located close to the lines. These particular regiments of "Bersaglieri," for whom the Casa was being opened, were under the command of Colonel de Ambrosi, one of the bravest and most quick-witted men of the entire Italian army. They had carried out their idealism to such a degree in beautifying an old house that they had made it into one of the most attractive spots imaginable. Around the grounds were flower beds representing the various phases of Italy's participation in the war. They had succeeded most remarkably in turning an old and dilapidated house into an architectural and landscape gem. In front of the house and camouflaged with leaves they had erected a platform which was to serve as a rostrum in the coming festivities. The time for the opening came. The air was serene and balmy, the first signs of spring were beginning to appear and the "Bersaglieri," always jovial, seemed to be in an especially good humor. The Italian soldier never forgets his mirth even under the most untoward circumstances. They had gathered in great numbers and were ready for the celebration to which they had eagerly looked forward. Our group of five American uniformed Y. M. C. A. men arrived, and it would seem extravagant were I to tell of the wild enthusiasm that burst from that group of four or five thousand men. I was escorted to the platform, where General Croce was awaiting us. When the time came, I arose to speak. Here was I, a son of Italy, for many years in far-away America, now come back to my native country to bring words of encouragement and cheer; and here I stood before them, the first man they had seen in an American uniform, and speaking the first words they had heard of America's entrance and participation in the war. I spoke for about fifteen minutes; in simple language I enumerated the reasons why America had not entered the war before, and why she had entered on the side of the Allies now; I spoke of her unbounded resources in men and means; I told them how American soldiers had already landed on European soil and that some of them would surely be sent to Italy. When I was through, wave after wave of uncontrolled enthusiasm burst from their throats. The air was vibrant with cheering. The enemy, not far distant, must surely have heard it.

When I was through speaking, General Croce met me, and in keeping with the Italian custom he kissed me on both cheeks, in token of deep friendship and appreciation. To me it seemed rather a strange performance, and looking round to my mates, standing near by, I smiled. They understood my embarrassment. The General then insisted that a picture be taken of him and myself, and another of the entire group of generals and other officers present, including our Y. M. C. A. men. These pictures were sent to the interior and published widely throughout Italy. Then a reception was tendered in the Casa to all the officers present.

So far as I was concerned, the incident was ended. To my surprise, however, the following day a messenger arrived from Army Headquarters requesting me to present myself that afternoon for a conference "regarding an important matter" with General Giuseppe Vaccari, chief of staff under the Duca d'Aosta. I went to the beautiful villa in which the command was housed and was ushered into the presence of the General. General Vaccari is a man of unusual dignity and poise, yet withal one of the most kindly men, as I came to know afterwards. As I came into his presence, every bone and fiber of me stood erect. I did not know or even suspect what I was wanted for. After exchanging the usual greetings, he spoke of the reasons why he had called me to him. He said: "His Excellency, the Duca d'Aosta, has requested me to thank you most heartily for the service you rendered us yesterday at the opening of the Casa. We heard of the speech you made and of the enthusiasm and encouragement which it evoked in our soldiery. He further instructs me to state that he would like to have you, at the expense of the Italian Army, to continue to render such a service, by going from place to place as may be directed later, addressing the soldiers along the lines." I answered that it was my duty and privilege to render any little service I could, and that, subject to the approval of my superiors, I should be happy to place myself at the Commandant's disposal and to do what I could in the name of my country, to serve the Italian soldier. With that we parted.

From that day until I left Italy, seven months later, when I came to America to bring a message from Italy, I was in the midst of incessant activity. Repeatedly I was called, early in the morning or late in the evening, to mount a car waiting at the door and go to some spot on the lines to speak in the name of my adopted country. On one occasion it was my privilege to speak to twelve battalions of "Ciclisti,"— the famous bicyclist sharpshooters; on another to nine battalions of the equally famous "Metraglieri di Sardinia"; one evening, just as the sun was setting, I faced a large body of men under the command of General Angelosanto, a daring Neopolitan soldier, and as soon as the address was over, they marched into the lines, not far away. On still another occasion on a hillside, on whose crest the enemy was deeply entrenched, I addressed five thousand men, who at the close of the meeting marched to their places in the trenches on the hill. And so the days passed, days of continuous activity, through which I was serving my native country in the name of my adopted country. Later at the instance of the military authorities and of the United States Committee on Public Information in Italy, I made a complete speaking tour of Sicily, reaching even the remotest hill towns inland. Sicily was at that time in a very low state of "morale," yet it rose to the occasion, and the unbounded enthusiasm of the people was manifested by the thronged theaters and other public buildings, and in the surging crowds that gathered in the open squares to hear of America. I carried with me small ribbon American flags, and distributed them by the thousands, especially to children who had relatives in the American Expeditionary Forces.

Those were the months of throbbing activity and of unequalled opportunity to observe the people and the life of my native Italy. I had occasion to confer personally with scores of the highest officers of the army, from the Duca d'Aosta to the Generals in command of the various armies and army corps, and with minor officers; I came into personal contact with many civilian officers and with leaders in the educational world of Italy. I had the privilege of escorting some leading American citizens and prominent men of other nationalities to the front lines, to interpret in some important conferences, and to carry between certain Italian and American authorities military information of the greatest importance. Above all, I had an unexcelled opportunity to observe the life and the institutions of my mother country with the eyes of manhood and in a way I never had before. I was given access to some of the most beautiful and cultured homes of Italy. I had the privilege of viewing the matchless natural beauties of Italy and of drinking in the invigorating sweetness of Italy's skies, rivers, lakes and seas. Opportunities were open for me to enter public life in my native country and to contribute to it what I had gained of experience and outlook in my adopted country. At times I almost entertained the thought of remaining in my native country. But something not entirely in the realm of reason or in that of patriotic sentiment kept tugging at my heart, pulling like a magnet toward America.

One day the final choice took place. It came in the midst of the splendor of a military occasion and unseen by human eyes. I myself did not realize its fullest significance at the time. At Messina, where I was to address a regiment of 1918 recruits, I was met by the venerable General Lang, who took me to the summit of the hill overlooking the Straits of Messina. It was late in the afternoon, turning toward sunset, as we reached our destination. On the very summit of the hill, lined up in military array in the form of an open square, some five thousand young soldiers were awaiting our arrival. Sighting our car, officers and men came to attention, while the band wafted out on the breeze the martial strains of "L 'Inno Nazionale," the Italian National Hymn. We exchanged the usual military salutes and then in a few simple words I spoke.

While speaking, my eyes were fixed upon the matchless sight before me. In the distance beyond the strait was Scilla; there too was my native country, Italy. Below, slumbering peacefully in the sunset glow, was Messina, with her mole-arm stretching out into the sea. The crystal blue of the Mediterranean was vying with the delicate tints, now rosy, now purple, of the western sky. Subconsciously I was thinking of the Italy of the Ancients and of the Italy I had known. Before my eyes the two national standards, each exemplifying so much, were waving triumphantly in the stiff breeze sweeping over the mountain crest. One stood for Italy, both ancient and modern, which the world respects; for the Italy of my childhood, for all the memories of my youth, of loved ones, for all that had been beautiful and lovely in my boyhood; for the tender memories of loved ones, living and dead. The other stood for all the suffering of the years, for the awakening of manhood, for the birth of freedom, for the unfolding of life. I loved not one the less, but the other more!

The address over, we exchanged greetings with the officers in charge of the occasion and returned to our car. Then followed a scene which will forever remain indelibly imprinted upon my memory and consciousness. The soldiers, even before being ordered to do so, spontaneously broke ranks and made a mad dash toward the road, where our car was waiting. Wave upon wave of "Evviva l'America" swelled. They massed themselves along both sides of the road, as our car began to move slowly down the serpentine way. The standards were still waving triumphantly. The band was now playing "The Star Spangled Banner." We moved on. The sun was just going down into the sea. The waves of cheers followed us, growing fainter and fainter like an echo. We gradually lost sight of the soldiers, their uniforms blending with the earth. But still we could see a mass of white in the distance; the boys with their handkerchiefs were waving the last possible farewell, the last "evviva" to America. All was now silent, save for the thud-thud of the engine as our car moved slowly down the hill. General Lang and I uttered not a word. Finally he broke the silence. His eyes were dim. "Memorabile!" he said as he looked back. Just then the sun sent forth its last ray. Looking back, the only thing I could see was the Stars and Stripes waving gloriously in the last radiant beam of light. I looked toward the west and in my soul I said, "Through the Western window comes the light." I knew where my heart lay.

An hour later I was on a northbound train and two weeks after that I was on my way to America. I called upon several of the civilian and military authorities to pay my respects, chief among whom was the Duca d'Aosta. He spoke deep and appreciative words of what America had done for Italy during her most trying hours, and requested me to repeat in America his appreciation whenever I had opportunity. At last I was on my way toward my adopted country. I was conscious that something vital had taken place in my life. *The final and lasting choice* had come and I knew it. Through my mind kept running the lines of Dr. Van Dyke, "It's home again, home again, America for me!" Years before, by a series of strange circumstances, I had been tossed upon the shores of America. Now I turned my steps by definite choice toward that country of which sages dreamed: AMERICA.

On September 28, 1918, sixteen years almost to a day, from the time when I first set foot on American soil, the U. S. Transport *Kroonland* anchored in New York harbor. As on the day when I had first sighted America, so now She, the Queen of the West, was again decked in festal array. It was the morning when the Victory Loan campaign was launched. The forts thundered their salutes. New York, the great city of the Western Hemisphere, was resplendent in one glorious canopy of matchless colors. I was again in America. I felt like kissing the ground, as Columbus had done centuries ago.

And yet a feeling of loneliness again came over me. Strange as it may seem, I felt as of old that I was alone. Had it not been for my American "Big Brother," whose voice over the telephone dispelled some of that feeling, I might have felt like a man without a country. Nor was this feeling without foundation, in a measure.

Soon after my return I was asked to take up work in the Middle West. A letter was shown from the man to whom I had been asked to report, saying he did not see how he could use a "foreigner" with such an "outlandish name." On my way West, a group of young men passed through the coach and taking me for a Jew began to shout: "Sheeny, Sheeny, how is beezness on Salem Street?" Of course within me I laughed heartily. And yet such incidents give one a feeling that no matter how much he is at heart an American, he is still *different* and will forever remain so.

I have now been in America for nineteen years; I have grown up here as much as any man can; I have had my education here; I have become a citizen; I have given all I had of youthful zeal and energy in serving my adopted country; I have come to love America as I do my very life—perhaps more—and yet they still call me a "foreigner." Not that I mind it. No, no! For I believe that with a real American a man is a man "though he comes from the ends of the earth." I *do mind* it though for the numberless men and women who do not know how to take it philosophically and humorously as I do, and who pass through life in this country under that ugly shadow, ever hanging over their heads, of being despised "foreigners" all their days.

As for me I care not! Though my features may always show something of my origin, of which I am far from being ashamed; though at times my speech may betray my foreign birth; though I should suffer unendingly; though Thy sons should ever dub me a "foreigner," still I love Thee, America. I am not blind to Thy failings, but Thy virtue and Thy glory far outshine them. Whatever betide, I am Thine and I claim Thee as mine own. In my veins runs blood, in my mind run thoughts, in my soul feelings and aspirations which Thou hast given me. Thy name is graven on my soul. I love Thee, Italy, my native land, with that mystic love with which men turn to their native country and as Pilgrims to their shrine. I love Thee, America, with manhood's strong love, born out of the unfolding of the mind, the evolving of the soul, the sufferings and joys, the toil and the larger loves of the years. I love Thy very life. I love Thee as I can love no other land. No other skies are so fair as Thine; no rugged mountains or fruitful plains so majestic and divine. I am of Thee; Thou art mine; upon Thy sacred soil shall I live; there I fain would die,—*an American*.

A Long Way From Home
Claude McKay

A controversial figure among Harlem Renaissance writers, Claude McKay was born on September 15, 1890, in Sunny Ville, Jamaica. McKay's mother sent him to live with an older brother at the age of eight, and it was in this home that he began to read classic literature and poetry. In 1906, McKay received a academic scholarship in Kingston where he was exposed to German philosophy and began writing poetry for *The Daily Gleaner*. These Jamaican dialect poems eventually formed the body of a greater work, *Songs of Jamaica*, published in 1912. Though he loved his homeland, McKay was opposed to the small but powerful landowners in Jamaica who kept the rule of the island in white hands. Intending only to leave Jamaica for a few years, McKay decided to attend the Tuskegee Institute in Alabama in 1912. The young author, however, would never return to Jamaica.

Dissatisfied with his studies at Tuskegee, McKay transferred to Kansas State College in 1913. Academic pursuits at Kansas also displeased McKay, and, after two years, he moved to Harlem. There, like many Jamaican immigrants, McKay worked in factories and at odd jobs, but he never stopped writing. Reluctant to distinguish himself in a new country, he published several poems under a pseudonym in the summer of 1919. The significant events of this "Red Summer," an era of intense anti-communism in American history, however, prompted McKay to publish his first major poem in America under his own name: "If We Must Die," published in the *Liberator*, a socialist weekly. This, and subsequent publications in the *Liberator*, as well as McKay's membership in the Industrial Workers of the World union, prompted the Justice Department to begin a file on his activities. In 1919, McKay escaped this scrutiny and traveled to England where he became more deeply interested in Marxism and began writing for the *Worker's Dreadnought*. In 1921, he returned to the United States and published his first widely acclaimed book of poetry, *Harlem Shadows* (1922), traveling to Russia soon after where he met Trotsky and gave lectures.

For the next ten years, McKay remained an expatriate in Europe and Africa, although friends encouraged him to take part in the Harlem Renaissance. Stricken with syphilis, McKay sought treatment in Germany and France. Lonely, ill, and impoverished, McKay published *Home to Harlem* in 1928, a novel which depicted what some readers considered a low-class lifestyle, while others praised its realism. In 1934, McKay returned to New York and published his autobiography, *A Long Way From Home* (1937), to good reviews but slow sales. In the last years of his life, McKay, partially crippled by a stroke, converted to Catholicism and wrote religious articles and poetry. He died of heart failure on May 22, 1948.

In Chapter 24 from *A Long Way From Home*, entitled "On Belonging to a Minority Group," Claude McKay describes an interesting meeting with a possible white benefactor. McKay is unwilling to accept this charity because payment might come at the cost of his own personal voice.

29

ON BELONGING TO A
MINORITY GROUP

It was in Africa that I was introduced to Nancy Cunard—an introduction by mail. Years before, when I saw her at a studio in Paris, she had been mentioned as a personage, but I had not been introduced. In Africa I received a pamphlet from Miss Cunard entitled *Black Man and White Ladyship*. The interesting pamphlet gave details about the Cunard daughter establishing a friendship with a Negro musician, of which the Cunard mother had disapproved.

Miss Cunard wrote that she was making a Negro anthology to dedicate to her Negro friend, and asked me to be a contributor. I promised that I would as soon as I found it possible to take time from the novel I was writing. That started an interesting correspondence between us.

Although I considered the contents of the Nancy Cunard pamphlet of absorbing interest and worthy of publication, I did not admire the style and tone of presentation.

After some months, Miss Cunard informed me that she was traveling to New York, and from there to the West Indies, including Jamaica. She asked me if I could introduce her to anybody in Jamaica who could put her in touch with the natives. I addressed her to my eldest brother, who is well-placed somewhere between the working masses and the controlling classes of Jamaica and has an excellent knowledge of both. From Jamaica Miss Cunard wrote again that she had landed in paradise after the purgatory of New York, where she was put in the spotlight by the newspapers, when it was discovered that she was residing in Harlem among the Negroes. My brother invited her to his home in the heart of the banana, chocolate, and ginger region of Jamaica, and she stayed there two weeks with her Negro secretary. Both she and her secretary wrote extolling my brother's hospitality and the warmth and kindliness of the peasants. Miss Cunard said she particularly liked my brother's face, and she sent me a snapshot of him.

Meanwhile I had come to the point of a breakdown while working on my novel in Morocco; and besides I was in pecuniary difficulties. Nevertheless I wrote an article for Miss Cunard's anthology and forwarded it to her on her return to France. Miss Cunard extravagantly praised the article and said it was one of the best and also that I was one of the best, whatever that "best" meant. She said she would use it with a full-page photograph of myself which was done by a friend of ours, the photographer, Berenice Abbot.

However, she did not accompany her praise by a check, and I requested payment. I was in need of money. Miss Cunard replied that she was not paying contributors and that my article was too long after all. She was doing the book for the benefit of the Negro race and she had thought that every Negro would be glad to contribute something for nothing. She had suffered and sacrificed a fortune for Negroes, she said.

I comprehended Miss Cunard's way of reasoning. Yet in spite of the penalty she had to pay for her interest in the Negro, I did not consider it my bounden duty to write for her without remuneration. Miss Cunard would have been shocked at the idea of asking the printers and binders to print and bind her charitable book without remuneration. But in spite of her ultra-modern attitude toward life, apparently she still clung to the antiquated and aristocratic and very British idea that artists should perform for noble and rich people for prestige instead of remuneration.

I might say that I too have suffered a lot for my knowledge of, and contact with, the white race. Yet if I were composing an anthology of the white hell, it never would have occurred to me that all sympathetic white writers and artists owed me a free contribution. I suppose it takes a modern white aristocrat to indulge in that kind of archaic traditional thinking.

As Miss Cunard would not pay for my article, I requested its return. She said she was going to take extracts from it. I forbade her to touch it. That made her mad, *comme une vache enragée.* My brother also was supposed to do an article on the Jamaica banana industry for Miss Cunard. He decided not to. And suddenly Miss Cunard did not like his face any more. She wrote that he was big and fat.

In her pamphlet *Black Man and White Ladyship* the reader gets the impression that the Cunard daughter enjoys taking a Negro stick to beat the Cunard mother. Miss Cunard seemed to have been ultra-modern in ideas and contacts without alarming Lady Cunard, who was a little modern herself. Then Miss Cunard became aware of the Negro by way of jazz in Venice. And soon also she was made aware that her mother would not accept her friendship with a Negro. Other white women have come up against that problem. It is not merely a problem of people of different races; people of different religions and of different classes know the unreasonableness and the bitterness of it. The mother Cunard drastically reduced the income of the daughter Cunard. The daughter replied with the pamphlet *Black Man and White Ladyship*, which was not published for sale but probably for spite. In telling the story of her friendship, Miss Cunard among other things ridicules her mother's American accent. Yet the American Negroes she professes to like speak the same language as her mother, with slight variations.

Writing in her strange, heavy and ineffectual giant of a Negro anthology, Miss Cunard has this to say of me: "His people [the characters of my novels] and himself have also that wrong kind of race-consciousness; they ring themselves in."

The statement is interesting, not so much from the narrow personal as from the broader social angle of a minority group of people and its relationship to friends who belong to the majority group. It leaves me wondering whether it would be altogether such a bad thing if by ringing itself in closer together, a weak, disunited and suppressed group of people could thereby develop group pride and strength and self-respect!

It is hell to belong to a suppressed minority and outcast group. For to most members of the powerful majority, you are not a person; you are a problem. And every crusading crank imagines he knows how to solve your problem. I think I am a rebel mainly from psychological reasons, which have always been more important to me than economic. As a member of a weak minority, you are not supposed to criticize your friends of the strong majority. You will be damned mean and ungrateful. Therefore you and your group must be content with lower critical standards.

A Fannie Hurst who is a best seller is interested in Negro literature. She is nice to Negro writers and artists. She visits among Negroes. She engages a Negro secretary. And finally she writes a trashy novel of Negro life. Negro critics do not like the novel. Fannie Hurst thinks they are ungrateful. I suppose the only way Negro critics could get around the dilemma would be to judge Fannie Hurst by social and sentimental instead of artistic standards. But that wouldn't help the Negro literature that Fannie Hurst desires to promote. I think Negro writers might benefit more by the forthright criticism of such southern gentlemen as H. L. Mencken and Joseph Wood Krutch than by the kindness of a Fannie Hurst.

A southern white woman who is married to a black journalist says, in a critique entitled, *Don'ts for My Daughter*, that she would not "want her to read *Home to Harlem*, which overemphasizes the carnal side of the Aframerican." I will confess that I may fall short of that degree of civilization which perfects the lily-white state of mind of the gentle southern lady. And that was why as a creative writer I was unable to make nice distinctions between the carnal and the pure and happened perhaps to sin on the side of the carnal in *Home to Harlem*.

Yet I once read in a Negro magazine some stanzas entitled, Temptation, by a certain Young Southern White Lady, and attributed to my pure critic, which sound like a wild jazz page out of *Nigger Heaven*. I remember some of those stanzas:

> *I couldn't forget*
> *The banjo's whang*

And the piano's bang
As we strutted the do-do-do's
In Harlem!

That pansy seal
A-tossing me
All loose and free, O, lily me!
In muscled arms
Of Ebony!

I couldn't forget
That black boy's eyes
That black boy's shake
That black boy's size
I couldn't forget
O, snow white me!

Now to the mind of this black sinner this piece of sophisticated lily-white lyricism is more offensively carnal than the simple primitive erotic emotions of the characters of *Home to Harlem*. But I reiterate it is possible that I am not civilized white enough to appreciate the purity of the mind which composed the above stanzas and to which *Home to Harlem* is carnal.

The white lady is raising her mulatto daughter on a special diet and periodically the child is featured as a prodigy in the New York *Herald Tribune*. But it is possible that when that child has grown up out of the state of being a prodigy she might prefer a plain fare, including *Home to Harlem*. I have not had the time to be an experimentalist about life, because I have been occupied always with facing hard facts. And this I know to be a fact: Right here in New York there are children of mixed parentage, who have actually hated their white mother after they had grown up to understanding. When they came up against the full force of the great white city on the outside and went home to face a helpless white mother (a symbol of that white prejudice) it was more than their Negroid souls could stand.

I think it would be illuminating to know the real feelings

of that white mother, who was doubtlessly devoted to her colored children. . . . I myself have had the experience of a fine friendship with a highly cultured white woman, when I first arrived in the United States—a friendship which was turned into a hideous nightmare because of the taboos of the dominant white community. I still retain a bitter memory of my black agony, but I can only try to imagine the white crucifixion of that cultured woman. . . .

I do not think the author of *Don'ts for My Daughter*, felt personally antagonistic to me, when she wrote in the leading Negro magazine that she did not want her child to read my novel. It is possible that like myself she has faith in literary and artistic truth. Perhaps she even desires to contribute something to the growing literature of Negro life. I have read an interesting article by her on "America's Changing Color Line," which emphasizes the idea that America is steadily growing darker in complexion, and is informing about the increasing numbers of white Negroids who are absorbed by the white group.

Without the slightest feeling of antagonism to my critic, I would suggest to her that vicarious stories of "passing white" are merely of slight importance to the great group of fifteen millions who are obviously Negroes. I would suggest to her that if she really desires to make a unique contribution to American literature, she has a chance of doing something that no Negro can—something that might be worthwhile for her daughter to read: she might write a sincere account of what it means for an educated and sensitive white woman to be the wife of a Negro in America.

Gertrude Stein, the high priestess of artless-artful Art, identifies Negro with Nothingness. When the eternal faddists who exist like vampires on new phenomena become fed up with Negro art, they must find a reason for their indifference. From being disappointed in Paul Robeson, Gertrude Stein concludes that Negroes are suffering from nothingness. In the ineffable Stein manner she decided to take Paul Robeson as *the* representative of Negro culture. Similarly, any other fadist could arbitrarily make Chaliapin or Al Jolson or Maurice Chevalier or Greta Garbo the representative of Russian, Jewish, French and Swedish culture respectively. When Gertrude Stein finds that Paul Robeson knows American values and American life as only one in it and not of it could, when she discovers that he is big and naïve, but not quite naïve enough to please Gertrude Stein, she declares: "The African is not primitive; he has a very ancient but a very narrow culture and there it remains. Consequently nothing can happen." Not long after she published this, something was happening: Negro Americans were rendering her opera *Four Saints in Three Acts* to sophisticated New York audiences.

Well, whatever the white folks do and say, the Negro race will finally have to face the need to save itself. The whites have done the blacks some great wrongs, but also they have done some good. They have brought to them the benefits of modern civilization. They can still do a lot more, but one thing they cannot do: they cannot give Negroes the gift of a soul—a group soul.

Wherever I traveled in Europe and Africa I was impressed by the phenomenon of the emphasis on group life, whether the idea behind it was Communist co-operative or Fascist collective or regional autonomy. I lived under a Communist dictatorship in Russia, two Fascist dictatorships in Europe, and the French colonial dictatorship in Morocco. I don't like any dictatorship.

Yet even the dictatorships were making concessions to the strong awakened group spirit of the peoples. Soviet Russia was hard at work on the social problems of its many nationalities. Primo de Rivera in Spain had organized two grand exhibitions: one for discontented Catalonia and another for unhappy Andalusia. Regional groups such as that in Brittany and in the Basque country were reviving their ancient culture. Labor groups and radical groups were building up their institutions and educating their children in opposition to reactionary institutions.

But there is very little group spirit among Negroes. The American Negro group is the most advanced in the world. It possesses unique advantages for development and expansion and for assuming the world leadership of the Negro race. But it sadly lacks a group soul. And the greatest hindrance to the growth of a group soul is the wrong idea held about segregation. Negroes do not understand the difference between group segregation and group aggregation. And their leaders do not enlighten them, because they too do not choose to understand. Negro institutions and unique Negro efforts have never had a chance for full development; they are haunted by the fear of segregation. Except where they are forced against their will, Negroes in general prefer to patronize white institutions and support white causes in order to demonstrate their opposition to segregation.

Yet it is a plain fact that the entire world of humanity is more or less segregated in groups. The family group gave rise to the tribal group, the tribal group to the regional group, and the regional group to the national group. There are groups within groups: language groups, labor groups, racial groups and class groups. Certainly no sane group desires public segregation and discrimination. But it is a clear historical fact that different groups have won their social rights only when they developed a group spirit and strong group organization.

There are language groups and religious groups in this country that have found it necessary to develop their own banks, co-operative stores, printing establishments, clubs, theaters, colleges, hotels, hospitals and other social service institutions and trade unions. Yet they were not physically separated from other white groups as much as are Negroes. But they were in a stronger position to bargain and obtain social and political privileges by virtue of the strength of their own institutions.

But Negro institutions in general are developed only perfunctorily and by compulsion, because Negroes have no abiding faith in them. Negroes wisely are not wasting thought on the chimera of a separate Negro state or a separate Negro economy within the United States, but there are a thousand things within the Negro community which only Negroes can do.

There are educated Negroes who believe that the color line will be dissolved eventually by the light-skinned Negroids "passing white," by miscegenation and final assimilation by the white group. But even if such a solution were possible in the future, it is certainly not a solution for the great dark body of Negroids living in the present. Also if the optimistic Negro advocates of futility would travel and observe or study to learn something of the composition and distribution of white racial, national and regional groups that are more assimilable than Negroes, and of their instinctive and irrational tenacity, they might be less optimistic and negative about the position of their own.

The Negro intelligentsia cannot hope to get very far if the Negro masses are despised and neglected. However poor it may be, the Negro intelligentsia gets its living directly from the Negro masses. A few Negro individuals who obtain important political and social positions among whites may delude themselves into thinking they got their jobs by individual merit alone against hungry white competitors who are just as capable.

But the fact is that the whites in authority give Negroes their jobs because they take into consideration the potential strength of the Negro group. If that group were organized on the basis of its numerical strength, there would be more important jobs and greater social recognition for Negroes.

And Negroes will have to organize themselves and learn from their mistakes. The white man cannot organize Negroes as a group, for Negroes mistrust the motives of white people. And the Negro whom they consider an Uncle Tom among the whites, whose voice is the voice of their white master, cannot do it either, even though he may proclaim himself a radical!

Many years ago I preserved a brief editorial from *The Nation* on the Woman's Party which seemed to me to be perfectly applicable to the position of the Negro—if the word Negro were substituted for "woman" and "whites" for men. It said in part: "We agree that no party, left to itself, will allow women an equal chance. Neither labor nor the farmer nor the business man nor the banker is ready to assume executive and political ability in women. They will steadily, perhaps instinctively, resist any such belief. They will accede to women's demands only so far as they wish to please or placate the woman vote. For every party job, for every political office, for every legal change in the direction of equality, women will have to fight as women. Inside the party organizations, the women will have to wage their own battle for recognition and equal rights. . . .

"After all, women are an indivisible part of this country's population; they cannot live under a women's Congress and a special set of feminine laws and economic conditions. They, as well as men, suffer when our government is prostituted, and lose their employment when economic hardship sweeps the country. They, like men, have a vote, and like men they will in the long run tend to elect people and parties who represent their whole interest. To be sure, apart from men they have a special group interest. . . ."

It would be altogether too ludicrous to point out that white women are by far more an indivisible part of this country's population than Negroes! Yet the advance guard of white women realize that they have a common and special group interest, different from the general interests of their fathers and brothers and their husbands and sons.

It goes without saying that the future of the Negro is bound up with the future system of world economy. And all progressive social trends indicate that that system will be based on the principle of labor for communal instead of private profit. I have no idea how the new system will finally work out. I have never believed in the infallibility of the social prophets, even though some of their predictions and calculations have come true. It is possible that in some countries some of the captains of capitalist industry might become labor leaders and prove themselves more efficient than many reactionary labor leaders. Who knows?

Anyway, it seems to me that if Negroes were organized as a group and as workers, whatever work they are doing (with or without the whites), and were thus getting a practical education in the nature and the meaning of the labor movement, it might even be more important and worthwhile than for them to become members of radical political parties.

A West Indian charlatan came to this country, full of antiquated social ideas; yet within a decade he aroused the social consciousness of the Negro masses more than any leader ever did. When Negroes really desire a new group orientation they will create it.

Such is my opinion for all that it may be worth. I suppose I have a poet's right to imagine a great modern Negro leader. At least I would like to celebrate him in a monument of verse. For I have nothing to give but my singing. All my life I have been a troubadour wanderer, nourishing myself mainly on the poetry of existence. And all I offer here is the distilled poetry of my experience.

Chinaman's Chance
No-Yong Park

The esteemed political lecturer, professor, and non-fiction author No-Yong Park fought difficult circumstances in both Chinese and American cultures to become what he respected most: a scholar. Born in a small farming village in Manchuria in 1899, Park was fortunate enough to attend a local school, a luxury not afforded to many of his relatives. In late nineteenth-century China, education was a privilege rather than a right, and Park learned to value his position through the classic Confucian teachings of social responsibility and order that his instructors strictly enforced. According to Confucius, the pen was a greater instrument of power than the sword, and Park retained this philosophy even after Japanese and European forces began westernizing his homeland in the early years of the twentieth century. Against the proud, nativistic instincts of his father, Park refused an arranged marriage in 1916, briefly entered a Buddhist monastery, attended a Methodist school in Japan, and left for New York at the close of the first World War. Only in the West, Park believed, could he gain enough knowledge truly to help China face the increasingly international political scene of the twentieth century.

Park entered the United States just before an onslaught of anti-Asian immigration laws passed through Congress in 1924, but he was not naturalized as a citizen. In New York, he found comfort in the familiarity of the sights and food in Chinatown, but was disgusted by the lack of jobs available to Asians. Often, Park felt encouraged to become a worker or businessman in the service trades of restaurants and laundries by both Chinese and white Americans. With a desire to escape these roles and to educate himself further, Park attended a radical Protestant school in Bound Brook, New Jersey, in 1921, worked as a traveling salesman in Chicago a year later, and eventually saved enough money to enter Indiana's Evansville College in 1924 as a foreign student. The taunting slang terms he heard thrown at Chinese immigrants in New York, such as "washee, washee" and "Charlie" became imbedded in Park's memory. He vowed to speak perfect English in the future and combat these slights.

In Indiana, Park found some acceptance and interest in his native culture, and there he began a career of political lectures that would sustain him for most of his life. As a lecturer on Asian affairs, Park traveled to ladies' clubs, churches, and universities across the United States and Canada, sometimes sharing the podium with political adversaries and sometimes with popular figures like Amelia Earhart. The knowledge of Western culture gained by these travels was invaluable to Park, and it brought him some solace to educate North Americans about the Opium Wars of the 1850s and 1860s, French Imperialism in Indo-China, and the Japanese invasion of Korea. Eventually the substance of these lectures was published as the historical work *Retreat of the West: The White Man's Adventure in Eastern Asia* in 1937 with some success. Between lecture tours, Park attended Northwestern University, the University of Minnesota, and Harvard, where he received a Ph.D. in 1932. Park later returned to the University of Minnesota as a professor of political science and international relations. He died in 1976.

In Chapter 17 from his autobiography, *Chinaman's Chance*, published in 1940, No-Yong Park attempts to integrate the frugality and social consciousness of his upbringing with the vast wealth of resources available in America. Writing just after the Great Depression, Park draws attention to what waste and harm can occur when the few, rather than the majority, have control over these gifts.

17

I came gradually, then, to believe that we live in a world where myriads of selfish interests constantly beg us, appeal to us and even compel us to form new wants and desires so that some profit can be made from the contents of our pocketbooks. If we wish to do all the things that we are told we should do, we must, in the first place, multiply our individual selves by the thousands, and then each and all of us thus multiplied must spend every hour of our lives doing what these interests demand. In a world of high pressure salesmanship, if one is to live the life of a free man and not that of a slave, one should endeavor to cultivate fewer and better habits and desires.

The idea of bringing up fewer and better children has already been exploited extensively in America, but mostly by the educated and sensible people. Only ignorant and stupid fools breed indiscriminately, causing poverty and misery within their homes and creating social problems of unemployment and relief. The more refined and cultured men first think of their responsibilities in educating their children, in feeding them, and in clothing them before they acquire families. Why not then give a little time beforehand to decide whether certain habits when acquired will help one to be happier or more miserable; whether they will make one a better human being or a more degenerate one; whether they will be liabilities for which one will have to work a lifetime to satisfy, or assets which will make one a better and greater human being?

With the forgoing ideas in mind, I started out first of all to eliminate all unnecessary wants and all desires for unnecessary possessions, for simplicity was to be the keynote of my new life. It is sometimes quite difficult, of course, to tell what is necessary and what is not, for what is for one person a luxury may be for another person a necessity. In fact all luxuries, when used habitually, become necessities. In terms of the definition of luxury which I set up, however, any article or habit which does not make a man a better being morally, intellectually, and physically, is a luxury. When I examine the ways of men in terms of this definition, nearly all of what are commonly called necessities are shown to be luxuries, because without them a man can be as healthy, and as desirable a citizen from the standpoint of society as with them. If every man were to examine his possessions and habits with this principle in mind, he would no doubt find many which he could get along without much better than he does with them.

I neither smoke or drink, but I am as healthy and as happy as any of my friends and acquaintances who smoke like chimneys and drink like fish. I play no cards and no games, I indulge in no gambling of any kind; I chew no chewing gum, nor do I chew "Red Indian"; I use no Burma Shave, no gargles, no tooth-paste of any kind. I have found that the best tooth-cleanser is plain white salt spread on the tooth-brush, and the best mouthwash is salted water. I think these are the best because to this day I have not found it necessary to have a tooth filled.

Having rid myself systematically of many unnecessary possessions and habits, I began to simplify the necessities such as food, clothing and shelter to the point where they can preserve my health and are conducive to virtue, but do not undermine my physical strength or lower my morals. Our shelter is very simple and inexpensive. During the winter we rent a student apartment, usually a two-room apartment, and during the spring, summer, and fall, we stay in a small shanty, a two-room cabin or cottage in the woods. While traveling I usually stay in tourist cabins whenever possible, not only because they are safer, healthier, cheaper, and more convenient, but because they save me the trouble of tipping. Tipping at hotels is expensive and bothersome.

You tip the doorman as you enter the hotel. You tip the porter who brings your luggage as far as the lobby and no farther. You tip the bell-hop who carries the luggage from the lobby to your room. When you check out, you have to go through this entire process again, in reverse. Thank God one does not have to tip the maids, the window washers, the hotel builders, the tree growers, the bricklayers, or the plumbers!

I could afford to live in a better house or apartment if I wished to, but I have no desire to do so for several reasons. First, I do not consider that my education and personality are magnificent, and for me to live in a big house would be very much like a mouse dwelling in a palace. Instead of wasting my money on household luxuries, therefore, I would rather spend it for improving myself, my mind and soul. Secondly, I have found out that when I move into a good apartment or house, I feel fine only for a short time, for as soon as I am used to it, the house makes little difference to my happiness. Moreover, after I have stayed in a better house, when I move into a poorer one I feel a discomfort which is far greater than the feeling of happiness which I receive at first in a big house. My idea, then, is this: that one need not be so particular about a house so long as it is adequate to help preserve one's health and render one receptive to virtue.

My clothes are as simple as my shelter. I have only two working suits, and one tuxedo which I dislike owning but which I am obliged to wear now and then when I lecture. During the summer I wear inexpensive clothes; my whole summer outfit does not cost me more than five or six dollars. This includes two pairs of trousers, one white and one black, three shirts (one of which is a polo shirt), several pairs of socks, two undershirts and two pairs of shorts, a pair of old shoes, one sweater, and a bathing suit which my wife made out of something, I do not know what. I have had the same outfit for the past three summers, and I have no chance to get new garments, because my "Charlie" mends the old ones so well that they always look new.

I should perhaps add by way of parenthesis that "Charlie" is my wife. I call her "Charlie" because that was her name for me when we first came to know each other. She used it because most Americans, who can think of no better name for a Chinese than Charlie or "Chink," call me by those names. My wife thought it great fun to call me Charlie as the Americans do, but now I get a kick out of calling her Charlie.

My Charlie likewise wears very simple clothes. Unlike most women, she is not much interested in competing with the other members of her sex in purchasing funnier, sillier, and ever higher-priced hats, dresses, shoes and the like. Unlike most modern girls who can meet the wolf at the door and come out with a fur coat, she does not pay much attention to what other women wear. She wears what she feels she should wear, regardless of the fashions and styles of the moment. In this respect my Charlie is more American than most American ladies, if Americanism truly spells freedom and independence, not regimentation or slavish imitation. I regard the tendency to "keep up with the Joneses" as the most un-American characteristic of Americans, for in this country all men and women are free to wear what they will. My Charlie is also not interested in competing with other women in squandering money for cigarettes, drinks, lipstick, rouge, and the like. She thinks that these things should be left to women who have nothing to be proud of except their outward appearance. Her primary interest lies in art and culture, not in fashions and styles. As a result, during the three years of our married life she has spent not more than forty-five dollars, or fifteen dollars a year, for her clothes, hats, gloves, shoes, "hand-me-down" dresses, yarns and so on, and yet she is one of the most neatly dressed women I know. The secret of her cleverness is that she makes most of her own clothes, and the best dresses she has are those she has made at a small cost for materials only. One day she asked me what size shirt I wore. Thinking she would make me a shirt, I told her immediately. She said gleefully, "Good, it will fit me. Now I can wear your shirt any time I want!"

Furthermore, she economizes on new dresses by making

use of her old ones. She never throws away her old clothes, not even her old shoes. One day I caught her mending old shoes between her painting hours; she did a good job, too, and I patted her on the shoulder with this compliment: "Charlie, if you are not a Michelangelo, you are at least a good cobbler."

Lest some jealous Scotsman might try to run away with my wife, I had best say that though she is frugal in some ways, she spends a lot of money for many things in which American women would not be interested. It is a fact, too, that women are about the same the world over: each is a thing of beauty with a perpetual spring in the jaw!

An American lady was once very much provoked by my criticism of the usual feminine weakness in listening to advertisers, and said to me, "Dr. Park, don't you think we are helping our industries and employment by changing our styles and by indulging in all sorts of silly things? Just think where all the dressmakers and the manufacturers would be if we did not change our styles, buy new dresses, redden our fingernails, powder our noses, and so forth!"

Her statement may be true, but why worry about the poor industries? Should we live for our industries or should our industries live for us? Consider the wisdom of a people who invent machines to gain a better livelihood and then work their heads off to keep those machines running day and night! It is not my affair, but it looks like funny business to me.

For those who are never satisfied with anything and are constantly seeking for funnier and sillier styles in wearing apparel, the following story of a vain and wicked king will perhaps reveal to what extremes of folly their weakness may lead them:

Once upon a time there was a wicked king who wasted all his life and treasure in seeking for luxuries. He built four marvelous palaces, one for each of the four seasons. He had hundreds of chariots and thousands of wives. He had all kinds of apparel made of silk, fur, brocades interlaced with gold and silver, fabrics decorated with jewels and precious stones, but he was satisfied with none of them.

At last a wise weaver conceived of a clever idea. He approached the king and told him that he could make a mysterious robe which would be so light that no one could even feel whether or not the king was wearing it. "The most mysterious thing about it," the weaver said, "is that the robe cannot be seen by anyone whose heart is occupied by evil spirits." The king was delighted with the thought that at last he could try something really new and something which would satisfy his desires. He gave all his remaining fortune for the making of the robe.

The weaver operated three large weaving machines day and night for three months. The king was very impatient, and he periodically sent his ministers to the factory to see what the cloth looked like. When the ministers made these visits, they could see nothing but the busily running machines. Pointing to the machines, however, the weaver repeatedly exclaimed, "Isn't it marvelous? Isn't it marvelous?" The ministers were dumbfounded. Each of them thought that he alone could not see the robe because his heart was filled with evil spirits, and so each of them repeated after the weaver, "Isn't it marvelous? Isn't it marvelous?" After each of their visits to the factory, all of them reported to the king that the new robe was marvelous beyond description.

The three long months slowly passed, and the weaver finally came to present the mysterious robe. In presenting it to the king, he said again and again, "Isn't it marvelous?" The king could see nothing and could feel nothing, but he feared he could not see the robe because his heart was filled with evil spirits. Therefore he likewise exclaimed that it was simply marvelous. At once he discarded his old clothes and put on the new robe, as advised. He felt very comfortable and pleasant in his new apparel, and thought he should ride out in the open coach to show his subjects what a fine new robe he had acquired. As he made his tour of the city, millions of spectators formed an endless line along the streets where the king passed. All of them had heard about the peculiar characteristics of the robe and each thought that he alone could not see it. So all of them likewise said again and again, "How marvelous! How marvelous!" The king proudly rode through the streets amidst the stares of his curious subjects. Alas! Toward the end of the tour, his joy was replaced by sorrow and his pride was buried in shame when he heard the little school children crying out, "Naked, naked, our king is naked!"

The simplicity of our shelter and adornment is matched by that of our diet. Our meals are ample but not elaborate, and cost almost nothing in comparison with those of an American family. I once had the pleasure of examining the kitchen in a middle class American home. To my surprise, I found that the cost of the cooking utensils alone would represent a sum which would be a great fortune in my old country, at least in the eyes of the average man.

During all the years of our married life, my wife has spent for cooking utensils not more than five dollars in all, yet she manages to prepare food skilfully and efficiently. Her utensils include a frying pan, a rice boiler, a soup kettle, a kitchen knife, a chopping board which we picked up at Cape Cod, two rice bowls, two soup bowls, a half dozen spoons of various sizes, two pairs of chop sticks, two glasses which came with pimento cheese, one inexpensive and yet very attractive tea set which is used only when friends visit us.

Now about our diet. We believe that over-eating kills a great many more people in America than undernourishment, for there is no more harmful drug, no more deadly poison than over-consumption of heavy, rich food. Profiting from the American example, we try our best to avoid over-eating. Our food is certainly very simple and inexpensive, and perhaps for this reason visitors do not stay at our shanty very long. In the first place, we have no heavy breakfast. All we eat in the morning is an apple or an orange, or perhaps a bowl of home-made vegetable soup. But we drink no coffee or tea. When we are in China we drink tea because the water is not pure, but here in America the water is so pure that there is no excuse whatever for drinking tea or coffee, beverages which are only spoiled water. At about eleven o'clock we have a very light lunch composed usually of just one dish and of not more than three dishes at the most. Sometimes we eat noodle soup with dish of salad or a dish of cooked vegetable, and sometimes we eat hot cakes made with flour, egg, squash, or sauerkraut. Occasionally we eat cornflakes with cream, or pudding with cream; and now and then we have boiled potatoes and some vegetable soup. The noon meal is thus ultra-simple, for supper, usually eaten between four and five o'clock in the afternoon, is our dinner, or major meal for the day. For dinner we prepare at least two fresh vegetable dishes and a large bowl of boiled rice cooked in Chinese style. We eat no pies or cakes or dessert of any kind, and have almost eliminated meat from our diet, using it only to season our vegetables.

One might ask if we are not tired of eating vegetables and rice all the time. My answer is an emphatic "No!" Americans who dislike vegetables and rice do so because they do not cook them properly. You prepare vegetables in America in such a way that only the cows and the rabbits, or possibly Popeye, can enjoy them. Chinese cooks know how to prepare them so that one can genuinely enjoy eating them.

No matter how well the vegetable dishes are prepared, we consider that if the rice is no good, the whole meal is spoiled, for rice is the most important part of any meal in China. We do not ask our friends if they have had dinner; we ask them if they have had rice, which means the same thing.

One day I asked a hotel cook to prepare some rice for me, as I was tired of eating American dishes. He promised to do so, and my mouth began to water a day before the appointed hour for the feast. When the time came, I went to the dining room with the expectation with which a suitor would meet his would-be victim. The cook brought out the rice which I think he had prepared in the following way: He put three teaspoonsful of rice into a big boiler which contained about three or four gallons of water. He boiled it half a day so that all the vitamins would be extracted. He drained and washed it thoroughly with cold water, lest any taste might still be left in the brew. He then spread it over a large platter and

brought it to me. I thanked the cook and whispered to him:
"You will have a warm reception after your death."

It may seem to many of my readers that our diet is too
poor to keep us in good health. But we believe that it is
wiser to be frugal than to pack our poor stomachs relent-
lessly with huge chunks of meat, potatoes, pies and cakes,
thus necessitating a hunt for doctors, liver-pills and other
poison to hasten our ends. Thanks to our simple, scientific
diet, so far we have patronized no cure-all medicine, no
hospitals, and no doctors save on one or two exceptional
cases.

Once when I was lecturing for Rotary International, I
caught flu, which was then prevalent in several states. I
thought it was just a little cold, and kept on traveling instead
of resting. As a result, I became very ill. Under the punctili-
ous care of the hospitable Rotarians, however, I was able
to recover before long. When I asked, after regaining my
health, what medicine they had been feeding me, their reply
was: "Hot toddy and Rock and Rye."

At another time when I was touring in the sunny South
my right cheek began to swell. It kept on swelling until I
lost my right ear and cheek bones. I was scared and called
on one of the most reliable doctors in Hot Springs, Arkansas.
The doctor examined me carefully and then said that pus
had formed underneath the skin and therefore he must drill
a hole in my cheek to drain it out for the good of all concerned. He asked me to come back at three thirty o'clock the
same afternoon to have an operation. I promised to come
back, but something within me rebelled again going back to
that doctor, the chief reason being that he was a medical
doctor, not a surgeon. I called off the appointment and
searched for the best surgeon in the city. To my surprise, I
was directed to a very young man, Dr. Berry Bowman, who
seemed to be too young to know anything. When I told him
what the other doctor had said, I asked him to cut it open for
me. He examined it once more and said, "Well, if you insist
upon being cut up, I shall be glad to cut you anywhere; I can
cut out a few ribs or a leg or an arm, or anything in no time,
but be patient and do as I tell you to do and then I will oper-

ate on you tomorrow, or maybe day after tomorrow." He then instructed me to dissolve a tablespoonful of Epsom Salts in a quart of hot water, soak a towel in the mixture, and pack my cheek with the towel. It all sounded silly to me, but within twenty-four hours after applying the hot towels, I rediscovered my ear and cheek bones! That young man could have opened up my cheek whether there was pus or not and could have made a handsome fee, but instead he cured me at the cost of ten cents, which I paid for the Epsom Salts, and he got absolutely not a cent. I do not suppose he will ever get rich in that way, but I hope he will manage somehow to remain in the medical profession, for otherwise the world of tomorrow will lose a promising surgeon.

Although our diet is simple and inexpensive, we derive from it some of the greatest pleasures in life. We got delight not only when we eat it but also when we prepare it. With our friends we have had some of the best times and the finest recreation while preparing our meals in the kitchen. When you play cards, you are suspicious of each other and you cannot talk freely or companionably, but the minute you enter the kitchen all formalities and pretensions fly away. We cook, chop, wash, or play with the cooking utensils as children do with toys on the playground. While we peel the potatoes or make Chowtze (a kind of ravioli) we joke, we laugh, we talk, and we discuss all the problems of the world with no fear or reservation. When we have forgotten all about the good movies we have seen, or the grand dinners we have had at fashionable hotels, we shall still remember, and shall never forget, the memorable hours we have spent in the kitchen with such good friends as Chang and Shih.

Chang, who now teaches at the University of Chicago, is one of the most thoroughly unspoiled Chinese scholars to be found anywhere, and is an excellent cook who can prepare dishes that were enjoyed by the scholars of many hundred years ago. Shih comes from Shantung, is now a graduate student at the same university, and is likewise a very good cook. I might say that I am not such a bad cook myself. In many of the colleges where I have lectured for a week or more at a time, I have spent an hour or two in the kitchen to show the cook how to prepare Chinese dishes out of American materials. Although I cannot vouch for it, I do not think that my cooking has killed more people than my lecturing.

When my friends and I get together in our little kitchen, we desire nothing more for recreation; we do not think of cards, of movies, of symphonic music; we are the actors, the musicians and the spectators in our own little show. I can think of no other that I would rather attend.

We have culinary fun not only with our Chinese friends, but also with our American friends. One summer we saw a little bird building a cute little nest right over the doorway of our small cottage. We thought it quite poetic that we were living with rare birds right under the same roof, and asked some American friends who lived nearby to come and visit us, adding that if they would come, we would be glad to prepare a delicious dish of bird's nest soup for them. Many of them came to call, but only one dared to dine with us—an old bachelor who was dean of a local college. Since he had no one dependent on him, he probably felt it safe to try our meal even if it should prove a fatal experiment to do so. He came in the afternoon, and the first thing he inquired about was the bird's nest. He examined it carefully to find out what part of the nest we took off. After a thorough examination, he seemed to be much relieved that the nest was as yet untouched. While my wife was preparing the meal, I took our guest for a walk through the woods and along the lake shores; then I took him back to the cottage and in by a back door so that he could not see the bird's nest again. At dinner he was so suspicious that he could not enjoy the meal, so we told him that we had saved the nest for some other day. The joke is that we do not make bird's nest soup out of the ordinary birds' nests, but do it with the sputum of certain birds dwelling in the South Sea Islands.

I believe that a man can enjoy his meals and his sleep much more if he has actually earned them with the sweat of his brow. For example, the worker who earns his meal by the labor of his own hands can enjoy his baked beans and boiled potatoes much more than a rich man who has never lifted a hand in earning or preparing it can enjoy an extravagant dinner replete with cocktails and full-blooded beefsteak. A poor hard-working man can enjoy a day of rest during the weekend as much as the rich man can enjoy his entire year's vacation. A poor man's son who works his head off to earn nickles and dimes can get as much enjoyment out of spending his hard-earned dollar as a rich man's son can out of wasting the millions inherited from his father. A poor man's son who fights and bleeds to win the heart of a country maid is as happy in his humble shanty with a homely wife as a rich man's son in his mansion with a modern Cleopatra. This is because the sweetness of life comes in proportion to the bitterness of sacrifice which one has to taste while struggling for it. Perhaps herein lies the chief reason why we moderns are not satisfied with all the comforts and conveniences we have today. We have not paid for them, we have not worked for them, we have not shed enough tears and enough blood to appreciate what we have.

With this idea in the back of my head, I try to feel the thorns of a rosebush in order to enjoy the fragrance of the roses. I try to feel the sting of a bee to appreciate the taste of honey. I try to experience cold, bleak, wintry nights in order to appreciate the sunshine and smiles of spring and summer.

When spring comes we go out into the fields and pick dandelions, garden spinach, watercress, and whatever plants are edible, and we make fresh salad out of them, or we boil them to make soup, or preserve them and make hot cakes or "chop suey"—I do not mean the kind served in America.

When summer and autumn arrive, we try to pick cherries, apples or potatoes. When we find no opportunity for this kind of work, we go out "nutting" in the woods. There we pick butternuts, chestnuts, and whatever nuts we can find. We get the biggest thrill of our lives when we race for food and struggle for life in competition with the squirrels and birds.

On these expeditions we enjoy watching animals greatly. Once we ran into a herd of elks, six of them in all, one male and five females. I immediately suggested that they were Mormon elks, for I assumed that the male had five wives. Naturally, my wife would not agree with me; she said that only one of the females was the wife of the male elk and that the other four were either his daughters or sisters, or perhaps distant cousins with the same surname. We argued for a long time, and in the end my wife won the debate as usual.

I was vindicated some time after, however, when we met some mountaineers who knew something about animal life. We asked them how many wives an elk usually has, and they told us that the sacred laws of the elk kingdom are comparable to the practices of the Democrats and Republicans; that is, all the wives go to the winner in a combat, as all the spoils belong to the victors in an election. They told us, for example, that one elk which had twelve wives once fought another elk which had only six wives and defeated it. As a result, all of the six wives of the defeated animal deserted him and followed the winner.

America is a land of plenty. Anyone who has as much common sense as the hill-billies have will never have to worry about his living. The land is covered with food which, if properly distributed, could without any difficulty feed all the races of mankind. On the very camp site where I spent the past summer, I actually saw rivers, valleys, and hills of apples, pears and other fruits. The fruit fell so thick and fast that it covered the hills, and then rolled down into the valleys to form rivers of apples. But no one cared to pick them or save them or sell them to city folk. Waste! I never understood the meaning of that word until I came to this land of plenty. As I was walking over those inoffensive apples, many old Oriental tales of economy and prodigality flashed into my mind as illustrations of the contrasting situation in Eastern Asia. Here is one of these stories:

One morning a fisherman came to sell fish at the home of an old woman miser. Her daughter-in-law handled the fish as if she were going to buy, but for the sake of economy she finally sent away the fisherman without buying any. Afterwards she washed her hands in the kettle and made soup with the water and served her mother-in-law, who exclaimed that the soup was really delicious. Hoping to be praised for her frugality, the girl told the story of how she had made the soup. Unexpectedly her mother-in-law shouted, "You squanderer! How extravagant! Why, if you had washed your hands in the sauce jar instead of in the kettle, we could have eaten fish soup all the year round."

The young lady was so chagrined that she told the whole story to an old woman who lived in the same town. Instead of expressing her sympathy for that unfortunate young lady, the old woman said mockingly, "You deserve a punishment ten times more severe. If you had washed your hands in the community well, the whole town could have eaten fish soup!"

I remembered another story of the same nature. An old Japanese miser said to another on a scorching hot day that he had made a fan last thirty years. When asked how he did it, he replied, "Instead of opening the fan all the way out, I open only one stick at a time. The first stick served me about three years, the second stick another three years, and so on to the end of the fan."

"Use a good fan for only thirty years?" exclaimed the second miser. "Why, this fan of mine has lasted my family through two generations, and I expect to leave it to my eldest son. I never wave a fan at all. Waving a fan! What wear and tear! What extravagance! No, indeed; I open my fan out like this and wave my face about it instead of waving the fan."

America Is in the Heart
Carlos Bulosan

The poet and author Carlos Bulosan was born on November 21, 1911, in Binalonan, the Philippines. At the time of his birth, hundreds of field workers and laborers were coming to California and Hawaii to find better wages. The letters sent home by these workers praised America and all the success to be found there. Some claimed to have moved up from fruit-picker to contractor in a matter of weeks. Deciding that he, too, would look for work beyond his mother's vegetable-selling in Binalonan, Bulosan bought a steerage passage on a ship in 1930.

From Alaska, Bulosan went directly to Lompoc, California, where he joined his brother Dionisio. Even with Dionisio's help, California was not what Bulosan expected it to be. The male-female ratio among Filipinos was fourteen to one, which encouraged some Filipino men to marry white women—a phenomenon that caused resentment among some white men. The sexual rivalry and job competition among many immigrant groups created tense relations between Filipinos and Americans. Bulosan would soon become frightened by news of violence committed, frequently without cause, against Filipino adults and children.

Soon after his arrival in America, Bulosan became ill, and went to stay with another brother, Aurelio. Bulosan spent his time in the library, pursuing a writing career while his brother found occasional work to support him.

In 1934, he began a bimonthy literary magazine of his own called *The New Tide*, a radical publication with a socialist slant. As a result of this venture, Bulosan met many literary luminaries, including the poet William Carlos Williams. In 1936, however, the aspiring Filipino writer was sent to a Los Angeles hospital for treatment of tuberculosis. Other ailments in his knees and kidneys would cripple Bulosan throughout his life, but it was during these periods of illness that he wrote most.

In 1939, Carlos Bulosan published his first collections of poetry, *Letter from America* and *Chorus for America*, to some acclaim. The publication of his third collection, however, *The Laughter of My Father*, in 1944, was an immediate hit that was translated into several languages and broadcast over wartime radio. At the urging of his publisher, Bulosan wrote his autobiography, *America Is in the Heart*, in 1946, but because of his affiliation with unions and radical politics, Bulosan's sales suffered. By the end of the McCarthy era, the alcoholic Bulosan was very ill, relying on his companion, Josephine Patrick, for support. He died on September 11, 1956. In this chapter from his autobiography, Carlos Bulosan looks back to his arrival in America, where he confronts American racial violence for the first time, a subject that would later permeate his writing.

CHAPTER 17

I reached Los Angeles in the evening. An early autumn rain was falling. I waited in the station, looking among the passengers for Filipino faces. Then I went out and turned northward on Los Angeles Street, and suddenly familiar signs on barber shops and restaurants came to view. I felt as though I had discovered a new world. I entered a restaurant and heard the lonely sound of my dialect, the soft staccato sound of home. I knew at once that I would meet some people I had known in the Philippines.

I sat on one of the stools and waited. I saw three American girls come in with three Filipinos. I thought I knew one of the Filipinos, so I approached him and spoke in Ilocano. But he did not understand me; even when I spoke in Pangasinan, he did not understand me. He was of another tribe, possibly a Visayan.

"If you are looking for your brother," said the proprietor to me, "go to the dance hall. That is where you always find them."

I asked him to direct me. It was still early, but the girls were already arriving. They went hastily up the stairs and their perfume lingered after them. I stood outside for a long time watching through the door until the guard closed it.

Filipinos started going inside, putting their hands high above their heads so that the guard could search them for concealed weapons. The guard was a white man and he was very rough with them. I went to Main Street, turned to the north, and found the Mexican district. The sound of Spanish made me feel at home, and I mingled with the drunks and the jobless men. In the old plaza some men were debating a political issue; a shaggy old man was preaching to a motley crowd. And farther down the street, near Olvera Market, I saw little Mexican boys carrying shoeshine boxes. They were eating sunflower seeds and throwing the empty shells into each other's faces.

It was now getting late. The crowd in the street was dispersing. The bells in the church tower began to ring. I looked up and saw devotees coming out of the door. It was already ten o'clock and the night services were over. The haggard preacher in the plaza leaped from his perch and disappeared in the crowd. I sat on a wooden bench and put my cap over my face so that I could sleep in the glare of the street lamps.

Toward midnight a drunk came to my bench and lay down to sleep. I moved away from him, giving him enough space to be comfortable. Then a young Mexican whose voice sounded like a girl's sat beside me. He put his hand on my knee and started telling me about a place where we could get something to eat. I was hungry and cold, but I was afraid of him.

I walked away from him, watching the church across the street. When I was sure no one was looking, I rushed to the door and entered. The church was empty. I went to a comfortable corner and lay on the floor. I saw on old man with a white beard coming in the door, and I thought he saw me. But he went to the candles and blew them out one by one, then disappeared through a side door. It was like heaven, it was so warm and quiet and comfortable. I closed my eyes and went to sleep.

I was awakened in the morning by the merry peals of tiny bells. I ran across the room and through the door, bumping into many people who were arriving for the morning services. I walked in the crowded street toward the Filipino district. I felt as though a beast were tearing at the walls of my stomach. The pain nauseated me: I was hungry again.

I thought I saw my brother Macario in a streetcar. I jumped on with all the power of my legs, but I was wrong. I got out on the next block and started walking aimlessly. I began to wonder if my life would always be one long flight from fear. When had I landed in America? It seemed so long ago. I crossed the green lawn of the new City Hall.

◆

I walked from Main Street to Vermont Avenue, three miles away. I returned to town by streetcar and went to First Street again. A Filipino poolroom was crowded, and I went inside to sit on a bench. The players were betting and once in a while they would give the table boy a dime. I waited until the men started coming in groups, because their day's work was done.

I was talking to a gambler when two police detectives darted into the place and shot a little Filipino in the back. The boy fell on his knees, face up, and expired. The players stopped for a moment, agitated, then resumed playing, their faces coloring with fear and revolt. The detectives called an ambulance, dumped the dead Filipino into the street, and left when an interne and his assistant arrived. They left hurriedly, untouched by their act, as though killing were a part of their day's work.

All at once I heard many tongues speaking excitedly. They did not know why the Filipino was shot. It seemed that the victim was new in the city. I was bewildered.

"Why was he shot?" I asked a man near me.

"They often shoot Pinoys like that," he said. "Without provocation. Sometimes when they have been drinking and they want to have fun, they come to our district and kick or beat the first Filipino they meet."

"Why don't you complain?" I asked.

"Complain?" he said. "Are you kidding? Why, when we complain it always turns out that we attacked them! And they become more vicious, I am telling you! That is why once in a while a Pinoy shoots a detective. You will see it one of these days."

"If they beat me I will kill them," I said.

The Filipino looked at me and walked away. As the crowd was beginning to disperse, I saw the familiar head of my brother Macario. He was entering the poolroom with a friend. I rushed to him and touched his hand. He could not believe that I was in America.

"Why didn't you write that you were coming?" he asked.

"I did not know I was coming, brother," I said. "Besides, I did not know your address. I knew that I would not stop traveling until I found you. You have grown older."

"I guess I have, all right," he said. Then suddenly he became quiet, as though he were remembering something. He looked at me and said, "Let's go to my hotel."

I noticed that he did not speak English the way he used to speak it in the Philippines. He spoke more rapidly now. As I walked beside him, I felt that he was afraid I would discover some horror that was crushing his life. He was undecided what to do when we reached Broadway Street, and stopped several times in deep thought. He had changed in many ways. He seemed in constant agitation, and he smoked one cigarette after another. His agitation became more frightening each minute.

"Why was the Filipino shot?" I asked, pretending not to notice his mental anguish.

"Someday you will understand, Carlos," he said.

Carlos! He had changed my name, too! Everything was changing. Why? And why all this secrecy about the death of one Filipino? Were the American people conspiring against us? I looked at my brother sidelong but said nothing. Suddenly I felt hungry and lonely and tired.

We turned to the north and came to a hotel near the Hall of Justice building. We took the slow elevator to the fifth floor. My brother knocked on a door and looked at me. There was a hunted look in his face. I heard many voices inside. A patter of feet, then the door opened. The strong smell of whisky brought tears to my eyes. It was so strong it almost choked me. I knew at once that there was a party. I saw three American girls in evening gowns and ten Filipinos. I was amazed at their immaculate suits and shoes.

"Friends," my brother announced, "this is my kid brother— Carlos! He has just arrived from the Philippines."

"More than six months ago," I corrected him. "I went to Alaska first, then came down to Los Angeles. I think I like it here. I will buy a house here someday."

"Buy a house?" a man near me said, his face breaking into a smile. But when he noticed that my brother was looking hard at him, he suddenly changed his tone and offered me a glass. "Good, good!" he said. "Buy all the houses you want. And if you need a janitor—" He turned around to hide the cynical twist of his mouth.

Then they rushed to me. All at once several cocktail glasses were offered to me. The girls pulled me to the table, tilting a glass in my mouth. The Filipinos shouted to me to drink.

I looked at my brother, ashamed. "I don't drink," I said.

"Go on—drink!" a curly-haired boy prodded me. "Drink like hell. This is America. We all drink like hell. Go on, boy!"

He was only a boy, but he drank like a man. I watched him empty three glasses, one after the other. My brother came to me.

"This is a wedding party," he whispered.

"Who got married?" I asked, looking around.

"I think that one," he said, pointing to a woman. "That is the man. I think he is twenty years old."

"She is old enough to be his mother," I said.

"They know what they want, don't they?" He winked at me foolishly and emptied another glass.

I gripped the glass in my hand so hard that it nearly broke.

It was past midnight when the party was over. I thought some of the men would go home, but it was only Leon who announced that he was leaving. The bridal couple started undressing in the other room, and the other men came to the outer room with the two girls. The curly-haired boy switched off the lights and the men started grabbing the girls.

I could see the red glow of their cigarettes moving in the dark. The girls would protest for a while, cursing the men. Then they would quiet down and go to bed, laughing yolkily when they threw their gowns on the floor. My brother took my arm and told me to follow him. We walked silently through the hall and down the stairs. I heard the married woman squealing and laughing, and I was bewildered and afraid. I wanted my brother to explain everything to me.

The sky was overcast and the lights in the streets were out. Newsboys were shouting the morning papers. We walked for hours because it was hard to talk. We had not seen each other for years, and it was difficult to begin. We could only pick up fragments of our lives and handle them fearfully, as though the years had made us afraid to know ourselves. I was suddenly ashamed that I could not express the gentle feeling I had for my brother. Was this brutality changing me, too?

At dawn we walked back to the hotel. What I saw in the room would come back to me again and again. One of the girls was in the bed with two men. The other girl was on the couch with two other men. They were all nude. Six men were sleeping on the floor and three others were sprawled under the bed.

My brother motioned to me to undress, switching off the

lights. I found a space near the closet, and I lay down hoping to sleep. My heart was pounding very fast. Leon came into the room with another girl. He cursed the sleeping forms and took the girl to the other room. They went to bed with the married couple.

I wanted to talk to my brother in the dark. But when I put my ear close to his mouth, I knew that he was already asleep. I could not sleep any more; my mind was wandering. I rolled over on my other side and tried to remember a prayer I used to recite when I was a little boy in Mangusmana.

A man named Nick was the first to wake up. He was making coffee in a big pot when I went to the kitchen. The girls were still in bed. My brother woke up suddenly and went to the bathroom. He was fully dressed when he came out.

"I'll look for a job today," he said.

"There is no use," Nick said. "I have been looking for a job for three months."

"I'll try, anyway," said my brother.

"Well, I hope some worker dies today," Nick said.

My brother looked at me. The girls woke up. They walked unashamedly in the room. The other men came to the kitchen and began drinking whisky again.

It was then that I learned their names. José, the curly-haired boy, was Nick's brother. They had both been going to college some months before, but the depression had deprived them of their jobs. Mariano, with the well-trimmed mustache, had been an agent for a clothing company that had failed. Victor and Manuel had worked in an apartment house in Hollywood. Luz, long out of a job, had come from the farm to live in the city. Gazamen was the life of the party: he was always singing and playing his portable phonograph. Leon was selling tickets in a dance hall: he was the only one who had a job. Alonzo was a college student, and had never worked as far as the other men knew. Ben was doing house work in Beverly Hills, but he seldom came home with money.

I found my brother Macario in a strange world. I could stand the poverty and hunger, but this desperate cynicism disturbed me. Were these Filipinos revolting against

American society in this debased form? Was there no hope for them?

One night Leon, who was the sole mainstay of our company, came home with a bottle of bootleg whisky. He brought a girl with him. She was small and dark. Suddenly, in the middle of the night, the girl started screaming. We rushed to the other room, but it was too late. Leon was dead and cold. The girl cried loudly and hysterically. Mariano struck her with his fist, felling her. The blow was so hard it stunned her. It was not that he hated her; it was that this was the sad end of a little world that had revolved around a man who sold tickets in a dance hall.

Barrio Boy
Ernesto Galarza

The economist and social activist Ernesto Galarza was born in Jalcocotan, Mexico, just as the Mexican Revolution was beginning. Desiring to protect her children from the swelling political strife, Ernesto's mother moved the family to the United States. They arrived in San Francisco in 1910, and later settled in Sacramento.

In Sacramento, Ernesto attended public school, while spending his summer vacations as a farm laborer. After graduating from high school, Galarza won a scholarship to Occidental College, making up the rest of his expenses by doing odd jobs. He married and attended Stanford University as a graduate student in economics. After receiving his master's, Galarza went to Columbia University on a fellowship to earn his doctorate. By 1934, Galarza needed only his dissertation to receive his degree, but his family, including two daughters, was in desperate need of money. He worked at the Foreign Policy Association, and then took a job with the Pan American Union as an education research associate. Finally, in 1944, Galarza completed his dissertation and received his Ph.D.

Galarza became director of the Division of Labor and Social Information of the Pan American Union in 1940. During World War II, part of Galarza's job was to investigate the *bracero* (Mexican farm workers) program. Through conversations with workers and visits to camps, Galarza concluded that the Mexican workers were being exploited by landowners with the help of the U.S. government. Unable to force much change among American politicians, Galarza left the Pan American Union in 1946 and joined the staff at the American Federation of Labor's National Farm Labor Union to help organize a strike against the Di Giorgio Fruit Company. Galarza was instrumental in many NFLU activities as he fought against landowners who hired illegal Mexican immigrants, and then exploited them through blackmail. Such successes made him unpopular among bureaucrats. Galarza was often slandered as a Communist by his enemies, and his family suffered the consequences of public ridicule and blacklisting.

Galarza wrote many books on farm labor, including *Strangers in Our Fields* (1956), *Merchants of Labor: The Mexican Braceros Story* (1964), and *Spiders in the House and Workers in the Fields* (1970). He left farm-labor activism after working for the AFL-CIO's Agricultural Workers Organizing Committee. The farm-labor movement died down in the early 1960s, with no signs of the *bracero* system ever ending.

Today Ernesto Galarza works as a consultant for projects concerning the plight of Mexican immigrants in America, speaks at conferences, and teaches. In the following section from Galarza's 1971 autobiography, *Barrio Boy*, the young Ernesto goes to California public school and encounters other immigrants. Soon after his family learns that their extended family will not be allowed to enter the United States, Galarza questions his desire to stay in such an unaccepting nation.

LIFE IN THE LOWER PART OF TOWN

In a corner of the musty lobby of the Hotel Español, we waited until it was our turn to talk with the manager. The place was filled with people stacking and moving luggage, some talking in Spanish, others in English and other strange tongues. The manager wore a long white apron and a blue beret and spoke *gachupín* like the Spaniards of Mazatlán. He led us to a back room, took our baggage claim check, showed us the dining room and returned later with our tin trunk.

The hotel was a prison, even more confining than the alley in Tucson. We were frightened by the traffic of mule teams, wagons, and the honking automobiles that passed by continuously. From our view in the lobby the street was a jumble. Up and down from the doorway of the hotel all we could see were shops and stores, warehouses and saloons, hotels and restaurants, few ladies and no children. Sacramento, I decided, was an ugly place, not like the vineyards and the eucalyptus trees with pastel colored trunks we had seen from the train.

For breakfast in the hotel kitchen we drank coffee with buttered hard rolls. Lunch was not served and since we were afraid to venture into the street, we did not eat. Supper was served in a room without windows, at a long table crowded with people who lived in the hotel and outsiders who came for meals. It was served by the manager, who was also the cook. Up and down both sides of the table he poured boiling soup out of a kettle into our plates, forked out pieces of meat, sawed thick chunks of bread from loaves as long as my arm, and poured wine. It was a noisy table, with loud talk and the clatter of dishes and the burly *gachupínes* slurping soup. But it was a show to us, funny and very un-Mexican.

In the corner of the lobby nearest the street window we sat for hours on a wooden bench, watching the pedestrians closely. At last we saw the two we were waiting for. Gustavo and José passed by the window, looked in, and stepped inside. With a shout I charged them and wedged myself between their legs, where I held tight. The three exchanged greetings.

"How are you, sister?"

"Very well. How have things been with you?"

After a little weeping by Doña Henriqueta we stood and looked at one another. My uncles were dressed in blue bib overalls and work jackets of the same stuff with brass buttons, and caps. Gustavo was the shorter of the two, chunky and thick-shouldered. Jose was thin all over—neck, arms, fingers, and face.

They paid our hotel bill and we gathered our things. We stepped into the cold drizzly street, my uncles carrying the suitcases and tin trunk and holding me by the hands. With the two of them on either side and Doña Henriqueta behind me I trotted confidently through the scurrying crowd on the sidewalks, the rumbling drays and the honking automobiles. I was beginning to lose my fear of Sacramento.

It was a short walk from the hotel to the house where we turned in, the tallest I had ever seen. A wide wooden stairway went up from the sidewalk to a porch on the second story, and above that another floor, and still higher a gable as wide as the house decorated with carvings and fretwork. The porch balustrade was in the same gingerbread style of lattice work and the wooden imitation of a fringe between the round pillars. We walked up the stairway and the three of us waited while José went inside.

He came back with the landlady. She was certainly a gringo lady—two heads taller than Gustavo, twice as wide as José, square-jawed, rosy-faced, a thin nose with a small bulge on the end and like all Americans, with rather large feet. She had a way of blinking when she smiled at us.

Standing as straight as the posts of the porch and holding her shoulders square and straight across she seemed to me more like a general than a lady.

Mostly with blinks and hand motions and a great many ceremonial smiles, we were introduced to Mrs. Dodson, who led us into the house, down some narrow, dark stairs and to the back of the first floor where she left us in our new apartment.

It consisted of one large room, a kitchen and a closet that had been a bathroom from which all the fixtures had been removed except the bathtub. Directly behind the kitchen was a cramped back yard enclosed on three sides by a board fence like all the other American fences I had already seen—dirty gray planks, streaked and cracked. Rising from the yard there was a steep wooden stairway resting on cement blocks. It made a right angle at the second story and turned back toward the house, continuing to the third floor. The stairway had panels on each side and a landing on each floor. From the yard the fire escape looked like a ladder into the wild blue yonder. Since people rarely used it, and the panels made private cubicles of the landings, I discovered that I could use them as private crow's nests from which I could survey the *barrio's* back yards for blocks around.

The apartment was furnished. In the living room there were three single beds, a clothes closet as high as the ceiling, an oil stove, a round dining table covered with checkered linoleum, a chest of drawers, and some chairs. In the kitchen there was a gas stove on a wooden platform, a table, a bench, and a dish closet next to the sink. A small icebox on the back porch dripped into a rubber tube to the ground through a hole in the floor. The bathtub in the big closet was covered with boards and a mattress on top of them. This was to be my room. It had no windows but an electric cord with a small bulb and a print curtain over the door connecting with the kitchen gave me quarters of my own.

We reached the front door through a long gloomy hall that opened on the street porch, from which we stepped to the sidewalk over a boardwalk. Along one side of the house there was an open corridor between the house and the fence, by which we got to the toilet and bathroom that all the tenants on the first floor used. We were enclosed from the street by a picket fence flanking the stairs, set off by a scraggly peach tree on each side. Because our rooms were dank and cheerless we sat on the porch or stood behind the picket fence, street watching, when the weather permitted. Mrs. Dodson's apartment was on the second floor back, with a door to a side porch from which she could look out over the yard and the street. This was the command post of 418 L Street, our refuge in a strange land.

Since Gustavo and José were off to work on the track early the next morning after our arrival, it was up to us to tidy the apartment and get the household into shape. As usual when we moved into a new place, we dusted and swept and scrubbed floors, doors, woodwork, windows, and every piece of furniture. Mrs. Dodson provided us with cans of a white powder that was sprinkled on everything that needed cleaning—cans with the picture of an old lady dressed in wooden shoes, a swinging skirt, and white bonnet.

The Americans, we discovered, put practically everything in cans on which they pasted fascinating labels, like *La Vieja Dotch Klen-ser*. Doña Henriqueta admired the bright colors and the delicious pictures of fruits and vegetables. We spelled and sounded out as well as we could the names of unfamiliar foods, like corn flakes and Karo syrup. On the kitchen shelf we arranged and rearranged the boxes and tins, with their displays of ingenious designs and colors, grateful that the Americans used pictures we knew to explain words that we didn't.

Once the routine of the family was well started, my mother and I began to take short walks to get our bearings. It was half a block in one direction to the lumber yard and the grocery store; half a block in the other to the saloon and the Japanese motion picture theater. In between were the tent and awning shop, a Chinese restaurant, a secondhand store, and several houses like our own. We noted by the numbers on the posts at the corners that we lived between 4th and 5th streets on L.

Once we could fix a course from these signs up and down and across town we explored farther. On Sixth near K there was the Lyric Theater with a sign that we easily translated into Lírico. It was next to a handsome red stone house with high turrets, like a castle. Navigating by these key points and following the rows of towering elms along L Street, one by one we found the post office on 7th and K; the cathedral, four blocks farther east; and the state capitol with its golden dome.

It wasn't long before we ventured on walks around Capitol Park which reminded me of the charm and the serenity of the Alameda in Tepic. In some fashion Mrs. Dodson had got over to us that the capitol was the house of the government. To us it became El Capitolio or, as more formally, the Palacio de Gobierno. Through the park we walked into the building itself, staring spellbound at the marble statue of Queen Isabel and Christopher Columbus. It was awesome, standing in the presence of that gigantic admiral, the one who had discovered America and Mexico and Jalcocotán, as Doña Henriqueta assured me.

After we had thoroughly learned our way around in the daytime we found signs that did not fail us at night. From the window of the projection room of the Lyric Theater a brilliant purple light shone after dark. A snake of electric lights kept whipping round and round a sign over the Albert Elkus store. K Street on both sides was a double row of bright show windows that led up to the Land Hotel and back to Breuner's, thence down one block to the lumber yard, the grocery store, and our house. We had no fear of getting lost.

These were the boundaries of the lower part of town, for that was what everyone called the section of the city between Fifth Street and the river and from the railway yards to the Y-street levee. Nobody ever mentioned an upper part of town; at least, no one could see the difference because the whole city was built on level land. We were not lower topographically, but in other ways that distinguished between Them, the uppers, and Us, the lowers. Lower Sacramento was the quarter that people who made money moved away from. Those of us who lived in it stayed there because our problem was to make a living and not to make money. A long while back, Mr. Howard, the business agent of the union told me, there had been stores and shops, fancy residences, and smart hotels in this neighborhood. The crippled old gentleman who lived in the next room down the hall from us, explained to me that our house, like the others in the neighborhood, had been the home of rich people who had stables in the back yards, with back entrances by way of the alleys. Mr. Hansen, the Dutch carpenter, had helped build such residences. When the owners moved uptown, the back yards had been fenced off and subdivided, and small rental cottages had been built in the alleys in place of the stables. Handsome private homes were turned into flophouses for men who stayed one night, hotels for working people, and rooming houses, like ours.

Among the saloons, pool halls, lunch counters, pawn-shops, and poker parlors was skid row, where drunk men with black eyes and unshaven faces lay down in the alleys to sleep.

The lower quarter was not exclusively a Mexican *barrio* but a mix of many nationalities. Between L and N Streets two blocks from us, the Japanese had taken over. Their homes were in the alleys behind shops, which they adver-tised with signs covered with black scribbles. The women walked on the street in kimonos, wooden sandals, and white stockings, carrying neat black bundles on their backs and wearing their hair in puffs with long ivory needles stuck through them. When they met they bowed, walked a couple of steps, and turned and bowed again, repeating this several times. They carried babies on their backs, not in their arms, never laughed or went into the saloons. On Sundays the men sat in front of their shops, dressed in gowns, like priests.

Chinatown was on the other side of K Street, toward the Southern Pacific shops. Our houses were old, but those in which the Chinese kept stores, laundries, and restaurants were older still. In black jackets and skullcaps the older merchants smoked long pipes with a tiny brass cup on the end. In their dusty store windows there was always the same assortment of tea packages, rice bowls, saucers, and pots decorated with blue temples and dragons.

In the hotels and rooming houses scattered about the *bar-rio* the Filipino farm workers, riverboat stewards, and houseboys made their homes. Like the Mexicans they had their own poolhalls, which they called clubs. Hindus from the rice and fruit country north of the city stayed in the rooming houses when they were in town, keeping to them-selves. The Portuguese and Italian families gathered in their own neighborhoods along Fourth and Fifth Streets south-ward toward the Y-street levee. The Poles, Yugo-Slavs, and Koreans, too few to take over any particular part of it, were scattered throughout the *barrio*. Black men drifted in and out of town, working the waterfront. It was a kaleidoscope of colors and languages and customs that surprised and absorbed me at every turn.

Although we, the foreigners, made up the majority of the population of that quarter of Sacramento, the Americans had by no means given it up to us. Not all of them had moved above Fifth Street as the *barrio* became more crowded. The bartenders, the rent collectors, the insurance salesmen, the mates on the river boats, the landladies, and most importantly, the police—these were all gringos. So were the craftsmen, like the barbers and printers, who did not move their shops uptown as the city grew. The teachers of our one public school were all Americans. On skid row we rarely saw a drunk wino who was not a gringo. The operators of the pawnshops and secondhand stores were white and mostly Jewish.

For the Mexicans the *barrio* was a colony of refugees. We came to know families from Chihuahua, Sonora, Jalisco, and Durango. Some had come to the United States even before the revolution, living in Texas before migrating to California. Like ourselves, our Mexican neighbors had come this far moving step by step, working and waiting, as if they were feeling their way up a ladder. They talked of relatives who had been left behind in Mexico, or in some far-off city like Los Angeles or San Diego. From whatever place they had come, and however short or long the time they had lived in the United States, together they formed the *colonia mexicana*. In the years between our arrival and the First World War, the *colonia* grew and spilled out from the lower part of town. Some families moved into the alley shacks east of the Southern Pacific tracks, close to the canneries and warehouses and across the river among the orchards and rice mills.

The *colonia* was like a sponge that was beginning to leak along the edges, squeezed between the levee, the railroad tracks, and the river front. But it wasn't squeezed dry, because it kept filling with newcomers who found families who took in boarders: basements, alleys, shanties, rundown rooming houses and flop joints where they could live.

Crowded as it was, the *colonia* found a place for these

chicanos, the name by which we called an unskilled worker born in Mexico and just arrived in the United States. The *chicanos* were fond of identifying themselves by saying they had just arrived from *el macizo*, by which they meant the solid Mexican homeland, the good native earth. Although they spoke of *el macizo* like homesick persons, they didn't go back. They remained, as they said of themselves, *pura raza*. So it happened that José and Gustavo would bring home for a meal and for conversation workingmen who were *chicanos* fresh from *el macizo* and like ourselves, *pura raza*. Like us, they had come straight to the *barrio* where they could order a meal, buy a pair of overalls, and look for work in Spanish. They brought us vague news about the revolution, in which many of them had fought as *villistas, huertistas, maderistas,* or *zapatistas*. As an old *maderista,* I imagined our *chicano* guests as battle-tested revolutionaries, like myself.

As poor refugees, their first concern was to find a place to sleep, then to eat and find work. In the *barrio* they were most likely to find all three, for not knowing English, they needed something that was even more urgent than a room, a meal, or a job, and that was information in a language they could understand. This information had to be picked up in bits and pieces—from families like ours, from the conversation groups in the poolrooms and the saloons.

Beds and meals, if the newcomers had no money at all, were provided—in one way or another—on trust, until the new *chicano* found a job. On trust and not on credit, for trust was something between people who had plenty of nothing, and credit was between people who had something of plenty. It was not charity or social welfare but something my mother called *asistencia*, a helping given and received on trust, to be repaid because those who had given it were themselves in need of what they had given. *Chicanos* who had found work on farms or in railroad camps came back to pay us a few dollars for *asistencia* we had provided weeks or months before.

Because the *barrio* was a grapevine of job information, the transient *chicanos* were able to find work and repay their obligations. The password of the barrio was *trabajo* and the community was divided in two—the many who were looking for it and the few who had it to offer. Pickers, foremen, contractors, drivers, field hands, pick and shovel men on the railroad and in construction came back to the *barrio* when work was slack, to tell one another of the places they had been, the kind of *patrón* they had, the wages paid, the food, the living quarters, and other important details. Along Second Street, labor recruiters hung black-boards on their shop fronts, scrawling in chalk offers of work. The grapevine was a mesh of rumors and gossip, and men often walked long distances or paid bus fares or a con-tractor's fee only to find that the work was over or all the jobs were filled. Even the chalked signs could not always be relied on. Yet the search for *trabajo*, or the *chanza*, as we also called it, went on because it had to.

We in the *barrio* considered that there were two kinds of *trabajo*. There were the seasonal jobs, some of them a hun-dred miles or more from Sacramento. And there were the closer *chanzas* to which you could walk or ride on a bicy-cle. These were the best ones, in the railway shops, the can-neries, the waterfront warehouses, the lumber yards, the produce markets, the brick kilns, and the rice mills. To be able to move from the seasonal jobs to the close-in work was a step up the ladder. Men who had made it passed the word along to their relatives or their friends when there was a *chanza* of this kind.

It was all done by word of mouth, this delicate wiring of the grapevine. The exchange points of the network were the places where men gathered in small groups, apparently to loaf and chat to no purpose. One of these points was our kitchen, where my uncles and their friends sat and talked of *el macizo* and of the revolution but above all of the *chanzas* they had heard of.

There was not only the everlasting talk about *trabajo*, but also the never-ending action of the *barrio* itself. If work was action the *barrio* was where the action was. Every morning a parade of men in oily work clothes and carrying lunch buck-ets went up Fourth Street toward the railroad shops, and every evening they walked back, grimy and silent. Horse drawn drays with low platforms rumbled up and down our street carrying the goods the city traded in, from kegs of beer to sacks of grain. Within a few blocks of our house there were smithies, hand laundries, a macaroni factory, and all manner of places where wagons and buggies were repaired, horses stabled, bicycles fixed, chickens dressed, clothes washed and ironed, furniture repaired, candy mixed, tents sewed, wine grapes pressed, bottles washed, lumber sawed, suits fitted and tailored, watches and clocks taken apart and put together again, vegetables sorted, railroad cars unloaded, boxcars iced, barges freighted, ice cream cones molded, soda pop bottled, fish scaled, salami stuffed, corn ground for masa, and bread ovened. To those who knew where these were located in the alleys, as I did, the whole *barrio* was an open workshop. The people who worked there came to know you, let you look in at the door, made jokes, and occasionally gave you an odd job.

This was the business district of the *barrio*. Around it and through it moved a constant traffic of drays, carts, bicycles, pushcarts, trucks, and high-wheeled automobiles with black canvas tops and honking horns. On the tailgates of drays and wagons, I nipped rides when I was going home with a gunnysack full of empty beer bottles or my gleanings around the packing sheds.

Once we had work, the next most important thing was to find a place to live we could afford. Ours was a neighborhood of leftover houses. The cheapest rents were in the back quarters of the rooming houses, the basements, and the rundown clapboard rentals in the alleys. Clammy and dank as they were, they were nevertheless one level up from the barns and tents where many of our *chicano* friends lived, or the shanties and lean-to's of the migrants who squatted in the "jungles" along the levees of the Sacramento and the American rivers.

Barrio people, when they first came to town, had no furniture of their own. They rented it with their quarters or bought a piece at a time from the secondhand stores, the *segundas*, where we traded. We cut out the ends of tin cans to make collars and plates for the pipes and floor moldings where the rats had gnawed holes. Stoops and porches that sagged we propped with bricks and fat stones. To plug the drafts around the windows in winter, we cut strips of corrugated cardboard and wedged them into the frames. With squares of cheesecloth neatly cut and sewed to screen doors holes were covered and rents in the wire mesh mended. Such repairs, which landlords never paid any attention to, were made *por mientras*, for the time being or temporarily. It would have been a word equally suitable for the house itself, or for the *barrio*. We lived in run-down places furnished with seconds in a hand-me-down neighborhood all of which were *por mientras*.

We found the Americans as strange in their customs as they probably found us. Immediately we discovered that there were no *mercados* and that when shopping you did not put the groceries in a *chiquihuite*. Instead everything was in cans or in cardboard boxes or each item was put in a brown paper bag. There were neighborhood grocery stores at the corners and some big ones uptown, but no *mercado*. The grocers did not give children a *pilón*, they did not stand at the door and coax you to come in and buy, as they did in Mazatlán. The fruits and vegetables were displayed on counters instead of being piled up on the floor. The stores smelled of fly spray and oiled floors, not of fresh pineapple and limes.

Neither was there a plaza, only parks which had no bandstands, no concerts every Thursday, no Judases exploding on Holy Week, and no promenades of boys going one way and girls the other. There were no parks in the *barrio*; and the ones uptown were cold and rainy in winter, and in summer there was no place to sit except on the grass. When there were celebrations nobody set off rockets in the parks, much less on the street in front of your house to announce to the neighborhood that a wedding or a baptism was taking place. Sacramento did not have a *mercado* and a plaza with the cathedral to one side and the Palacio de Gobierno on another to make it obvious that there and nowhere else was the center of the town.

It was just as puzzling that the Americans did not live in *vecindades*, like our block on Leandro Valle. Even in the alleys, where people knew one another better, the houses were fenced apart, without central courts to wash clothes, talk and play with the other children. Like the city, the Sacramento *barrio* did not have a place which was the middle of things for everyone.

In more personal ways we had to get used to the Americans. They did not listen if you did not speak loudly, as they always did. In the Mexican style, people would know that you were enjoying their jokes tremendously if you merely smiled and shook a little, as if you were trying to swallow your mirth. In the American style there was little difference between a laugh and a roar, and until you got used to them you could hardly tell whether the boisterous Americans were roaring mad or roaring happy.

It was Doña Henriqueta more than Gustavo or José who talked of these oddities and classified them as agreeable or deplorable. It was she also who pointed out the pleasant surprises of the American way. When a box of rolled oats with a picture of red carnations on the side was emptied, there was a plate or a bowl or a cup with blue designs. We ate the strange stuff regularly for breakfast and we soon had a set of the beautiful dishes. Rice and beans we bought in cotton bags of colored prints. The bags were unsewed, washed, ironed, and made into gaily designed towels, napkins, and handkerchiefs. The American stores also gave small green stamps which were pasted in a book to exchange for prizes. We didn't have to run to the corner with the garbage; a collector came for it.

With remarkable fairness and never-ending wonder we kept adding to our list the pleasant and the repulsive in the ways of the Americans. It was my second acculturation.

The older people of the *barrio*, except in those things which they had to do like the Americans because they had no choice, remained Mexican. Their language at home was Spanish. They were continuously taking up collections to pay somebody's funeral expenses or to help someone who had had a serious accident. Cards were sent to you to attend a burial where you would throw a handful of dirt on top of the coffin and listen to tearful speeches at the graveside. At every baptism a new *compadre* and a new *comadre* joined the family circle. New Year greeting cards were exchanged, showing angels and cherubs in bright colors sprinkled with grains of mica so that they glistened like gold dust. At the family parties the huge pot of steaming tamales was still the center of attention, the *atole* served on the side with chunks of brown sugar for sucking and crunching. If the party lasted long enough, someone produced a guitar, the men took over and the singing of *corridos* began.

In the *barrio* there were no individuals who had official titles or who were otherwise recognized by everybody as important people. The reason must have been that there was no place in the public business of the city of Sacramento for the Mexican immigrants. We only rented a corner of the city and as long as we paid the rent on time everything else was decided at City Hall or the County Court House, where Mexicans went only when they were in trouble. Nobody from the *barrio* ever ran for mayor or city councilman. For us the most important public officials were the policemen who walked their beats, stopped fights, and hauled drunks to jail in a paddy wagon we called *La Julia*.

The one institution we had that gave the *colonia* some kind of image was the *Comisión Honorífica*, a committee picked by the Mexican Consul in San Francisco to organize the celebration of the *Cinco de Mayo* and the Sixteenth of September, the anniversaries of the battle of Puebla and the beginning of our War of Independence. These were the two events which stirred everyone in the *barrio*, for what we were celebrating was not only the heroes of Mexico but also the feeling that we were still Mexicans ourselves. On these occasions there was a dance preceded by speeches and a concert. For both the *cinco* and the sixteenth queens were elected to preside over the ceremonies.

Between celebrations neither the politicians uptown or the *Comisión Honorífica* attended to the daily needs of the *barrio*. This was done by volunteers—the ones who knew enough English to interpret in court, on a visit to the doctor, a call at the county hospital, and who could help make out a postal money order. By the time I had finished the third grade at the Lincoln School I was one of these volunteers. My services were not professional but they were free, except for the IOU's I accumulated from families who always thanked me with "God will pay you for it."

My clients were not *pochos*, Mexicans who had grown up in California, probably had even been born in the United States. They had learned to speak English of sorts and could still speak Spanish, also of sorts. They knew much more about the Americans than we did, and much less about us. The *chicanos* and the *pochos* had certain feelings about one another. Concerning the *pochos*, the *chicanos* suspected that they considered themselves too good for the *barrio* but were not, for some reason, good enough for the Americans. Toward the *chicanos*, the *pochos* acted superior, amused at our confusions but not especially interested in explaining them to us. In our family when I forgot my manners, my mother would ask me if I was turning *pochito*.

Turning *pocho* was a half-step toward turning American. And America was all around us, in and out of the *barrio*. Abruptly we had to forget the ways of shopping in a *mercado* and learn those of shopping in a corner grocery or in a department store. The Americans paid no attention to the Sixteenth of September, but they made a great commotion about the Fourth of July. In Mazatlán Don Salvador had told us, saluting and marching as he talked to our class, that the *Cinco de Mayo* was the most glorious date in human history. The Americans had not even heard about it.

In Tucson, when I had asked my mother again if the Americans were having a revolution, the answer was: "No, but they have good schools, and you are going to one of them." We were by now settled at 418 L Street and the time had come for me to exchange a revolution for an American education.

The two of us walked south on Fifth Street one morning to the corner of Q Street and turned right. Half of the block was occupied by the Lincoln School. It was a three-story wooden building, with two wings that gave it the shape of a double-T connected by a central hall. It was a new building, painted yellow, with a shingled roof that was not like the red tile of the school in Mazatlán. I noticed other differences, none of them very reassuring.

We walked up the wide staircase hand in hand and through the door, which closed by itself. A mechanical contraption screwed to the top shut it behind us quietly.

Up to this point the adventure of enrolling me in the school had been carefully rehearsed. Mrs. Dodson had told us how to find it and we had circled it several times on our walks. Friends in the *barrio* explained that the director was called a principal, and that it was a lady and not a man. They assured us that there was always a person at the school who could speak Spanish.

Exactly as we had been told, there was a sign on the door in both Spanish and English: "Principal." We crossed the hall and entered the office of Miss Nettie Hopley.

Miss Hopley was at a roll-top desk to one side, sitting in a swivel chair that moved on wheels. There was a sofa against the opposite wall, flanked by two windows and a door that opened on a small balcony. Chairs were set around a table and framed pictures hung on the walls of a man with long white hair and another with a sad face and a black beard.

The principal half turned in the swivel chair to look at us over the pinch glasses crossed on the ridge of her nose. To do this she had to duck her head slightly as if she were about to step through a low doorway.

What Miss Hopley said to us we did not know but we saw in her eyes a warm welcome and when she took off her glasses and straightened up she smiled wholeheartedly, like Mrs. Dodson. We were, of course, saying nothing, only catching the friendliness of her voice and the sparkle in her eyes while she said words we did not understand. She signaled us to the table. Almost tiptoeing across the office, I maneuvered myself to keep my mother between me and the gringo lady. In a matter of seconds I had to decide whether she was a possible friend or a menace. We sat down.

Then Miss Hopley did a formidable thing. She stood up.

Had she been standing when we entered she would have seemed tall. But rising from her chair she soared. And what she carried up and up with her was a buxom superstructure, firm shoulders, a straight sharp nose, full cheeks slightly molded by a curved line along the nostrils, thin lips that moved like steel springs, and a high forehead topped by hair gathered in a bun. Miss Hopley was not a giant in body but when she mobilized it to a standing position she seemed a match for giants. I decided I liked her.

She strode to a door in the far corner of the office, opened it and called a name. A boy of about ten years appeared in the doorway. He sat down at one end of the table. He was brown like us, a plump kid with shiny black hair combed straight back, neat, cool, and faintly obnoxious.

Miss Hopley joined us with a large book and some papers in her hand. She, too, sat down and the questions and answers began by way of our interpreter. My name was Ernesto. My mother's name was Henriqueta. My birth certificate was in San Blas. Here was my last report card from the Escuela Municipal Numero 3 para Varones of Mazatlán, and so forth. Miss Hopley put things down in the book and my mother signed a card.

As long as the questions continued, Doña Henriqueta could stay and I was secure. Now that they were over, Miss Hopley saw her to the door, dismissed our interpreter and without further ado took me by the hand and strode down the hall to Miss Ryan's first grade.

Miss Ryan took me to a seat at the front of the room, into which I shrank—the better to survey her. She was, to skinny, somewhat runty me, of a withering height when she patrolled the class. And when I least expected it, there she was, crouching by my desk, her blond radiant face level with mine, her voice patiently maneuvering me over the awful idiocies of the English language.

During the next few weeks Miss Ryan overcame my fears of tall, energetic teachers as she bent over my desk to help me with a word in the pre-primer. Step by step, she loosened me and my classmates from the safe anchorage of the desks for recitations at the blackboard and consultations at her desk. Frequently she burst into happy announcements to the whole class. "Ito can read a sentence," and small Japanese Ito, squint-eyed and shy, slowly read aloud while the class listened in wonder: "Come, Skipper, come. Come and run." The Korean, Portuguese, Italian, and Polish first graders had similar moments of glory, no less shining than mine the day I conquered "butterfly," which I had been persistently pronouncing in standard Spanish as boo-ter-flee. "Children," Miss Ryan called for attention. "Ernesto has learned how to pronounce *butterfly*!" And I proved it with a perfect imitation of Miss Ryan. From that celebrated success, I was soon able to match Ito's progress as a sentence reader with "Come, butterfly, come fly with me."

Like Ito and several other first graders who did not know English, I received private lessons from Miss Ryan in the closet, a narrow hall off the classroom with a door at each end. Next to one of these doors Miss Ryan placed a large chair for herself and a small one for me. Keeping an eye on the class through the open door she read with me about sheep in the meadow and a frightened chicken going to see the king, coaching me out of my phonetic ruts in words like *pasture, bow-wow-wow, hay,* and *pretty,* which to my Mexican ear and eye had so many unnecessary sounds and letters. She made me watch her lips and then close my eyes as she repeated words I found hard to read. When we came to know each other better, I tried interrupting to tell Miss Ryan how we said it in Spanish. It didn't work. She only said "oh" and went on with *pasture, bow-wow-wow,* and *pretty.* It was as if in that closet we were both discovering together the secrets of the English language and grieving together over the tragedies of Bo-Peep. The main reason I was graduated with honors from the first grade was that I had fallen in love with Miss Ryan. Her radiant, no-nonsense character made us either afraid not to love her or love her so we would not be afraid, I am not sure which. It was not only that we sensed she was with it, but also that she was with us.

Like the first grade, the rest of the Lincoln School was a sampling of the lower part of town where many races made their home. My pals in the second grade were Kazushi, whose parents spoke only Japanese; Matti, a skinny Italian boy; and Manuel, a fat Portuguese who would never get into a fight but wrestled you to the ground and just sat on you. Our assortment of nationalities included Koreans, Yugoslavs, Poles, Irish, and home-grown Americans.

Miss Hopley and her teachers never let us forget why we were at Lincoln: for those who were alien, to become good Americans; for those who were so born, to accept the rest of us. Off the school grounds we traded the same insults we heard from our elders. On the playground we were sure to be marched up to the principal's office for calling someone a wop, a chink, a dago, or a greaser. The school was not so much a melting pot as a griddle where Miss Hopley and her helpers warmed knowledge into us and roasted racial hatreds out of us.

At Lincoln, making us into Americans did not mean scrubbing away what made us originally foreign. The teachers called us as our parents did, or as close as they could pronounce our names in Spanish or Japanese. No one was ever scolded or punished for speaking in his native tongue or on the playground. Matti told the class about his mother's down quilt, which she had made in Italy with the fine feathers of a thousand geese. Encarnación acted out how boys learned to fish in the Philippines. I astounded the third grade with the story of my travels on a stagecoach, which nobody else in the class had seen except in the museum at Sutter's Fort. After a visit to the Crocker Art Gallery and its collection of heroic paintings of the golden age of California, someone showed a silk scroll with a Chinese painting. Miss Hopley herself had a way of expressing wonder over these matters before a class, her eyes wide open until they popped slightly. It was easy for me to feel that becoming a proud American, as she said we should, did not mean feeling ashamed of being a Mexican.

The Americanization of Mexican me was no smooth matter. I had to fight one lout who made fun of my travels on the *diligencia*, and my barbaric translation of the word into "diligence." He doubled up with laughter over the word until I straightened him out with a kick. In class I made points explaining that in Mexico roosters said "qui-qui-ri-qui" and not "cock-a-doodle-doo," but after school I had to put up with the taunts of a big Yugoslav who said Mexican roosters were crazy.

But it was Homer who gave me the most lasting lesson for a future American.

Homer was a chunky Irishman who dressed as if every day was Sunday. He slicked his hair between a crew cut and a pompadour. And Homer was smart, as he clearly showed when he and I ran for president of the third grade.

Everyone understood that this was to be a demonstration of how the American people vote for president. In an election, the teacher explained, the candidates could be generous and vote for each other. We cast our ballots in a shoe box and Homer won by two votes. I polled my supporters and came to the conclusion that I had voted for Homer and so had he. After class he didn't deny it, reminding me of what the teacher had said—we could vote for each other but didn't have to.

The lower part of town was a collage of nationalities in the middle of which Miss Nettie Hopley kept school with discipline and compassion. She called assemblies in the upper hall to introduce celebrities like the police sergeant or the fire chief, to lay down the law of the school, to present awards to our athletic champions, and to make important announcements. One of these was that I had been proposed by my school and accepted as a member of the newly formed Sacramento Boys Band. "Now, isn't that a wonderful thing?" Miss Hopley asked the assembled school, all eyes on me. And everyone answered in a chorus, including myself, "Yes, Miss Hopley."

It was not only the parents who were summoned to her office and boys and girls who served sentences there who knew Nettie Hopley meant business. The entire school witnessed her sizzling Americanism in its awful majesty one morning at flag salute.

All the grades, as usual, were lined up in the courtyard between the wings of the building, ready to march to classes after the opening bell. Miss Shand was on the balcony of the second floor off Miss Hopley's office, conducting us in our lusty singing of "My Country tiz-a-thee." Our principal, as always, stood there like us, at attention, her right hand over her heart, joining in the song.

Halfway through the second stanza she stepped forward, held up her arm in a sign of command, and called loud and clear: "Stop the singing." Miss Shand looked flabbergasted. We were frozen with shock.

Miss Hopley was now standing at the rail of the balcony, her eyes sparkling, her voice low and resonant, the words coming down to us distinctly and loaded with indignation.

"There are two gentlemen walking on the school grounds with their hats on while we are singing," she said, sweeping our ranks with her eyes. "We will remain silent until the gentlemen come to attention and remove their hats." A minute of awful silence ended when Miss Hopley, her gaze fixed on something behind us, signaled Miss Shand and we began once more the familiar hymn. That afternoon, when school was out, the word spread. The two gentlemen were the Superintendent of Schools and an important guest on an inspection.

I came back to the Lincoln School after every summer, moving up through the grades with Miss Campbell, Miss Beakey, Mrs. Wood, Miss Applegate, and Miss Delahunty. I sat in the classroom adjoining the principal's office and had my turn answering her telephone when she was about the building repeating the message to the teacher, who made a note of it. Miss Campbell read to us during the last period of the week about King Arthur, Columbus, Buffalo Bill, and Daniel Boone, who came to life in the reverie of the class through the magic of her voice. And it was Miss Campbell who introduced me to the public library on Eye Street, where I became a regular customer.

All of Lincoln School mourned together when Eddie, the blond boy everybody liked, was killed by a freight train as he crawled across the tracks going home one day. We assembled to say good-bye to Miss Applegate, who was off to Alaska to be married. Now it was my turn to be excused from class to interpret for a parent enrolling a new student fresh from Mexico. Graduates from Lincoln came back now and then to tell us about high school. A naturalist entertained us in assembly, imitating the calls of the meadow lark, the water ouzel, the oriole, and the killdeer. I decided to become a bird man after I left Lincoln.

In the years we lived in the lower part of town, La Leen-Con, as my family called it, became a benchmark in our lives, like the purple light of the Lyric Theater and the golden dome of the Palacio de Gobierno gleaming above Capitol Park.

With safer bearings of our own we were ready for another attempt at a family reunion.

One had already failed. The Lopez's had left Jalco and reached Mazatlán but had returned to the village to await better times. Now the revolution was moving south again, making travel by rail to the United States unsafe. It was agreed that they would make the journey by sea to San Francisco.

By the kitchen calendar we counted the days. On the last one Gustavo, my mother, José and I took the train for a trip that was a fiesta of smiles and anecdotes, and a great deal of reminiscing about our last days in Jalco when we had last seen our relatives. Together again we would be four men accustomed to *trabajo*, sufficient to support the women and the young.

On the waterfront we boarded a launch that took us across the bay to Angel's Island where our kinfolk were in quarantine. The boat churned up a heavy wake and seagulls swooped around us, squeaking. As she always did, my mother nodded her head this way and that, explaining the things or the people she was calling to my attention. I watched the pilot turn us smoothly alongside a wharf. A man in uniform took us through a building and out into an open courtyard from which we could see the city across the bay. A strong sea wind was blowing, cold and salty.

The Lopez family were standing at the far end of the yard: my aunt, slender and poised in long skirts and a shawl; Don Catarino, in freshly washed work clothes, a coat and a felt hat which he held clamped down with one hand; Jesús,

Catarino and a younger brother wrapped in blankets. Huddled between them were two wicker baskets, each with a twin, born on the trip.

There was no laughter, no shouting for joy, no back-slapping at the reunion. The excitement was inward and it came out only in the smiles and the formal, gentle *abrazos* all around. Following the cue of the adults I merely said: "How are you, Jesús? How are you, Catarino?" And they answered, "How are you, Ernesto?"

My cousins were shy and I just stood by them, staring at my relatives, one by one. My aunt and my mother were talking. Gustavo and José were listening to Don Catarino.

The women took our hands, the men carried the cribs and together we went inside the building. After a long wait the man in uniform joined us. An interpreter was with him.

The immigration officer, through the interpreter, was explaining. The Lopez's would not be allowed to enter the United States. There were papers on the desk in front of him. He explained the rules and the laws and the orders and they all made the same point: the family would be detained for a few days on the island and would then have to return to Mexico the way they had come.

So it was hello and good-bye in one afternoon. We left them by the wharf. From the launch we waved and lost them in our wake.

The trip back to Sacramento was like returning from a funeral. My uncles exchanged puzzled questions, bitter and despairing, anger and grief in their faces, staring out of the window to avoid looking at each other.

They paid little attention to my comments, caught up in their own distress. The man in uniform had merely shown us some papers but he had not told us why. He had not even said what would have to be done to bring our family back and take them home with us. I saw him vividly in my mind, ugly and menacing, and silently called him all the names I could think of, like *gringo pendejo*. But my secret revenge did not make me feel better as I tried to guess what Gustavo meant when he had said on the launch: "Es una injusticia." Our hopes had been denied and our joy had been turned to sadness by people we were powerless even to question. My own response to injustice seemed the only way to get even. I turned to Doña Henriqueta and said: "Let us go back to Jalcocotán together." She smiled compassionately, as if there were still many things I had to learn, and said nothing.

Quiet Odyssey
Mary Paik Lee

Mary Paik Lee was born Kuang Sun Paik in the northern province of Pyongan, Korea, in 1900 to a large family of scholars and teachers. Although most women in nineteenth-century Korea were not allowed to read or write, Lee's grandmother learned these skills from her husband, read the newly translated King James Bible, and encouraged all of her kin to convert to Presbyterianism. As Christians, however, the Paik family would suffer greatly when Japanese forces took control of Korea in 1905 (the Japanese viewed any educated Koreans associated with Western nations or beliefs as a threat to their power). Fearful of persecution, even death, Lee's father, Paik Sin Koo, a Presbyterian minister, contracted with a Hawaiian sugar cane farmer as a laborer and boarded the S.S. *Siberia* with his wife, Song Kuang Do, five-year-old Kuang and her eight-year-old brother, Meung.

In Hawaii, Paik Sin Koo worked at hard labor for extremely low wages. His contract expired after a year, allowing the family to travel to San Francisco in 1906, but in California the wages and hours of farm labor were also poor. Mary Paik Lee would recall in her memoir, *Quiet Odyssey*, published in 1984, how often the family went hungry, even though her father sometimes held several jobs and traveled great distances to find better work. By the time Lee reached adulthood, the family had grown to ten children, and Paik Sin Koo and Song

Kuang Do were unable to settle permanently in any farming area in the western United States. Everywhere the Paiks went, they found WHITES ONLY signs posted on stores, restaurants, and public drinking fountains.

At school, Kuang and Meung suffered countless racial taunts, and found that teachers and students alike could not remember their Korean names. The elder sibling pair renamed themselves, and the younger Paik children, with American names they liked. Their father praised them for their ingenuity and understanding of American ways. As a Christian who had escaped Japanese rule with the help of American missionaries, Paik Sin Koo felt an appreciation for America that his children did not. Often confused by her father's forgiveness of white Americans, the newly named Mary watched Paik Sin Koo grow old before his time, laboring at a fruit farm, and once handling toxic materials at a quicksilver mine in 1918. When Mary's parents spoke of the atrocities occurring in Korea at this time, however, their emigration and subsequent poverty made more sense. Contacts at church brought news from Korea that hundreds had died in what came to be called the March First Uprising of 1919. Frightened by thousands of mourners at the Korean Emperor Kojong's funeral, Japanese soldiers attacked the crowd with gunshots and sabers. In Mary's home province of Pyongan, Grandmother Paik was struck and blinded in a similar skirmish. After hearing of the horrors, the American Paiks looked to President Woodrow Wilson to help their relatives escape Korea, but Asian immigration to the United States had already been seriously limited under President Theodore Roosevelt's Executive Order 589 in 1907.

Mary Paik married Hung Man (H. M.) Lee, also a Christian-Korean immigrant, in 1919. At this time, H. M. was a successful foreman at a rice farm in California, and the couple continued to grow rice until the market fell in 1921. Following this failure, H. M. and Mary made their living by farming idle land and taking care of abandoned homes in the Anaheim area. Such arrangements between Asian immigrants and white land owners were illegal at the time under the 1913 California Alien Land Law barring "persons ineligible to citizenship" from buying or renting land. As a result of this law, the Lees could only make verbal agreements with landlords; with their three children, Henry, Allan, and Tony, the couple sold produce at vegetable stands to make a sustainable income until the end of World War II. Although Henry and Allan served in the U.S. military forces, the Lees were often accused of being "Japs" by white community members, and they watched fearfully as Japanese friends and neighbors were forced into internment camps. Unwilling to face such harsh conditions, the Lees moved to Los Angeles soon after the war ended.

As fruit sellers in a more accepting community in Los Angeles, H. M. and Mary finally fulfilled their dream of owning property when they became landlords of an apartment building. They were naturalized as U.S. citizens in 1960 and celebrated their fiftieth wedding anniversary in 1969. H. M.'s death in 1975 prompted Mary to write her memoirs with the help of Allan. *Quiet Odyssey* remains a rare form of Asian-American autobiography that is useful to social scientists and common readers alike insofar as it details the working-class life of a determined and thoughtful woman. In 1990, the historian Sucheng Chan edited this work for the University of Washington Press, bringing Mary Paik Lee's story national attention. Mrs. Lee still resides in Los Angeles and acts as an interpreter for new Korean immigrants.

In Chapter 5 from *Quiet Odyssey*, entitled "Idria," Mary Paik Lee details the extreme hardship she experienced as a child, as well as the small pleasures she took from the plentiful California wildlife around her.

5

IDRIA

We were told that there were only a few quicksilver mines in the United States, the largest of which was in Idria. On the way to Idria, we had to stop in Sacramento, because Mother became very ill. We stayed at a boarding-house owned by a Mr. and Mrs. Lee, where another brother, Young Sun, was born February 26, 1914. Mother was so weary and ill she almost died that night giving birth. Young Sun, also named (but never called) Lawrence, was born more dead than alive, a blue baby. Father and I had to place him in hot and cold water alternately and massage him vigorously. It took a long time to get his circulation going.

After a day or two of rest, we continued to Tres Piños, a very small village some distance south of San Jose, to catch a wagon to Idria. It was a big haywagon with benches on both sides, hitched to four large horses, which took us up the mountains. It took half a day to reach the place. We crossed several creeks and stopped to move big rocks that had rolled down the road from the mountain. The scenery was beautiful—tall pine trees and hilly country—with very few houses along the way. Every time we moved, we came to a different kind of world. This was the best so far. The pine trees smelled good, and the cool air made us feel refreshed.

Mr. Lee had found an old house for us. It had four small rooms, and a shack in the back served as a kitchen and dining area. There was a big oven in the shack and a picnic-style board table with benches on both sides. The house had a small wood stove for heat. The mines, the company buildings, the hotel, the store, the houses of a few Caucasian families, and the boardinghouse for Caucasian workers all had electricity, but there was no electricity in the shacks for the rest of the workers—mainly Mexicans, with a few Koreans. We were back to our old way of living, but we felt happy to be in such a beautiful, wild country. Meung and I had to hunt for firewood again. There was a water pump outside the house, and the outhouse was halfway down the hill.

Mr. Lee took Father to the company office and asked if he could work there. He was accepted and was given a card to record the supplies from the company store which we bought on credit. Father bought kerosene lamps, a sack of rice—and a big ham. It was the first time we children had ever seen such a luxury. The ham tasted wonderful, and we enjoyed it very much for several weeks.

Father got a basket and took us up in the hills to see what could be picked for food; he showed us what was good and what to avoid. In a shallow stream, we saw crayfish, which hurried to get under the rocks when they heard us coming, and soft green watercress, which grew on top of the water. All kinds of wild vegetables grew there. They had a light green color. The celery had thin stalks and smelled a bit like the celery we buy in the stores now. The lettuce looked like romaine, the same shape and size, but was soft green in color, with thin and very tender leaves. Little cucumbers on vines climbed on the tall bushes nearby. Also, gooseberries and blackberries took the place of other fruits that did not grow in that location. Nature had provided a great wild vegetable market for all the poor people living there. As we sat around the table for our supper that evening, Father thanked God for leading us to this place.

The short stay on Roberts Island had been a wonderful experience for us children. We learned a lot about all the wild creatures who share this world with us. This new place, Idria, was yet another exciting experience—an interesting new way of life.

Around the house of every Mexican family in Idria were two or three burros, one or two pigs, and some chickens. We found that burros were a necessity of life in those mountains. They were the only means of getting around because of the numerous rattlesnakes. We needed two of them to bring the firewood down from the mountains, so Father and I went to a neighbor who had several and asked if we could

buy two. He brought the burros out to us and told them in
Spanish that this man was to be their new owner, that they
should go with him and should stay at his house and not
come back. The burros just blinked their eyes and stood
waiting while Father paid for them. The owner patted their
backs and told them to go with us. I asked if we should tie
them up. He said that was not necessary, that they knew
what to do. Also, he said there was no need to feed them,
that they would go up the mountains at night to feed on the
grass there. I didn't believe him but waited to see what
would happen. The burros followed us home. All my brothers were so excited and happy to see them. They brought
water for them to drink and played with them all day. I
thought the burros would run away at night and not come
back, but the next morning I looked out the window and
there they were, standing meekly by the kitchen shack. It
was a wonderful surprise to see them there.

Meung and I took the burros up the mountains to look for
firewood. There was plenty everywhere. We had to chop the
wood into shorter lengths so we could pack bundles on both
sides of the burros. We first put down a layer of sacks to protect the burros' bodies; then we tied the bundles of firewood
tightly. The burros knelt down to let us tie the bundles with
ropes around their bodies, but they would not get up when
ordered. We were told this might happen, so we just left
them there and returned home. They came home later when
they felt like it. They must have received harsh treatment
from others and expected the same from us. They were
showing their feelings in the only way they knew. When
they got home, we took off the loads, and the boys brought
water for them and petted them. They seemed to enjoy the
attention and love shown to them. After this happened a few
times, they decided not to be so stubborn. They stood up after the loads were tied and walked home with us. It was a joy
to have such cooperation from them. On weekends we made
as many trips as possible to gather wood. We had to pile up
a lot of wood by August, because our neighbors had told us
that the winter might bring snow storms and that sometimes
it might be impossible to get wood. We made a shelter for

the woodpile so it would not be covered with snow or get soaked with rain.

Father worked in the furnace area of the mining company, stirring the rocks so they would burn evenly. He had to wear a piece of cloth over his nose so he would not breathe the poisonous fumes whenever the lid was opened. It was a hard, nasty job that few men wanted to do, even though the pay was five dollars a day, an unheard of amount in those times. But Father was desperate and felt compelled to take it.

The fumes from the furnace were poisonous not only to humans but to plant life as well. Nothing grew where the fumes went. Because quicksilver was used to make explosives, soldiers guarded the entrance to the mines. When the quicksilver was being shipped out, several soldiers accompanied the cargo to its destination. No one was allowed to walk around the mining areas or furnaces.

One day Mother asked me to see if the store had fresh meat to sell. The clerk said meat was sold at the back. A big hole had been made in the side of a hill and boarded up, just big enough to hang one side of beef and one of pork. An electric bulb was hanging in the back. It was a spooky place; I had to chase a snake away from the entrance. The so-called butcher asked how large a piece I wanted. I told him I wanted a small piece about the size of my fist. He just cut off a section from the side of beef, put it on a piece of paper and gave it to me. I told him to put it on my father's account.

When we were fairly settled, we looked around for the schoolhouse. It was on top of a low hill not far from our place. Meung and I discovered it was another one-room schoolhouse with a teacher who taught all eight grades. We registered and started going to school the next day. There were about thirty Mexican children at that school, mostly little ones, though some were big boys who looked about twelve to sixteen years old. They had never been to school before and spoke very little English. They were so noisy the teacher had a hard time. She didn't have time for Meung and me. She was forced to tell the boys to go home, but they couldn't understand what she said. I had picked up a few words of Spanish, so I told them what she had said. They were so startled to hear me speak Spanish that they got up and left. After that, the rest of us could learn our lessons.

There was a wood stove in the middle of the schoolroom. The teacher built a fire at noon and heated something in a small pot which smelled so good I asked her what it was. She said it was a can of Campbell's soup that she had bought at the store. That was my first introduction to Campbell's soups. I told Mother about the soup, and she bought one can at the store. She said it was good but that we couldn't afford to buy enough for the whole family.

I noticed that there was no one to sweep out the schoolroom, so I went to the company office and talked to the supervisor. He was a kindly man who listened to my story. I told him that I wanted to earn enough money to buy my books when I got to high school. He decided to hire me. My job was to clean the blackboards, sweep out the room, chop the wood for the stove, keep the outhouse clean, and ring the school bell at 8:30 A.M. so the children would know it was time for school. He would pay me twenty-five cents a day.

I had also been helping in the boardinghouse kitchen every evening. A couple there cooked and served about forty men every day. The wife paid me twenty-five cents every night and gave me leftover roast meat and rolls, which my family enjoyed. One evening while we were all busy in the kitchen, the couple started to argue about something. The wife said something that made her husband so angry he picked up a small can of lard and threw it at her. She screamed and fell to the floor. I was so frightened, I dropped everything and ran home. Father told me not to go there anymore.

Instead, he wanted me to do something for him. He told me to look for two stones of a certain size and thickness. He said he wanted to make a millstone to grind beans, so we could make our kind of food to eat. There were lots of big boulders around, but very few small ones of the size he wanted. It took me several days to find the right kind. When I did, I loaded them on the burros and brought them home. Every day after work, Father would chip away at the stones with a hammer and chisel. He made a beautiful two-piece mill. The top stone had a small oblong hole on one side and a handle inserted on the other side. On its bottom was a small hole, exactly in the middle. The bottom stone had a metal bolt, which fitted into the hole of the top stone. When the two stones were put together and the beans were put into the hole, the upper stone was turned around. It ground the beans into powder—a very ingenious machine. It must have been invented by someone like my father in the ancient days. He was always thinking up ways to improve our living conditions, always making things out of materials other people had discarded. We never had much, but he always tried to make our lives as comfortable as possible—even though harsh circumstances made that difficult most of the time.

Life in Idria was exciting; we had something new to learn every day. In the fall, when the cones on the pine trees were large and ripe, the boys climbed up with hatchets and cut them down. They buried them in hot ashes. The cones opened up in the heat, exposing the big nuts. They tasted better than peanuts and were very delicious. Then the bright red holly berries and small trees made everything look like Christmas. We cut lots of berries and pine tree branches to decorate the schoolroom and make it smell good. Meung cut a small tree for our house, and I went to the company store and bought bright tinsel and decorations for the tree with the money I had earned as a janitor. What a difference from our last Christmas in Colusa!

About two weeks after Christmas, Meung and I walked through the alleys in town to select the best tree that had been put out for the trash man. We picked out one that had some tinsel on it. We took it home and decorated it with strips of colored crepe paper. Our little brothers were happy to see it. Our parents never said a word; they just looked at us with sad faces. I was too young at that time to realize how they must have felt to see such a pitiful sight. On Roberts Island we had decorated a tall bush outside our house and had pretended it was a Christmas tree. The little children were happy with anything we did to pretend it was a special occasion.

In Idria the snowfall was heavy that winter. We couldn't open the front door and had to crawl out the window to shovel the snow away from the door. In the spring, after the snow had melted away, the sun brought all the beautiful flowers to life. The mountains were covered with different flowers and were full of color. It was a wonderful sight. Their fragrance filled the air. Every weekend people from San Francisco, Berkeley, and San Jose drove up to enjoy the scenery and to get some flowers. All the children came out to pick flowers, which we sold for twenty-five cents a bunch. We used to look forward to making a little money. The people were afraid to get out of their cars because of the numerous snakes, especially the rattlesnakes. But somehow, none of the children ever got bitten, perhaps because we always made enough noise to scare the snakes away.

We saw tarantulas for the first time in Idria—giant spiders with big, round, black velvety bodies about two inches in diameter, eight long hairy legs, and piercing eyes. They are scary but very fascinating creatures. They dig holes in the ground and camouflage the openings so cleverly that it's easy to pass by and not see them. We were told that their bite is poisonous, so we always carried a long stick with a sharp point. Whenever they heard any sound approaching their hole, they would lift the cover a bit and peek out. We just stood and watched them.

There were also ugly little horned toads in the mountains which were born fighters. The Mexican boys would put two together in a box. The toads would squirt blood from their eyes and tear at each other until one was dead. That was about the only amusement the boys had; they bet on their favorites and had as much fun as watching a cockfight.

One hot July afternoon as I was walking in the hills, I noticed a strong, peculiar odor that was very unpleasant. It seemed to get stronger as I climbed higher. I found a big pile of rocks with an opening in the middle, and when I climbed up and looked down the opening I saw a curious, frighten-

ing event in progress. A huge gathering of snakes was en-
twined and entangled, just moving around in one huge
mass. A heavy silence in the air made me shiver, so I quickly
walked away.

I asked the teacher if there were large wild animals in the
higher mountains. She said that mountain lions and red
foxes had been seen, but the Mexican men did not go hunting because they did not have hunting rifles.

Whenever it rained on a school day, all the mothers of the
Mexican children in school got together and made big
tamales with everything good stuffed in them. One apiece
was enough for each person. The Mexican families were so
generous—they always remembered to make extra ones for
Meung and me. They didn't have much, but they were willing to share with others. Their generosity turned rainy days
into picnics.

I saw a motion picture for the first time in 1914. Some
film company showed a cowboy movie in front of the hotel.
It was a free preview to advertise the real picture at the
dance hall that night. The movie showed cowboys drinking
in a saloon. They were staggering out, laughing and firing
their pistols. When they saw an old Chinese man walking home on the other side of the road, they said they
wanted to see if he could dance. They started firing at his
feet, and they laughed as he kept jumping to avoid being hit.
Of course, their aim was not accurate, and he fell wounded.
That made them laugh louder. They told him to get up.
When he could not, they kept shooting until he was dead.
Then they walked away, laughing as though it were a big
joke. I was so shocked, I vowed I would never go to see the
pictures again. That movie reflected the attitude toward
Orientals in those days. Our Mexican friends didn't like it,
either. They remembered the days when their people were
also treated that way. They had bitter memories of how their
country lost California.

During our stays in Idria, Mother had time to sit down
and talk to us once in a while. We wanted to know how our
grandparents and uncle were getting along in Korea. So for
the first time, we learned about the tragic events that had

taken place since we had left in 1905. After Japan took possession of Korea, the Korean people were treated like second-class citizens. They were not allowed to possess any kind of weapon to protect themselves; they could have only one kitchen knife to a family. They were deprived of all their property and had no rights under the new Japanese laws. Names of towns, streets, and persons were changed to Japanese; the teachers in all the schools had to speak Japanese and teach from Japanese textbooks. All Korean books and Korean flags were destroyed. It was the complete humiliation of an entire nation. Since all letters leaving Korea were censored, the tragedy was unknown to the rest of the world. But there were letters from people who had escaped to China or elsewhere. We could not do anything to help our loved ones; we had only the agony of hoping and praying. Life was just one crisis after another.

AMERICAN CLASSICS

☐ **SPOON RIVER ANTHOLOGY** by Edgar Lee Masters. Introduction by John Hollander. A book of dramatic monologues written in free verse about a fictional town called Spoon River, based on the Midwestern towns where Edgar Lee Masters grew up. This landmark work is an American classic.   (525302—$4.95)

☐ **SELECTED WRITINGS OF RALPH WALDO EMERSON**
Foreword by William H. Gilman, University of Rochester. Fourteen essays and addresses including *The Oversoul, Politics, Thoreau, Divinity School Address,* including poems *Threnody* and *Uriel,* and selections from his letters and journals. Chronology. Bibliography.   (524047—$5.95)

☐**EVANGELINE** and Selected Tales and Poems by Henry Wadsworth Longfellow. Edited by Horace Gregory, poet and translator. Includes *The Witnesses, The Courtship of Miles Standish,* and selections from *Hiawatha,* with commentaries on Longfellow by Van Wyck Brooks, Norman Holmes Pearson, and Lewis Carroll. Includes Introduction, Bibliography and Chronology.   (520033—$5.95)

☐**LEAVES OF GRASS** by Walt Whitman. Introduction by Gary Wilson Allen, New York University. The text of this edition is that of the "Deathbed," or 9th edition, published in 1892. The content and grouping of the poems were authorized by the poet for this final and complete edition of his masterpiece. Index and Bibliography included.   (524853—$5.95)

☐**TARZAN OF THE APES** by Edgar Rice Burroughs. Introduction by Gore Vidal. This is the classic story of the ape-man Tarzan, and how he learns the secrets of the wild to survive—set amidst the vibrant colors and sounds of the African jungle.   (524233—$4.95)

☐ **CLASSIC AMERICAN AUTOBIOGRAPHIES** Edited and with an Introduction by William L. Andrews. The true diversity of the American experience comes to life in this superlative collection. Included are *A True History of the Captivity and Restoration of Mrs. Mary Rowlandson, The Autobiography of Benjamin Franklin, Narrative of the Life of Frederick Douglass, Old Times on the Mississippi,* and *Four Autobiographical Narratives of Zitkala-Sa.*   (628527—$6.99)

Prices slightly higher in Canada

Penguin Putnam Inc.	Bill my: ☐Visa ☐MasterCard ☐Amex _____ (expires)
P.O. Box 12289, Dept. B	Card#_____
Newark, NJ 07101-5289	
Please allow 4-6 weeks for delivery.	
Foreign and Canadian delivery 6-8 weeks.	Signature_____

Bill to:

Name_____

Address_____City _____

State/ZIP_____

Daytime Phone #_____

Ship to:

Name_____ Book Total $_____

Address_____ Applicable Sales Tax $_____

City_____ Postage & Handling $_____

State/ZIP_____ Total Amount Due $_____

This offer subject to change without notice.